DIARY
of the
GERMAN OCCUPATION
of
GUERNSEY
1940—1945

This Diary covers the five years of the German occupation of Guernsey to within a few weeks of the liberation.

Mr. Sauvary records how the island's economy was adapted to food production, and it is a day to day account of the effect on the islanders of the gradual encroachment on their life and liberty. As the Germans tightened their grip his philosophical acceptance of the situation helped many to come to terms with this daunting experience, and he helped one and all.

Mention is made of what could be observed about the immense fortifications being built by slave labour, what he calls the "foreigners" about whom he had to write guardedly because of the risk of the Diaries being found.

In addition to having the common experience of Germans billeted on him and being turned out of his house, he had unusually wide experiences (some of which were unique) of dealing with the enemy because of his fourfold role of Builder, Grower, Churchwarden and Douzenier.

The deportation of British born residents makes poignant reading as does the long wait until Red Cross messages began to arrive. These stopped after D Day and thereafter comes the increasingly grim situation as starvation faced both islanders and enemy. The relief and joy when Red Cross supplies began to arrive is vividly recorded.

His interest in nature runs like a thread through the narrative as he records the changing seasons, and his observations of human nature are revealing. Although he often mentions his loneliness, the fatigue of bicycling instead of driving his car, and his regret at being cut off from expert medical treatment as his health failed there is no self pity. He faces the bleak prospect of not surviving to see his children again with the courage shown by the 23,000 people who endured five years of German occupation.

ALDERNEY
N
HERM
SARK
GUERNSEY
JERSEY

ENGLAND
HERM
ALDERNEY
GUERNSEY
SARK
JERSEY
Not to scale
FRANCE

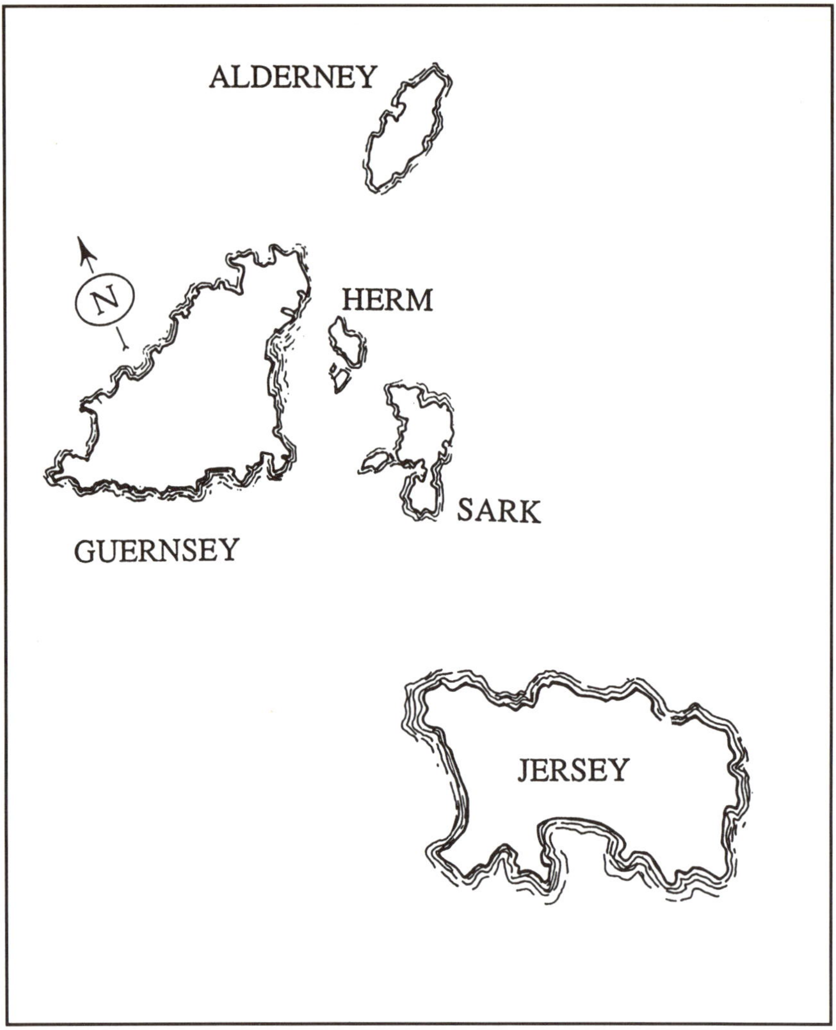

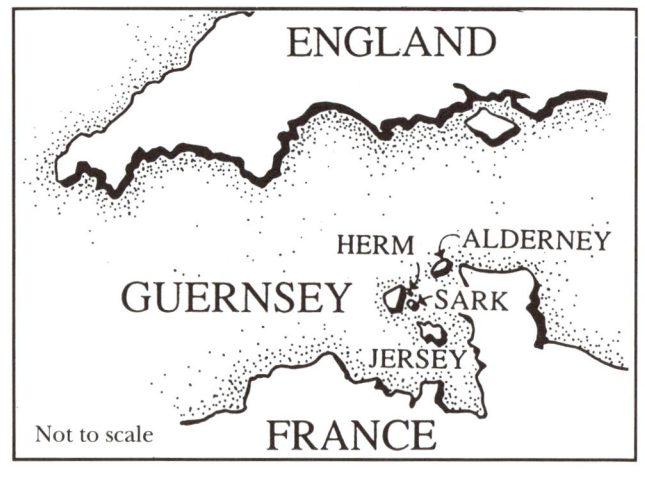

DIARY
OF THE
GERMAN OCCUPATION
OF
GUERNSEY
1940—1945

By
J.C. Sauvary

Builder, Grower, Churchwarden, Douzenier

© K.A. Sauvary 1990

All rights reserved. No part of this publication may be reproduced, stored in a retrieval system, or transmitted, in any form or by any means, electronic, mechanical, photocopying, recording or otherwise, without the prior permission of K. A. Sauvary.

First published 1990 Hardback
Revised edition 1995 Paperback

ISBN 0-902550-56-X

Published by The Guernsey Press Co. Ltd.,
in conjunction with K. A. Sauvary

British Library Cataloguing in Publication Data
Sauvary J.C.
   Diary of the German occupation of Guernsey 1940–1945
   1. Guernsey. Occupation by German military forces, 1939–1945
   I. Title
940.5342342

Made and printed in Great Britain by
The Guernsey Press Co. Ltd., Guernsey, Channel Islands

This Diary is dedicated to
the 23,000 people of Guernsey
and with particular gratitude to
Mrs Rowe, Tom Roberts and Mary Ayres
(*née* Sauvary)
who endured five years of
GERMAN OCCUPATION
with unflinching courage
and certain faith in eventual liberation

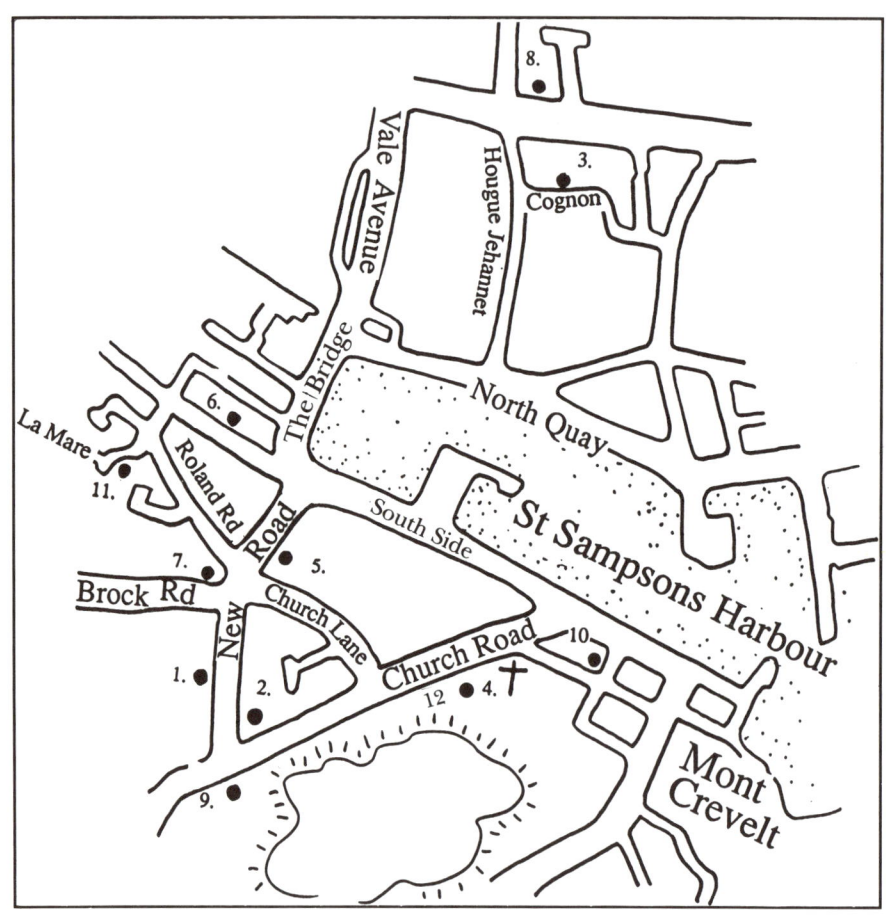

Part of the area covered by much of the Diary

1. "New Road"
2. Dr Jones' House
3. Dr Jones' House '2'
4. St Sampsons Church
5. Methodist Church & Hall
6. Salvation Army
7. "1449"
8. Minnie & Bill Le Maitre's House "Cliffdale"
9. Church Schools
10. Carpenter's Shop
11. Allendale
12. The Old Rectory

CONTENTS

	page
Maps	2
Road plan	6
List of Illustrations	9
Foreword by Sir Charles Frossard to the first edition	10
Foreword to this edition by Sir Graham Dorey	11
Brief notes on the Occupation of Guernsey 30 June 1940 – 9 May 1945	12
Relevant events of the 1939-45 war	13
Principal persons mentioned in the Diary	17
Photograph of the writer of the Diary "Jack" Sauvary	22
Introduction	23
Reproduction of a page from the Diary	24
THE DIARY	25
Extract from a letter	287
Valediction	289
Reproduction of a Red Cross message	290
Inscription on a family tombstone	293
Orders of the German Commandant	295
Guernsey recipes	297
Glossary	301
Calendars of Occupation Years	307
Index	313

Thanks

I would like to thank the following people for assistance relating to specific Diary entries or for help given in other ways:-

The late Dr Charles Cruickshank (author of the German Occupation of the Channel Islands), Mr J.H. Lenfestey (States of Guernsey archivist), Mrs Butt (St Sampson's Douzaine), Dr Maurice Burton (naturalist), the Librarians of the Guille-Allès Library, Guernsey and of both the Selsey and Chichester branches of the West Sussex County Library, Dr Osmond Roussel, Mr Vernon Luff, Gwenyth Wiltshire, Malcolm Vivyan, Eleanor Gibson, Peggy Evans, Keith Rudland and Shirley Harris.

In addition I thank Mrs Moira Crimp and the late Quill Bisset for taking special photographs, Mrs Sheila Berrett for typing the first transcript, Mr John Hyatt for proof reading and Judith Fiennes for help with the technical details of publishing.

Lastly I would like to make particular acknowledgement of the invaluable help given me in editing our father's Diaries by my sister Flo.

Thanks (second edition)

First my sincere thanks to the very many readers of the first edition who wrote so appreciatively about my father's Diary, some of whom even thanked me for making his record of the Occupation available to them. I also thank the numerous people who encouraged me to reissue it.

In addition I thank Mr Carel Toms for the use of several photographs from his fine collection of the Germans in Occupation, and Mr G R Farnham for his photograph of The Old Forge, then known as "1449".

My thanks are again due to Shirley Harris, Peggy Evans, Eleanor Gibson and my sister Flo for their continued help and encouragement, and to Judith Fiennes in particular for her patient and stalwart help in the preparation of this new edition of my father's Diary.

ILLUSTRATIONS

Germans marching past the Royal Hotel (cover picture) *

p.23   Mr J C Sauvary (Jack)

1. The beauty of the sea from The Banques
2. Mr & Mrs Sauvary
3. Flo with her daughter Rosemary
4. Jack with his daughter Jane
5. Jack in service uniform
6. Kit in nursing uniform
7. Flo's husband "that grand lad Ted"
8. Mr Gervase Peek, Guernsey's "Grand Old Man"
9. "New Road", built by Mr Sauvary in 1914
10. The Old Ford outside "New Road"
11. View down Church Lane from "1449", The Old Forge
12. "Pullman Car", horse drawn bus*
13. Tom and the "Skipper"
14. Mrs Rowe, owner of "1449"
15. Mary Ayres (née Sauvary) given in marriage by her uncle
16. Delancey Monument*
17. St Sampson's Church
18. St Sampson's Church "sheltering under the old elms"
19. Channel Queen Memorial
20. The grave in "the sunny jib patch"
21. The cinema in St Julian's Avenue*
22. Smith Street – Queue for Sweets – The Pollet*
23. German Observation Tower at Fort Richmond*
24. Machine gun at Fermain*
25. German transporter, Weighbridge, St Peter Port*
26. German light railway, Glategny Esplanade, St Peter Port*
27. SS Vega, Red Cross supply ship*
28. Liberation Fleet*
29. War memorial

* CAREL TOMS COLLECTION

FOREWORD
by Sir Charles K. Frossard, Bailiff of Guernsey 1982-1992

Les Lierres
Rohais
St Peter Port
Guernsey

I am privileged and honoured to write a foreword to these diaries of the late Mr J.C. Sauvary whose daughter is editing and publishing them as a work of love to the memory of her father.

The diaries record the thoughts and activities of a Christian Guernsey gentleman during the time the Island was under enemy occupation in the World War.

I was privileged as a young man to know Mr Sauvary, and I am sure that there are many, especially of my generation, who will appreciate the thoughts and feelings of Mr Sauvary and will be encouraged by the Christian steadfastness he showed in these difficult times.

Bailiff

FOREWORD
to the second edition
by Sir Graham M Dorey, Bailiff of Guernsey 1992

La Hougue ès Pies
Vale
Guernsey

Fifty years have now passed since the Liberation of the Island on the 9th May, 1945. Memories edit facts continuously over a period of time; so this contemporary account of the occupation is unexpurgated, and therefore of great value.

Mr Sauvary's Diary gives a true and balanced picture of life during the Occupation and is a patently honest presentation of the hardships that had to be endured. His determined spirit is typical of the will of the Islanders to survive with dignity and honour.

Bailiff

BRIEF NOTES ON THE OCCUPATION OF GUERNSEY
30 June 1940 – 9 May 1945

The outbreak of the Second World War on 3 September, 1939 began relatively quietly for the island of Guernsey, the second largest at 25 square miles, of the Channel Islands lying 80 miles South of England, but only 30 miles from the French Coast.

With the German invasion of Holland, Belgium and Luxembourg in May 1940, and the bypassing of the Maginot Line via Belgium, France was overrun with unexpected speed. A glance at the map will show that the defence of the Channel Islands was impossible without reducing them to rubble, and so their occupation was inevitable.

The British Government demilitarised them and made provision for the evacuation (in this order) of men of military age, school children, mothers with children under five and lastly anyone else wishing to leave.

Controversy persists about the way in which the British Government and the Island Authorities coped with this sudden, tremendous upheaval, and this is dealt with fully in Charles Cruickshank's Official History.

This first conquest of British soil had tremendous propaganda value for the Germans who began an immense building of fortifications which continued until 1944. Railways were laid, quarries re-opened and thousands of tons of material were imported for these buildings. They were constructed by Organisation Todt who employed thousands of European civilians of many nationalities to do the work. In addition, thousands of German troops were brought in. Some were billeted on residents, and other residents were turned out of their homes.

The island's economy was at once adapted to provide food, and trade with France was greatly increased by the importation of necessities especially food and fuel.

In 1942 there were two waves of deportation of British born residents. There is still doubt about the reason for this. (See Chapter X in the Official History.)

Following the Allied landings in Normandy, 6 June, 1944, it soon became apparent that the Channel Islands were to be bypassed. They quickly became isolated and were soon in a state of siege. Islanders and Germans were left to starve and freeze together, and there were many ugly scenes as the struggle for food intensified.

After long-drawn out negotiations the Red Cross was at last allowed to send food and other necessary supplies, and when these arrived at the end of December 1944, semi-starvation was averted. Further supplies arrived, but when one failed to bring flour, the islanders were without bread for three weeks.

Thereafter they had to wait patiently until they were liberated on 9th May 1945.

Some events of the 1939-45 war, relevant to Diary entries

1939   Britain and France declared war on Germany

1940
April   9   Germany invaded Denmark and Norway
May   10   Germany invaded Holland, Belgium and Luxembourg
               The Maginot Line bypassed via Belgium, and France overrun
         20   Germans reached the English Channel
         24   Dunkirk – evacuation of 338,000 British troops, completed by June 4
June   10   Italy declared war on Britain and France
         14   Germans occupied Paris
         19   Evacuation from the Channel Islands began

June   21   J. C. Sauvary's Diary commences

June   22   France capitulated
         28   Germans bombed St Peter Port Harbour, Guernsey
         30   Germans occupied Guernsey
July   10   Battle of Britain began
Sept   7   Big blitz on London began
         17   City of Benares, evacuating children to Canada, sunk by Germans
         27   German-Italian-Japanese mutual assistance pact
Oct   28   Italy invaded Greece
Nov   20   Hungary joined the Axis
         23   Rumania joined the Axis
               Roosevelt re-elected President of the USA
Dec   9   British offensive opened in North Africa
         29   Great fire raid on City of London

1941
Jan   Fighting in North Africa with varying results
         22   British took Tobruk
March   Bulgaria joined the Axis
         11   US Congress approved lend-lease
         24   Yugoslavia government joined the Axis
         31   Rommel attacked in Libya
April   17   Yugoslavia and Greece capitulate
               German Baedeker raids on Britain began
May   14   Hess landed in Scotland
         18   Battle-cruiser Hood sunk in the North Atlantic
         20   Germans captured Crete
         27   German battle-cruiser Bismarck sunk
June   22   Germans invaded Russia

	29	Rommel halted at Egyptian frontier
July	16	British invaded and occupied Syria
August		Churchill and Roosevelt meet off Newfoundland – Atlantic Charter formulated
	25-29	Anglo-Russian forces occupied Persia
Dec	5	Germans drive on Moscow halted
	7	Japanese attacked USA at Pearl Harbour
	8	USA and GB declared war on Japan
	11	Germany and Italy declared war on USA
	15	Battleships Prince of Wales and Repulse sunk off Malaya
	24	Meeting of Roosevelt and Churchill at White House
	25	Benghazi retaken by British
		Fall of Hong Kong

1942

Jan	21	Rommel opened Libyan offensive
Feb	15	Fall of Singapore
		Much activity in the Far East
May	27	Rommel's second Libyan offensive opened
June	21	Fall of Tobruk
	30	Rommel halted at El Alamein
Aug	19	Dieppe raid
		Battles for El Alamein
	25	Duke of Kent killed in air accident
Nov	3	Rommel began retreat from Egypt
	8	Allied landings in French North Africa
	27	French warships at Toulon scuttled

1943

		Russian winter offensive
Feb	2	German surrendered at Stalingrad
		Much fighting in North Africa until the . . .
May	12	Axis forces in North Africa surrendered
July	10	Allies invaded Sicily
Aug	18	Conquest of Sicily completed
	25	Fall of Mussolini
Sept	2	Italian surrender signed
	12	Italian fleet surrendered
Dec	27	Teheran Conference

1944

Jan		Allies advanced in Italy
June	6	Allied landings in Normandy
		(It was at once evident that the Channel Islands were to be bypassed)
		Concentration camp of 1,222 men and 46 women moved from Alderney to France
		All OT workers left Guernsey but 13,000 troops remained
June	13	Rocket bombing by V1s of SE England began
End June		SS penal instruction brigade ordered out of the Channel Islands by Hitler himself
	27	Cherbourg taken
	30	Attempted assassination of Hitler
July		By the end of the month shipments of food from France ceased
		Shortage of bread became acute
		Rations down to three months' supply
		German High Command considers evacuation of civilians (thereby allowing more food for the troops, but this was left too late)
Sept		Rocket bombing (V2) of South England began
	12	Leaflets for Germans dropped on the island
	17	Airborne assault on Arnhem
End Sept		Rations down to absolute minimum
		Thereafter the situation became most involved, with protracted negotiations between the British Cabinet and the German High Command via the British Legation in Berne – all unknown by the islanders until Nov 11.
Nov	3	Fred Noyon and Enitcott escaped with detailed information about the food situation and eventually reached England on Nov 12
	7	War Cabinet finally agreed to the sending of food parcels to supplement the basic civilian rations which were the responsibility of the Germans
Nov	11	The Bailiff informed the islanders that he had sent a wireless SOS to the International Red Cross about shortages and asking for immediate help and a visit from a Red Cross representative
		The Germans were determined to retain a garrison in the island at all costs
Nov	21	Germans requisition island's stock of potatoes
Dec	26	SS Vega arrived with food and medical supplies
Dec	31	Food parcels distributed

1945

Jan-May		Allies advanced towards Germany and victory
Feb		Possibility of removing sick and German wounded from the Channel Islands considered but no Hospital ship was available
Feb	6	SS Vega arrived with a second consignment of food parcels but no flour; and soap left behind in Lisbon
March	1	Islanders three weeks without bread
April	2	Last entry in Diary
April	**5**	**Mr Sauvary died**
April	28	Mussolini murdered
	30	Suicide of Hitler
May	8	Victory in Europe Day Mr Churchill in his broadcast to the nation said:- "Our dear Channel Islands will be free"
May	9	The surrender of the Channel Islands was signed on HMS Bulldog at 7.14 am.

PRINCIPAL PERSONS MENTIONED IN THE DIARY

RELATIVES

Mrs SAUVARY, Florence Susannah – Mother – Mum. Mr Sauvary's wife, the daughter of an army schoolmaster (10th Brigade, Royal Artillery). She was a teacher at the Capelles Schools. She had a beautiful alto voice, and was recruited to augment the choir of St Sampson's Church for festivals by her sister, Kate Honey, who sang treble in the choir. Mrs Sauvary became a lifelong member of the choir, and together with her husband played a prominent role in every aspect of church life, notably in the Mothers' Union and in fund raising. She did her husband's bookkeeping to within six months of her fairly sudden illness, and she died in June 1939, just three months before the outbreak of war. So it is small wonder that Mr Sauvary missed his wife so greatly, left alone in his big empty house, his second daughter having evacuated and with a severely depleted work force including his gardener.

GRIFFIFTHS, Florence, Flo – Mr Sauvary's first child. She taught music in Oxford until her marriage to Ted Griffiths in 1932. They lived in Surrey and had one child, Rosemary, born in 1937, who had spent two summer holidays in Guernsey and was very dear to her Grandpa.

SAUVARY, Kit, Kitty – Mr Sauvary's second child. Following her return from Canada in 1934 she taught at the Froebel Demonstration School in London. She did not evacuate with the school, intending to live with her widowed father. But in both the Winter and Spring terms she was asked to help at the evacuated school, and her father urged her to go, saying it was a call to war work. She returned to the island at Easter, determined to remain at home. But "Man proposes..." and she evacuated, to become a Nursing Auxiliary of the Civil Nursing Reserve, and eventually returned to teaching.

SAUVARY, Jack – Mr Sauvary's third child. He worked in the Midland Bank, first in the island and then in London. His war service was in the North African Campaign and the Middle East. He and his wife, Josephine had one child, Jane, born in 1938, a second granddaughter who Grandpa longed to see again. A second child, Robin, was born in 1947.

SAUVARY, Tom – elder of Mr Sauvary's two brothers, married to Alice. He worked at the Electric Station. Two of their sons were fishermen, hence the many generous gifts of shell and other fish.

SAUVARY, Willie – Mr Sauvary's other brother. He was a grower and evacuated with his wife Winnie. Mary was their only child who did not evacuate. The other five went or had already left the island.

SAUVARY, Mary – fifth child of Willie and Winnie. She visited her uncle regularly and he always tried to give her a good meal and food to take back. She, in her turn, was a great help in many ways, not least always accompanying him to put flowers on the grave. She worked in the Red Cross Bureau, so often gave him early notice of messages, and could dispatch his replies. She married Ted Ayres during the Occupation.

LE MAITRE, Minnie – one of Mr Sauvary's sisters. Her husband, Bill or Billie, was a grower who, before the Occupation, took Mr Sauvary's tomatoes to the boat. They had three sons and twin daughters who evacuated. Minnie, often supplied her brother with most welcome extras.

LE MAITRE, Vernon – eldest was a Billeting Officer, Percy and Ronald ran a bakery and confectionery business on the Bridge.

HONEY, Ned, Uncle Ned – widower of Mrs Sauvary's eldest sister, Kate. He had had an ironmongery business, and although already in his eighties, was in constant demand for repairs of pots and pans, as shortages became acute. Auntie Kate had been a prominent church worker, and was a brilliant needlewoman, even making altar frontals. She ran a guest house in the lovely Old Rectory (now demolished) for many years. He continued to live there alone to try to save his home from the damage of German Occupation.

HONEY, Marjorie – only daughter of Ned and Kate. She was a teacher and evacuated with her school.

HONEY, Percy – second son of Ned and Kate. He and his wife Edith would have liked his father to live with them after his daughter evacuated.

WEST, Edith, Edie – youngest of Mrs Sauvary's sisters. She was known to Mr Sauvary's children as their 'poor, poetic aunt', because she was always quoting poetry. She died in 1940 and her considerable number of books was stored at New Road awaiting disposal.

OTHERS

AUSTIN, George – Chief Health Inspector. He was able to give news of conditions in totally evacuated Alderney. A member of the church choir.

BACHMANN, Peter – An engraver at the Jewellers and Silversmiths. The firm was founded by his father Emil W.J. Bachmann, a skilled watch-maker, an emigrant from the island of Fehmarn in the Baltic, then a dependency of Denmark. Peter married Kitty Head, a school friend of Mr Sauvary's daughters, and she continued to be known in the family as Kitty Head, to distinguish her from Mr Sauvary's daughter, Kit, who had been called Kitty while at school. Kitty 'Head' and Peter had one daughter, Diana, who evacuated with her school. A second child, Peter John, was born during the Occupation.

BISSON, Henry – He fished from Bordeaux harbour with his uncle Pilot Charlie Corbet before the war, and then acquired his own boat. They sometimes took Mr Sauvary and his daughter crabbing and fishing.

BROWELL, W.M. – A one-time guest at the Old Rectory which Mrs Honey once ran as a guest house.

CLARKE, Angelo – He had once owned the little island of Brecqhou, off the coast of Sark, and Mr Sauvary did all his building work there, an interesting, but at times hazardous job. His eldest son Philip married Freda a fellow student of Mr Sauvary's daughter, Flo.

CORTVRIEND, G.B. and V.V. – Gussie and Violet were family friends. Gussie was a Belgian who was badly wounded in the First World War, and was sent to Norfolk to convalesce. Here he met and married Violet in 1917. He eventually moved to the Guernsey branch of the Midland Bank. Their four children evacuated.

ELLIS, Lily – A neighbour whose brother had worked for Mr Sauvary. When she lost her job at a bakery, partly to help her, Mr Sauvary opened a greengrocery and barter Shop next to "1499".

ELSIE – Mrs Godfray's personal maid. A lively, energetic and humorous character.

ERWIN – His correct name was IRMA. He worked for the German civilian construction company FIRMA IRMA, so was probably one of the family owning the company. His home town was Mosel. His birthday is 30 April. It has recently been learnt that he was eventually moved out of New Road but remained in the island.

FROSSARD, The Rev. and Mrs E.L. – Mr Frossard came to be Rector of St Sampson's parish in 1918 following service as Chaplain to the Forces in France. His mother was French, his father English. Mrs Frossard was Scottish and had served in France with the Scottish Church Canteen. Both their children were born in the island, and their son is the present Bailiff. They soon endeared themselves to their parishioners, Mr Frossard giving particular pleasure by preaching in his fluent French to the congregation at the daughter church of St Clair. He was Dean from 1947-1967 and died in 1968.

GODFRAY, Mrs A. – The sister-in-law of Mr Tom Godfray, Mr Sauvary's Sark friend, known as the Grand Old Man of Sark. Both he and Mr A. Godfray died before the war. Mrs Godfray, who lived at Belle Vue, St Andrew's, was already in her late eighties at the beginning of the Occupation, and Mr Sauvary was assiduous in providing her and her sister with any extras he could get. Unfortunately every visit involved tiring cycle rides up hills.

HOUSTOUN, Miss Mary – A Guy's nurse, a great friend of Mrs Sauvary's sister, Edith West, from her nursing days. She retired to Guernsey where her brother Jack joined her.

HUNKIN, Reg & Belle, his daughter. His second wife was Winnie Le Poidevin, and they lived at Fosse André. He was a builder.

JONES, Dr Charles – A family friend of very long standing, a widower who had recently retired. He lived at Newington, a stone's throw from Mr Sauvary, until he too was turned out of his house.

LAINÉ Jack – Dr Jones' chauffeur.

LAWTON, Mr W. and Miss – Possibly from Poland. Mr Lawton helped Mr Sauvary with his bookkeeping when Mrs Sauvary became ill. Mr Sauvary subsequently befriended them.

LE POIDEVIN, Mrs – She lived just a few doors away from Mr Sauvary in New Road. During the Occupation she lived with her daughter Winnie and her husband Reg Hunkin. Amy and Nellie, her twin daughters, both headmistresses at the Vale schools, evacuated with their schools. Amy was married to Major Hampton.

LIHOU, Miss – Mrs Godfray's sister. She too was provided with many extras.

MARTEL, Gerald – One of Mr Sauvary's three employees who did not evacuate. As Mr Sauvary's health and strength failed he gradually took over more and more responsibility for the undertaking side of the business.

MATTHEWS, Miss Dorothy – A retired nurse who had been a great friend of Mrs Jones, and when she died she took over the running of Dr Jones' house. She was a great lover of cats.

MESSERVY, Arthur – Mr Sauvary's foreman, and one of the three who did not evacuate.

MONSELL, Evelyn – The aunt of Mary Sauvary and sister of Winnie. She was a sister at the Emergency Hospital during the Occupation, and she kept an eye on Mr Sauvary right up to the time of his death there.

OGIER, Jim – He had a little shop almost opposite Mr Sauvary's house, where he sold confectionery, tobacco and newspapers etc. His son, Jackie, was organist at the parish church for a time.

OGIER, Stafford, Staff – (no relation of Jim Ogier). Mr Sauvary's fellow churchwarden. He was a custodian of the houses of evacuees. He and his wife, Emmie, lived at Les Gigands, a lovely old Guernsey farmhouse. Their hospitality to Mr Sauvary was boundless and did much to alleviate his intense loneliness, in addition to providing him with many a good meal. Of their three sons only Lesley evacuated. Lionel and Bryan ran a wireless business.

OPPENHEIM, E. Phillips – The popular novelist of adventure and intrigue. He owned a big house in the Vauquiedor and a Martello Tower at L'Ancresse. Mr Sauvary did all his building work, and Mrs Oppenheim liked him to show her the birds' nests in her garden. Their maid looked after the German officers billeted in their house.

PATTIMORE, Mr – For many years the family lived opposite Mr Sauvary. "Rooster", as he was popularly known, had been a foreman of the stevedores. He was a widower and lived with his widowed daughter, Elsie Carré, in Roland Road. She was a very amusing character. For a time she was a great help to Mr Sauvary in making cigarettes.

PEEK, Gervase – A personality of the island. He was a manager of the Guernsey Press Company, still with a hand on the helm in his eighties. He withstood every set-back of the Occupation with characteristic good humour, remaining cheerful and active to the end. He died in March 1943.

ROBERTS, Tom – An employee of the family retainer type. He was devoted to the family and came to be regarded as a friend. This very intelligent man, because he ranked as a labourer could never rise in the hierarchy of the building trade. He was Mr Sauvary's right-hand man throughout the Occupation, and with Mrs Rowe did everything for the "Skipper" that the children were not there to do.

ROMERIL, The Rev P– The Wesleyan parson who lived next door to Mr Sauvary in the Manse, with his wife and family. Mrs Romeril died in February 1943.

ROWE, Mrs – She lived at the Old Forge, "1449" Brock Road, just a stone's throw from Mr Sauvary's house. She was the equivalent of the present day Home Help. Soon after the Occupation she took over the running of Mr Sauvary's house, and undertook many extras. When he was turned out of New Road he lodged at "1449", and Mrs Rowe made his last years comfortable, doing as Tom did, all that Mr Sauvary's children would have liked to have done for him. After the Liberation she told his daughter that her one regret was that, because he had to spend his last weeks in hospital, she could not look after him to the end.

SANTANGELO – A musical Italian family who settled in Guernsey. There were three children, Albert a violin player, Ida, and Peppino who played the cello and after a career in music returned to Guernsey. He became a Conseiller, was a member of the Investigating Committee looking into feasibility of the island taking over the Post Office, and became the first President of the Post Office Board following its independence of the UK on 1st October 1969.

SHERWILL, Major Ambrose – The Attorney General, known as the Procureur in the island. At the beginning of the Occupation he became President of the Controlling Committee. He was 'released of his office' on the 24th December 1940 because the Germans discovered he knew there were 'spies' in the island and had kept silent.

STUBBS, Mr & Mrs R. – Fellow parishioners. Mr Stubbs was the chief engineer of the granite firm, William Griffiths. They were most helpful in providing tobacco coupons.

"Jack" Sauvary

INTRODUCTION

These Diaries were clearly written in ink in eleven hardbacked notebooks from the day the Germans bombed Guernsey prior to occupying it two days later on 30 June, 1940 to within a few weeks of its Liberation on 9 May, 1945.

To shorten an inevitably long five-year record some repetitive matter has been omitted. Mr Sauvary never got over the rather sudden death of his wife in June, 1939. They had had an unusually close partnership, working together in his business and in church and parish affairs, and many entries about his feelings of loss have been omitted. Also left out are full details of various matters in which he was called upon, as always, to act as arbitrator and peacemaker, because they might cause offence.

Otherwise apart from paragraphing, a very few spelling corrections, the omission of a few personal details about people mentioned and with just the occasional word altered or added to elucidate the entry, the text has been left exactly as written. Punctuation has been added, but not inverted commas for speech which has just been preceded by a comma and begun with a capital letter.

Readers should bear in mind that Mr Sauvary had to write guardedly because of the possibility of the Diaries being found by the Germans, especially when they were billeted in his house. For instance slave labour is always called 'the Foreigners'.

The relative value of money should also be remembered. In real terms:-

the 1940-1945 £1 is the approximate equivalent of £18 in 1990
the old shilling (s.), twenty to the pound, about 90p in 1990
and the old penny (d.), 240 to the pound, 7½p in 1990.

2/6 per lb. I think I will get some to mix with Rhubarb, but just then the price shocked me, I am recovering so may get 1 lb. I have a nice lot in the field, but will, like last year wait till they are properly grown. I forgot to mention, Mary had a cup of coffee, a slice of dry bread with a nice taste of stewed Rhubarb, I could see she enjoyed the little snack. Most of the Germans are gone from around here, its so quiet & normal again, that I feel perhaps the end is nearing. I hear Mr. Cross, can have his House back again the Germans have been in the last 12 months or more, they also had D. Jones Garage & Store, & they are practically all gone from the Church Schools, I hope for ever. The red & white pinks (that sounds funny) are all in bloom outside study, I will put some on Mum's Grave on Friday, its 3 years on Friday she died, on a lovely morning such as we are having today.

Photocopy of a page from the original diary

JUNE 1940

Darling Flo, Kit, Jack, Ted, Jo, Rosemary and Jane,

Now I am going to try to write up a Diary of Events, starting Kit from the day you left by the Courier, that eventful evening, Friday, June 21.

I was really glad in many ways that you decided to go, and I had practically made up my mind to go as well, but only (I think) because as you all stated, we ought to be all together. *But* in my own mind, if I had had to choose and advise, I would have taken the risk and recommended us to stay here. Of course, in the end, I did not have the choice, events happened too quickly, and I am here.

I was, as you know, very anxious to get the best of my crop of tomatoes off in order to get the cash, and hoping against hope that the Occupation, which I was convinced was coming, might have been delayed a few days longer. I must say I had foreseen it, and I had looked facts straight in the face. My conclusion was that it was better to be starved to death than bombed to death, I think I favoured the former. But there was the fact that, if in England, we could have done war work and helped the cause, while here we would be in camp and able to do nothing, a great problem.

You know darlings that I am getting old and to start life again is not very encouraging, not at 64. Even, Kit, had we gone to Canada, I did not relish the change.

Well here I am. My carpenter shop was getting depleted. Ellis and Horace went, also my gardener Ralph. Messervy my foreman fell off his bicycle and broke his arm nearly at the shoulder, I understand in a very bad place.

Darling Kit, Saturday passed very quietly. I was lonely and wondered how you got on.

On Sunday Stan Simon came down (I thought he had evacuated) and said there was a cargo boat in, so we started to pick and pack tomatoes. The order was not to grade. I got through 66 baskets and was dead beat, it was such a rush. The carter, Bill Le Maitre, was there at 7 in the evening. That done I got some tea, no Ethel to do my housework.

From Monday to Friday, the 28th, we continued watering and picking the rapidly ripening crop, killing work, but we were getting ahead.

Friday, June 28. The eventful outrage. I packed 39 baskets. Billy Le Maitre fetched them at 3 o'clock. I had a little snooze, then went to Town by bus to get my hair cut (in case I slipped off). I told Tom I might go as far as the White Rock. Wilfred Robin got in the bus at Mr Poat's, and said he was going to Smith Street to hear Mr Sherwill's broadcast.

I was finished at 5 to 6, and followed the crowd up High Street and met Mrs Cortvriend. She persuaded me to stay, and we chatted

JUNE 1940

about the pros and cons of going or sticking it out here. She agreed Kit was wise in getting away.

The broadcast was finished at a quarter to 7, and hundreds besides myself ran down the Quay Steps. I ran along the front and managed to get the bus, which proved lucky for me, though I would not have minded walking to St Sampson's.

I reached home, went through the house and when opening the back door heard terrible machine-gun firing. I guessed what it was, so ran to my shelter (the little office under the bathroom), put on my tin hat and sat in the corner, expecting Tom and Stan Simon to come. They were working that evening, and I had told them I would always leave the house open for them to shelter in case of a raid. I was worried that they did not come and was just going to fetch them when the bombs dropped and I flew back.

A minute later I heard them scampering down. Tom came so fast he slipped on the cement path which startled me. However after blowing them up for keeping me in suspense, Tom explained they had been taking a bird's eye view by climbing on top of the packing shed, thinking it was a scrap between English and German planes. While the Pop-Pop was going on they stuck there, when suddenly the bombs dropped and clouds of smoke flew up. In their fright they rushed down, and poor Tom was terribly pale. He said the Town looked on fire. This continued for 15 minutes, then things were quiet.

Simon would insist on going home to his wife in Trinity Square, against my advice. He was lucky to get home because when by the Generator four bombs dropped. I think they were trying for the Gas Works, missed and hit the Fruit Export sheds and blew the gable out. The concussion nearly blew him off his bicycle. A lucky miss for him.

As the planes were approaching for their attack the Courier was just passing Bordeaux, returning from Alderney with a cargo of pigs and cattle. They dropped three bombs but all fell behind the ship. Captain Ingrouville, who knows the rocks well, ran for St Sampson's harbour. The crew and helpers waded ashore.

The Germans had also machine-gunned the ship, and the men hay-making in the fields at Bordeaux who were wounded. All that was happening while I was in the bus.

The White Rock got it and the roof of the Weighbridge was partly blown off. About 20 lorries loaded with tomatoes were burned. Some drivers who took cover under their lorries were burnt to death. Some 30 people were killed and many wounded. [*See illustration 29.*] Hundreds were going to the mail boat with their portmanteaux which made a good target. Hundreds were going home after the broadcast. A bomb fell in the Strand. Mr Le Feuvre who lives in front of us had three of his toes blown off. His

JUNE 1940

little boy with him was not hurt.

Philip Clarke's house came in for a smash. A bomb dropped in his garden, intended I think for Steve Duquemin's Racecourse. I expect they thought it was an aerodrome. I saw the Royal Hotel, Munro's, the Pollet, all a picture with hundreds of bullet holes in the cement fronts. I am keeping the Presses. You will find better reports there.

Saturday, June 29. Air raid warnings all day, naturally as bad for the nerves as bombing was. Tom and I ventured to the church and took shelter there while a plane passed, reconnaissance, I think, to photograph the damage. Tom went to Town for my provisions, though I told him not to go, he risked it. He did not like it. Many people were on their nerves, rushing from shop to shop.

Sunday, June 30. On my way to church I saw a large Blenheim bomber flying very low over the harbour and around the Vale Castle, in fact it was lower than the castle. It was a funny Morning Service, only two men, Ogier and myself, no choir boys or ladies, and very few at the service. Mr Frossard took for his text, Luke 12, verse 32, "Fear not, little flock, for it is your Father's good pleasure to give you the kingdom." The Collect, 5th Sunday after Trinity, also very appropriate.

In the evening I arrived early and Mr Frossard told me that two German planes had landed, and one hovered around then flew off. We knew by then that the Germans would be in occupation that night. So they were, and by 8 o'clock it was broadcast that all had to behave and not talk in groups. It's now official that we are in camp.

Monday, July 1. This morning the orders are that we are to take all firearms to the Royal Hotel. I took the bus to Town and there were already hundreds in front of the Royal, some with as many as four guns slung on their backs. I saw swords and bayonets, curios of every sort, muzzle-loading guns and revolvers (not service). It was a sight to see all those German officers standing in the lobby. Mr Peek was much in evidence accompanied by his big cigar.

I decided that I had better send my revolvers so Tom took them in that afternoon. He was delighted, said it would make history. I had tied the three together, and when he presented them butt end, the officer just handled them and said, Curios I suppose, oh you can take them back.

Tuesday, July 2. All clocks to advance one hour, (making us two hours in advance of sun time). Only beer, cider and wine to be sold. All buses to be taken off the roads.

The States are offering to take over all greenhouses. I have

JULY 1940

handed mine over and put Tom in charge. They pay him £2 a week.

Friday, July 5. I went to the Douzaine Room, where hundreds called for their first pay out, collected by the foreman. I also drew pay for myself and Simon, but I know they won't pay for three on my small vinery.

Saturday, July 6. Kit, we are religiously keeping the garden clean. Weeds are growing like mad. It's awful outside the house evenings, not a sound except the few men who collect outside Ogier's little shop discussing our future.

The tomatoes are ripening by the hundreds. My houses look a sight. It's heartbreaking not to be able to export them, but people don't worry as much as I expected, I think because we are all in the same boat.

Orders now are that we are to grow food in the greenhouses for the winter, but my tomatoes are looking so well that for the present it's decided to keep them watered till November.

All the Rectors were called to be informed that England had demilitarised the island and did not intend to protect us as the island is of no strategical value. Personally (although not unanimously agreed) I think they were very wise in their decision. The cost of protecting us was too great, and a small island like this could have been smashed from the French coast.

Of course this came as a terrible shock to Guernsey, as Kit knows. She will have told you of the great muddle about the evacuation. They should have said definitely that all children and men of military age should evacuate. Instead they said 'advised', and consequently these men had their wives, mothers and sweethearts advising them all sorts of different ways, making it difficult for them to decide. The authorities should have given them a definite lead. Now we have left here hundreds of men who would have been useful for our war work in England. [See C. Cruickshank's *Official History*, pages 43, 44 & 45.]

Mrs Cortvriend insisted that I should spend my weekends at The Hollies, only 100 yards up the Fosse André from their home, Essex House. They have taken charge of the place. After putting flowers on Mum's grave I went and had a jolly good time.

Oh! by the way, I had to buy a bicycle, £5.15.0. I hadn't ridden one for about 24 years. Tom suggested that I should have a practice first, but my patience would not allow this, so I rode off right away. Of course I did not feel too comfortable the first time.

The weather was superb, I was boiling hot, and when I reached The Hollies where they were waiting to receive me, I had hardly a dry stitch on.

JULY 1940

Monday, July 8. The Hopper I bought from Jack West, 26" frame, I found too high, so I took it back and got a 24", just in time, the last one. I got him to fix a 3-speed gear, 35/- extra, so now I am fixed up.

The States had decided to take over all unoccupied houses and are sending men around collecting first of all perishable goods. Then they will collect bicycles, then sell the coal.

We are picking hundred of baskets of tomatoes. The Alliance vinery took two tons away. It's really heartbreaking, the waste. The cows eat as many as you like to give them. In the country it's a picture to see the gulls getting at the baskets and boxes piled in the fields. Stevens, Banana Market, has had two tons, up to now, for his pigs.

The 'elite' of St Sampson's collect outside Ogier's shop after work, waiting for the Press. Some nights they have had to wait up to two hours, it's very irregular. I expect they will get in proper stride later. I expect everything has to be censored.

Darlings, you would not know New Road. The least sound now seems to make you jump. It's really funny and worrying. Every sound is magnified, and startles you, even the rustling of leaves, sounds which in normal times were not noticed but now seem different.

More bicycles are moving about nowadays. Pammett and a man from L'Ancresse are running "Pullman Cars" as people call them. They consist of a skinny horse attached to a very old and neglected van raked out from some old barn, with crates around which are covered with a sort of bed ticking. One has red stripes, the other blue. I decided to go to Town in one this week to make history. I could have walked there quicker. Then when your shopping is over you have to wait about 1½ hours before they return.

I see Mr & Mrs Lake start off for Town at 8.30 walking, about twice a week, returning at 12.30 loaded with parcels. Everybody is now trying to get in a store for the winter.

Stevens is allowed a car but often has no petrol. He has improvised a funny kind of trailer which carries ½ ton of tomatoes. Herbert Wright has a sort of little dog-cart he tows behind his cycle to take out wirelesses and batteries. His wife evacuated and he is boarding at Luxon's. Lily Parsons asked me if I wanted to board there, but for the present I am cooking for myself making my own bed but never cleaning the house. Washing up dishes is as far as I go.

On the Bridge a few days ago I saw three women having a terrible row as I thought. But when I arrived at the spot, one of them I know very well (lives at the Grandes Maisons) was indignant because one of the others, discussing the war situation, said, *If* we win. The other was bullying her, in fact shouting, *If* we win, don't

AUGUST 1940

you say that. It's *WHEN* we win. She appealed to me, What do you think this awful woman is saying – If we win, IF we win. Of course we will win and don't say that again. It was time to laugh so I left.

I forgot if I told you about the boy at the vinery who was sent to get a Press and returned saying, Warsaw is captured. They caught him early this morning.

We had two Germans at our church the other Sunday morning. They told Mr Frossard one was a Catholic, the other a Protestant. He showed them the way to the Catholic Church but they preferred to remain at our church together. One of them sang very heartily.

August. The month opened with marvellous weather. We are having a hot summer as in 1911 and 1921. It's awful weeding, the ground is so hard, and it's out of the question to dig our potatoes. But the weeds grow. They catch the heavy dew. Your pickling onions, Kit, are now as big as golf balls.

I am eking out the fowls' food with boiled potatoes and crusts of bread. They are laying fairly well and I am pickling a few each week. I got water glass from Boots. I am using our casserole to pot 4 lbs of butter.

I wonder all the time where you all are and if Jack is in the army. Week after week I turn things over in my mind, and think perhaps I ought to have gone to England to relieve your anxiety. Then I decide not to bother, but to leave everything to Providence.

We are quiet and comfortable here, have sufficient food, and the wireless until our electric supply is exhausted. They say we can carry on till Christmas. Coal is getting short, gas they think will last till November.

The States have a battalion of men cutting down trees all over the island under the supervision of Mr Lloyd De Putron. Stone carts and vans take them to depots. Later they will sell the wood to eke out the coal.

I don't worry about this winter. Hundreds of greenhouses are growing beans, carrots and other foodstuff, but water will be the problem as most of it is pumped by electricity. They are putting up a windmill at Manuelle's quarry behind the house, so I am likely to get water as I draw from there. All my crops are good, and your onions, Kit, are nearly as large as footballs. But I intend to pickle them for you all the same. I got a gallon of white wine vinegar, Vinaigre-de-Table.

Friday, August 9. Our English planes paid a visit to the aerodrome this afternoon, dropped several bombs and I believe did a fair amount of damage. We could see smoke rising but don't get to know the extent of the damage.

AUGUST 1940

Sunday, August 11. Darling Kit, I went to wish you many happy returns but you had flown, and I really hope and trust it was for the best. I felt sad that I could not even write or send a telegram. But I went to Town on Saturday and got your presents, Lavender Water, French Fern Talcum Powder, etc. I often wonder if you will ever get them. However I am trusting to Providence that all will work out well for us, but time will hang so, and I worry with all this devilish bombing.

Things are tightening up here in every way. Clothes are to be rationed. Butchers open only Fridays and Saturdays. Another new order, all fishing must be done from St Peter Port harbour, and all other boats not afloat must be parked on the Castle Walk. You cannot even keep a boat in your garden or garage.

Wednesday, August 21. I arranged about an air raid shelter at Delancey Schools (they opened last month) to be built of concrete blocks and capable of holding 70 children. We will put four loads of shingle on the flat roof.

I took Miss Lawton a large bunch of Muscat Grapes nearly as big as plums, 6d per lb. I wish you were all here to eat them, particularly Rosemary and Jane. It's awful to think of the loss to the growers.

In the afternoon (as the season was swiftly passing) I went to Richmond Corner for a bathe. Mr Poat was there. He bathed his feet to keep me company. I was the only real bather. Many women were shrimping, a poor catch. I remember being there with you one afternoon, Kit, and you swam out to the Flie Rock.

It was again perfect weather, not one single breath of wind, sun beautiful but not burning, but the water in the rock pools was burning hot. You know what Guernsey is like when it is really fine. It took me 2½ hours to bathe and parade the beach. And all the time there was a terrible bombardment going on sometimes to the S, sometimes towards Cherbourg.

When I returned Messervy, who is now out of hospital, had come to see me with his wife and daughter. Dr Jones was chatting with them in the garden. I made them all tea, including Tom who fetched a few cakes from Plummer's.

Wednesday, September 4. I saw the States Supervisor about the air raid shelter at Delancey Schools. What awful raids over England! I often wonder where Jack, Jo and darling Jane are in these awful times. I trust they are safe and don't get disturbed nights. And I wonder if Jack has to go up to London every day.

The week passed quietly. The boats are now catching plenty of mackerel. This week we have two "Pullman" bus services, the other from L'Ancresse.

SEPTEMBER 1940

Undated. Went to the Cortvriends for the weekend as usual. Had a quiet time, nice rest, but very depressed wondering where you all were and how you are sticking it. I was worried one evening when I heard on the wireless that a woman had been knocked down and fatally injured in Kensington. Being in that district, Kit, I imagined it might be you. I think with the strain and worry we imagine all sorts of things. I dream about poor little Rosemary and Jane, and wonder if I will ever see them again.

Violet was also in the dumps, especially after the wireless announcement of the sinking of the City of Benares on September 17th, evacuating children to Canada. [The full story is told in *E. Huxley's Atlantic Ordeal*, 1941.] So many children lost 100 miles from land.

I understand a noisy night but not till 5 o'clock did the bangs wake me. From the landing window I had a good view of the display of fireworks. They dropped No. 1 English News Leaflet with photographs of the King and Queen, his speech and other news. It seems they are not aware that we have wireless. I am told thousands fell over Cobo and the Câstel.

Sunday, Sept. 29. Decided to spend my birthday at home. I knew you would all be picturing me in the old place, New Road. So here I am without a soul to greet me or wish me many happy returns. This is sad but I can bear it if only I knew where you all were and if you are still alive and well. It's the first time in 42 years that I have not had greetings from Mum and the children. She used to think so much of birthdays. There was always the great ordeal of choosing presents, and on the 29th the 'surprise' of two or three pairs of lovely hand-knitted socks from Mum.

Well I am 64 and must not dwell on all that. I told Violet my reason for not going this weekend and sent her a bottle of wine to drink my health. Miss Matthews insisted I should go there for lunch, and I have promised Mrs Stubbs I would go there for tea. They are worrying and want my opinion on an air raid shelter, so after all I won't have been at home as I intended.

Tom generally takes on the garden and fowls on Sundays, when he gets the eggs. But he thinks the fowls must know as it's generally the slackest day!

Very few people at church. Jack Ogier is organist now Mr Guillemette had to leave, owing to pressure of work with the Bailiff.

Mr Stubbs' shelter has about 75 bags of stone dust between his and Mr Mallett's house. Mrs Stubbs is very upset not to have got away. She blames Dick for studying his firm too much. There was a trail of vans going to Town with boats, some with as many as three on and towing another on a cradle.

OCTOBER 1940

After church Uncle Ned came in and drank my health in a bottle of beer. He is looking well but thinner. He is living with Percy and goes to the Old Rectory every day to ventilate.

Tuesday, October 8. It was a wonderful day and a beautiful moonlight night. I pictured the moon also shining over you wherever you all are. The world so wonderful yet all this savagery. We now have Socials on Tuesday nights at the Church Schools and I look forward to them. We had an enjoyable whist drive and singsong tonight.

All clothing and boot shops are closed for nine days for stock taking, the second time in two months. We have been issued with index cards for clothing. Coupons – suit 60, overcoat 60, handkerchief 5. Shop hours, food and tobacconists 10–12.30, 2–4. Therefore people have to rush and there are queues. I waited ½ hour for a packet of soda and they had none.

I now have Mrs Rowe looking after the house. After 2½ months I was sick of trying to keep things going. She cooked a mackerel for my dinner. I dine quality hours, about 2.30.

I went to see Mr Finey at the Câstel Hospital. He has been there five weeks, nervous breakdown. Last week he went to the Forest Rectory, it had been broken into and all his silver stolen, and the place like bedlam. His wife and the kiddies evacuated with the Forest School. It's in the hands of the police but I don't think they will trace anything.

I went to see Mrs Carré, my first visit since the Occupation. She thought I had gone away. She gave me lovely sweet grapes which are selling at 4d per lb. Yellow grapes as large as walnuts are 6d and 8d per lb. I have a small crop of pears, I cannot eat them all so Tom benefits.

Mrs Godfray phoned the other day to know if I was ill as I hadn't called for six weeks. It's such a long uphill way on a bicycle.

Undated. It's such a lovely day I asked the Lawtons to tea. Miss Lawton rests in the swing hammock, her brother in a camp chair. I leave them to read or sleep and go for a bathe. Mrs Rowe (who is now looking after the house) offered to stay and give them their tea, but being such a fine day I would not keep her, so I will do the honours myself.

What an awful raid on London. An enormous number of planes brought down. I still wonder where you all are.

This morning we dug the potatoes, then I went to Town. Got paté and charcuterie. The paté lengthens out my butter. Got my rations from the Bridge, 1/- worth of meat, 4 oz sugar which looks like 50 grains, salt etc. There seemed to be a fair amount of tinned fruit but not on sale while fresh fruit is about. Tinned salmon and lobster are still on sale. I get a tin each week to build up my stock. But it's

OCTOBER 1940

impossible to get cheese, and cereals are almost out of the question.

I went to the bank with the collection money, £4.10s. not bad. The bank man had counted 24 boats heading for the Town on his way down. A notice in the Press says this is a reprisal because eight men, with a fair sized boat, slipped away about 10 days ago. (I don't know if they reached England). [They did.] If any other men go the Germans say they will take all other men to France. The women would get a grand time looking after things here!

Friday, October 18. Mrs Rowe had prepared a stuffing, onions, sage, parsley which I baked with my small joint of veal and parboiled potatoes. I had to wait till 5 o'clock, bad management, but I enjoyed it very much after fasting for eight hours. Milk pudding with skimmed milk. We are reduced to ½ pint of skimmed milk.

Mrs Rowe put out some of mine and Mum's clothes. The pants of my dress suit are completely spoilt, moth eaten. The sunshine lines were packed with clothes, most I think ruined. I should have got someone in to deal with them before. However these are only details which don't worry me.

Saturday, October 19. The week passed very quietly, usual Social, Choir practice. Curfew now at 9. I hear there was a funeral at the Fort burial ground on Saturday. It's reported that German officers were inspecting land-mines at Fermain and an explosion killed two officers. We hear a lot of reports but don't know what is true.

I had a Douzaine Meeting this afternoon. Everyone now has to have a Registration Card and the Douzaine is responsible for registration. All to be done by Saturday, so we are in for a busy time.

Kit, I have your onions in the greenhouse drying, a lovely lot, some weighing over 1lb. There will be no scarcity as we have imported a lot from France, also 200 tons of sugar, biscuits which require better teeth than mine to crunch (it will take a sledge hammer to break them!), hundreds of tons of cereals (some for seed), cheese which I have not yet had, salt butter, and I hear salt, (but we are making our own with sea water). We have Mr Raymond Falla and Mr P.A. Mahy in France buying for us, trading from Granville.

The Germans are buying up all our motor-cars and lorries, the 1939s and 1940s. I am told they are paying a fair price for them, and that Stan Noel is one of the valuers. I wonder what they will give for my old Ford (I mean as a curio!). They are paying for them in Francs, and we use that money for buying our goods.

On the wireless last night I heard the talk on the Channel Islands. Was glad even to hear that news. It seemed like home even hearing Fulford's voice. He was Master (Masons) the same year as I was.

OCTOBER 1940

This week I have been fixing a stove in the church near the font. All electric and gas heating is cut off. We are still allowed both in the house. This week the coal man has left me only ½ cwt. They have had to give the Gas Company 600 tons, leaving us short.

They are digging peat from Steve Duquemin's Race Course. I saw some at Helman's Brickfield where they are drying it in open sheds. Some of the oak is solid yet, and I saw elm branches with all the grain.

I have two or three weeks' work for Mr Peek, but am otherwise earning nothing except an occasional funeral, and some material I had in stock I pass with the little work I get.

I hear it's costing the States £10,000 per week for wages etc. as they've taken over most of the vineries and outside ground. I have kept the field, but not wise as it brings me in nothing.

Week Oct. 21. Work slacker than usual. At times I wonder if I was wise in delaying my departure till I could not get away. I worry for your sakes, but whatever happens don't ever worry about me. I had so many things to keep me here.

I have been at the Church Schools all the week. The Douzeniers and Constables have to check and witness the signatures of people bringing back their Registration Forms. Next week their Identity Cards will come and everybody will have to come again and we will have to check their signatures.

I have looked into more ladies' eyes this week than I ever did in all my life! Had I been colour blind I might have got out of the job! A Dutchman described himself as blonde. It amused me for he was dark, one more dip and he would have been black. Some could not even sign their papers. We had to visit those too old or infirm to come. The charge was 1s. but of course we have not taken the bob. (The weather was cold and dreary but we had a nice fire.)

What a blow on the wireless today. Fancy losing the Empress of Britain, 42,000 tons. Now Greece is in the struggle. Where will it all end, and will we ever meet again at New Road, a united family.

I am getting enough food, for certain enough fruit. I have dozens of Chaumontel pears in the attic, and lovely Blenheim Orange apples.

I bought five cwt of small potatoes to fatten all my cockerels and lengthen out the ration of meal.

We got 1,000 tons of coal from France this week, and lots of beef, chestnuts, lemons, cheese, etc. Many shops are closing down, stocks depleted. We won't have tea much longer.

Many things I don't write about. It might not be prudent. I never know how things will turn out nor whose hands this epistle might get into.

OCTOBER 1940

Thursday, October 31. A sad day for us all, Mum's birthday, and already a second one she has gone. I am sure all our thoughts were concentrated on her. She often said, Death is so final. After I had called at the Schools to see if I could be spared I put sprays of yellow chrysanthemums from Mr Purse on the grave. For the past weeks I have put Belladonna Lilies from our garden, and we still have Mignonette, Roses, Pansies and Carnations, and Mrs Rowe had given me a lovely bunch of Chrys.

I was at the Schools all the afternoon with Mr Poat and Frank Dorey. The weather was so bad only nine people came.

Mr Trouteaud was riding, the Bouêt or Longstore, a S gale was blowing and he fell off dead. What a tragedy for the family. I expect the head wind was too much for him. Jack Lainé's father died this morning. I am doing the funeral. All this added to a depressing day on Mother's birthday, has not helped to brighten things. I am getting to hate going out, even the sea and the islands don't seem the same. I hardly look at them now. This isolation is having a bad effect on us all.

I don't know what the Germans intend doing here. They say 300 engineers came today. Some groups are wearing different caps and clothes.

We had an awful drive to the Town Hospital in an open van, a gale, no rain but cold. A heavy and slow horse walked slowly both ways. There was a high spring tide and seaweed and stones were strewn along most of the road. We missed the sprays which startled the horse. When it jumped aside I wondered if we might be thrown out.

I went to Mr Trouteaud's funeral at 2.30, St Sampson's Church. Jackie Ogier played the organ and Mr Frossard said, as usual, a few words about his virtues.

The gale increased tonight, it has never blown harder nor rained more heavily. At night the gusts woke me and I thought it was thunder.

We have finished the first part of the Registration. Elsie Ellis was the last to register, 5 minutes before 7.

Sunday, November 3. It is still pouring and only 18 in church. The big stove I fitted under the belfry will, I am afraid, do no more than dry the belfry which is always damp. After the afternoon service at 4 Mr Frossard would make me go to the Rectory for tea. I got back at 8, made a big fire and read till 12.

Monday, November 4. Tom called me at 9, the time he now starts work, a new order. The weather is devilish, raining as much as ever, first a S gale, then a W one. I am making a few bills. I don't know how long I will be able to keep on the business.

NOVEMBER 1940

Saturday, Nov. 9. It would be impossible to describe the severity of the gales and rain this week. Dr Jones went to the Bridge and was nearly blown over the quay. Returning, the gusts compelled him to sit down, and some Germans helped him as far as the Chapel. He is really frail and is silly to venture out, and I told him so.

Everything is flooded and we are busy at least this week repairing leaks. I am happily in the dry, but the misery of the place. I got some tobacco yesterday and may get a pipe, but I hear they are sold out.

Darlings, perhaps you would hardly believe it – the gale subsided yesterday, and for three hours this morning it has been dry. Then it started to come down again. The ground cannot take any more.

I went to the Douzaine Meeting at 5. A small Blue Book, just five items. I am delegate for the States Meeting on Friday. One item is to pass a vote of thanks to our purchasing commissioners, Mr Falla and Mr Mahy. 1,000 bags of flour are stored in the large hall at Delancey Schools.

I hear we are to have our wirelesses taken. This is the last straw. Mrs Rowe was so upset she nearly cried. I am getting more and more worried and think I should have come to England. I would have come had things not happened so quickly, but it would have been only for your sakes. I am all right and you will have to forgive me for not coming. But how I would like to know where you all are and if Jack is in the army. I was afraid that if we all got killed with bombs there may not be even a small stone to mark Mum's grave.

I am in fairly good health except for a fluttering on the left side of my face and neck. Dr Jones said it might be nervous worry. Perhaps it is too much smoking. But the nights are so long and the suspense is great, and there is the uneasiness of not knowing what is going to happen next. Mrs Rowe is very kind and helps me all she can. I see today my hair is nearly white. I think it showed up more as I wore my Guernsey Frock. Mrs Rowe did laugh and said it did not become me, it made me look too workish.

The postman collected my wireless on Sunday. They are stored at St Sampson's and the Vale Schools. Mr Frossard told me there are 1,100 in the big room near Feldspar. An awful loss if fire broke out.

Up till now we have heard all about the bombing over London, the Midlands and Coventry. I don't think we will get our sets back till after the war, so now we are quite cut off from news except German communications in the papers. To me it's going to be just awful, but I will try to keep my balance. The papers say it's owing to sabotage. I hear they have taken Mr Marquand away.

Tom is pulling up tomato plants in the span. They are going to plant potatoes. My chickens get a fine run in the greenhouse, but they have turned out nearly all cockerels. My Light Sussex laid her

NOVEMBER 1940

first egg after the moult, a double yolk, 3½" long. It's impossible to get eggs now, so I give away a few to sick people as I am strong and can do without such luxuries.

An oil boat came from France on Sunday with 250 tons of oil, and they are discharging her in St Sampson's harbour. We got 1,000 tons of coal from France and 500 tons from Alderney, so we can expect gas until Christmas.

Thursday, Nov. 21. I could not explain the dense blackness when I left Dr Jones at 8.55. I managed to get across the road safely. I could tell one person was coming by his cigarette, so I called, Keep to the right.

Again it's been very distressing with no wireless news all day. I wonder and wonder how you all are. If Jack and Ted are still working in London it must be nerve-racking constantly running down to shelters. I wonder if they go home or stay in the night shelters we heard about on the wireless. It's a case of wondering, nothing certain.

Thursday, Nov. 28. It's been a mild week, of course rain on and off. People soon won't have any pillow slips. All you see is people flying to the shops or rushing on their bicycles with white bags on their backs.

Orders come out every few days. The men may now again fish from St Sampson's harbour. They get a permit to go out and return it when they come back. The Germans guard the harbour. 12 – 20 of them live in the harbourmaster's office.

Tuesday, December 3. Christmas soon here again. How I remember last year Kit, when you were delayed by fog and arrived as I was coming out of church, and the turkey at the old Rectory waiting for you to devour it. Now all is changed. Many, many years Mother went carol singing with me. I had many happy Xmas festivities, and I think you children must retain happy memories of those days, mostly due to your dear Mother who put heart and soul into the true spirit of the season. The hours I spent choosing cards and presents! Well it's nice to reflect on this, but I'm afraid there won't be peace on earth for many nations and people this year.

I am hoping and longing that I will get a letter from you all (via the Red Cross) to say you are safe before Xmas. That would be better for me than anything. I am keeping two or three cockerels in case a miracle happened and you all came across, and one each for Tom and Mrs Rowe.

I had a week at the Schools to check up and sign for the Identity Cards. We were in the food cutting-up room as the other end is

DECEMBER 1940

packed with over 1,100 wirelesses. I enjoyed the week. Some women were a little nervous but most were humorous. Although I have always lived in St Sampson's I could not identify half as many as Mr Bourne. We got him there for that purpose, but he could not sign anything, only Constables and Douzeniers could. It's all over now and things are flat again.

One man thought we were very mean not to supply envelopes. Other remarks are not fit to report here, but when we meet will be time enough.

Undated. Elsie, Mrs Godfray's maid, came down to see my chicks and rabbits, which she thought looked like nanny goats. She thought the chicks had got on well and might lay next week.

I invited Tom in to tea with us. He's that humorous and she is very funny, it was better than a play. Mrs Rowe made me a nice cherry and sultana cake. We made a fair gap in it. Dr Jones joined us and Elsie told him that my war-time tea was better than pre-war. I told her it came only once a week.

Monday, Dec. 9. I had a very poor day on Sunday. Got up late but being the first Sunday in the month thought I had better go. Half washed and shaved, half a breakfast, the fowls got about the same, and I believe the rabbits got none, but I was early for church.

By lunch time I was feeling an aching void. Had lunch at Dr Jones, curry, but not equal to it, but enjoyed a large cup of tea. Then like a fool went to church again. Came home feeling funny down my spine, pains in fingers, darts in ears, so packed off to roost. I had a beaker of milk and of course a speck of brandy (no more as it is nearly all gone and we cannot buy it). Got into bed with coat and dressing gown on top. I thought I was in for it.

But no. Tom called me at 8.40, and said they were ready for the Town Hospital. But I did not move, no fear. Told them to go without me. But the telephone went so many times that I had to get up, feeling quite fit! And the funeral was carried out by myself in the afternoon. I see by the Press (I have to be journalist as well) that only 18 friends attended, no relatives here, born in France 84 years ago.

The bread is poor. I agree with the people who say that it's potatoes with every meal, especially with the French flour in the bread.

Darlings I cannot write too much in detail or I could say things much more interesting, but this book might get into anybody's hands. You may never see it at all, but if you do, up to now I have been very comfortable. I was glad Kit decided for herself what to do, and I have never regretted not going to England (for my part). But I often have a nasty feeling, and wonder if I did my duty rightly, for I was the only one left to move and then we would have been altogether, and you would not have had to worry. Was I right or wrong? I don't know.

Thursday, Dec. 12. We get a fine day occasionally, but have had four horrible gales of wind veering SE to N, and deluges of rain. It's impossible to do much work outside. Things are about the same. We are getting short of tinned food, and charcuterie and paté are unobtainable unless you arrive at Madame Pommier at 10 when the shop opens.

It is so quiet that when we get a calm I can hear four clocks strike the hour. I often hear the Vale and Town Church clocks during the night. I hate the stillness, you can almost hear it.

Kit, who do you think was at the Social last night? I saw this man in a lovely light suit, beautifully groomed. He said, Good evening, and I said the same, and was left wondering whoever he was. Then this Tuesday I arrived early and he was sitting by the fire with two flappers and a friend of his, all laughing and giggling. It was Henry Bisson with whom we have often been fishing.

It had been blowing a gale all day and he told me they had been trawling on the banks off Brehon. I told him they were risking it and he agreed. He is now working in partnership with Jack Corbet (Ginger). I really believe they will come to grief. The girl is very young for him, but they may only be flirting. I never realized he was nice looking before.

I have cut down on smoking and bought a pipe. Have also bought chewing gum to wean me off. I called on Mr Pattimore tonight. Elsie is as saucy as ever. He is worried about you all and wishes Kit had stayed. He would have given her a lady's bicycle he has.

I went with Mr and Mrs Frossard to the Cortvriends to tea on Friday. Mr Finey is living with them at The Hollies. The Forest Church is closed. We had a nice tea and an enjoyable time.

I am killing my cockerels. Miss Lihou and her sister had three and the Doctor one which I helped him to eat in the curry. I still go there on Sundays. One Sunday I went to the Stubbs to tea and this Sunday to the Frossards with Finey and Mrs Stafford Ogier.

Monday, December 16. What an Xmas to look forward to! I have not been asked out anywhere and don't know if I feel much like going, although I know several would be glad to have me.

New German orders again. All dogs must be on the leash. I expect another order in a few days, as men now ride bicycles with the dogs running and trailing from the cycle, much more dangerous than the dog running loose.

I hear from Mr Pontin that by the end of the year we will be without tea. Mrs Frossard tried to make parsnip coffee and Mr F.

DECEMBER 1940

did not know the difference! While I was there on Sunday there were five large boats in the roadstead. One, about 8,000 tons, looked like a French boat.

The RAF paid the airport a visit on Monday, Dec. 6 at 1.30. I think it was a stick of bombs, a heavy bang and then like a roll of thunder. I believe a direct hit on the new hangar only completed the day before. It was camouflaged to look like a greenhouse, and supposed not to be detected between the other greenhouses. I hear it was a shambles.

Unfortunately one of our Guernsey carpenters, a youngish man, Anderson, was killed, and a Martel had his arm injured. I hear the men had no business there in the dinner hour, but four of them went in to play cards. The other 50 or 60 stayed in the greenhouse and came out safely.

Wednesday, December 18. I have not had a Red Cross letter from any of you yet. Mrs Gerrish showed me one she had a few days ago. I am now hoping as a German called on me on Monday and said:- You are Mr J.C. Sauvary. I agreed. You work for the States Occupation. I said, Yes. I immediately thought he had a job for me, but oh no. Have you any children evacuated? I have a daughter who went away, she is a schoolteacher in England. Oh, any other children? Yes, one son, one daughter. Oh, how long has your son been in England? Eight or nine years. Oh, what is your daughter's name? Mrs Griffiths. Oh, thank you very much. A very nice place you have here.

The last remark I did not like! He spoke English beautifully and was exceedingly polite. The next day I felt more contented. I believe they call on all those people who have letters from families in England, and before they let people have them get all particulars.

The Lawtons are coming to tea again. They seem to love it. I generally give them stewed Chaumontel pears. I still have candy sugar and Mrs Rowe prepares them splendidly.

Thursday, December 19. I got up in glorious moonlight at 8 o'clock. I went out to Saumarez Park (the States Offices are now there), I had to see the Income Tax administrator re my income which I said was nil. However it was a satisfactory interview. In the evening I went to choir practice at the schools, anthem, psalms and hymns, all of course very sad for me. But I feel the only thing left is to live it out.

I wrote you each a letter via Lisbon and one each via USA. I had five of the six returned. They had not left Guernsey.

I went to see Mr Pattimore who is fairly fit at over 80, but his heart is groggy. Elsie makes me cigarettes. On an awful patent machine she made me 50 out of 2 oz of tobacco. It's quite an entertainment going there. They gave me home-made ginger biscuits.

DECEMBER 1940

We hear we may have our wirelesses back. Rumour I expect. It's awful not having proper news. We get the German reports in the Press and Star. What a loss in our shipping this week, (100,000 tons).

A few days ago they buried that Anderson who was killed at the airport. The Germans attended and placed two wreaths on the grave. (You can see the report in the Press of Dec. 20, 1940.)

No sign of turkeys this year. It will be the first year I have not eaten turkey on Christmas Day for at least 45 years, and many of those years I had a slice off at least six.

Saturday, December 21. The Germans have raised the curfew for civilians on Xmas and New Year's Eve to 3 am. I would rather have had Xmas night. It's now 11.30 and I am still very much awake. I hear a German plane passing over for about the sixth night in succession. I have watched once or twice. They put up a searchlight from the airport.

It's Jack's birthday on Monday. I can imagine us all wondering where each of the others are, and about presents. I will make it up, Jack, when we all meet (and as I always remark, if ever.) The silence and the lonesomeness in this house is anything but pleasant, and the darkness tonight unbelievable.

I made a Guernsey cake today, but it was not very successful. It did not rise as last week's. A pity as I put more butter, the last of the 4 lbs I potted, which kept well. I have started Kit, on your potted eggs.

I have a Douzaine Meeting next Monday, the Budget for 1941. We have a net deficit of £360,853 to carry forward and budget for next year. If the figure for the revised estimate materializes the year 1941 will commence with this deficit. The total income is given as £578,754 and the total expenditure £1,208,831. Where is all this coming from? Ask me another!

Sunday, December 22. I rose much too early in order to get to church by 10.45. I have a fair amount to do – warm my rain water on the gas (no geyers allowed), shave and wash, which you know takes me a fair time, get my own breakfast, general clearing away of dishes, feed the fowls and rabbits, collect eggs (one or two daily).

It was a very cold morning, strong NE wind. Mrs Frossard said I was the only man there without an overcoat, and I made her feel cold all through the service.

After church at 4 I went with Mr and Mrs Frossard to Stafford's, Les Gigands for a nice high tea, tongue and other pressed meats, salad, bread and butter, cakes of all sorts in a nice cosy room with huge logs burning. We left at 8.30 after a glass of whisky and soda, the first I had tasted for months. Very cold walking home with the Frossards.

Mrs Ogier asked me there for Christmas Day to help them

DECEMBER 1940

through a fat goose. Today Miss Matthews asked me there, but I had promised the Ogiers. I think the Doctor is a little put out, but I was in a difficult position. Mrs Ogier asked me straight out, Are you invited anywhere for Christmas Day? What could I say although I knew in my mind they had intended asking me to Newington.

Monday, December 23. Elsie fetched the cockerel and brought me a present of Benedictine from Mrs Godfray. Miss Lihou sent Peppermint.

I went to Town this morning, The Banques were bleak and cold. Tom said I would never stick it, but I did. In Town I pictured the French Halles with four rows of turkeys and each pillar draped with another three rows, the market with meat with wonderful yellow fat, and great farm turkeys and geese. Then I looked at the real picture today, only bare stones. It was not possible to buy a small bird or even a pigeon. I tried to get a cockerel for Dr Jones but could not, so I killed him the one I had saved for myself.

I have been really busy today and thinking about Jack. It's his birthday and I cannot send greetings, don't even know where he is, perhaps gone for ever, perhaps injured in these devilish raids. However I will hope for the best, wish him many happy returns and trust in Providence.

I saw Angelo Clarke in Town this morning. He has injured his hand. Had a chat with Mr Browell who is looking very thin. I also met Mr Santangelo and I am glad I did for he is going to keep my spirits up! I bought some lovely yellow spring flowers for Mum's grave tomorrow. I put violets and rambler roses from our garden on Sunday.

Tomorrow we have Choral Communion at 5, then our Social at 8 till 11, but our curfew is extended till 3. Pubs have to be shut at 2.30. Very few people are satisfied. I will have to leave the Ogiers at 8.30.

Oh Kit, I dug your leeks today. They are enormous, the parsnips are fine, B. Sprouts also good. I gave Elsie Carre four broccoli, they were pleased.

We do hear some funny things. In spite of being in prison camp people are humorous. I hope I remember all the things to tell you. Some are not fit for publication, others I would not like to write down in case these books got into other hands.

Mona is flying round. A plane, German I presume, flies around every evening for about three hours, very high, and you only hear this humming.

Xmas Eve. I got off the perch a little earlier today as I have a few extra jobs. We are having a little extra meat and fat and an extra ration of butter. I've started on the eggs you pickled, Kit, and the four dozen I added, and gave half a dozen each to Tom, the doctor

DECEMBER 1940

and Miss Lawton. They were pleased. Then I packed a little Xmas parcel for Mr & Miss Lawton, cigs, tobacco, dates, figs and some cake.

Oh, what a change of news. We are to get back our wirelesses, it's official. Crowds are outside Ogiers waiting for the Star and Press with the information, and hundreds outside the Schools. I went inside and the Constables and Officials were spreading out the 1,100 odd sets in both big rooms in order to find each person's number. I did not stay as I had to collect holly from Dr Jones which I put with the spring flowers on Mum's grave. I met Miss Dyson who had never seen such lovely berried holly. I gave her some.

Then it was time for Choral Communion and on my return the Official papers were out, with the great proclamation of the trial, (held I think in Paris). 2nd Lts Nicholle & Symes having been in Guernsey, in civil clothing with a reconnaissance order, are guilty of espionage. Emile Nicholle, Elsie Nicolle, Frank Nicolle, Hilda Nicolle, Louise Symes, Rachel Symes, Wilfred Bird, Walter Bird, Elsie Bird, William Allen and Jessie Mariette have given refuge and assistance to the two officers, they have therefore been guilty of high treason and of having lent assistance to espionage. Mr Sherwill had, before the publication of the notice, made declarations contrary to the best of his knowledge and acted against his appointed duty. He has therefore been guilty of favouring the above and acting disloyally towards the German Inselkommandant etc. etc. etc. (See Press and Star, Dec. 24, 1940.) Mr Sherwill will be released from his office [President of the Controlling Committee] as further co-operation with the German authorities is no longer possible. All the others are freed and the matter is therefore settled. The wireless receiving sets confiscated in the island of Guernsey will be returned to their owners for use until further notice. etc. etc. etc.

Xmas Eve was freezing cold and sleeting later. Now at 7 everybody carting home their sets on wheelbarrows, carts, greenhouse trolleys, prams and bicycles. I helped one man on the Bridge in difficulties. This game was going on till about 9 o'clock. Mine is at the Vale School so I will get it on Friday. It was a pathetic, yet amusing picture. Strange that this news did not get through from Jersey till Xmas Eve.

Of course our Social could not take place in the Church Schools, so the Chapel people lent us theirs. A big crowd turned up. We were not allowed to play cards or dance, and we sang hymns and carols till 11.30.

I asked the Rector and Mrs Frossard to come home and have a decoction. They readily agreed but on second thought the Rector said that if we went to the Rectory we could have both the news and a refresher. So we trotted on there. A nice fire in his study. Had a nice supper of tongue with bread and butter, then hot brandy. At

DECEMBER 1940

12 o'clock I told Mrs Frossard that the news would be on, but she said 12 o'clock our time is 1 o'clock English time. Still it was worth waiting for after being deprived of our sets since November 17. It was most exciting hearing the announcer again.

Christmas Day. Out to the Ogiers, Les Gigands, after church. A lovely young goose, quite up to the standard of any Christmas dinner I have ever eaten. I then went to Stafford's father to feed the fowls, and he would insist on my having a drop of whisky with him. Stafford and the boys were at the Schools between meals delivering wireless sets. By the night there were still 500 to be delivered. The Post Office will do this as they are the responsible authority to return them.

I got back at 8.57, just in time for the curfew. I have lumbago, or something in my right hip. Have a pain only when trying to stand after sitting. Had to roll out of bed this morning.

Boxing Day. Had breakfast in the study by the fire, the first morning fire this winter. Generally I have it in the kitchen standing up. I won't know what comforts are if they ever come my way again. Miss Matthews said the Doctor wanted me for lunch (and to hear the news). A lovely cockerel, and I went there tonight as well, cold tender sirloin.

Tomorrow my men start work again, only three, and I am not making any money. But if it were not for the uncertainty of your whereabouts and knowing you're worrying about me, I would say things could be much worse. Most people seem to have had a good Christmas under the circumstances. I was delighted to hear the King's speech and Greetings from the Empire. England is wonderful and sticking it well, but what destruction.

Friday, December 27. Mild and much warmer, a real spring day. I had my first pullet's egg. The Lawtons came, Dr Jones called and actually had some stewed pears and cake. Then Uncle Ned came in, had a cigarette and a glass of sherry with the Lawtons, and we drank England's health, then the family's à la mode de Paris (clinked glasses).

Tom fetched my wireless. It cost the States £800 to collect them but it won't cost as much to return them as most people fetched theirs. One man made 27/- fetching them for people on Xmas Day.

I forgot to tell you about a trip to Town about a fortnight ago. There was a gale blowing, it was raining heavily, and one of my men got soaked with spray coming down to work. It was high spring tide and the waves were flying over at the Salerie (the papers said 40'). We were 20 in the Pullman car and the poor horse almost refused to face the wind and rain, dragging us along at a creeping pace. I was perished with the cold and much regretted turning out for 3 oz of tea which I could have got later.

DECEMBER 1940

Instead of waiting two hours I managed to get a return much earlier. Now after this preamble I will come to the funny part.

As our van was loading up a strange man got in (who I don't think has ever smiled). Emile Noyon came next and I remarked as he got in, to the amusement of the dozen women, that all was well, we had a pilot to take us down through this awful weather. Emile had been in Town all day, hence the fun. He looked at me and said, Ladies, we are better off than others for, if the worst happens, we have the undertaker. Then to everybody's amusement Mr Frossard got in. Emile, being very excited, said, And we have the Parson to pilot you aloft.

Now all this talk about a bus ride to St Sampson's only because there is an account of it in the Press tonight. I had told Mr Pattimore, Dr Jones and others about the fun, and they were much amused to read it there. I think the stranger who never smiled was the culprit. I must remember to tell you some of Emile's jokes, and Mr Frossard also kept the fun going.

I pass my time hanging fat (when I get it) and nuts on the beech tree by the study window. Just now I have six beautiful tits hanging upside down, swinging in the wind. My robin and my lovely blackbird wake me in the morning. Mrs Rowe is quite excited. She has never seen birds so tame. There are so few interests here now we have time to notice the birds more.

Tuesday, New Year's Eve. Darlings, the last day of the year broke badly, and it poured a deluge all day. I asked the Lawtons up to listen in to Mr Morrison's [the Home Secretary] important announcement. They came up in all that weather, like me wondering what it would be all about. Nothing important to us after all. Still they enjoyed the news and a glass of wine with cherry cake. They drank all your health, and mine, wished you all the best and hoped I would soon get news for you. Their wireless has not been returned yet.

I went to the Church Social at 8. I had the booby prize at whist again, three times in two months. That's five prizes since we started, but I have not kept any.

The Frossards came back with me at 11.30, just to drink your health and mine. They wished you all the best of luck in the coming year, their children as well who are in Scotland, and wondered how everything will pan out for us. They are also very distressed about their children.

What a terrible raid on London on Sunday night. It makes our blood run cold here, to listen to such news. They went on to Dr Fox for the late news and to see the Old Year out. I did not wait till 1 o'clock, and think I slept it out which was best.

I went to the Frossards again on Sunday, and am going the next

JANUARY 1941

Sunday too. The Rev. James is preaching and the Peeks are also going.

New Year's Day. Nice chicken dinner with white wine at the Doctor's. Had supper there as well. Went for a brisk walk while Charles was sleeping. It was blowing half a gale from the NE and freezing cold along the Banques. Went to the cemetery to see Mum's grave, all so desolate. Called on Uncle Ned, and thought what a change in one year, Marjorie gone, and a very cold, empty house.

Uncle Ned came back with me, had a glass of beer and cake, and we talked of all of you. He also is very worried, has heard nothing from Marjorie yet. I dread to think of the months we may have to put up with this yet. We are warm and have enough food, but it is the strangeness and uncertainty of when we will all be united, and I will add as usual, if ever.

Sunday, January 5. My darlings, I have been listening to a service in an air raid shelter. The last hymn was Abide With Me, and I could hear the altos (not very good) and it made me think of Mother and the many times I heard her singing that hymn when she sat just behind me in the choir. I have so many associations with nearly every broadcast service I listen to, that although I am strong it takes a lot of standing up to.

It's been devilish cold with ice ³/₄ ins thick in the fowls' bucket. I went to Town by 'bus', driver J. Burrows, who gave me a cigar, because he said I was kind to him and gave him cabbage leaves for his rabbits. Several times I wished he had kept it as I kept getting nicotine in my mouth and could not spit.

I got tongue for Dr Jones and pressed beef for myself. There is now a States' Tax of 1/8 in the £1 on all sales, but not on labour, which makes my bill making complicated. Some time ago I had to stamp a bill 35/- not out of my pocket, but it makes the bill look high.

I had to wait 1¼ hours at the Town Pier for the next bus. I perished to the marrow. (Oh yes, I had my great coat, Guernsey Frock and thick flannel shirt, and what a boon they have been this winter.) Emile Noyon and others were there and we laughed and joked and the time passed. Henry passed with his friend, rather a nice looking young girl.

Saturday, January 11. A horrible week, heavy frost, then sleet and a little snow which did not lie here, but they say the Fort field was white and hundreds of lapwings were there. But they could not get shot for people are not allowed to shoot. It must be very cold on the continent. From the Red Lion I saw dozens of duck on the sea. Kit will remember the kind of weather for she was held outside the

JANUARY 1941

harbour in such a wind all night on one of her crossings.

On Friday, January 10 I was excited. The post brought the news that a letter was at College for me from the Red Cross. Of course, bad as the weather was I went in by bus. I was only allowed to read it there and answer at once, 25 words allowed. As you will know Kit it was from Mr Peyton Houston, 290, West 11th Street, New York, asking if I were at home, Katherine is busy, working very hard and asking me to reply soon. I replied, Darling Kit, so glad to receive news. Miss you all very much. Am well, comfortable at home. Have heard nothing from the children. Love Dad. I signed and dated it Jan. 10, 1941.

I had to go to the Caledonian Nursery to pay my men, so called at The Hollies to tell Violet and Gussie the good news. They were very pleased and excited, but have not heard anything of their children and are anxious. Finey, who was boarding with them, is back in hospital. I am afraid all is not well with him.

I had to wait until 4.30 for a bus. It was worth it to get even that little news. Even now I do not know if Kit is in England or Canada. I am hoping soon to hear from Flo and Jack and the darlings Rosemary and Jane. I am most anxious as to your safety. The drive back was awful. I had to sit outside as all the passengers were women, and I did not get warm that evening.

Sunday, January 12. It's warmer now and lovely moonlight. I went back twice to see Kit's letter, first because I could not remember the contents and I was perplexed about the address, New York, the second time as I had not taken the date it was written.

Saturday, January 18. First I must speak to Darling Flo. It's your birthday and I have wished you many happy returns many times during the day. I have been thinking about the morning you were born and when I was allowed to see poor old Mum. She said, Now come and see what you think of your firstborn. There was much excitement when it was all over. Mrs Jones and Auntie Kate were, I think, just as proud as we were. Mother was a born mother by nature and knew how to bring up children.

Just fancy, your three birthdays, Flo, Kit and Jack, and I have not been able to send greetings. I wonder how long this awful situation will last. Judging by the wireless and Mr Churchill we have to stick it another year. I do hope you are safe and sound and do not have to spend your nights in shelters.

We get a lot of meat from Granville. I saw several lorry loads at the King's Weights in Market Square. A steamboat, the Holland, comes nearly every week and brings flour, wheat and cheese. We had a few oranges (I had ½ dozen and gave some away), also nuts, dates and figs. I hope this continues but I don't see how it can, for

JANUARY 1941

we hear on the wireless about the shortage of food in France. Yet we are getting so much. We have about 1,800 sacks of flour stored in Delancey Schools Hall. Another steamer, the Diamont (French, I think) often comes.

They are always bringing troops here and taking others back. These soldiers buy tons of materials, boots, etc. and the shops are nearly empty.

We are coming to the end of our tinned food. Spring is coming and we can carry on for sure without imports till September. But without them we cannot go through another winter. We will be short of coal in two months.

The weather has been hellish, very cold, two falls of snow two inches deep stayed on the ground. On Wednesday night the snow melted as it fell on the roads until there was about one inch of water. Then a heavy frost set in. I have never before seen the roads like this in Guernsey. They were like sheets of glass and many people fell.

Mr Frossard came in very distressed. His brother Guy was killed at Calais on May 23, 1940. He got the news from the wife today. I am so sorry for him. They were such pals.

The States have decided to plant my greenhouses with potatoes. Tom is digging and soaking the ground. Kit, the pullets are laying and the devils are eating their eggs. But I have stopped their little game. It's fun now to see them laying. They look around for their egg, but it's dropped behind the curtain. One turned around so much it must have got giddy, then it looked up very sad, then got into the next box, but did not find it. (I did.) We keep them running in the greenhouses until next week.

Sunday, January 19. Mr Frossard got through the services very well though much upset at the news of his brother's death. Lunch at the Doctor's as usual. He opened a bottle of lovely old Burgundy. Miss Matthews and I got through the greater part of it. He does not care for it.

Tonight I got a very good reception of President Roosevelt taking the oath. My greatest relief of this war was when he got in as President for the third time. A lucky stroke for democracy. He was the strongest man we could ever get for the job.

I have been reading several books. One I rather liked by E.V. Lucas was Over Bermertons. I thought of your house, Flo, when I came to a poem beginning,

> When I am at Epsom or on Banstead Down,
> Free from the wine and smoke and noise of the town

JANUARY 1941

Mrs Hurford told me going to church this morning that I was getting thin. When I told the butcher, lifting up my Guernsey Frock (I have been wearing it this cold weather) he said it was the Guernsey stretching! I don't know who is right but I feel well enough. But I think, Kit, that I have lost my Little Mary which you were always teasing me about.

The Germans have stopped the fishing again. I don't know the reason. It's a pity as we are short of beef and it's a drain on tinned food. I saw Mr Browell in Town. He is getting thinner. Uncle Ned is in bed with a cold. Mrs Frossard is in bed with flu.

What terrible casualty lists of civilians in the air raids given on the wireless today. I often think one of you might be on them. I ask myself, why not you as anyone else. I cannot imagine where any of you are. Jackie perhaps joined up. Then I think Kit must be in Canada, or why in her message did she not include any of you. Then I think she asked Peyton to write, and he omitted to mention any but Katherine who was busy and working hard. Then I drop all and trust to providence.

Tuesday, January 21. I carried on the Social at the Schools tonight. Mr Frossard did not care to come after the news of his brother's death. Our Socials are very nice and the only outing we get now. Henry was there and got second prize. The girl Brache he is courting and another family are renting Feldspar, Mr Brooks' house. He was in England during the evacuation and couldn't get back, so the house has been let furnished.

I enjoyed the Cardinal of Westminster speaking on the wireless, and very much truth in it.

I have been busy these few days securing with keys etc. some of the many houses evacuated. What a mix up. Some have been occupied by the Germans (they say all those who left the island are their enemies) who have moved furniture from one house to another. It will be most distressing for the evacuees when they return.

We have had a lot of deaths lately, old people between 85 and 95.

Friday, January 24. I have this afternoon partitioned off a small part of the lean-to for my pullets who are now laying. I have had no corn for them for the last three months, and am allowed 33 lbs mash per month for 20 fowls. They feed mostly on potatoes, poor food for egg production.

The Red Cross letters are now coming through very quickly. They get through about 300 a day, so I expect one or two out of the 1,500 awaiting replies.

The news from Africa is very good. The Italians are having a bad time.

JANUARY 1941

Lorries are off the road except those used by the Germans. They are carting tons of paving stones, stone dust and siftings to the airport and are building hangars.

Saturday, January 25. It was one of those mild and silent warm spring mornings that opened into a lovely day, a little cloudy at first which made it seem all the sweeter when the sun broke through. So I visited Mrs Godfray and Miss Lihou. I took candles (they cannot get paraffin) and tea. I had a nice tea and Elsie insisted on my taking two eggs, as her fowls are laying better than mine.

The other day Elsie chopped off the top of her thumb. She took it and ran to Bailiff's Cross, to a lady (who trained in First Aid with Kit) at St Andrew's who stuck it on after the usual antiseptic treatment. Next morning she went to Dr Sutcliffe, who looked at it and rebandaged it. Elsie says the tip is not on very straight. (I hope it's not on back to front!) Mrs Godfray was very frightened. Elsie is very funny and said, Fancy Mr Sauvary, I did not even faint! She told them she liked coming down to see my fowls. You're treated like a lady, get a jolly good feed and always something to take back.

Sunday, January 26. Lunch at 'Docker' Jones as Rosemary says it, tea at the Stubbs, then church at 6. Nice to hear J.B. Priestley on the air again.

Monday, January 27. By chance I got to know it was Mrs Le Poidevin's 85th birthday. I got Soleil d'Or and Mimosa from Purse and called at 6. The old lady was delighted, the usual kissing and hugging and nearly dropping a tear. She only hopes to live to see Nellie and Amy [evacuated with the Vale Schools].

She made me take two jibs of a lemon sandwich Mrs Ryan had sent. Winnie gave me a glass of whisky and a piece of cake, very nice. But later Reggie gave me another whisky. He would have women were no use serving whisky. I drank it as the first was not a big drop. I managed to cycle quite well but my face was rather flushed when I got to the Doctor's.

Tuesday, January 28. I again took charge of the Social. Only Mrs Frossard came. The death of Mr Frossard's brother has been a great shock to him. The Social went well. We played 12 hands of whist, had singing, then Mr Symons, butcher, gave two nice turns. He is a bit of a comic.

This morning when I was at Tozers getting my Star, six Germans came in. (There are always a lot of them on the Bridge.) They wore peaked caps, looked more like cadets re dress, but rather older. They all gave me a salute, bowed slightly forward and said, Good morning, in good English. They are really very polite, never appear

FEBRUARY 1941

awkward, confused or self-conscious, they just carry on as if people were not around.

I wonder when I will get a Red Cross message from Flo and Jack. Lots of people have been getting them. How much longer will I have to wait. I have had the humps today and feel awful when I get these moods.

I went with Tom Roberts to Mrs Giffard's place, Braye du Val, a choked drain. They have only the Hungarian maid there looking after the place.

I went to see Mrs Carré, Hougue Guillmine. She still sleeps on the sofa in the kitchen. I cannot understand how she got on in that cold spell two weeks ago. I am going to do a small job there. Good nights Darlings. I hope you are all safe.

Saturday, February 1. I got my rations from Le Riche. I put down 30 items and about 20 were crossed out. I can get salmon, sardines, tinned fruit, marmalade about once in four weeks. Small shops are closing. I hear you cannot get a reel of white cotton. Still up to the present I cannot grumble. I am comfortable but earning little money.

I hear that Mrs Le Masurier, the wife of Jack's Manager at the Midland Bank, is back from France. She had been interned there for three months for an offence.

Jack Ozard is clearing up his garden and told me I could have two apple trees. They were enormous, but as they were supposed to be Orange Pippin or Blenheim, I decided to take one which we dug out, but found we could not carry it. I then started cutting away branches. The only way to get it to my land was via the Alliance Vinery border, then over the wall. Tom said Ozard was mad, but we must be worse! However with all the arguments about the wisdom of transplanting such a tree, and in spite of the drizzling rain, we got it planted by the small span. Although stripped of some if its branches it looks a fair shape yet, and I am hoping it will take and you will all be here this summer to share its fruit. I had a few apples from my other trees and a beautiful flavour.

Sunday, February 2. An awful day which started with a quiet rain, and very, very cold, but by the time we left church (and only 40 people there, Choral Communion) the wind had increased to nearly gale force and the rain fell in sheets mixed with sleet and snow. We had only 18 for the Evening Service, the choir had a larger number. The collection was 13/- and £2.0s.6d. for the day. Almost the lowest on record since my tenure of office, now 21 years. Not too bad. Elected seven times. I think this will be my last, young blood for a change will I think be better.

The job for the coal and wood stove under the belfry cost £22,

FEBRUARY 1941

but as I superintended and did the plastering it's very satisfactory!

Monday, February 3. Cold NE wind and by 10.30 it started to snow and blow like the devil. By 11.30 there was about three inches of snow over our garden. I started to feed the birds, our dear little robin. I have missed my cock blackbird this last week, but a hen blackbird comes each day.

Then a telephone message from the Matron of the Vauquiedor Hospital, a patient has died. In spite of the awful weather I set off in my rubber snowboots Dr Jones gave me, extra pullover and my lovely Guernsey which Tom insisted I should wear. He also made me take gloves, one white woollen right hand I found in Kit's drawer, a brown suede left hand of Mum's I found in the attic. Thus completed with mackintosh I managed to get there without falling off.

It was a man Humphries. Family kept a tobacco shop in the Pollet. Elsie Carré and Mr Pattimore (who by the way is about as usual and always asking about all you children and that grand lad, Ted [*See illustration 7.*]) knew about them as Elsie used to work for the daughter. He has no family here now.

I am expecting to bury Mr Humphries at the Foulon in a day or two, depending on weather conditions, when the funeral will be attended by the undertaker and parson (Mr Greenhow, who is Chaplain of the Hospital). It seems sad that when the war is over his daughter and brother will return to hear he had been buried by the authorities in the poor law grounds. However, such is life.

The boat from Granville brought many porkers. Symons had about a dozen down today. They have a very dark skin like smoked bacon. It's because they singe the hair off instead of, as we do, scald it. I like our way better because we get the roots out.

Tuesday, February 4. Warmer but still very cold. I have had a lot of difficulty over this funeral of Mr Humphries. I had such few particulars but after telephoning several of the family, only to find they had evacuated, I found a brother at Jerbourg who will be at the funeral. I also found the wife's grave where I will bury him, instead of in the poor ground. I had a lot of cycling over the matter, but the brother was very pleased that I found him. I always seem to drop in for these problems. I don't get any more pay for it, but I suppose I must take it as a duty.

We had a very nice Social. I was MC again. The Rector has a very bad throat and Mrs Frossard says it has settled on his chest.

A German order. We have to collect all old car tyres. I don't know what price they are giving.

I do hope I will get news from some of you this week. I don't know why my news is so long in coming, for I know you all must

FEBRUARY 1941

have written after you received the wireless news of a Red Cross service for Guernsey.

Mrs Rowe is keeping the house very nice and clean. She made me a cake again this week. I am getting on very well regarding meat and ordinary foods. I sometimes wish I had made Kit stay here, except for helping doing war work in England. Up to the present she would, I am sure, have been better off here, but at the time I felt she would be better gone. Even now we are not sure about all this.

Now for the news, then I will read a little. I am wading through Ivanhoe. I like it but the print is so small it tires me.

Wednesday, February 5. I went to the Foulon this afternoon for the funeral. It was sleeting as I rode along the Banques, and what a relief to turn the corner inland at the Red Lion. By that time my hands were numb. (Oh yes, I wore my gloves). I got there at 3.15 and had to wait till 4. I went early as I was afraid of a blizzard. The ground was white and the cemetery looked desolate. It was a sad spectacle, just one mourner, one vicar, one undertaker, four carriers and the grave-digger. Had his daughter been there she would have thought it a lonely scene.

I got back at 5, made a cup of tea and was joined by Tom and the Doctor. Then my headache, which I had had since morning, passed away. I think it was the effect of the cold wind when riding my bicycle yesterday. It is blowing a gale and if it freezes tonight we are in for another awful day getting about. I am comfortable with a lovely fire, and after the news will have a treat for my supper, cold sausage over from my boiled vegetable Guernsey dinner.

I went to choir practice tonight in that cold School, but it lasted only 20 minutes, and I have not been cold since my journey back from the Foulon. I don't know if all this news will interest you to read, but it will give you some idea of how we fared during the Occupation.

Another German order out today, warning people not to go anywhere on the South coast and from Pleinmont around to Lihou Island, as it is all dangerous.

If fine I will start on my Cadastre work tomorrow. It won't take long this year as the alterations and changes and new buildings won't be many. *But* I am hoping we will get the same pay. We should as when we had big years we got no more pay, so I am standing out that we take the fat with the lean years. Do you all agree? I think you will.

Friday, February 7. Damp, dull and drizzly. The walls of the dining-room were streaming. I asked Mrs Rowe to light a fire and it soon dried out. I had a really good night's sleep and my head is much

FEBRUARY 1941

better today, but I am not really A1.

Mr Bird is without coal, only coke, anthracite and logs to be had. Some people have not had coal for weeks. I don't know how they are managing this cold weather. Granville has had a foot of snow, and the coal expected has not come because the bad weather has made transport difficult.

Saturday, February 8. It was pitiful to see the queue outside Plummers shop waiting for the small portions of cake or scones they can get. We are getting hard put for luxuries. From now onwards it will be plain necessities. I got a few Guernsey biscuits and a piece of plain cake from Minnie's boys, Percy and Roland.

Mr Fossard called this evening, very excited. He had received news of Charlie and Pansy. They are both in Edinburgh, Pansy nursing and Charlie in the Gordon Highlanders. I would like to see him in kilts. He said 2,000 letters had arrived via the Red Cross, so I am expecting to hear from all of you. He is going to the College to help them next week.

I dreamt about Mum last night. I miss her a lot these days now the evenings are lighter and longer. We can see till 8 o'clock, Greenwich time 6.

I bought a lot of seeds, sweet peas, asters etc, etc 8/6. I feel if I plant the flowers as other years, perhaps by August a miracle might happen and you may all be here enjoying them as usual. For sure there will not be a plentiful supply of tomatoes owing to water shortage (lack of petrol for the electricity for pumping). We are all in the air now regarding our future.

When I was in Town this afternoon Henry was in the harbour with his boat. They had been trawling and had a fair catch of ray and flat fish. Petrol is very short and I believe they go trawling under sail. He and Ginger (Jack Corbet) are real workers.

Sunday, February 9. Sunday again, always a very sad and dull day for me. I was at the Doctor's for lunch as usual and the wireless was playing the Blue Danube. I remember being at a ball at St Julian's and waltzing it with Mum. It was encored several times and I did enjoy it, Mum was such a good dancer. After all those years, 40 or more, I could remember it with the brass band, and sense the same feeling which carried me back all those years and made me sad all day.

Tea at the Stubbs. After church Stafford asked me to go out to the Gigands to hear the Prime Minister's speech. I went, thinking that in the mood I was in, sleeping out there might be better for me. We had a nice tasty supper of tinned beans and chip potatoes.

Then Mr Churchill started. What a speech! I am sorry I did not copy a few passages. It seemed to buck us all up.

FEBRUARY 1941

Monday, February 10. Nice breakfast of baked pork fat. On the way back went to see my men at the Park Schools, then changed, shaved and called Tom in for a cup of tea. Did Cadastre work in lovely sunshine this afternoon. A little tired riding my bicycle.

Violet rang up very excited. They had had news from her sister that the Froebel School and her children are well. She thinks that I will get news for sure this week.

Jurat Arthur Dorey has had news that his daughter, Dr Claire, in Transjordan, had a car accident and has lost the sight of one eye. Ted Dorey had news of his wife. All this is in the Star this morning. I hope my news will be good.

I wonder if I have told you about the marking of all cross roads. It's a yellow line and 12 inch letters LANGSAM, which presumably means GO SLOW. Men's lavatories are marked MANNER, very nice word had they added 'S'!

This war seems to have had a bad effect on people. I hear that the mental home is full, and we certainly have two or three people down here who are going mental. It must have been the shock. It certainly is not because of any great pressure placed on them. Of course the 9 o'clock curfew is bad for people who want amusement. I don't. It's months since I have been to the pictures.

Tuesday, February 11. A mild day, lovely sunshine and quite warm. We had quite an enjoyable time on the Cadastre work around the Capelles and the Coutanchez.

This morning I helped Tom dig up our lilies of the valley on the greenhouse border. I wanted all that couch grass out, but am afraid I have left it rather late.

We had our usual Whist Drive. I was MC but Mr Frossard came in after 8 o'clock. He had been at the College all day. They are dealing with this batch of 2,000 Red Cross letters in alphabetical order. Again a delay for us. He does not think 'S' will be called much before next week. Even then there might not be a letter for me. I think there will be all the same. Next batch they will start with 'Z'.

Thursday, February 13. A mild day with clear blue sky, so I finished the Cadastre work. I now have to make up the books at the Douzaine Room. We got through quickly as no new building had been done since the Occupation. Yesterday returning from Portinfer we passed Pulias where we used to stop with darling Rosemary to see the Nanny Goats. Everything is now bare. Sad to reflect back on those lovely summer days when Mum and all of us were just like kids centring ourselves only on the baby. I can still hear her say, Ah gu, ah gu. Days like those are gone for ever, happy days that pass all too soon.

FEBRUARY 1941

I hear that a cargo of coal, 800 tons, has arrived from France, but they say it is of poor quality, mostly dust. I have enough to last me three months. Logs are 2/6 a cwt. I believe the States sell 80 to 100 tons a week. Maison du Haut in Brock Road is being well stripped. More than 40 trees are cut down already. Mrs Carré, Hougue Guillmine, is annoyed that they have cut down many on her farm.

Sunday Evening, February 16. Still no news. Mr Frossard said they got through 1,200 messages last week, but I told him that the organisation is wrong. It is now 17 days since these Red Cross letters came, and all should have been disposed of in less time. There should be some quicker method. I told him I could find a quicker plan. I also complained about the poor people of the Vale and St Sampson's having to go to College. Even *when* they can get a ride it costs 8d. On Friday it poured and the women had to walk back and got soaked.

I offered to help and make a Depot at the Church Schools and give four or six hours a day, and could get plenty of help. How about the men whose wives are evacuated, they have to lose ½ day's work to go in and see the message. I really cannot understand the world. They seem to love making difficulties.

After lunch at the Doctor's I called to see my sister Minnie at Cliffdale as I hadn't seen her for five or six weeks. I was unlucky, they were out. On the way back I met Henry, Kit. When I told him my weather glass was the lowest I had ever seen it, he said he would take a reef in the mainsail. I told him to take a reef in the rudder. He laughed and passed on.

Violets and Soleil d'Or are now 2d per bunch. People in vans and carts are trying to sell them. A good joke in the Press tonight titled, Not a French word. A shop had on a board – Soleil d'Or at so much per dozen. A customer asked if the commodity was rationed and could she buy some. When shown the popular bloom she exclaimed, "Oh, I thought it was some foodstuff just arrived from France!"

Wednesday, February 19. Mrs Rowe had news from her daughter. They are all well. It has bucked her up. I am wondering when I will get news. I know for sure you all have written. Mrs Frossard told me another 500 letters had arrived.

I have some funny experiences but I don't care to write them here. I hope I will remember to relate them when we meet again.

This afternoon Tom and I started clearing the lean-to. I planted scarlet runners and transplanted lettuce. I will save some seedlings from the Calendulas. The carnations are not looking too promising, but I am preparing everything as other years, hoping. I got a man

FEBRUARY 1941

to prune the apple trees.

I went to practice as usual in the Schools. We started on the Easter anthem, Christ is Risen. We had it some 30 years ago. Mum sang in it. I remember those days so well, happy days never to return. As Mum used to say, Death is so final, and it came to us so suddenly. But I always knew, Keep your lamp and be ready for the midnight call, but I never took heed, hence my shock.

Monday, February 24. I must tell you about Wilfred Robin, Mr Poat's male nurse. He went to the pictures on Thursday evening. Mr Frossard was sitting behind him and they joked all the evening. They had a little snow storm on the way home but it was not very cold. He went into the kitchen and asked Mrs Honey to help him take off his coat and said, Mind my left arm. Mrs Honey told him he had a nice fire in his bedroom, turned to attend to the gas stove, and heard a fall. He was down by the chair dead. He told me only a few weeks before he would drop like that.

Saturday was a vile day with SE gale. I put off Town till the afternoon when the rain had slackened, but the wind had increased. When I reached Richmond Corner and saw the sea mountains high I nearly turned back. But the wind was a little on my side till I got to the Banques. Then, oh my, the rain began to lash down as you know it can on the Front. I managed to weather the Red Lion and Longstore, but head wind to the Salerie. Most men and all the girls were walking their bicycles. I stuck it to Glatney, then that hellish corner. I kept close to a man in front of me almost to danger point. Had he fallen I would have been over him. Twice I was blown into the gutter but managed to stick on. The second tack frightened me. Again I got into the gutter, a dead stop, a dead calm for five seconds, I was saved. My next spurt I was around and believe me I was soaked. I could not feel my hands (no gloves as usual). When I got to the Avenue I had had enough, I walked up the Pollet.

Returning, Don Bisset drew my attention to a boat making for Town. Sometimes we could not see it for minutes. I am sure it was Henry Bisson. They are too venturesome. They must have reached the harbour for I have heard of no accident.

Mrs Rowe and Tom went to College to see their Red Cross messages. Both got soaked. Mrs Rowe got three and I know of others who have had five. Cliff Hall's daughter had her first little daughter and it died after 1¼ hours.

Stafford again invited me there after lunch at the Doctor's and I decided to go. I hate Sundays at home now. They had company, plenty of good fodder and the usual decoction or nightcap. I slept there and came back at 9, very cold riding along the Banques in my thin suit, but really only 7. Still I survived.

A barrage balloon passed over the island yesterday and dropped

FEBRUARY 1941

in the sea near Sark. Was washed up at Grand Havre. It had about 80 yds of cable and marked some number and Kent. I hear the Germans have it in a shed at Hoûmet du Nord.

Thursday, February 27. Another week nearly ended and still no news from any of you. I know it's not your fault. For certain you have written many times.

Mr Frossard was rather upset as this week he had further news about his brother Guy. He was wounded at Dunkirk, taken to Calais where he died in hospital five days later.

The Lawtons came to tea today. They bring their own butter. Elsie came yesterday with a nice lot of shallots. I gave her tea with cake. For many weeks now Mrs Rowe has made me a cake.

New orders. We have to clear out all inflammable goods from our attics. I don't know what I will do with our lot. I think I will leave the chairs there. All motor cars must be jacked up off their tyres. Fancy, mine are hard yet, and it's eight months since I last used it. I think the last time was when I took Kit to the boat, June 21, 1940. The Courier was going out of the harbour at 6 o'clock.

I had a letter from Miss Houstoun telling me that she went to College for news from Doreen, who says she often hears news from Marjorie, Flo, Kit and Uncle George. It was dated Dec. 11, so it seems you were all well then. Nothing about Jack. She has not yet heard from her own people. My sister Minnie has heard nothing of her twins, nor of our sisters or Willie.

Pancake day on Tuesday. Mrs Rowe said she would make me some. But when I went to Elsie Carré for my cigarettes, she was making some and swearing they were either burning or breaking in pieces. The batter was quite brown with the flour and the milk skimmed, and little fat, so I will wait till you all come over and you can make me some.

We should dig the greenhouse potatoes in May. I wish I could believe the war would be over by then. It is a jolly time of the year to take a holiday, but I will be out of cash by then. I make very little profit on my men and still have expenses of ground and store rent. Allendale is empty, nothing coming in from there.

Dr Jones has a message, he cannot walk much now, so I went to College with him in a hired Chair. It turned out to be an old Victoria, built in the year dot, with curtains all around and scarcely room for your knees.

At the College, which had tables and dozens of people answering their letters, Mrs Frossard and then Mrs Cortvriend, who are both helping, came up thinking I had received news from you (but oh no, not yet). *But,* as I was leaving, Léonie Trouteaud came running down to me saying there was a letter from Flo, but I would not get

FEBRUARY 1941

the notice until perhaps Tuesday. She told me roughly the contents which you can guess greatly relieved me. Flo is at Horsham with Grandma, and all those I am thinking about are well. It was very kind of her to let me know.

It is very curious here now, everything has changed. It takes hours now to get on with a job. I started a job at Miss Mauger's St Martin's. The van came yesterday at 10.15 instead of 9 o'clock. The rain poured so terribly he had to go back. Came this morning just as late, did not get away till 11.15. The slow transit and delays are awful. I had had to wait two days as all the horses were vraicking. We have no other way of getting chemicals to manure the ground.

Many of the contraptions for conveying things are amusing. I am enjoying the funny sides which, among all the depressions, I can see. Tom and I have many jokes.

They only brought the seed potato down from Jersey this week. With luck we might dig them before the outside crop. I hope to plant the field on Monday. I may yet give it over to the States in order to keep Tom constantly in the garden. For now that the greenhouses are planted they might take him away.

They have ploughed part of Delancey Park for planting wheat. Our beaches on the Front are cleared of limpets and seaweed. People besides eating limpets get them for their cats. Miss Matthews still has eight and finds it difficult to get food for them. There is one remedy?

Soleil d'Or and violets are selling at 1d per bunch. I expect next week they will give them away. The loss Guernsey is making is terrible. I am sure I lost £600 on my tomatoes. Still if the war could be over and we could start again, I would not worry.

Sunday, March 2. What distressing news on the wireless this morning about Bulgaria which I said many weeks ago would happen. It only remains for the others to show their cards. I said many months ago that now the Axis consisted of Germany, Italy, Russia, Spain, (Portugal did not count) the remainder of Europe would be forced to fall into line. Now we see it all happening according to my prophecy.

Mrs Cross died and the funeral is tomorrow. Uncle Ned came into the Doctor's tonight after church. It seemed very sad, the Doctor, Uncle Ned, Mr Cross and myself, all lonely widowers. I don't know why but around this way the men seem to be left alone. I could mention another twenty more in this district.

Mr Stubbs had a fall at the works, cut his ear and injured his knee. He had been home a week. Mrs Stubbs has a carbuncle on her shoulder. She has had three messages from her people in England.

I had to go about a funeral at Grosse Hougue, a Mr Hamelin, 78 years.

MARCH 1941

I put Primo, Soleil d'Or, violets with roots, primroses, forget-me-nots, wallflowers and snowdrops on Mum's grave, flowers mostly from our garden. I have had a lonely day today. Was a little depressed about the war.

Tuesday, March 4. At last, on Monday, March 3, I had a Red Cross letter, Flo, to say there were two messages from Mrs Florence Griffiths. I had such a busy morning, going to the Town Hospital, rain and wind as usual, then to the Vale Rectory, then Vale cemetery, all pedalling which is now the quickest method of getting about in Guernsey. By that time it was 1 o'clock, had a quick dinner, wash and shave and change then to St Sampson's Church. After the funeral, although by then very tired, I went to the College to see your two messages. They were practically the same. I was glad to receive the reassuring news that houses and yourselves are all well. You will have received my reply. I hope soon to hear from Jack and Kit.

I saw Mary Sauvary there. She is the only one of their family left. She had called to see me once but I was out. I asked her down. I had a chat with Léonie Trouteaud.

I am just back from the Tuesday Social. The curfew is extended one hour owing to a boxing match. I was glad to hear you are all together in Horsham. I expect Grandma and Grandpa spoil darling Rosemary. I am longing to see her. She will have forgotten me. Jane, of course, was too young to remember me.

Wednesday, March 5. It is Mrs Godfray's 89th birthday. I took her a bouquet from the Nursery, also a bottle of nice Sherry wine and ½lb tea. (People are getting only 1 oz this week. I have a little stock left.) She was delighted and said I was a naughty boy to give her such nice presents these times. She looks very well, is proud of her age and still reads without glasses. We celebrated over a glass of wine and cake and I told her my news from Flo. I had a nice cycle ride back, downhill, awful uphill going out.

I am going to Delancey Park Schools at 7 to elect a new constable to replace Mr Frank Dorey. I think they are putting up Mr Collas, Ernest Villa.

More orders on the paper tonight. We cannot use electric light after 11 pm and not after 7 am. Again calling in all war weapons of any sort.

Friday, March 7. We have had a lovely day. I wish we could get lovely war news. Instead it's spreading to the Balkans.

For the benefit of all concerned the Press is printing the information on practically all Red Cross letters received. I have had so many inquiries about all of you that I decided to let the Press have

MARCH 1941

my news. Therefore tonight's Press has plenty about the Sauvarys, Kit's news via New York, the news from Flo, news of Uncle William's death in Maidstone about 13 November, aged 73 and that he married Eliza, daughter of Mr J.J. Sauvary (my father), their daughters, Mrs Brooks and Mrs Le Quesne send news that they are well, also the death of Mr Langlois from Delancey Lane who married Miss Edna Sauvary from the North Side (my great uncle's daughter) and finally a funeral supervised by Mr J.C. Sauvary. It's funny all this came out in the same Press and Star, March 7, 1941.

Saturday, March 8. A terrible day. It started with a gale and rain. The rain stopped and the wind increased. It was East, and thinking it nearly a side wind, like a silly I started for Town, always so anxious to get my tea ration. The seas were mountains high. I got blown off my bicycle at the Banques. The basket with the chicken and sprouts for Elsie got untied and began swinging. I got blown off again, then walked some distance. I was glad to leave my basket at Cox where Elsie had left me three tins of fruit. Pontins were out of tea and coffee.

Another order, to fill up more papers for bread rations, 6 lbs for workers, 4 lbs for others. I am claiming 6 lbs.

Our potatoes are up. I am handing over half the field to the States. I am digging up the remainder of my leeks, carrots and parsnips, they are lovely and fine.

Uncle Ned has had news of Marjorie. I am so glad as he was always worrying. She sends greetings to him and Giff who, I notice, calls at the Old Rectory some Sunday afternoons.

I hear that the Germans took from the airport their searchlights etc. and sent away a few hundred soldiers. They say that the decks of the boats that left were packed. About 100 Germans passed this morning going towards L'Ancresse with full kit.

The Lawtons came to tea. I worked in the field, mostly picking up worms for the fowls, food is scarce. I bought three bowls of limpets for them, at 2d per bowl. I cooked them, cut each in three. The fowls loved them but I think enjoyed the enormous worms even more. At last I am getting two eggs per day.

Gussie rang up this morning for a sitting of eggs. I gave him six Elsie had given me and managed to buy three more. I am always called to the rescue.

Wednesday, March 12. Tom took them out on Sunday afternoon. I am not supposed to be well although I have never felt better. But Dr Jones said don't cycle too much, so I rode as far as Tom's house and he finished the journey, all hills.

I went to the Stubbs to tea and they gave me three cigarette coupons, good going I thought. Mr Stubbs is not a smoker. I will

MARCH 1941

probably write later of my slight indisposition, nothing I think serious, not worth taking note of.

Friday, March 14. It has been a lovely, real Spring day. I made Mrs Carré's bill and took it to the Hougue Guillmine. She is still the same, living in the kitchen, sleeping on the couch, just as Flo and Kit will remember when we took Rosemary to see her.

She wrote out my cheque, wonderfully done for a woman of 83 years. She is staying alone, a neighbour calls each day to see her and open the greenhouse lights. The garden is still a wilderness.

Dr Jones called as usual to have his cup of tea, and said the Press was out with further orders. This time better news. The curfew is extended to 10 o'clock, much better, it is still light at 9. Tonight I cannot get the news on 70, and only very indistinct on 80. I hate missing it as I follow the news very closely, more so with the raids on England. It must be awful there now. But I won't complain. I have had a nice supper, toast, pork fat mixed with sausages and a hot drink (not tea), all enjoyed after a perfect day. Everybody has been brighter. So have I.

I had to go to Mr Monsell's pub to meet Mr Downing, Mr Randall's Works Superintendent re a job, which did not develop into the big one we had expected.

On my return I missed Tom. He had run away to try and get me some ormers, as he was told the tide was good. As he crossed from Little Hoûmet to Mont Crevelt, he got his great hip boots full of water. He was soaked to the waist when he eventually came back with four large and eight small ormers. He said he knew I like them very much. Mrs Rowe seemed satisfied to prepare them for me. I write this only to make your mouths water.

Mr Cross and Miss Mauger also paid their bills today, so I have a nice pocket full. But I can spend it only on a little food and materials for the shop. Must stop. The clock is striking 11 and we are not allowed electricity after then. Good night darlings. I hope you are safe.

Saturday, March 15. It has been the most beautiful day imaginable. Had I known it was going to be, I would have gone to Herm with Henry. I met Barlow Corbet who said I was a fool to miss the chance.

I went to Town this morning, no tea ration, only barley coffee. I have a little reserve, some awful Lapsang, a China tea with a very smoky flavour. It's quite dear, 4/- per lb and they say an acquired taste. Quite so for those who take sugar and can kill the taste! Even so you cannot kill the smell. Still I expect I will have to put up with many things yet.

MARCH 1941

Undated. I hear the curfew is put back to 9 o'clock because of sabotage, cutting telephone wires which, by the way, have been fixed on many roads. I have several insulated wires passing from Carpenter's opposite, the Holly tree to the Manse, thence through my big garden to the telephone pole in the vinery. I omitted to say that on my return from Miss Houstoun I saw the Fort Road strewn with wires on both sides. The primroses and buttercups on those lovely fields facing Morley Chapel looked exquisite.

I see by the paper tonight that Mrs Santina Lucretia Santangelo, Ida's mother, was fined 2/6 in Court for losing her Identity Card. I met both in Town last Saturday and they made me promise I would go and see them. It's the third time I have promised so I will have to go this time.

Elsie came down this afternoon with a nice rabbit, a doe. I think I will breed from it, meats, etc. are getting so scarce. I gave her a bottle of wine for Miss Lihou and Mrs Godfray. They cannot get these things as I can, and they are very kind to me in other ways.

Thursday, March 20. Just had a telephone message, urgent Douzaine Meeting at 6 tonight. I will have to leave the Lawtons who are coming to tea. They have no wireless, so I will show Mr Lawton how to manage it.

Friday, March 21. It was an important meeting. Somebody has been cutting the German telephone wires near the Forest Road in two places. Hence an urgent States Meeting for Friday. Jurat Leale will then also explain our food position which is not too rosy. See Press, March 21, 1941.

Because of this sabotage we have to find 60 men every night to guard these wires from 8.30 pm to 8.30 am, two hours on, two hours off. And I hear there may be a fine or some other punishment. All this is very unfortunate. It could be anybody, perhaps irresponsible boys. Of course, if found, the penalty would probably be death.

Diva came down today. She slept the night as the van was going back to Town so early. Mrs Rowe made her up a bed in Jack's room. She goes back on Saturday at 2.

Mary Sauvary rang up to say she had heard from her father. All the family are well at High Wycombe. Another batch of Red Cross letters has arrived and she thinks there are some for me.

Saturday March 22. Pontins were out of tea and barley coffee. Quite a long ride for nothing. However I brought back other drinkables! The shops are decked with the most wonderful blooms, and it's difficult for them to get even 1d per bunch. Hundred of lettuces, very tender but no hearts, grown in greenhouses, radishes and new potatoes were all fairly cheap.

MARCH 1941

I met the postman coming from Town. He was excited and said he had a RX card for me. But it was another disappointment, although I was glad to get the card. The message is from my brother Willie. But Mary had already told me she had received news. I had hoped it would be from Jack.

Undated. I listened to Greek Independent Day celebrations. I am afraid now that Yugoslavia has signed the Axis pact her country is doomed. I don't see how she can stand up to such forces.

The reduced bread ration started today. I get a 2 lb loaf Tuesdays and Saturdays, and a 1 lb loaf on Thursdays. I think I can manage. Men on hard work get 6 lbs.

Another funeral, an old Mr Le Poidevin, next door to Mr Sebire, The Orchards. Kit will remember where we used to get apples with dear Mum.

It's been a bit of a strain, once to Town, twice to the Courtillon which is near Noirmont. All this on my bicycle which I am not used to. I do miss my car. The service will be in the Chapel, in French, with hymns. The old gentleman had been there all his life, and he died in his 99th year, so I expect Mr Beaugie will elaborate on all the changes since the old man was a boy.

I went to the College to see my brother Willie's letter. I was pleasantly surprised as he gave me good information about all of you. Dated Feb 6, 1941, he wrote he often saw Jack, Ted, Flo and Kit and all well. I was very anxious and dare say I will get some news from some of you this week from the 2,000 more letters arrived. I don't make many comments on the progress of the war or war news, as you hear it as well on the wireless.

When I passed Brookdale Nursery at L'Islet, I saw the whole of that big field in front of Mr Roussel, Grand Fort was one sheet of yellow. It's terrible to see the flowers wasting. Of course vergées have been dug and thrown away, but I suppose lack of time and perhaps to save a few tons of bulbs, hence the sight. In ordinary times we did not see that beauty, because they were always picked before they came into full bloom. This year they have not been damaged by the wind.

I met Kitty Head on the Front this morning. She was glad of your news. She has heard of her daughter, Diana, and Bachmann's people, but nothing yet from her father, mother and family.

Mary Sauvary came down on Saturday and I gave her a nice tea. I had a little bread to spare as rationing had only just begun, and my butter ration was not exhausted as my pork fat lasted well. We had blackberry jam, the last pot, marked Chouet 1938. I think Kit made it. It was hard and dry but she loved it and with extravagant helpings we nearly cleared the lot. She finished with Mrs Rowe's sultana cake, made with two eggs.

MARCH 1941

That day one of my fowls laid a double yolk which I gave her. She stands more than six foot and is as thin as a wafer. I don't know how these growing girls are going to get on with only 5 lbs of bread per week and 1/4 lb of butter.

I went to see Mrs Cortvriend while visiting my men at De Putron's Nursery. They were glad to see me, and that morning had 10 chickens out of the 11 eggs I got for them after much trouble. I find Violet much thinner and she finds me much thinner. I expect we are all falling away somewhat.

This morning my man Martel rang from the shop to say the Germans were going around the South Quay warning people to open their windows, as at 11 they were firing their guns from Mont Crevelt. Hart, the Chemist, an ARP man, was warning people on the Bridge.

The Star, this morning, has new orders. We are not allowed coal fires. We can have a wood fire, and people cooking on open fires must put them out when the cooking is over. I am wondering what the next restriction will be.

If you read the Presses I am keeping you will laugh, see Jersey News, March 29. A farmer's wife was taken to Court for water in her milk. Her excuse was, first she was tethering her cow on German prohibited pasture, the day before the cow had eaten her Identity Card, she was in a hurry and nervous not being allowed where she was, was taking water in the milking can for the cow and perhaps forgot to empty it! Excuses which of course did not work with the Court. However it seems her husband's reputation saved her a little.

The men helping Tom trenching the States half of the field are collecting worms for my fowls. The boy helping them is very thin and looks half-starved. I joked with him and said, I don't expect you would fancy an egg, it's possible you might find one of those big worms in the egg! He said he hadn't eaten an egg for six months, so worms or no worms, he would chance it. Now the joke was that I couldn't leave out the man. So I called out, Could you tackle an egg for breakfast? I could sir, but I *likes* a couple! Tom and I could not stop laughing. It was fit for Punch. Tom thought he deserved the two. So I had to part with four eggs, and there's Tom to think of too.

Mary told me she went through all the S's of the 2,000 letters but there were none for me. She thinks I ought to be satisfied as some people haven't heard anything yet. About six from her father for different people came through. She thinks some have been lost.

I met Mr Oppenheim's housekeeper in Town yesterday when I called at the College for a permit for Mr Lawton for chemicals. She told me she now has Germans in the house, six officers I believe. She is alone there but says they are very nice to her.

I am always hoping, and I bought dozens of sweetpeas from

MARCH 1941

Gussie and am planting them. My own will come on later, so if the war finishes in July I will have some sort of show for you all, and if in August I will have my own. Good night till we meet again, and as always I add, if ever. Life today is so uncertain. I often wonder how you all feel and whether you are losing your nerve in this nerve-racking terrible time. Live in hope is all we do today.

Tuesday, March 26. I went to St Martin's to see my men at Miss Mauger's, Delmery. I met Mr Browell. He has left his bungalow on the Jerbourg Rd, I hear the Germans are fixing heavy guns at Jerbourg. He is now in a boarding house on the Calais Rd. He asked me to lunch but I put him off. The fields in front of the Fort still look lovely.

In Town Lipton's window is filled with lettuce, radishes, broccoli at give-away prices. But new potatoes are 6d per lb, much too dear. I gave Mrs Frossard some carrots. She has made lovely marmalade with lemons. I don't know the recipe. She gave me a pot and I am enjoying it, but I don't suppose I would have looked at it a year ago. Hunger is the source of cure for all fads.

Not so many at the Social tonight. There was a boxing match in Town and the skating is going strong. Henry was there. They had a lovely catch of mullet on Monday, over 100, nearly £8 worth. They are also catching ray but it is not plentiful. We had a long chat. He really is a nice boy.

Tuesday, April 1. A wonderful week of news and I hope and trust these successes will soon end this infernal war. I am getting sick and impatient although there is not much yet to complain of. Food is scarce and I am short of butter. Mary Sauvary is coming again on Saturday and I am determined to give her a good tea.

I was at the Doctor's last night, Mr Cross was there and I happened to mention that I'd have to go without butter till Saturday. As we left at curfew hour Mr Cross said, Come in a minute. As I had only four mts. I did not want to. His assurance that he would keep me only one mt. made me go. To my amazement he gave me 1/4 lb of States butter. I got home, cut a full round of a 2lb loaf, coated it with butter, then on top a liberal layer of turkey and tongue paste, then washed it down with a drop of hot gin. That butter was a real present.

Jack Corbet brought me two dozen roselet [smelt]. I have cleaned them and may take them out to Miss Lihou and Mrs Godfray. It's impossible for them to get fish. The queues in Town are pathetic. I saw 50 people waiting while a dog fish was being skinned, and there was not enough for a quarter of them.

Friday, April 4. I have a job at Dr Sutcliffe, Shaw's house in the

APRIL 1941

Grange. I sent the roselets to Mrs Godfray. Elsie came down for a few 'rations'. I don't like to think of these old ladies being short of food at their ages (89 and a few years less). I gave them a little sponge cake, a milk pudding, a piece of sultana cake Mrs Rowe had made me and vegetables. Elsie brought me four eggs, two of which I gave Mrs Rowe.

Mr Frossard called to tell me there was a letter for me, and Mary rang about it. It's from Flo. I still get no news from Jack.

Saturday, April 5. Mrs Bim Honey came to see me (the first visit since Mum died). She brought me two packets of Mattee tea. Mary came and I gave her a nice tea with plenty of bread and butter and two wedges of sultana cake. She left later than usual, as the unexpected happened, the curfew was put back to 10 o'clock, with the warning that if anything happened again the punishment will be more drastic.

Sunday, April 6. I had a miserable day. Palm Sunday and the Easter Festival coming remind me so much of Mum that I cannot feel bright. The cold reminded me of our primrosing in the perishing cold. But Mum would always go. She liked giving some to Auntie Kate for the font.

I wish you could see our little back garden. The primrose clusters are enormous, and there are several in the front garden too. The cemetery man fetched a basket full for a border on the little wedge plot, left of the front entrance.

Monday, April 7. I went to Town to see Flo's letter. Dated Feb. 7, 1941, she says she has not heard from me yet. I have answered three so you should soon hear. Mrs Trouteaud attended to me and Mrs Hickey came up to ask if I'd had news of the children.

I do wish this infernal war was over. Now the Balkan trouble is developing wherever will it end. I have been listening to extracts of Mr Churchill's talk or statement in the House of Commons. Some parts seemed disappointing and distressing, and what a raid on Coventry. Can there be any town left. I note the Kiel had two visits.

Thursday, April 10. Uncle Ned came to listen to the 2 o'clock news. It's his 82 birthday, he looks well, is active but his sight is very bad. He runs into every obstacle yet insists he can see. The news was not very bright, nor was I. I have a shivery feeling down my spine so am resting. Had hot milk for supper. Sent Tom out to Mrs Godfray with provisions and a few bunches of the narcissus type flower as an Easter Egg for the old ladies.

Good Friday, April 11. I did not feel too fit but got up at 8.15 (really

APRIL 1941

only 6.15). The very first Good Friday I remember without Hot Cross Buns. Church at 10.45. When I returned Dr Jones had called. He thought I would have stayed in. Tom called to open the greenhouses and feed the fowls. My dinner was a bake. Mrs Rowe had called to see to it and I gave her a dinner out of it to take home.

I think the young people had cycle picnics. About fifty passed in one group. The order that you must not ride two abreast was not observed. I would not be surprised to see Court cases in the Press next week.

Wilfred Haysom took Mr Pattimore out in his wheel chair. He had not been out for 10 months. He can scarcely walk, his heart is groggy, I cannot understand how he lasts. I believe while people can keep their spirits up they prolong their lives.

Coventry and Birmingham must be in a terrible state, and the casualty list will be awful to hear.

Holy Saturday, April 12. It's pitiful to see the display of mostly bulb flowers on the Bridge. I bought several bunches, lovely large blooms much like pheasant eye, not exactly the flower I wanted but much the same perfume, all for 2d per bunch. The whole house was scented with them. Mrs Frossard is going to do the altar, and I think the Malletts might do the font. No other decorations this year.

I saw the oil boat in St Sampson's harbour, they say with 100 tons, in which case we will get electricity till June.

I am feeling a little more fit today. I did not ask the Lawtons to tea this week as I did not feel equal to it. Our work is getting on the slack side. I hope something will soon come in.

Mary brought a large bunch of flowers for Mum's grave. For tea we had a potato cake Lily Ellis had brought me down from Plummers (she is working in Town now the St Sampson's shop has closed). It's a mixture of potatoes, sultanas and milk. I warm it in the oven. It's very nice but I am sure I would not have eaten it in peace time.

After putting Mary's flowers on the grave she wanted to see Grandpa Sauvary's grave, which we forked and weeded. Then she asked where Grandpa Monsell's grave was. It was overgrown with weeds, so we forked and weeded it too. I gave her a nice lot of lettuce seedlings and two eggs for her Easter Egg. She seemed to be thinking about Peter (her young brother), they were pals. She typed my answer to Flo's letters.

Easter Sunday, April 13. A happy Easter to you all. I got up much rested and fresh. The weather was fairly mild, the air crisp, and I went to the 8.30 celebration. It was really only 6.30. There were 65 and at the 7.30 Mr Frossard said there were 50. The Easter collections, up to now, look as if they will be very small. I walked to

APRIL 1941

church with Mrs Frossard. She was not looking very fresh. Back to the quiet, empty house.

At the 10.45 service we had a nice little anthem, Christ is Risen. Jackie, our organist, does very well. We have ten girls in the surplice choir now. The men looked very nice in their clean surplices. The altar looked nice and Mrs Frossard thought the flowers beautiful. There were also about six dozen Arums.

Mrs Le Poidevin, Winnie and Hunkin came down for the 10.45 service in a Chair. They could not get one to take them back till 2.30, so the old lady stayed at Jack Lainé's till then. She could have come to my house, but they did not like to ask me as they knew I always went to the Doctor's.

An RAF airman came down off Lihou Island I think about 3 am and landed in a rubber boat or somehow. They think he was flying a fighter plane and either lost his way or ran out of petrol. I have heard about six different versions! However he went to one of the cottages who let him in and kept him there for the night. They had no telephone and because of the curfew could not go out. He was reported in the morning and is now a prisoner of war. Scotchman, I believe. I don't think anything was seen of the plane. It was heard flying around some time previously.

After Evening Service Stafford said, Come along, get on your bicycle and come to the Gigands. You are free. As I was still moody I just packed away the collection and we sailed off.

We went to see the old people. They are well but Mr Ogier has lost a lot of flesh. Meantime Mrs Ogier and her daughter-in-law had been preparing an enormous plate each of chip taters and beans from a tin. As I had had no tea I thought it safe to devour the lot, washed down with a bottle of cider, their own make and very good, followed by an enormous cigar which I just managed to finish. I did not sleep till 4 o'clock, but will leave out my midnight trouble. I should not have been tempted.

For breakfast a nice egg and my first taste of barley coffee.

Easter Monday, April 14. Booked four seats for them at the North Cinema. I am not going, not feeling too well. Have sat by the fire and slept when not feeding the fowls. Had only toast and milk for dinner.

Uncle Ned came in at 2 for the news. We each had a fresh egg for tea and as I am not eating freely I was able to spare him bread and butter. He left soon after 7 to close The Old Rectory.

The sun is trying to peep through the study windows while I write this, and our back garden is looking wild and neglected. I hope I feel better tomorrow as I want to get on with my gardening. The beech has its pointed twisted leaves all ready to untwirl, which might happen with this wind and rain. It's marvellous how it breaks out and covers itself with leaves so quickly.

APRIL 1941

I seem to be full of trouble just now. I have a nasty, tender patch under my right foot, and have difficulty to walk with the pain. Miss Ross came last week, but I think the trouble is that all my boots are thin and have served on the brake pedal of the old Ford. This gets the boots out of shape, and now I am on the cycle pedal. With rheumatic pains in my head this morning at 4 o'clock (which is now better) you know all my troubles and ailments.

I suppose I can't always expect to feel well. The Doctor gave me two blue pills, said they act on the liver. Miss Matthews laughed as I swallowed them without water, and they were not small.

Friday, April 18. We have had a couple of hot, sunny days but I could not enjoy them. I am shivering all down the back and this is the third day I have not eaten a dinner. Dr Jones gave me a tin of Apricot Conserve, Australian. The flavour was lovely and I was tempted and ate some on a small piece of bread.

One of the Sisters, Cotîls, has died and I had to make the funeral arrangements. I don't feel very fit, but had to go out. (I don't feel sick but have lost all my will power. While in bed I feel well.) I think you will remember the Sister. She was only 62 but looked 80. She was the old one who looked after the cows.

The morning of the funeral they rang to say it would be impossible for them to walk to the Foulon in the rain, and could I get a car. It took half an hour to get through the various departments of Civil Transport, but with great difficulty I did. A blessing as I made one of the cars fetch me and bring me back. Tom had been trying to persuade me to get a Chair, but I had intended to cycle as there was no wind.

About April 22, 23. I have had lunch on only two occasions during the past nine days, at the Doctor's on Sunday, and on Tuesday at the Frossards. The Doctor had said that I was off my food and he thought my meals were not varied enough. Mrs Frossard was having oxtail soup and thought it would be a little change for me. I ate a lunch but did not feel much benefit from it. Tom gets half my bread ration.

Dr Digby Roberts has died. Dr Jones went to the funeral in Dr Cambridge's car. When at Mr Wheadon's to get onion plants, I met Dr Wilson and we had a long talk. He said Dr Digby Roberts had collapsed six hours after a successful though serious operation.

At Candie I met Mrs Cortvriend who was much upset over the doctor's death. They have been rather friendly lately, especially Madam, who is staying with her at The Hollies for a few days. Mrs Cortvriend said she could not leave her alone in that big house in Queen's Road.

APRIL, 1941

Mary came down on Saturday, and her boy friend (as she calls him) came to call for her at 8 o'clock. When she arrived she was excited as she had two messages for me from Flo. You can guess I was also excited. As she works at the College she brought me copies, one from Dec. 15, 1940, the other March 4, 1941. On Monday I had the PC to call to see the messages, so I was able to prepare my answers. There were hundreds there, and I was in the queue for nearly one hour. I was glad of the news of your safety. Fancy Flo, your going back to Burgh Heath. I expect one place is as safe as the other. I also sent a message to Ralph's parents.

We have some nice rhubarb, but I have no sugar. I am offering one dozen eggs for 5 lbs sugar, but up to now with no success.

I saw Henry last night coming from Town. He called out, You ought to have been with us today. It must have been awful, strong E wind, the sea on the Front was white foam. They go out any weather and I am afraid get very little fish, and have to sail mostly, very little petrol.

Friday, April 25. I am staying in again, have a nice wood fire and will try to get some booking and bills cleared up.

The few shops open on the Bridge have enormous displays of tulips of the most vivid colours. Anemones of the brightest colours also make a marvellous display. Of course other years all the best flowers were exported. The lovely tulips Mum planted outside the study are just opening.

I hear there has been more sabotage. (I don't know if it's true.) They say wires have been cut at the Vardes. It might be by someone not accountable for their actions, and why should the population be punished for such a slight offence. In fact we are getting several cases of suicide, one only yesterday, a Star office clerk, Mr S.N. West.

Thursday, April 30. Yesterday it blew a buster, wind still NE. I've stayed in the house practically two days. My back and side pain me a lot. I have not asked the Lawtons. In fact it's been too much trouble to go down there to give them the news. They cannot use their set owing to no dry batteries.

I am a little better and my appetite is coming back. My butcher's bill this week was 1½d. I laughed when I saw it, and that was my allowance for fat. (I say a fat lot!)

Mrs Rowe made me a rhubarb tart (and it was very nice) with part of a tin of Atora suet I found on the top shelf of the kitchen cupboard. She said it smelt. I know it had been there for more than eight months. Still I knew it was good (or at least the tart was). Tom had a big piece.

Tom is a grandpa today. His daughter had a little girl at the

APRIL 1941

Emergency Hospital at 8 this morning, and there had been a lot of excitement and telephoning today.

The curfew is to be extended to 11 from May 1. Our sugar ration is to be reduced to 3 oz. Our meat ration is 6d per person.

The Germans have taken over Delancey Park Schools, and I hear they are going to sleep 90 men there. They have guns on the Park but people can still use the bowls and tennis courts. The children are coming to the Church Schools, 65 boys and girls I believe, and I am making an air-raid shelter under the floor. I have to make the place ready by Monday.

I have just heard Churchill announce that at least 45,000 of our troops managed to evacuate from Greece. I was glad to hear that news but worry about the awful raids on England. Plymouth got it badly this week. I do wish this raiding could stop. It seems too awful to believe.

Our beech tree is now in full leaf. The early part of the week there were dozens of sparrows picking something out of the inside of the leaf as it uncurled. I think there must be something inside. I don't think it is an insect, as I see something like white blossom dropping out. [The white feathery substance is a tomentum (soft down of matted woolly hairs) so the sparrows were eating either the flower buds which are known to have a high oil content, or some insect such as aphides. Information from Maurice Burton.]

Dear Mum's tulips are in bloom. I took a dozen to the grave on Saturday. I did not go the week before, it was so rough and I very poorly. Someone had removed all the old flowers and put a bunch of Iris in one of the pots. Tom came with me. We took the wheelbarrow with fresh soil. I put five pots of flowers, all from our back garden. People spoke of the beautiful colour of the tulips, a sort of bronze. Do you remember them?

I see by the papers that 30 tons of flour, 25 tons of sugar, cheese etc have arrived from Granville, but no meat this week.

Mrs Dredge came in for trouble in the Fish Market I hear. One woman smacked her face with a whiting. There was a large queue, but owing to booked orders she could not supply them all. Two women had a free fight and the police had to be called. I think fish will have to be rationed now.

Sunday, May 11. The Doctor has rice for only one more Sunday. We had gooseberry tart, crust very hard, I think only flour and water. Miss Matthews gave me a nice cup of cocoa after. They are out of tea.

Tea at the Stubbs. They gave me four cigarette coupons. I took her a nice bunch of Lilies of the Valley. If I can get her 3 lbs of flour (if I can spare it) she will give me a pair of lady's shoes worth £1 or more, and another pair I can give Mary Sauvary.

MAY 1941

Mary came as usual yesterday. I gave her a nice tea and two eggs to take home. We put a huge bunch of Lilies of the Valley and other flowers on Mum's grave, where the birds had played havoc sunbathing. It was a profusion of flowers.

We had our Parish Meeting on Wednesday, passing my accounts. Mr Frossard elected me his for another three years. If I complete it I will have served 18 years as People's Warden and six as Rector's. I should then come in for a pension, or at least deserve one! Stafford Ogier got in again, though there was opposition which fell flat. Later we went to Court and were sworn in for another term.

What a terrible raid on London. I dread to hear the account. I wonder how you are all getting on. It must be terrifying. We are so quiet here. Scarcity of food is our problem. I weighed in last week, 10 stone 12 lbs so have lost 9 lbs, but I was eating very little for eight days. But I have sufficient food for some time.

We have had companies of Germans marching through New Road this week. They sing very well in parts, often to our English tunes, It's a long way to Tipperary and so on.

It's been a noisy day, many fast fighter planes passing over, it seems returning from England. I saw three medium-sized boats come into the harbour, about the size of the New Fawn. They have been unloading coal today. This traffic on Sunday is funny. I hear she had 700 tons. I hope so as they have left me anthracite for two weeks, which you know is difficult to burn without force draught.

Monday or Tuesday, May 12/13. I went to see Auntie Minnie. I was lucky, they made me stay to dinner, vegetables and haricot beans with the gravy of a fowl. I quite enjoyed it and it will lengthen out my rations.

Mrs Stubbs is hard pressed for food. They gave away their collected provisions, thinking they were evacuating, but missed their chance, leaving it too late. She has lost 2 stones, 2lb. I gave them the flour and she gave me the shoes which I gave to my sister. She also gave me a pair of trousers. I have had three callers cadging for pants. They were wearing only overalls in this cold weather. I felt sorry for them.

George Austin, the MOH Inspector, who sings in our choir, has been to Alderney for two weeks clearing up houses. There are a lot of Germans there. They are fixing up guns at Fort Albert. They have cut holes in the tower of the church, and get out on a plank and use it as a lookout. He says the place looks awful, no furniture in the houses. The Marais, you will remember the Square with the big drinking fountain, is named Hitler Square, and they have German names for all the streets. We have a Guernsey contingent there planting the Blayes with wheat, barley and potatoes, 500 vergées I think. I hope so, we will want it all.

MAY 1941

At last they have hit the Houses of Parliament, and how sad about the Abbey. All those beautiful carved stalls now, I suppose, in ruins.

I have a litter of rabbits today and can see three. I am keeping them for meatless weeks.

I am wanted at the Church Schools. The children have broken down the nets on the tennis court. A job to mend those posts. That's only the start now the kiddies are there.

I called this morning to wish Mr Pattimore many happy returns – his 84th birthday. I took him two new laid eggs, all I had. He wanted me to drink his health, but I hate drinking in the morning, so called again tonight and drank a glass of gin.

Wednesday, May 14. The Occupation Account will be enormous. Guernsey will never be able to pay it up. Then we have to pay the children's living and school expenses in England.

Fancy having one of the Nazis as a refugee in England, Rudolf Hess, one of the Fuhrer's third in command. I wonder what it all means. He was lucky not to have been killed and also that his plane was not attacked.

I noticed three small French craft in the Old Town Harbour this morning, kind of motor boats converted from sailing sloops. I think they brought the meat I saw at the King's Weights. I got a nice cheese from Le Riche, 1/-. It's very soft and I spread it on bread and save my butter. It's the first time I remember eating dry bread and cheese.

Fish is now rationed and we are allowed it once a week.

Saturday, May 17. I got up early this morning as I did not expect Tom. He had a cold and an awful pain in his side yesterday. He went to stay with his daughter who had just returned from the Emergency Hospital with her baby daughter (much excitement), and I am afraid he slept on a damp bed. However he came, but did nothing except look at the nice litter of rabbits, six I think, plump and strong. It was from the doe Elsie gave me. (I am giving her one or two.)

Mary brought me a fillet of whiting, much enjoyed. It is months since I had a bit of fish. We picked the flowers for the grave including dark blue iris, you will remember from the gable of the house by the drawing room. In one vase I put a huge bunch of Lilies of the Valley with tender light green leaves from underneath the myrtle bushes in the front garden. We cut the stems of the bronze tulips (Mary's idea) from last week, they were wide open and blended beautifully.

We straightened the ground where the birds had made great hollows. It's a lovely corner, a real birds' sanctuary. I am sure Mum

MAY 1941

would have been pleased with the display, all from her garden and a lot of what she herself had planted. It seems a shame she could not have lived a few more years with me to enjoy life, but it was not to be. It's two years, the 5th June, she died.

I am now planting the greenhouse and garden at Allendale. The Greenhouse Control took it over but have not used it owing to difficulty about water. But I am going to take the risk, planting sunflowers, tomatoes, cucumbers and sweet corn, and outside late potatoes (very late). There are two vines. The Muscat has 100 bunches, the Alacant not so good. Jack Lainé is trimming the vines, Mrs Rowe will do the thinning.

I met Mr De Putron, for now was my chance to get the trees at the top of the garden cut down. Crops have never done anything there because of the shade. I am promised they will be cut down but won't feel sure till I see it done.

I built a small span greenhouse there, I think 49 years ago, in the second year of my apprenticeship. I got all the timber ready by hand that winter (evenings) and got leave for one week to put it up and glaze it.

While in Town this morning I went to Elizabeth College for my fish coupons, and Dr Jones' too. But it was at the Ladies' College, so I had to climb further. Oh, what remembrances of Speech Days and your little plays in the hall while I waited my turn (not long). Last week the queues were two or three hundred.

The rain is at last coming down. It's a godsend otherwise our summer crops would have been a failure. The beech tree looks lovely weighed down with the rain, the lower branches nearly touching the ground. Mr De Putron was pleased with the tree.

After tomorrow I will be out of tobacco. I hear that if they can get continental tobacco from France we will get 1 oz. I have been smoking a pipe on and off for four weeks now. One evening Dr Jones was without and came down at 10 to 11. He said Miss Matthews was nearly demented, dying for a smoke. I gave him 10 home-made and he rushed off just in time before the curfew. I did not happen to go there that evening, and being alone and expecting me any minute, I think got on their nerves. Being lucky I had three extra coupons last week, or would not have been able to help them. I am wondering what they will do if we really have to go without.

While at the Pattimores Tom came to tell me that there was a large fleet of barges and escorts coming down past St Sampson's, forty one in all. Everyone thought it was the Invasion fleet. So I rushed home to get my bicycle. Mr Romeril from the Manse, next door, decided to come with me. We went by the Oil Tanks. The weather was rough (probably they came in for shelter). A fine drizzle was falling, I could see only nineteen, still worth seeing. But after 5 mts in the cold wind we rushed home for the 9 o'clock news.

MAY 1941

These barges, 100 ft long, are tucked into the Town Harbour. I hope they clear out, otherwise our people will come and bomb them.

Mary came as usual and we had another hot potato cake. They are like a pancake, 7½d each. Besides the usual flowers we put London Pride, Kit, that you planted, on Mum's grave. They have bloomed well. I think the Pinks will be out next week. The Laburnum and Chestnut are in full bloom.

Sunday, May 18. Had a right royal lunch at the Doctor's today, a small joint of beef with yellow fat (so Guernsey), nicely browned potatoes, parsnips and new cabbage. I told Miss Matthews it was, as Mum used to say, fit for the gods. I can assure you I can do with it, to make up for the lost 9 lbs.

What a shock about the battleship Hood and practically her whole complement gone.

A new order out. We cannot do any painting or decorating without special permission. In fact, for almost any work now we have to get a permit, and if it is not absolutely necessary it will not be granted. I expect now, small as my show is, it will go to pot.

Sunday, May 25. It blew a gale from the S and poured with rain, worth thousands of pounds to Guernsey, just in time for our outdoor vegetables and fruit, all we have to depend on for the winter. Even now I think the Red Cross or someone will have to step in before next winter.

Ascension this week with remembrances again. Mother was such a personality, and we talked over and worked over all details of seasons and customs, that nothing happens, even for a day, that I am not reminded or her. I try to keep myself occupied but find I am dreaming. Fortunately I am sleeping better.

Undated. We mostly live on potatoes. 40% are put in our bread I believe. Still I find it fairly good. But with only ¼ lb butter per week and nearly all my jam gone, I am wondering how I will get on. I have been so glad of Mum's plum jam of 1938, and the apple and sloe jelly, Kit's I think, which have helped me through up till now.

I have a funeral this week, a Mr Duquemin, 63 years. Luckily I had the oak. It came an awkward week, Whitsun, and we had to work on Sunday. I say we, but I didn't have to do much work.

I managed the three Whit Sunday services, 8, 10.45 and 6.30. Had lunch at the Doctor's. The other day he had a heart attack at Dredges, the fish shop. We got an ambulance to take him home, and he was chopping wood again in the afternoon.

Mary came with Kit's message from Mrs M.A. Kundert, Florastrasse 9, SOLOTHURN 7, Suisse. Dear Mr Sauvary, letter

JUNE 1941

sent you returned to me. News from Kit which is good. She is nurse in an Emergency Hospital. Write through Red Cross, Geneva, then will send it to your family. Best wishes, M.A. Jecker Kundert. Sent May 5, 1941. I replied, Many thanks welcome news. Well, comfortable at New Road. Mary (Sauvary) tea Saturdays. We attend Mum's grave regularly. Often think of your welfare. Fourth reply. 31.5.41.

Tuesday, June 3. At last I am through Whitsun. People say Mum and Auntie Kate are out of all these troubles, as Mum would have worried so much about your safety. But still I won't agree. Even if selfish, I would rather Mum had been here with me. Although I can bear it alone I would rather she'd been here. And to those who say it's a blessing they are out of all this, I feel like saying, pop your wife off out of all this misery, and they would soon sing another song.

We are getting lovely crops of potatoes out of the greenhouses, as much as 4 cwt to the perch, and excellent vegetables, but no fat to cook them with.

We have scarcely seen the sun for eight days and the weeds are taking charge in the garden. I boiled new potatoes, carrots, etc. with red cabbage and pickled onions (a great help to get the dinner down). Went to see Miss Lihou and Mrs Godfray. Elsie made tea before she left for a Euchre Drive. She gave me four eggs. Fancy, I have eighteen fowls and have not had an egg for three weeks. I had a ducking riding home, but all downhill on my nice new Hopper.

Wednesday, June 4. The middle aisle of the church was packed for Mr Duquemin's funeral. There were twenty seven wreaths and again I had to report for the Press and Star. A lot of work but the others do it and I have to follow, otherwise I lose the advertisement.

Thursday, June 5. The second anniversary of dear Mum's death. With the wind blowing so hard, and the cold and rain, I had no energy, so I made a good fire and did the time sheets. Had my dinner again of the 10d joint stewed with vegetables. Of course I have to wait till I am very hungry, otherwise I could not get through the meal. I now have a glass of skimmed milk at 11.30.

This afternoon after seeing my men who are working at Mr Bird's, I rested and slept till 6 o'clock. Rather cold as I forgot to put the rug over me. Then feeling fresher I took a lovely bunch of yellow Iris and some red flowers from Mrs Godfray to Mum's grave. All the other flowers from Saturday were fresh.

My seven baby rabbits are doing well. It has been a lonely day for me. I am longing to see you all. I do hope we will all get through. I must add that I am comfortable, but the place is dead.

JUNE 1941

Friday, June 6. Lots of lorries are carting stone of all descriptions to St Martin's. The Germans are doing a lot of work of some kind.

Mr Browell called yesterday. He is much thinner. He sends his love to you all. He does not know where his son is, but has had news from his family from Horsham.

The Laburnum is one solid mass of gold bloom hanging down in festoons. In fact all the Laburnums, including the one in front of the Manse, are looking lovely. So is our Chestnut. The Beech is again a splendid sight, so is our garden (except for some overgrowth). The sweet smelling Pinks around the borders and the pink ones just outside the study window are out in masses, the Pansies are also marvellous especially the black, the Foxgloves are almost out and about 6 ft high, the Briar is a mass of Roses.

Sunday, June 15. I have never known such cold weather in June. It is still necessary to have fires. We have had rain for about four days this week and it's impossible to keep the weeds down. I am keeping turnips for seed in the big garden. They are about 7 ft high. I hope the high wind won't blow them down.

The Doctor and I are going to the Frossards to tea. I am taking Madam a large bunch of red and white Pinks (that sounds Irish). Mrs Stubbs also wanted me to go to tea and the Ogiers to go there for the evening. I am out every Sunday if I wish it.

Have been busy all the week. Two funerals from the Vauquiedor Hospital. I do all their Poor Law Burials. I now have a fair amount of other work too. I had a lot of cycling and was very tired. Gardening tires me a lot, but I must keep on if I want vegetables.

I wish you could see the field now, Luxon's end planted with parsnips for the States. There is not a patch in the island looking better. Everyone passing stops and looks at it, even the Germans. I cut the dead wood from the May tree which is in full bloom, a mass of white, and the smell is superb. It looks better since I trimmed it.

Mr Kilshaw preached at Evening Service. I think it was arranged because he preached down here 14 years ago tonight. He said he remembered me well as warden. I did not.

The fishermen are bringing more boats from Town for the mackerelling season. There are a fair number of Spider Crabs at 10 – 15d. each, and Lobsters anything from 5-10/- I don't buy them. Rationed fish is very dear.

I hear electricity is being cut off next week if no oil arrives, then there will be no wireless. That will be awful. Coal merchants are not allowed to sell any more coal until October. I don't know how people will cook as the trees which we are cutting down (by the hundreds) are green and will not burn. Still we must not worry, though I cannot help it sometimes. Other than the food problem I am comfortable in the lonely house in New Road. Mrs Rowe

JUNE 1941

comes every afternoon except Sundays. She comes when she likes.

The laundries are closing this week (no soap). They merged into one at the Anchor, Nocq Road.

I bought some soft and half dozen stiff collars from Cox. I had to give 80 coupons for eight. I will soon be short of working suits. Mary took my coat and waistcoat to mend the pocket and sew on buttons. Mrs Rowe attends to my socks and underwear. It is very kind of them.

Another fleet of barges arrived last night. I think they come for shelter. The last lot stayed for nearly a week. I don't know what they use them for.

I weeded all day yesterday in the field. I nearly broke my back! But I had a nice whiting which Mrs Rowe fried for me with chip potatoes. Dr Jones called over the wall to come up at 7 to pick a kipper, which turned out to be four small lobsters, with nice salad, two of the lettuce from my garden. We did justice to the meal. Then had coffee which I took up as they have none, even barley coffee is finished now. To celebrate we had a liqueur, Pére Chartreuse. I then came back and planted 25 red beetroot, and so ended a perfect day.

I listened to the Derby. Fancy being able to carry on racing with a war raging.

Elsie is bringing down a broody hen to lend me. I *managed* to get six eggs. It's very late but I might get a cockerel or two for Xmas. I don't know where I will get the food for them. I have only potatoes and very little mash for my 20 hens, and can you believe it, I haven't had an egg from them for six weeks. If they don't lay soon I'll kill the lot!

No tea or coffee ration again this week, but I am not yet without, nor have I used Kit's Typhoo, or the China tea I found only last week in a tin on the kitchen mantelpiece.

Had such a good roast dinner that I could not eat any rice pudding. Not enough man, as dear Mum used to say, one of her jokes.

I wasted part of my morning trying to get a tobacco coupon. Tom was without cigs, and I managed to cadge a coupon from Mrs Stubbs. She is now trying to exchange them for flour or sugar, but that's what I am short of myself.

We get only 1oz tobacco and 20 cigs per week, we draw on Mondays and by Wednesday are mortgaging our next week's. But it's stopped now. Ogier won't do it. I had a mind to 'do' him. I just went in with the coupon I had been given and I think he was more worried about where I had 'scrounged' it, as he remarked, that he charged me only 1/- instead of 2/-. Tom didn't want me to take the 1/- back, and offered to toss me for it. But honesty being the best policy, my conscience would not allow that. He just gave a grunt when I gave him the bob.

JUNE 1941

Everything is very silent this afternoon, and with the stillness there was not a ripple on the water in the harbour this morning. A nice day for fishing. I hear the Mackerel have started.

Friday, June 20. It was just a year ago that I took Kit to the boat. Little did we think that after 12 months we would still be separated.

I have just made up the men's wages, only three. Tom goes to the Douzaine Room to collect his wages for looking after my place.

It's a glorious day. The only thing I can hear is the birds singing. I was at a funeral at the Foulon when the blackbirds, thrushes and other birds were singing so loudly that I could not hear the priest. They seem to have sung more than ever this year only a fancy I expect. Things are so silent it's almost like Sark. A thrush sings in the May tree in the field practically the whole day. There are very few nests, not one in the garden.

Saturday, June 21. It's a sweltering hot day, impossible to work in the garden. Everything is silent except the Germans singing in parts on the Park. Cars or lorries were passing it seemed all night. People seem generally more depressed than usual. Tom had the jitters this morning, and I, now being alone, am starting to feel the same. It's awful being stuck here like this. I feel it more Saturdays and Sundays. I think I will go to the beach and perhaps have a dip and pick limpets for the fowls. I have had two eggs this week, the first for nearly two months. I am loath to kill them yet, they have cost me so much.

Bill Le Maitre called with tobacco plants for Allendale and brought me a nice piece of soda cake. I'd almost forgotten the taste.

I saw Jane's cradle and Rosemary's beach can and wonder if they will ever come and fetch them. In any case not in the St Patrick, another of our mail boats gone. And fancy, ninety eight of our ships lost last month, and all their valuable cargoes. It won't be possible to find crews for the ships soon, especially engineers and stokers.

I am just back from my bathe, and what a disappointment. When I got to my 'private' spot between Mr Poat's beach and A. Dorey's house, to my amazement there were 80 to 100 Germans there. It was half tide and out of the question to dip there. In fact there was no place to undress but under the wall. At least 20 were undressing on the mound where the seat is.

I had no choice but to go underneath the wall in front of Mr Burgess's, then walk over the stones. I had to go down on all fours, the stones nearly burnt my feet, and even now I can only just stand the burning pain. I have never known anything like it in Guernsey. Still I got to the water only to find I was amongst 20 children, and the Germans on the Town side. They are a fine stamp of men, say

JUNE 1941

nothing to the girls and children bathing, but just mind their own business. One on a hoopie said something, I think Hallo, as he nearly collided with me.

Mr Poat was on the wall and told me that the vans of furniture which were passing were from Jack Leale's and Miriam's houses. They are putting two hundred men down there, but letting the Shaws, Leale's and Dorey's store their furniture in Town.

Sunday, June 22. Weather fine but foggy, and I think and hope that rain is coming. I rose early and went to Allendale to open up. I have that job to do now. I am never finished and judging by the weeds I pulled up in my dreams last night, I didn't expect to see any this morning. But it *was* only a dream.

Then I listened in and to my *very, very* great surprise heard the announcement that Hitler had declared war on Russia. I really did not expect that. I was not right this time.

I suppose you imagine me at church and that our thoughts are then united. Mr Frossard often speaks of those who were brought up and confirmed in the old Church, a monument of centuries.

This morning I had also to take on Kit's job, looking after the broody hen while out on her morning patrol. The first two mornings she did not go back of her own accord. Now she does. But I will not get fourteen chicks this time, Kit, as there are only eleven eggs. I have to cook potatoes for the fowls every two days. Another egg so I hope they have started in earnest, as I haven't potted any yet. Those Kit potted came in most useful, especially for cakes.

Saturday, June 28. Since I last wrote there have been many changes here, and the Russians are now in the conflict. The Germans are taking over two blocks of the Vauquiedor Hospital, the Capelles, Vale and, I think, St Andrew's Schools, the greater part of Manuelles Stables and many more houses. The nearest they are to New Road is Cranbrook. Mrs Hotton's bungalow is occupied.

Mrs Godfray telephoned that they have taken several houses in St Andrew's, and she is getting nervous about her house. Miss Lihou is not well. I told Mrs Godfray that they could both come and stay with me.

Now there is another trouble, continental riding on the roads and we have to keep to the right. I am such an awful dreamer on the road that I am afraid to go out. I set off yesterday to Allendale and on my return kept to the left. But I remembered when I got to Roland Road and kept extra well to the right. Just passing Jack West's cycle shop a young chap popped out bang into my front wheel. Luckily it got between his legs and he grasped the handles and saved us both from falling. That was my first experience of – Keep to the Right.

JUNE 1941

I have my baby rabbits out with the mother in a chicken run. They love it and carry out some wonderful acrobatic manoeuvres. But rabbits cannot stand too much sun so I shade part of the run.

I noticed going out that the Germans have occupied Amy Hampton's house. I don't know if Hunkin has moved any of the furniture.

It's a most glorious day and I am writing this sitting in a camp chair. All is quiet except the noise of the new mill at the quarry by the field, and the breeze is so light it scarcely turns. Then a car passes occasionally. Were it not for the Occupation it would be really lovely here with the scent of the Pinks just at my side, Antirrhinums of all colours in front of me, the shade of the lovely beech tree, and the Sergeant Majors, I mean the Foxgloves, standing in a straight row, fifteen of them, at least 8 feet high, white and red. Then on my left against the Ivy wall is the Orange Blossom tree (as I call it) loaded with bloom. Everything in our little house garden is lovely except the half-cut lawn waiting for hay-making.

Undated. My dinner consisted of dry bread, a tomato (no flavour), the first I have ever bought in my life, and a tender salad from my garden. It was not very appetising but I never start my ¼ lb butter ration till Saturday.

I have made good progress weeding, the garden is straight and I have at last planted the Sweet Peas. I work till after 9 and am always tired. It's a back-aching job and I sometimes wish I had given all to the States. Then after looking after my three men I could have had all afternoons and evenings free. But then I begin to think I might have been more miserable.

The Germans are having all mattresses collected from the Town houses. It would have broken the hearts of people who were living in Queen's Rd if they had seen, as I did this week, their lovely blue and red striped mattresses being piled into lorries. I hear they want hundreds, possibly thousands. I suppose they will be around our way some day. I hope they won't take this house.

Tuesday, July 1. After tying the runner beans which should have had their strings weeks ago, I had a wash and shave, curled my hair and decided to go to Kennilworth, Grosse Hougue, to get my photo taken. They have about 20,000 to take for fixing on our Registration Cards. There were streams of people but I was not kept waiting long. I hope you will like my permanent wave!

I then went to see Miss Lihou who is very ill. The ambulance took her from her house, Vauquiedor, to Mrs Godfray. I found her very weak and am afraid she won't get over it this hot weather. I managed to get from a friend a bottle of Valentine's Meat Juice, and also took an egg custard and sago pudding Mrs Rowe made me, a packet of Kit's Typhoo tea, a little coffee, a bottle of Lavender

JULY 1941

Water, good make 5/- and four large lettuce.

I cannot describe the beauty of the sea from the Banques as I rode out at 5 (really only 3), a lovely low tide. I would have loved a bathe but no time to spare. It was extremely hot and all uphill. I call the hills lovely when I am free wheeling down them! I had no hat and very light clothes which are falling off me. I had a nice tea there with *Brown Bread.* Oh the difference! I hear what we are getting has 40% potatoes. Still I don't complain, it suits me.

Then I worked here and at Allendale until 11 o'clock curfew. Mrs Rowe has finished thinning the grapes. It would be delightful if you were here to eat them.

Undated. Albert Bichard, Heathdale, Banques, telephoned that his mother had died after an operation at the Emergency Hospital. Last Sunday I walked to church with her. I went to the house at 10 o'clock. It was again a most lovely scene. Right across to Herm it was like a lake, and the motor fishing boats as they glided through were forming rings. Then from Richmond Corner the Town, Côtils etc could be seen reflected in the sea. It's real Guernsey summer weather. But I must have my dinner and get to work. I hate riding now keeping to the right. What I hate most is the cars rushing past me on the left.

I went out to the hospital via Camp du Roi, and paid a bill for Dr Jones at Mrs Carré, Four Cross. I have never ridden in such heat. The country is looking lovely and the scent of Broad Beans and every sort of flower fills the air. It's a real Rose year, and could not be excelled in England, the land of Roses. As I told you the Briar at the gable of the house is so loaded you cannot see the tree.

On to Mrs Godfray where I put on the mortice lock I had taken to be repaired. She was so pleased to get it done so soon. I saw Miss Lihou who I find weaker. When I reached the Banques I wished you could have seen the sea front, like a sheet of glass. It was half tide and the reflection of the rocks was as is often seen in photographs. I would have loved spending the afternoon on the beach, but always seem so busy. The garden takes much of my time, and what's unusual for this season, I am getting so many funerals. Still it's real summer now, and I do wish you were with me to enjoy its loveliness, instead of this infernal war going on.

In the evening the sights along the Camp du Roi were strange. The whole atmosphere has changed. There were old women resting, their baskets filled with rabbit food, girls and men, some with back carriers loaded with milk thistles, others with sacks of hay providing bedding for the winter. People are breeding hundreds of rabbits, but I hear the young are dying a lot, some say disease, other too much green food. I saw, as I said before, Roses in profusion. Rose Day in England. This year we could have provided you with

JULY 1941

thousands.

By the Star this morning we are in difficulties with the Germans. I expect through the broadcast the other evening. Someone has been chalking up Vs near the Royal and if the culprit is not tracked down within 72 hours, penalties are to be inflicted.

Saturday, July 5. More trouble and Mrs Bird is very ill. I called to convert a chair for moving her about. Ruby was very upset. She said the Germans were going to take over all Mr Bird's stores, offices, etc. and he had to move 1,400 tons of anthracite and tons of logs of wood by Wednesday night.

What a wonderful moonlight night. After several quiet nights 'they' disturbed me soon after 12 going S, and at 1.30 one passed so low that it woke me again. I looked through the window, Guernsey has never been more still and quiet. There were a few dotted clouds in the W and the ³/4 moon was so bright that it was nearly daylight. My windows were bang open but I could not see the plane. I am silly to get up as I never do see them at night.

I had a nice dinner of baked conger. Mrs Rowe stuffed it with tomatoes, spring onions, parsley, thyme and bread, no fats, and baked it in milk. She made me a rice pudding (I expect without sugar) and rhubarb in casserole.

I saw Ida Santangelo and her mother in Town, also Miss Kane. She inquired about all of you. She thinks we must not bother but trust to luck.

Mr Frossard gave a short address at Mrs Bichard's funeral, about her church work and the Work Party since its inception. Jackie Ogier was at the organ. There were 24 wreaths. I was no sooner home, not even time to give the fowls their midday meal, than the Star rang up with the usual apologies about transport, and could I give them particulars. This took more than 20 minutes but I must do it.

Mary came. For tea dry bread and real bitter, acid rhubarb. Mrs Rowe would not let me put gooseberries as it would have made it worse. We had a nice cup of tea. My tea ration this week is bramble leaves. I have not tried it yet and probably won't. We did the grave with Sweet William, Sweet Peas, Antirrhinums, Pansies and those lovely dark red Roses from near the study window.

Sunday, July 6. Went to the 8 o'clock, first of the month, (60 there) and to Choral Com. at 10.45. Again a glorious day with a lot to fit in. I hate going out Sundays now, as my suit, which was already on the large size, is falling off me. I have lost a stone since January, *and* my 'Little Mary', Kit!

I saw Uncle Ned. He said he was shaky on his feet and could I notice it. (I could). His face has gone to nothing and he has shrunk

JULY 1941

I am sure 4 inches shorter.

I was awakened at 12.45 by the explosion of bombs, then the tracer bullets flying up and the searchlights going. The British were bombing the airport.

Monday, July 7. My chickens were born yesterday, eight out of 11 eggs, three not fertile. When Tom came to work five of my young rabbits were about the garden faring on the fat of the land. They greeted him, then waltzed sky high!

I have ten old car tyres for the Civil Transport. They fetched my Marconi Radio. I don't know who called, but they found the door open so took it and left a receipt. Now I hear we must send in all rags, bones and old bottles.

The Germans are closing in on St Sampson's harbour, and have taken most coal stores, yards and houses on both side. I don't know what they want them for. They have not taken my Carpenter's Shop.

Tuesday, July 22. Went to see Mrs Godfray. Took two cakes, an egg custard, a tin of sardines for Miss Lihou who is fond of them, and two small bottles of English ale for Mrs Godfray who loves it.

Tom and I listened to Mr Churchill's speeches at the Civil Defence Inspection in Hyde Park and at the luncheon following. We did laugh at some parts.

Mary has just telephoned that there is a Red Cross message from Jack. It is written in German and she is bringing it down tonight.

I hear that all the Germans billeted on the North and South Sides have, after only one night, gone to L'Ancresse. They say there are too many rats here. I hope they don't bring any more troops. They say there are thousands, they are everywhere but very quiet and never speak to anyone.

This morning the men came to collect mattresses. They took two and one pillow. They gave me a receipt for which the States will pay me 37/6 (when I don't know). I was lucky they did not want box mattresses, so the one from our bed and the nice one in the attic they left.

Had a phone call from the Douzaine Room. The Germans want to know the amount of greenhouses on each estate, amount taken over by the States, amount kept privately, running feet of glass under GUB Control. I have to do this work on half the parish, the part nearest the Banques and Sauvagées. Of course I will be paid for this work. It's like my Cadastre work.

I went to the Red Cross office which is now in the High Street. Jack is inquiring about my welfare and is worried. Dated 6.6.41. I don't know why it is written in German. I answered I was well comfortable at New Road and carrying on business as usual, and

JULY 1941

was surprised you had not heard anything from me as I had answered three messages from Flo and two from Kit.

I sincerely hope you will soon get my messages. I know they will relieve and clear your minds. I am of course lonely. I miss you all and I miss Mum very much. I am longing to see Darling Rosemary and Jane and wondering if I ever will. I hope their nerves will not have been shattered with all the bombing.

Tom is still digging potatoes. We are going to plant beans, food for the winter. I will be glad when we can get proper food. I am losing weight fast now, lack of fats and only half ration of meat. Many people have lost weight. My good suit is falling off me and looks so bad that I wear my black coat and vest on Sundays.

Had tummy trouble but went to church, then to the Doctor's for lunch, but ate very little. Had just a cup of milk for tea and supper. I called to see Mrs Stubbs. She has the same complaint and fainted. She is now a little better, but has lost $2^1/_2$ stone. I have lost one. It's impossible to keep up your strength on the ration. I drink a fair amount of skimmed milk.

No house coal now and only people without gas can buy logs, $^1/_2$ cwt per month.

There must be 7,000 Germans here now. I hear them drilling on the Park every morning, and plenty of singing. This morning I passed 100 on bicycles. This afternoon there was a full company in shorts or bathing trunks, no vests or socks, singing away as happy as could be. I think they had been for a dip.

We have them in the stores all around my shop on the South Side. They have taken over Huelin's Timber Yard, are working Leale's Engineering shop and I hear they are at Manuelles' Cracking Machines and that they are going to pump out the quarries and work them. It won't make any difference if they provide their own food. But in spite of all this I don't worry. There is the humorous side and I hope I'll remember and be able to relate all the funny things.

Mr Frossard has just called for me to sign a few cheques, but when he opened his wallet he had left them at home! After a chat, a smoke and a gôut he left. He had only 7 minutes before curfew. I laughed to see him running along the road.

I had an egg for breakfast, my last. Those infernal fowls won't lay. It's the bad food. My eight chicks are growing fine.

Did you hear the Bishop of Winchester's talk on the Channel Islands? Very cheering to us all to hear his voice.

I saw a very large steam boat in the harbour towering above the White Rock walls. Later two large steam boats left, and there were several motor barges going in and out, more shipping than I have seen for some time.

JULY 1941

Don Bisset told me more troops had arrived. They say L'Islet district is crowded. They are bringing big guns, I cannot see that they will be of much use. They seem to be digging themselves in properly.

We have had a lovely day but being so busy I could not get a bathe. The summer is passing, and if I don't take a proper holiday I will miss my bathing altogether.

Thursday, July 24. It's just beautiful weather so after lunch I called Tom from the greenhouse and we went to Richmond Corner, he to bathe his feet and pick limpets for the fowls, I to sunbathe and then a nice dip in the briny. This took me two hours, the tide was very low, lovely sand, but the water was rather cold, so it was a long time before I really dipped. Had two good swims then sunbathed.

I cooked the limpets and gave the fowls a good feed. Then I made bills, about £60 worth, so should be well in funds next week.

Mrs Rowe picked the loganberries. She went to Dredge for fish and waited from 6 – 9, but got a whiting, 11d. My coupon had not been stamped for a month so she was served first. But what a waste of time waiting in a queue.

Uncle Ned has just called. I gave him a glass of Johnny de Kuyper which he relished.

Mrs Rowe made five pots of jam. I supplied the fruit (including 3 lbs of raspberries Mrs Godfray sent me), she the sugar, and we went halves. I will try and keep this jam for a rainy day.

I have had fairly good food this week, spuds, broad beans and fried tomatoes from my garden, and for tea a little extra butter as the fat ration this week was Guernsey butter, and nice loganberry jam.

I am still clearing up Allendale. The grapes are coming nicely. I have cucumbers and tomatoes in the greenhouse, and outside potatoes, sweet corn and horse-carrots for winter store for the rabbits. It's now awful to feel the days are already shortening.

The V sign is beginning to give trouble here. In the Press tonight the Germans are taking the wireless sets from a mile radius around Beaulieu Hotel, St Martin's. I am afraid it will not stop as so many people are without wirelesses owning to no dry batteries, so they will not care. It will be awful if we get ours taken away too. The V sign seems so silly. All the Germans have them on their cars that are at the St Sampson's Harbourmaster's Office, the Crown Hotel, La Piette and, I expect, all other places they occupy.

I expect by tomorrow we will have Japan in the conflict, then America, then the whole world will be at war. I do wish something could end all this.

I get very tired these past weeks and am resting more. It must be the food telling on us. Many people say the same, although I have put on $3/4$ lb this week.

JULY 1941

Friday, July 25. This morning the bank had no small silver, and I had to take small change in marks. I cannot understand where all our silver has gone, but if every German leaving the island took half a dozen coins as souvenirs, hundreds of pounds would have gone.

Saturday, July 26. A glorious Guernsey summer morning. I went for my rations, $1/10^1/2$ worth, not much to live on. Still, I am managing.

I am building gate pillars for R. Le Maitre and when I went this morning my sister gave me six scones. Lily Ellis brought me another potato cake. I don't like them but Mary is coming this afternoon and it will save my bread.

I went to Mrs Godfray in the afternoon as I had managed to get 6 lovely peaches from Mr Langmead (one weighed over $^1/2$ lb). He says I am first on his list. They were 1/- each. This sounds dear but they were 2/6 in Town; (I was glad I went as I heard it's Miss Lihou's birthday tomorrow). They say I am much too good to them but I can get things for them that they could never find. I brought back a bowl of raspberries.

I was back in time for Mary who brought me the best news I have received from any of you yet, that Kit had received news from me. So now you know that I am still at New Road and no drastic changes yet.

Sunday, July 27. I got Tom to get me carnations from the Ozannes who had given me a lovely bunch when I went there on Cadastre work. He also got me fern from Bill Le Maitre. I made a birthday bouquet for Miss Lihou and a bunch for Mrs Godfray. Tom took them out in the afternoon. I could not face cycling there again today, so much uphill.

A large barge came into St Sampson's harbour on Saturday with 300 tons of oil for the Electric Station, so if we do not lose our wirelesses over the V business, we are fixed up till September. I don't mention war news as you get the same on the air.

I am feeling a bit better these days. I think I get a little more food, and I am trying to rest afternoons, so much recommended by Kit.

Thursday, July 31. I went to the Red Cross. It is over Burton's, High Street, now the Germans have taken Elizabeth College. I was glad to see Kit's message (May 23) saying she had had my news, and one from Flo (April 16) that she hadn't heard from me yet, both received the same day. I don't know if Kit had received my reply to the New York or the Swiss message. However, I am satisfied, and you will know that I am still at New Road and still carrying on my business, and if you read between the lines, am as comfortable as can be expected.

JULY 1941

I went over the Park this afternoon on Cadastre work, but could not pass right through but had to turn back and cross to the gate opposite Mr Peek's house. The Germans were playing football on one pitch. Others were playing skittles or some such game, all with only a pair of shorts on. The big pitch has been planted down with wheat.

I hear they go bathing from the Park at 7 in the morning, sometimes a hundred or more. They never take a towel and seem to stay undressed all day. I am sure they are getting a good time, and by what I hear think there is no place like Guernsey.

I got 2 cwt from my perch of early potatoes, a very good crop. Now I will plant cauliflower and first broccoli. As I write this by the study window the silence is so strained I feel I am in Sark.

A large boat arrived this morning, and lorry loads of tables and frame work boarding piled sky high passed this way. I think it's wooden huts from France. I hear they have brought lots of horses. While I was at Mr Matthews' house this morning on Cadastre work (it is occupied), Mr Martel from next door came into the garden with me, and he said there were seven horses up there. I did not see them as I had no business on that part.

Peter Bachmann and Mrs Cortvriend telephoned to say they had heard from Flo, and was there any message I would like to send. As I had just replied to two, and only 25 words are allowed, I said Peter could just say 'no need to worry about me', and Violet nothing. She was glad as she had so much to get in.

When Marjorie arrives back at the Old Rectory she will hardly know it. The States are cutting down all the trees around. Then they will do the same in the cemetery. The dear old church will not be sheltering among the old elms.

Sunday, August 3. First Sunday of the month so I went to the 8 o'clock service. A glorious morning. All the trees on the NE of the Old Rectory are cut down. What a gap.

At the 10.45 service the organ would not function, so two of the men volunteered to blow. They had a warm time, only to find after the service that the switch had not been turned on!

I hear the Germans have brought another 90 horses. I don't know where they will get the fodder.

Edward Roussel, Marie Dorey's husband, drowned himself in their well last Sunday. He had been at the Vauquiedor Hospital since the Occupation and came out three weeks ago. He did it while they were in Chapel. One of the sons stayed home with him, but he managed to slip away.

Uncle Ned has just been in. He is very depressed and wanted a bottle of O be Joyful. I did not feel like sparing it but can never refuse. He says he is not surprised that people commit suicide going

AUGUST 1941

through these times. I am glad I don't get depressed to that extent.

Mrs Frossard rang to ask me to have tea at the Rectory with Mr Kilshaw and escort him to our Evening Service. The Rector will go to St John's and Mrs Frossard would like to go with him. She suggested I should bring the Doctor along. We had a very nice time there.

I am now out of tobacco and cigarettes and cannot get my ration till Tuesday. Bank Holiday tomorrow. I will be glad when it is over. I hate holidays now.

We get few planes here lately. People tell me there was very heavy bombing towards Cherbourg during the night and the sky was ablaze with light in the NE and everybody's windows rattled terribly.

I forgot to say that Charlie Frossard is in India Officers Training Corps. They had news two weeks ago.

Monday, Bank Holiday, August 4. I went to the Bridge and got a whiting (lucky boy) and three mackerel, and a packet of saccharine for Mrs Godfray and myself 6/- each. Elsie came down and I also gave her snacks for them. Then fog set in and it turned to rain. I saw them setting out with baskets and bathing-suits, then by 2 o'clock felt sorry to see them returning in the gale and wind. Mrs Rowe fried me a nice dinner.

A very dull day for me, only the fowls and rabbits for company. I saw Uncle Ned on the Bridge, still very depressed. I don't know why except that he feels all his friends have left him. I reflect and say to myself it's the usual. While you have an open house such as they kept you have plenty of friends, but when you're down and alone you get nobody.

The only thing I had to smoke today is a cigarette this morning and a blooming old strong cigar I found in the study. It's awful to be stranded like this. I save every cigarette end and smoke them in my pipe.

Tuesday, August 5. The apple crop is poor and this wind will have brought a good many down. I bought 1 lb from Mr Blampied for 8d. I am feeling better these days, I think mostly because I have had better meals. I must try to look into my diet more in the future.

A pair of beautiful horses passed this morning, harnessed as on the continent with no blinkers, pulling a long wagon. It did not seem like Guernsey at all. One man described them well, said they reminded him of Pharoah's chariots. The horses are frisky. I believe people can hire them free, just for their feed.

I had a nice afternoon measuring the greenhouses etc. I did Camp Code Lane, Delancey Lane and part of Vale Road. Most people seem scared to see me around again so soon and wonder what it all means, getting these particulars. I simply say it's another order.

AUGUST 1941

I have a fair amount of work. Some weeks I think it's slackening and then other jobs come in.

Mrs Peek, the Malletts and others I met going to church on Sunday were so glad to know that Kit had at last received news of me. Mrs Godfray too, and to know that Kit was Nurse Sauvary, just the girl for the job, she said. [*See illustration 7.*]

Saturday, August 9. Mary has been down as usual. I was glad to see her especially as she brought good news, another Red Cross letter from Kit. She did not get a chance to copy it down as they are very busy. About 7,000 have arrived during the last few days. I will get it by Wednesday.

The Germans are building long rows of huts on that tip between the oil tanks and Mont Crevelt. I expect they mean to station more troops here.

Sunday, August 10. I had rather a bad night, another attack of dysentery or diarrhoea. This is the second attack in three weeks. There seems to be an epidemic, two of my men were bad and I have heard of others. They say it's too many vegetables.

I am expecting a litter of rabbits in the morning. It will be Kit's birthday, easy to remember, August 11.

I have a fair amount of tobacco this week. Mr Stubbs gave me his ration. I lent Tom five this morning, he has already borrowed 11, so I don't expect I will want them back. The barter going on over smoking is too funny for words. And people are smoking anything, dried bean leaves, coltsfoot, rose petals, dock leaves, bramble leaves, etc.

The apples and grapes are coming on. Muscats 4/- per lb, peaches 1/- to 2/- each, figs 1/- to 1/3. Onions are 1/- per lb and tomatoes almost given away. Dredge gave me two baskets for my fowls.

Bread seems to be the problem with most people. They cannot satisfy themselves and are falling away to nothing. I saw Bob Valpied (who spoke of poor old Auntie Edie) and hardly knew him. He has lost 3 stone 2 lbs. He was, I suppose, wearing his usual collar, about a 17, and today a 13 would be loose on him. In spite of a doctor's certificate the Food Control Board would not grant him extra bread. Dr Jones and Miss Matthews are walking shadows. If the war keeps on I expect we will all get the same. Still I am not worrying. Mr Frossard says he only lives from day to day.

Owing to Vs marked somewhere near Victoria Hospital, Mary's boy friend with others has to patrol the district affected each night. They make them walk up and down 15 yards between the men. At St Martin's they took their wirelesses away as well.

Monday, August 11. I am still poorly so will stay in. I am lighting a fire. Fancy doing this on the 11th August. It's your birthday Kit.

AUGUST 1941

Many happy returns. This is the second birthday away from you. I had the litter of rabbits this morning. Mary has just telephoned your message. I was glad to get it on your birthday, to know that Rosemary and Jane are well and that you like your new work nursing. Now I am not worrying quite so much about all of you.

Mr W.S. Mahy has telephoned me about a funeral, a Mrs Cohu, 85 years old. He has given up that work and is passing it on to me. He tells me two Germans are working in his shop. (I hope they don't come to mine.) Later I went there and saw them. One, a huge man about 6 ft, was sleeping on the shavings in a corner. They have been making a large table, 9 ft in diameter, for Curr's Tearooms at Cobo. One spoke French and said it was for a writing table (and I expect a map). It was of beautiful seven ply oak.

Now that the Germans have taken over the whole of Huelin's timber business and La Piette Sawing Mills, I am wondering if I will be able to get any more timber. It will be unfortunate for me if not as I am getting a fair amount of trade.

There is no silver in the island and it is difficult to get change. The Press has printed 5/- and 2/6 notes, but now they say we have to use marks. But the half mark is 1/0½ so it means a pocket full of coppers.

Tuesday, August 12. We have had a nice day, lovely sunshine, a stiff breeze and the sky dotted with white clouds. A good mackerelling day.

This afternoon as I went to Camp-du-Roi funeralling. I saw everybody harvesting and the wheat is ripening well.

I heard the Kitchen Front this morning. They have taught us to eat lettuce leaves, now they tell us how to cook and eat the stump when the lettuce bolts. I expect the next talk will tell us how to cook and eat the roots!

Another order out. Funerals must not have processions, only the hearse. Only two carriages are allowed and they must not follow.

Wednesday, August 13. I had a nice baked dinner. You would have laughed to see my little ball of meat, as tough as hell, but the tough fat did not make bad gravy, and with stuffing of onions, tomatoes, sage and thyme and all my own vegetables, it was a good dinner. I am now feeding better. I had been rather careless about meals.

Thursday, August 14. Slept badly, and had just gone into a doze when a thundering noise woke me. I tried to think what it could be. I knew it was not a picture. I knew of no chair that could have fallen off a dressing table. It was not the sound of saucepans slipping. I finally decided it must be the blackout Kit manipulated in the bathroom, so went there first. I was right. The rod fell and rolled.

AUGUST 1941

You might not fancy so, but it was quite a big noise in the dead of night.

Elsie has just phoned from Mrs Godfray. She will come tomorrow for a few things I get for them and is bringing me some cigars, (lucky again). I managed to get two mackerel this morning.

Friday, August 15. Almost incredible for August but it's poured a deluge. My rabbits in their outside pen were almost swimming, so I put them in their new hutches in the ¾ span with a nice bed of sweet hay. I got almost soaked going to the bank. Pay day again.

I try to go on quietly, but there are always calls, Midland Bank in Town roof leaks, gate pillar down at Mallett, Vale Road (some lorry). I have to charge this to the States Occupation Account. When this war is over the expenses will be not thousands but millions. England will have to come to our rescue. [It did most handsomely.]

Saturday, August 16. Yet another order in the Press. Someone scratched V RAF on the back of a car outside the Victoria Hospital. Now as a punishment the curfew tonight and on Sunday is at 10 o'clock.

Went to Mrs Godfray this afternoon. Miss Lihou is better but still there. I took a little cake Mrs Rowe made, a bottle of special wine and ½ dozen nectarines. I chatted and made the old people laugh, stayed till 9.15 so had to hurry home owing to the earlier curfew. It was fun to see hundreds of cyclists and others hurrying home.

Sunday, August 17. I went to church. A nice service.

I have been stewing some of my large apples (windfalls). We had an extra pound of sugar.

There has been a constant flow of lorries from the White Rock bringing tons of timber, 1½ x 9, 3 x 4½, enormous pit props (for firewood I should think). I saw lorry loads of rusty wire, barbed wire by the mile, tons and tons of cement. What they want all this for I do not know.

I had tea at Mrs Stubbs'. She seems awfully worried about all these movements. I explained that whatever happened she was helpless, so why worry. I just let things take their course. While we can get a good shelter and sufficient food, just to live is all we can expect, for the time being anyhow. I know the winter is looking gloomy for us.

Now gas is rationed. I am allowed 200 ft per week. We each have a diagram sent to us. It's going to be awful to read the meter every day. It means that if I burn my month's ration in two weeks (which I have no doubt I will, being a careless boy) I will be cut off till next month.

A heavy shower of rain with a west wind direct into Kit's room where I sleep woke me. The window was wide open so I was flooded, even my bedding was flooded. Summer time so it did not matter. The bathroom was flooded too.

I went to borrow 10 lbs of dry mash for my fowls from R. Le Maitre till I get my ration next week. I get only 33 lbs per month. I am going to try mixing new potatoes with a little mash. People say it's better than boiling the potatoes, and more satisfying. They say anything and write letters to the Press. But I have tried all ways, even boiled limpets, and they won't lay.

When I got back people were waiting for me to arrange the funeral of Jas Marriette, 79, lived in Roland Road. He had been blind for some time. I was then rushed for I had to go to St Martin's where I am putting a new slate roof on Miss Mauger's cottage (I managed to get 750 slates) and cycling up those blooming hills is a killer for me. I just think I am getting on with a job when I have to leave off for a funeral.

I came back dead tired, went to choir practice only to find Lily Mallett and Miss Cleale coming back, no practice for some unknown reason. J. Ogier had sent round but I was not at home. Did not make much difference other than I would not perhaps have had to hurry back from St Martin's.

Mrs Rowe has been poorly today. Her turn for dysentery. Everybody seems to be troubled. It must be constantly eating vegetables and not enough bread and fats.

I met about 20 of those wagons each with a pair of lovely horses. They take their time, only walking them. I hear they are going to make the airport larger, and pull down that little Catholic Chapel and several houses.

Thursday, August 21. The Germans have now taken over the Salvation Army Hall in Nocq Road for a canteen. I saw Le Feuvre's men carting the benches and chairs to the Chapel Schoolroom, and asked him if it was for the Sunday School Treat. He saw the joke and said the weather was not fine enough.

Dr Jones brought me $1^{1}/_{4}$ lb of sugar, so with the African blackberries Mrs Godfray gave me I made jam this afternoon with Mrs Rowe helping me. I added $1^{1}/_{2}$ lbs of my fallen apples and three sticks of rhubarb. It did not set hard and will not keep. I will eat it straight away and save my butter. I will give Tom a pot. It's impossible for people to make jam now (no sugar).

They brought some little cakes from France. We were allowed one per person, $2^{1}/_{2}$d each. Two mouthfuls and they were gone. Mrs Rowe would not buy one.

Saturday, August 23. No fish again. What a disappointment.

No child under the age of 16 is allowed to go to any picture show

AUGUST 1941

or entertainment. This seems to me a rather wise move as you see them coming out of the cinemas and flying away on their bicycles, not caring how they ride and making a devil of a row. It seems to me they have made a rod for their own backs. Of course I don't know the reason for this order.

I went to Town but no tea ration for the third week. I am getting nice Quarenden apples for my breakfast, and Elsie gave me ½ dozen eggs. I gave one each to Tom and Mrs Rowe.

Going up Victoria Road, what a change! The smith's shops were busy shoeing horses and the street stank of burning hoofs. In the Bordage chalked up in the ironmonger's shop window was, Trépieds made to order. There is so little gas. The Normand, a steam boat that has been trading here since the Occupation, brought 1,000 tons of coal for the Gas works, but what rubbish. Still it's something.

Nearly all shops are now closed in Smith Street, High Street and the Arcades. Only about three stalls in the Fish Market. Depressing, and people cannot stand going to Town now.

We still have Pammett's bus (the rickety old van) running from the Bridge, and one twice a week from Bordeaux.

Henry Bisson is working very hard fishing and, I think, making good money. I am glad for his sake, having laid out so much money for his boat. Very large catches of mackerel are coming in.

Monday, August 25. Again a deluge of rain with wind, which woke me up, and a blessing it did, as the rain was pouring in on my bed. The carpet was again soaked. I had the windows wide open as usual. I found the bathroom flooded as well. I didn't bother to mop it up but bounced into bed again.

Miss Ozanne (Eliza) Watville, the eldest, died rather suddenly this morning. Mr Poat sent his man down for me as they could not get me on the phone for some unknown reason. I was in the study all the morning.

It is quite cold and still raining. I am afraid the potatoes will be diseased. A lot of people harvested on Sunday. (Some would not). I think the corn will have suffered.

I have a Red Cross letter from Doreen. She hears regularly from Flo and Kit, sometimes from Jack, and Uncle George sends his love. This is the first news I've had of George.

Joseph Williams, of Nocq Road (you may not know him) was knocked down by a motor lorry, right opposite the PO Bridge, by a German. I arrived just after the accident. They took him into Brache's shop. He was badly cut about the head. The Germans were quite concerned and all bunched in front of the engine arguing. I passed on as a huge crowd of sightseers assembled.

AUGUST 1941

Wednesday, August 27. I had an appointment with Jack Mahy at the Câstel. The Germans are pulling down the old-fashioned house, Sous l'Eglise (which joins the Câstel cemetery) belonging to Zelia Mahy who valued the old building very much. She bought it because it formerly belonged to her grandparents, and just before the war I was to reconstruct the place. You will remember the roof fell in and I covered part of it with tarpaulins.

The Germans have already taken away the top storey and there were four Germans pulling down the walls lower down. They have three or four large guns in a field.

Oscar Guilbert, the architect, met us there, in the interests of the States, I to represent Mr Mahy and the German. We sent for one who could speak English. The German said the States had been informed, which at the moment nobody seems to know. He said Jack Mahy could take away the old arch, and that they wanted these things for war purposes and that the States had plenty of money. He also said he was an architect and it hurt him to see old buildings like this destroyed, and wanted to know why it had not been renovated before. They saluted, we returned the compliment and then parted.

If the States are responsible for all these things I don't know where it will all end. Guilbert said it was the first case they'd had of demolishing buildings. It's very difficult to assess a valuation of this kind, as it's more of a sentimental value than a real value.

Another order. We have to send in information of all wireless sets, make and all particulars, and say if we sleep where the sets are, and if any sick person resides there. It looks as if they intend calling them in. It will be awful if they do. We don't know what to expect from day to day. Things are tightening up all the time.

Thursday, August 28. Town owners of cars have to send in all tools belonging to their cars. And a civil order, no tobacco this week, and once a fortnight in future, which is a cut of 20 cigarettes and 1 oz pipe tobacco. It's our only comfort. Things are so dull and lonely we will miss it more than ever.

It's been blowing hard so I stayed in sending delayed bills, which are awful to make now we have to charge a States' Sale Tax, 1d on 1/- materials, there is no tax on labour.

After bills I looked after the "farm" which takes quite a time. I now have 14 rabbits but don't think I will keep them all, it's too much bother to collect food. The devils can eat all day long!

I used a month's allowance of gas in four days! Now I have to boil water for tea, dishes etc on the fire. But now I am cooking on the fire I think I can catch up. I always have a kettle of boiling water ready.

SEPTEMBER 1941

Sunday, August 31. We had a lovely moon last night, so different going to bed with no black out. It's impossible to black out the moon.

At last we have a real glorious morning. Mr Frossard preached his sermon on trees, and quoted from the Old Testament where, during their wars, they were warned to cut only trees that bore no fruit. I forget the text. St Sampson's is now looking bare of trees. Manuelles' little hill next to Stanley Brooks' house, where you used to play, has just a dozen small, lanky sticks.

I went to the Stubbs to tea. Lucky for me he gave me 1 oz of tobacco and 20 cigarettes.

I find it lonesome here when night falls and will go to the Doctor till 11. I miss dear old Mum mostly I think because few people interest me. Life is very disappointing, very few people are sincere. I could fill a book with things that happen now which leave me stunned. Although many here can run with the foxes and hunt with the hounds and be quite happy and comfortable in their minds, I often think they can have no power of thought.

Tuesday, September 2. I have been tying up sunflowers which are not very fine this year. I made about 15/- on seed last year, but will want it for the fowls this year.

I have had a hectic day. Miss Baker marched in unexpectedly at 12.30. Luckily I got two longnose from Dredge this morning and had a lot of potatoes boiled, so only had to pick runner beans. Mrs Rowe fried the fish, spuds and tomatoes and we had an enjoyable dinner. She had to catch the van back at 3.30, and I gave her tomatoes, carrots and some brandy. She has been rather poorly lately, and is coming here for a weekend, Friday to Tuesday. Of course if it's like last time she will not come. She can never make up her mind about anything. If she does come, Mrs Rowe will come here on Sunday too.

I am sitting on the oak bench outside the study, with coat off and sleeves rolled up, it's so mild. I wish you could see my brown face. Years ago when in a restaurant in London, Flo laughed and said all the people were looking at me, I was so tanned. Well I am browner now. I sleep with my windows bang open, so if I cannot get enough food, I am determined to get fresh air!

Wednesday, Sept 3. Tomatoes are now down to 2d per lb, cucumbers, melons, cantaloupes and grapes very plentiful, but grapes very dear at 1/- to 1/6 per lb. The Germans buy them. At lunch time I see them run across to Dredge and Guilbert, who are sold out in 10 mts. Hence the high price. I cut the first bunch of Muscat of Alexandre last night. I wish you could sample them, small but a lovely flavour.

Messervy has just rung up from the shop. A German corporal is there and wants some cold water paste. They have at last found my

SEPTEMBER 1941

shop and will now probably always be calling for things. I was without, but he took three packets of size which he said would do as well.

I am going into the garden to do a little more. I will never catch up on the work, and I now get so tired that I often have to rest. It's either old age creeping on or the food.

Thursday, Sept 4. A wonderful day. The stillness and dead calm are strange. Not a leaf is moving, just now and again I hear a dog bark, otherwise not a sound. No Germans singing in the Park tonight. Perhaps they get Thursdays off.

I have been in the vinery garden all day, repairing the roof of the old fowl house, trying to make it watertight for the winter. The sun was scorching. I thoroughly enjoyed my day except that I got so infernally tired, otherwise everything was lovely.

The Germans are building a wooden bridge across from the Crock to the Electric Station side. They have a crowd of men hammering on the patent slip, it sounds like the old days when the shipwrights were there at work. I can see no earthly use for it except to give the men practice bridge building.

Now I hear some heavy guns firing towards the airport, but I don't hear any planes.

We never had a more beautiful moon, the sky is lovely and clear and it points to a beautiful night.

I managed to get longnose and a nice piece of conger, so it will be something extra if Diva Baker comes tomorrow for a few days.

Friday, September 5. Miss Baker did not come. I was awakened during the night by heavy peals of thunder and strong flashing of forked lightning, then a steady rain which, in 10 minutes, developed into a deluge. I had not intended getting up to close the windows, but at last I was bound to and got nearly soaked. I banged up my two windows, then ran to the bathroom which was fast flooding, then the lav windows top and bottom. Then I got into bed to find my pyjamas soaked at the bottom. So I kept my legs one side till the sheet had soaked up some of the dampness, then I moved over to the opposite side. By this time the storm was overhead with peals of cracking thunder, which lasted on $3/4$ hour, and then I went to sleep.

Sunday, Sept 7. I went to the 8 o'clock service. Wind NE, dull sky and cold air, real autumn. The altar looked lovely with the electric lights. Mr Frossard referred to the King's order for a day of prayer. Quite a lot of people, nearly 60.

This afternoon I shelled my broad beans, and have a chip basket full of nice seed. I have just lit up my last smoke, a small cigar. As

SEPTEMBER 1941

I write this outside the study window I can hear the Town, Vale and harbour clocks all striking 9, only 7 Greenwich time.

Most people now complain of always feeling hungry. I don't feel too bad yet. I fill up with apples, but the crops are very poor this year. Last week I successfully helped the Doctor through three melons. One he paid 7/6 for, a fine one and I did justice.

Monday, Sept 8. This afternoon there was excitement along the Banques. Our planes attacked a convoy of tugs, barges and a tug boat carrying a large floating crane. The convoy was in the Déroute passage behind the islands. I heard the planes high over the Town, but thought it was a skirmish in the air. I believe they sank one and damaged one. The convoy then came into the roadstead.

At 6 I was awakened by what I thought was a bomb dropped on the airport, and much firing for 5 minutes, then all was quiet.

Tuesday, Sept 9. Last night, just before 12, our people were over the airport again. I watched from my bedroom window and could see the tracer bullets coming down, but when the searchlights started pointing towards the house and the guns banging, I thought I ought to take shelter, so ran downstairs to the small office, put on my brass helmet and waited. When all was quiet I went back to bed and was soon asleep.

We don't get to hear about any damage, but I think there were a lot of casualties from the convoy. This morning it was reported that the Ambulance was running from the White Rock part of the night, but I don't know if this is authentic. What a terrible slaughter this war is.

Mary came in for a few minutes and said I had another RX letter. I don't know from whom and she will bring it down on Saturday.

As I write everything is so quiet. I can hear someone hammering and now and again one of those infernal hooters, then the silence is broken by a car passing. It's been a wonderful harvest moon.

Miss Lihou doesn't want to leave her house permanently. She went back last week with a new housekeeper who now won't stay. She finds it too dull. Mrs Godfray asked me to go out. At her age Miss Lihou should give up her house and live with her sister.

Friday, Sept 12. It's been blowing a stiff breeze but now it's a dead calm and a lovely cloudless setting sun. Have been busy all day in the office (pay day) and garden. There has been a lot of shooting, practice I suppose.

Mary came down last night with my RX message. It's from Rosemary. She says she is growing and learning dancing. We wrote the reply and to one from Flo which came the same day. Mary

SEPTEMBER 1941

brings the form and I sign it.

I am looking at the beech tree outside the study. The leaves are already turning their autumn shade. It seems only a few weeks ago I was telling you about the leaves unfolding. They will soon be dropping again. Seasons just fly past and in spite of being isolated, the time is not long. I have not heard a complaint of the time hanging. It seems awful for us to be here earning nothing and simply growing our own food.

I made Mr Bird's bill yesterday, a long job because of the sales tax on materials. He paid me this morning. What a relief as I had put off making it for the last three weeks and probably would not have done it then only I wanted the cash.

Saturday, Sept 13. Mary came down as usual. We had a nice tea, a potato cake and I stewed some of the beautiful cookers (apples) from my garden. They take very little sugar. I bought a large melon, 4/6, and also gave some to Mrs Rowe and Tom.

Sunday, Sept 14. A lovely day except for a NE breeze. Went to church, lunch at the Doctor's, tea at the Stubbs' (of course I take my bread ration). Then I went to Mrs Godfray's, had a snack, a nice drink and came home by 9.

There has been a constant rush of lorries since 6 this morning until 7 pm. While at Mrs Stubbs' we watched a large steamer, about 5,000 tons, come into the harbour. She had two escorts. Our air force was not about. The convoy of last week left yesterday.

Monday, Sept 15. Elsie came down. I had bought a nice melon for Mrs Godfray and her sister. I also let them have half of the 12 lbs of apples I had bought for storing, 8d per lb. It worked out at 4d each. What a terrible price! There are few apples and no late potatoes. I hear they intend to ration them this winter.

I am living mostly on fish these days. I casseroled the conger with toms, onions, parsley, thyme, potatoes and water, no fats but very tasty.

Tuesday, Sept 16. I had a poor night. It was so still and silent, I believe that's what woke me. I couldn't explain the stillness, not even a cow lowing.

Wednesday, Sept 17. Much activity during the night, machine gunning, bombs dropping, anti-aircraft guns in action, the dropping of bright lights which looked exactly like sheet lightning. I could not catch my sleep again, then daylight came and I got up. We don't get very much news of what damage is done.

SEPTEMBER 1941

Saturday, Sept 20. Mary came as usual. Unfortunately I could not give her any bread for tea as my ration has been cut, 1 lb this week. We shared a potato cake, and I gave her an apple, a pear and a fig.

Sunday, Sept 21. A glorious hot sunny day with clear sunny sky. I have very little to smoke, but am now enjoying a lovely cigar Mr Stubbs gave me. He's giving me his ration tomorrow, and with mine I have to make it last two weeks.

I hear a German was killed this morning along the Braye Road near Coloma. He was scorching on his motor-cycle, and I suppose lost control.

I hear 6,000 Germans left here this week. We got 500 tons of gas coal which will carry us on a bit further. But we have no house coal in the island for the winter, and are now allowed only ½ cwt of logs per week.

Mrs Godfray rang up on Friday most excited. She had received an RX post card to say there was a letter from Flo. She immediately sent Elsie's niece, Una, to the High Street place to read it. I am glad Flo wrote, she was so pleased.

I am picking the grapes at Allendale, and glad to have them, they are so dear. I think the States should have controlled the price so that everyone could have had a share. But it's the way of the world, things are all wrong. For instance, some fishermen could not go out for two days because they had to unload a coal boat for the Gas Company. Other men could have discharged the boat. Fancy, the mackerel season and not sending the men out. There were dozens of women waiting for fish on Saturday, but people had to go without this weekend.

On Saturday for dinner I had four hard baked potatoes, which I ate with two raw apples. Could not spare any bread. I have not gone really hungry yet, but things must not get worse or I shall. Still in spite of these hardships I am not worrying at all, and I don't feel too bad yet. It's funny to see the men with their coats hanging on them. Mrs Rowe said she could not help laughing to see Mr Carpenter, opposite, with his coat drooping in front, it looked as if he had no shoulders.

Monday, Sept 29. I know you will all have been thinking of me, 65 years old today. Thinking of the many years you would bring your presents to our bedroom before I was up, and how dear old Mum would prepare so much, perhaps helped to depress me. Also the stillness of the last few days. The old saying, Look forwards, not backwards, sounds nice, but is not easy. Still I carry on.

Mary did not want me to be alone as last year, and came down early to tea. She sent me a nice birthday card by post this morning, and gave me a nice present, a tobacco pouch. She brought her own

SEPTEMBER 1941

bread and butter. I stewed a dish of apples, Mrs Rowe kindly made me a lovely cake and brought in six little chocolate cakes. (I will tell you when we meet, or write out the cake recipe, made with no butter or eggs.) I made a nice brew of coffee sweetened with four tablets of saccharine (I am out of tea now). Then Mary, Mrs Rowe and myself had our nice little birthday tea party, followed by grapes from Allendale. I gave Mary a slice of the melon I had bought for the occasion and four pears to take back.

So I had a nice birthday under abnormal circumstances. We must be grateful for small mercies. Earlier Mr Frossard had called to wish me many happy returns of the day, and we drank a glass of port. I now start another year and wonder what my 66th will bring. The end of this infernal war I hope.

Tuesday, Sept 30. I was up a bit early as I had to record my vote for the election of a Jurat. There were two candidates, Le Pelley our former Greffier and R. Johns. Le Pelley got in by 29 votes.

I had the funeral of Mrs Duquemin, aged 95, at the Vale Church. It was well attended, even by great-grandchildren, and there were 13 wreaths. That gave me a lot of work as reporter afterwards.

Gussie has rung up. He talks of building a pigsty. I tried to talk him out of it. He has asked me to buy him two goats. He already keeps rabbits.

New Road has been very busy with Germans trying to find billets for another batch of men. They have taken Nellie Le Poidevin's house and the Church Schools (where only a few weeks ago I fitted, for about £30.0.0, an air raid shelter for the children because they had taken Delancey Park Schools). When passing Vale Road I saw Lily Mallett in a great state because the Germans said they must clear out of their house.

Sunday, October 5. Up early as I could not sleep. I know I am bound to have a clear out (which I will not do) so will have to billet or give up bedrooms for sleeping accommodation.

Harvest Festival, another hard time remembering the many years Mum did the altar decorations. We are having only two sheaves of corn and a few bunches of grapes. We had a photograph of the Choir as we now have a girls' Surplice Choir.

In the afternoon I spent my time catching my little rabbits. They had fun dodging me. I let the older ones out, they are easy to catch.

Monday, Oct 6. A German came who spoke English fairly well. He wanted one bedroom so I showed him Flo's. He liked it then asked if I could spare another, so I showed him Jack's. I told him to send men who would look after the place. He said I would have no work or bother as a batman would come in. That sounds as if I might get officers.

OCTOBER 1941

Major Langlois and Vernon Le Maitre are billeting Officers, and Major Langlois came in later. I told him of a scheme I had. They need a place for the school children, so I suggested the use of the drawing-room and dining-room and the piano. This would suit me better as I could close the house when the children leave.

They have taken Cross's house, Dr Jones' garage for a field kitchen, Mr Higgs', Mr Peek's and part of Mr Poat's houses. Still I won't leave here even if I have to billet three or four of them, although it will be very awkward with my business.

Tuesday, Oct 7. Again slept badly after our friend's visit, so was up before 8 (really 6). The dew was so heavy everything was soaked. I went to the Church Schools where everything was in an uproar, with lorries, vans and crowds of men moving out the school gear. Mr Frossard was already there. There was only one redeeming feature, the weather was perfect.

I had a funeral from the Vauquiedor Hospital this afternoon. It was exhausting riding out. When I arrived the Sexton was asleep on the grass. I did not wake him but lay down and had a burning sun on my face, and nearly slept. Half an hour later I heard them arriving, the first sound for half an hour except the flies humming, not even a bird singing. Not one person attended.

I came home tired. Nobody had called so it is not certain when I will have to billet these men. I am not going to worry further but trust to luck.

Wednesday, Oct 8. I was just shaving when Mrs Rowe told me two Germans were downstairs. It was to see their bedrooms, so now I am occupied. I had not got the rooms ready, so Mrs Rowe and I had to hurry. What an upset moving all the clothes.

They have now brought their gear. We are not supposed to have any bother and one of the men eats in the bedroom. He is the NC as the man with him seems to be his batman. He asked what time I locked the house. I said 2 minutes to 11. One came in at 9.15, I don't know about the other. It seems funny to have people in. I had to move about so quietly.

I slept well till 4 then in snatches and dreamt, planning and seeing difficulties having to leave the place unlocked.

When the Company came from St Saviour's it was like a fair along New Road. Church Lane too is full of them. Mr Peek has gone to Lady Ozanne's place in Hauteville, Mr Higgs to the White Cottage, Jurat Arthur Dorey to the Hawthorns, Mr Cross to Roseland in the Vale.

Ned came in late to say a German had just come to the Old Rectory to say he was sleeping there that night. I was sorry for Uncle Ned. I could see it upset him. I advised him to see Percy and

OCTOBER 1941

perhaps they could both sleep there that night.

All this confusion is awful, but I must say they are very quiet and seem reasonable. I am staying in this morning, doing some writing and these notes of information to let you know how we fare.

Thursday, Oct. 9. Again a very mild and beautiful day, our first with our new visitors (billeting). I dreamed a lot about arranging the rooms. They were on the move early, so I got up, wanting to be about, not knowing what the arrangements might be.

They seem to have some meals in their bedrooms, and asked if they could use Flo's mahogany table. I told him he must have a cloth and we also gave him 2 plates and a cup. The only inconvenience so far is a lot of running up and down stairs, but that I don't mind as long as they leave me quiet as things have gone today.

Unfortunately at 6 this evening Bob Valpied phoned to say his wife had just died at the Emergency Hospital, and I had to go, there and then, right out to St Martin's to make arrangements. I was dead beat when I got back. I find cycling tiring and had to rush as I have no lamp. He wants the funeral on Saturday, a struggle as we cannot use lights in the workshop.

Poor Bob has had a trial with a very delicate wife always ill. They took her to hospital only yesterday. I feel shaky after riding so hard, so Goodnight Darlings, X X X for the babies, much love Dad.

Friday, Oct. 10. At the hospital who should I see but Evelyn Monsell. She is doing night duty.

This morning soon after 6 the batman came and the officer let him in. I came down soon after and to my surprise found the batman had left quite a lot of bread for the fowls. Mrs Rowe had a piece. I don't care for it. It's made of barley flour.

My No. 1 officer introduced a No. 2 officer as his friend who would sleep in Jack's room that night and leave in the morning. He said he was going to the pictures (Gaumont) and asked if I had a bicycle. I said I had but it would be of no use to him as I had no lamp. He said soldiers did not need lamps, so I was in it! Then I was worried that he would leave it anywhere and get it stolen. However, he got back safely at 11.45.

Saturday, Oct 11. The house was alive before 6, so I got up soon after. The batman tells me they are going out to Fort Le Marchant tomorrow. I hope so then I can have a quiet day.

My funeral was at 11.30. There were only 4 there. Poor Bob Valpied was very much cut up. It rained on my way back and I got drenched.

Mary came as usual and I sent a RX letter to Kit this time and

OCTOBER 1941

hope she will get it for Christmas.

Sunday, Oct. 12. My first officer was about at 6 and there was quite a bustle, so I got up. Sure enough they packed off and I was quiet all day.

So I went to the Stubbs after the 4 o'clock service. They have been in awful trouble this week. A German officer wanted to take the house furnished. But after a big fight and fuss with the Billeting Officer, they found Andrew White's house (next to Mr Jeremiah's) so they got away with it. I told them they could come and stay in my house and this might put me in a better position. I am now dreading almost every day that they may take this place.

They have taken the Old Rectory, and Uncle Ned said there were about 7 sleeping there last night. I had to send a carpenter to fix one of the shutters and see to some of the locks.

It is difficult to understand their movements. They came into this neighbourhood from St Saviour's this week, fixed themselves in the Church and Chapel Schools (the field kitchen in Dr Jones' garage feeds these men) and billeted a lot of others. My officer came on Wednesday, went away Sunday morning, it's now Monday night and I haven't seen him since, and he said nothing to me. I left the front door open all Sunday night in case he came late, and will do so again tonight.

Tuesday, Oct. 14. Uncle Ned has just called. He sleeps at Percy's but goes to the Old Rectory every day. He is now plumbing, making cans and saucepans. He made me a copper can. He has plenty of work and considering his age it is wonderful how he turns them out. Of course it's awkward for him with 6 Germans occupying rooms, but I think they do their own work. He does not seem to worry as much now.

I gave him a livener before he left at 8, then nearly dark. As he walked through the hall he said, Just fancy, this house was such a lively spot full of brightness, and now dead. He feels it's all for the best that Kate is out of all this trouble, but I cannot feel that about Mum. I know that while I stood up to things she would not have worried. However this was not to be.

My officers have not returned. I believe a lot went off by boat this morning. About 200 in full kit marched past our house this morning singing merrily.

I have had a quiet day, just cooked my dinner, visited my jobs and looked after the animals. Mr Peek rang this morning and I sent my man out to fix him a copper at Mr Ozanne's house, Hauteville. We have to take everything out on the trucks, half a day has gone before you get there. I was rather busy but thought I had better oblige the poor old chap,, after being turned out of his house

OCTOBER 1941

Delancey, and had to leave furniture etc. behind. It's a blow at his age.

Friday, Oct. 31. I have not written for some days and there have been many changes and new orders. Probably owing to mine-laying we are not allowed on any of the beaches, and people in houses near the shore have to leave. Uncle Tom has had to move from the front and has gone to Les Amballes. We have to fill in census papers of how many people in each dwelling, to make it easier for billeting, I understand.

A few days ago a German officer came with Vernon Le Maitre. They want to billet 2 people here, a civil servant and a lady typist, and I have to provide a room for them to work in. I said they could have the dining-room. They are to bring their bedding, towels etc. Up to now no coal or anything has arrived, so I don't know when to expect them.

In the meantime it is very cold and I am on the sick list with awful pains in my left shoulder, side and under my arm. I slept very little for 5 nights. Dr Jones gave me K 11s which eased the pain a little. Bill Le Maitre painted it with iodine, Mr Hart said try Wintergreen. Then Dr Jones said it sounded like herpes (shingles). Later when he saw the blotches and red spots he said there was no doubt and I had to keep warm. I can tell you it's been a very painful job, and last night I had my first night's sleep since it started. Dr Jones said the cause is being run down, but we cannot get good food to pick up on. Mrs Rowe comes in to give me a little breakfast, then I get a little dinner at about three. But I am 50% better today and would not like another week like the last.

Elsie came down from Mrs Godfray with two eggs. Tom is looking after the farm and other things. Mr Frossard came in to see me and brought a RX message from Flo, saying you are going to Kit's country school for a holiday, but you never say what Jack is doing. The school is, I think, Kit's school from London [The Froebel Demonstration School evacuated to Little Gaddesden, Hertfordshire] where she went to help them the first autumn and spring terms of the war.

Although I was well and with little pain yesterday, I had a very poor night as regards sleep. It was stormy and rained and hailed practically all night. Mrs Rowe cannot come on Friday mornings so I had to get up, and before I could even light the fire someone was at the door. Yes, the worst had happened, it was a funeral, a Mr Thorn about a funeral for his father at Oberlands, St Martin's. So half-dressed, half-washed and with no fire I had to fix up this man.

Tom did the other funeral at the Foulon this afternoon, and if I don't feel better will have to do this one too. He went to the bank for me.

Dear old Mum would have been 68 today. I could not get Chrys.

NOVEMBER 1941

anywhere but Mrs Rowe gave me a nice bunch and Tom took them to the cemetery. How I look back on the past. Not many regrets. Perhaps a few things could have been altered, but we cannot foresee everything in life.

I am cosy by a large wood fire feeling much better except shoulder and chest very tender. Spots now breaking and my vest very stained.

Sunday, Nov. 2. Again I was called up by telephone soon after daylight. It was Andrew White ringing for Miss Enid Leale to say her sister had died and they wanted me to arrange the funeral. I explained I was ill but would do the necessary. (Just fancy, 3 the week I am ill). Went back to bed and later Mrs Rowe brought me my breakfast (what luxury!). At 11.15 I heard tramping on the stairs. Mrs Rowe thought it was Dr Jones. When I heard them in Flo's and Jack's rooms I knew it was the Germans. I dressed quickly but they had gone. I expect it was the chief showing someone the rooms. It's 3 weeks now but no one has arrived.

I have enjoyed listening to the news, and you would have laughed to hear me singing bass at the 2 services. This is my third winter alone. I will be glad when this period of my life is over. I have so much time to think and wonder. I ought not to complain too much as I have had only one real set back in my life, dear Mum's death.

I sent a RX letter to Flo this time and hope you will get it before Xmas, then you will know I am spending it at the Ogiers, Gigands.

Tuesday, Nov. 11. Very good night. Pain and tenderness much improved and have felt much better today.

Thursday, Nov. 13. More changes down this end. The Germans have taken over the 26 Dorey's Cottages, Grosse Hougue, and the people have a week to find other places. Tom tells me they have also taken over the houses in Victoria Avenue from the Cycle Track both sides to one house before his. He says it's pitiful to see all the lorries and vans moving beds and furniture (what they are allowed to take). 50 or 60 men from the greenhouses are helping to load the gear. I don't know where they will find houses for all these people. One blessing it's dry, the one redeeming feature.

Up to now my visitors have not arrived.

Saturday, Nov. 15. Mary telephoned to say she had been at home all the week with a severe cold. I am not surprised, for the place where the RX work their business, over Burton's, High Street, has huge plate glass windows, the doors are open all the time with queues of people, and they are not allowed a fire (no fuel).

NOVEMBER 1941

I received a PC today to say there is a letter from Kit. If Mary goes on Monday she will telephone the message. The house Kit, *up to the present,* is much the same as you left it.

What bad news this morning, the Ark Royal sunk, at last. Luckily only 1 casualty, wonderful luck.

Sunday, Nov. 16. Lily Ellis came for the RX PC and will bring me the message from Kit. Dr Jones called in the afternoon and Uncle Ned after church. I have again been singing the hymns following the wireless. It must have sounded terrible as my voice seems nearly gone. My visitors have not yet turned up.

I am always quoting Tom, but he is practically the only one to bring me news. He said the spirit of those people who have had to leave their houses in Victoria Avenue is wonderful. In spite of all their troubles they brighten up, laugh and whistle, and find the humorous side. Still, that's the spirit that built England. One woman told a German that it was awful to be turned out of their houses. He replied, You must blame Churchill and Duff Cooper.

Tuesday, Nov. 18. I had a very good night. A mild morning after storms. I made bills and read most of the day. I am wading through Nicholas Nickleby and enjoying it very much.

The Constable has just telephoned about a job. He was telling me the work they are getting, 45 families changed addresses this week. A lot of people are suffering from dysentry, and such a lot going to hospital for operations for rupture. I suppose the lack of fats weakening the stomach muscles.

The siren went this morning. All have been warned that when the alarm goes they must take shelter wherever they are. People knew there was no air raid and just carried on. Instead it was a sham invasion. People were stopped in Town and on the Front, and the Germans fined them on the spot, 2/- some 4/2. Those without money had their names taken and I suppose will appear in court.

Saturday, Nov. 22. Mary came and was soaked. I was sorry she came after being home with a bad cold last week. I don't think she has enough warm clothes. I gave her 3 woollen vests, Mum's or yours Kit, in any case I know Mum (and you) would have been pleased. She liked Mary.

Although the beaches are closed, the men were allowed to go ormering for 2 days, but only along the Front from Town to St Sampson's.

My German came again today, the usual civil servant and an officer in uniform. When he was introduced he clicked his boots, gave me such a salute, and shook hands. They asked my permission to see the 3 rooms again, chatted there for a few minutes and went

NOVEMBER 1941

away. It's funny that these people supposed to come by the next boat have not arrived, and it's now 7 weeks since they took the rooms. Still, it suits me very well.

I hope Kit will understand the message I sent this week and buy Rosemary and Jane nice presents. Only 4 weeks to Xmas and the days will lengthen. It's awful being penned in like this, although nobody minds the Germans being about. They are quiet, look and speak only if you say good morning, otherwise you would swear they saw nobody. They can look through space.

I had another job today, to open up the main drain in Cognon Vale. This is the third time it is badly choked.

The wireless quoted tomato prices, 1/6 to 1/9 per lb. We sell ours for 2d to 4d and give them to the fowls. Jack Mahy brought me a nice bunch of grapes. He cut the last 2 and gave one to his mother and one to me.

Mr George Dorey who worked at Leale's and lived next to Jurat Arthur Dorey, was at Chapel in Town on Sunday morning and fell dead in his seat. He had gone to stay at Chilcott's for a few days. His father died only 6 weeks ago. Perhaps this shock and being turned out of his house, and the poor food caused his death.

Wednesday, Nov. 26. Soon after 10 three Germans came in, the Boss, his aide-de-camp, I suppose, and an officer, loaded with files, stationery, boxes, coal, wood. When I saw the amount in their car I thought I had better empty the sideboard. I had quite a busy time and filled the kitchen table with decanters (I found half a decanter of gin), glasses, china and the devil knows what.

There was a terrible lot of in and out all day. In the evening the officer came to my study and asked for 3 glasses. I had to give him Mum's nice sherry glasses, had nothing else. Then he wanted an extra one for me. He opened a 5 star Peach Brandy and poured me a glass.

An hour later he knocked again. They wanted me in there to celebrate. They had a small harpsicord or some instrument like it. They played and sang. I don't know what outsiders (if any) could have thought. I had bread and paste. As I left he filled my glass again. I did not want it and tried to stop him, and he spilt more than another glass full. I mopped it up with my handkerchief. (I drank it next evening.)

I had rather a bad head next morning, what with cigarettes and neat spirits. I have never been a drinker and don't know how they can stand it. I had only 2 glasses and that was one too many.

Since then they have been in and out. I hear they are going home for Xmas on the 15th. I hope this is true. On Sunday they were in and out all day. Only 1 sleeps here so far. I have a lot more to say but will tell you later.

NOVEMBER 1941

My side is still sore, otherwise I am not too bad. My appetite is good but the supply is small. Dr Jones said perhaps I could drink a bottle or two of port. Mr Frossard kindly brought me one today, so I am trying that. Stafford Ogier called on Sunday.

Now we only occasionally have cigarettes or tobacco. I smoke Lipton's tea mixed with lavender, rose petals, bean leaves, chestnut leaves, anything we can get hold of and dry. But it's awful stuff and dries the mouth up. And it takes me all my time, after filling my pipe with the infernal stuff, to take the prickles from my forefingers.

I rose at 8, really 6 and pitch dark. It was a funny scene from Kit's window. Every light was on in the windows of Delancey Cottages, Mr Peek's and Mr Higgs' houses, it looked like a barracks, they stood out so bright. Then I heard the Boss in Flo's room getting up. I try to be down first to open up for the girl who comes to clean up their grate, sweep and make the bed.

I am going to sell Mum's coats, the moths are such a bother. I put Kit's fur coat out as often as possible and hope it won't be spoilt.

I went down to the Bridge to get my hair cut. I saw they have passed electric wires through from Potter's house to Miss Le Poidevin's. All the windows were flung wide open and the paper was falling off the passage walls. The drawing-room and dining-room are turned into a barber's shop. As you pass you can see the men stretched out on chairs, their faces plastered with lather. The only thing missing is the barber's pole! Potter's house and Easterbrook in front of the chapel are Red Cross places.

Saturday, Nov. 29. Mary came down as usual. She brought four RX messages from Ted, Flo (Sept. 8), Rosemary and Mr Lazenby (June). We had a meagre tea, so little bread and butter, grapefruit from a tin, very nice, and coffee substitute with saccharine.

Sunday, Nov. 20. Weather so rough that, although I am feeling better I did not go to church. Mrs Rowe made me a nice apple tart. Mr Johns' gave me a little fat and liver, and I managed to get a plaice, all because I am sick. I think I had better keep being sick!

Dr Jones called this morning saying that as I had been out, Miss Matthews sent him to say I should go there to dinner, which I did.

Monday, December 1. Got up at 6.45 as my lodger in the next room was about. I turned on the wireless to hear that Japan was at war with America. (I quite expected it.) Now it's a world war; whenever will it finish? Tonight I heard the American President broadcast the declaration. What a cheer! If cheers can do it they will win the war.

Another job now. All the drains at Braye du Val are choked and flooded. It's not surprising considering the septic beds are built for a family of about 10 persons and now they have 180 Germans

DECEMBER 1941

living in the place. If poor Sir Henry Giffard were alive and saw his place he would faint. I have to charge to the German Occupation and the States will pay me.

Undated. This has been a hectic week. The German civil servant, the Boss, who is now occupying part of my house (they have their office in the dining-room) told me he was going to Berlin for his holiday and would be back for Xmas. Most of their lorry drivers have already gone for Xmas. He wished me goodbye on Tuesday, but the boat did not go. It was also cancelled the next day owing to rough weather, when he came back with his portmanteau and baggage. However the next day he again wished me au revoir and now he has gone.

The house is quiet except for a German officer who calls to make up orders for the lorry drivers. On Sunday evening he came to the study with another officer and asked to use the telephone. I was obliged to ask them in. We chatted. His friend could speak a little English which he said he learnt in Germany. He had a motor garage and used to drive English visitors about his district. I had the wireless on for the church service. He told me he was an R.C.

They were quite nice and kept me going with cigarettes which were very acceptable considering we had not had a ration for 5 weeks. We drank a glass of whisky. They did not look at all pleased when I told them I thought the war would last another two years now the Japs were in. They thought that however long it lasted in the end it would mean a round table talk, and neither side would be any better off. They did not like war.

Tom has undertaken the last 4 funerals but I took one today, a Miss Domaille. While we were at the graveside someone went into the church and stole a pair of ladies' wellington boots with a lovely pair of gloves inside. I was annoyed because I had told the lady they were safe under the seat just inside the little door. It's awful the things that get stolen now. I had had 2 cycle pumps stolen.

After the funeral I went to the Parish Meeting and was again elected as Douzenier for the fourth term. Should I complete this term (which I know I will not, or at least I feel I won't) that will be 24 years.

Friday, Dec 12. Today I got up early for a States Meeting to elect another Jurat to replace Mr Drake, deceased. A Mr Sarre from Torteval was elected.

This afternoon I went to see how the drain at the Cognon was getting on, so am rather tired. I have managed to get some special port wine, so am drinking a few bottles (not all at once of course!).

I got a RX message from Kit on Saturday. She will receive my answer in February I should think.

DECEMBER 1941

If the war keeps on the food problem will be acute. There is the great shortage of potatoes owing to the failure of the late crop, and the Food Control don't want to release the beans till after Xmas. I hear the price will be 1/7 per pint. I had 2 oz of cocoa extra to my coffee ration today.

I went to Town to do a little church business. I had to receive interest on investments for the Churchwardens' Trésor account. The Town looked dreadful, just 2 stalls with vegetables in the French Halles, no rows of turkeys on the pillars, and in the meat market no hundreds of quarters of beef and dozens of pigs at every stall. The meat market was not even open. One stall in the vegetable market had made an attempt to decorate with a little fancy paper, a few Japanese lanterns and a little holly. A sad sight and I could see it made other people sad. I could stick it, it takes a lot to depress me.

But how I thought of the many years we went to Town with dear old Mum and had tea at Le Riche's, and later at Le Noury's, and you kiddies with bags of roasted chestnuts. And of course we had to parade you through all the toy shops. Yesterday only one, Le Cheminant, was open. The few other shops that were open had only vegetables, and would you believe this, it was not possible to buy a potato! I don't know what people will do if we cannot get any up from Jersey. I am sure if ever you read this, you won't be able to picture the scene.

We are to get extra rations Xmas week, 1 oz meat, 1½ oz tea, 1 oz salt, 2 oz sugar. I am reduced to a cup of tea on Sundays only.

Saturday, Dec. 20. I went to Town early to be sworn in Douzenier for the 4th term. The Town as depressing as yesterday except for flowers, Violets 3d. per bunch and Chrys. 3½d per bloom. I bought some for Mum's grave. I also bought Talcum Power at Boots, French 3/6 (rubbish I expect). I was glad to get out of Town.

Mrs Rowe was quite upset to see a lorry with the German Xmas mail and parcels stop at our house to give out some to the Germans here. It set her in a rage to think she could not send or receive a parcel. I thought she was going to break down. She said, Well, we are definitely in prison, it's awful. But I told her our day will come again. She said, Yes, perhaps for our children.

Mary came as usual and we had a tin of fruit salad. Tomorrow is the day I have been longing for, Dec. 21st, shortest day, long night. (Where is the time we had Guernsey biscuits and Port Wine for Long Night). When it's past I feel the winter has turned, sun rising earlier, days lengthening, and although we have to go through our Guernsey winter, the spring is coming.

I hear there are about 18,000 Germans and Frenchmen here. They are taken to different jobs by bus. And now we have dozens and dozens of these 2-horse 'chariots' (I think they must be Dutch

DECEMBER 1941

wagons), and lorries by the hundreds. It's a constant stream of cars etc. Of course our people have to walk or cycle. We have just our 2 vans which still ply between Town and St Sampsons.

Monday, Dec. 22. I have a busy day before me. I am going into the garden now to kill 3 fowls (how cruel), for Mrs Godfray, Miss Lihou and Elsie. Tom will feather them and I prepare them for the table. With them I am sending out a bottle of Port, one of Sherry, Chaumontel pears, one of dear Mum's small Xmas puddings, and a few other knick-knacks including a small cake and an apple tart.

Tuesday, Dec. 23. Many happy returns Darling Jack. I began the day early as I have so much to get in. I went to Town and bought scent and bath salts for Elsie, Mrs Rowe and Mary. Mrs Frossard bought for me two pairs of nice gloves for Mrs S.T. Ogier and her daughter-in-law. The Frossards and I are going there on Xmas day. I sent Diva an Xmas pudding (one of Mum's 1938), some potatoes, parsnips, carrots and cabbage.

Elsie came and she was quite loaded when she left, but she telephoned to say she got back safely with the parcels. Mrs Godfray sent me a nice pair of gold cuff links and a stud, and Miss Lihou had already given me a sovereign.

Wed. Dec. 24. There were crowds of people on the Bridge this morning, queuing and all they could buy was 2 lbs potatoes, onions, parsnips, carrots, cabbage and red beetroots. It really was a pitiful scene, but everybody was bright, and they laugh and joke about it. Of course the women say, If only we had a little more bread.

I got the flowers for the altar as usual, Chrys. incurved, rather fine, 3/6 per doz. I put 1 doz. white, 9 yellow and some nicely berried holly from Dr Jones on Mum's grave.

The service was at 5 owing to the black out. Nearly 200 present. We had a nice anthem, There were shepherds. Mr Frossard spoke about absent relations and friends and nearly broke down. I think he worries about Charlie who is an officer in India. He said it might be the last Xmas separated, and trusted that by next year it would be peace on earth.

After the service Stafford came for the brussel sprouts and took the gloves. Good for me, I am always bashful giving presents. Mary had called with my present, a black carrier bag for my bicycle. I am sorry I missed her as I had bath salts and 2 pears ready for her. I had given her the money to get a handbag which was what she wanted for her present. I gave Tom 20/- for his Xmas box. He had been very good while I was laid up looking after the poultry.

During the week I have listened to the carols on the wireless.

DECEMBER 1941

And I have thought of the many evenings spent getting the cards ready. Mum and I spent a lot of time to find appropriate words. These things make me sad but I must not dwell on them.

The many Germans around here are making quite a lot of Xmas. I've seen them up and down with Xmas trees.

It's now 11.30, our time. I have just returned from the Doctor's and am having a piece of apple tart and a glass of hot whisky. I am listening to a broadcast from America, some of the carols I don't know, but 'O come let us adore Him' brought a little lump in my throat feeling we are so separated. Still I have hope and if I count my blessings I have a lot to be thankful for. Now an announcement that our Prime Minister will be speaking.

I heard him and the President from the White House (and laughed at Churchill's, 'Some chicken, some neck!') I could write a lot about the unity of our 2 great nations, and what Xmas can bring to earnest folk fighting for a good cause. Although I can see the faults of both our nations, I still see our cause is far the most righteous one.

Saturday, Dec. 27. I spent a very nice time under the exceptional circumstances. I completed my duties on Christmas Eve, presents and 5 or 6 cards sent, the grave arranged, and those around me sent off to spend a happy Xmas with their Xmas boxes, as much as I could afford. (They were pleasantly surprised as they did not expect anything this year.)

On Xmas morning I went to early communion, back to the empty house and had breakfast standing up at the kitchen table. Mrs Rowe (who had taken on the job of looking after the animals) came in and laughed when I said, Xmas Day in the workhouse. Still despite all, everybody's spirits are high and they can laugh.

After the 10.45 service I walked out to the Ogiers with Mrs Frossard. Mr Frossard came along later after Communion and a christening. I wheeled my bicycle and carried the 2 enormous bottles of Champagne they were taking, which went down very well with the dinner of goose, beef and Xmas pudding (not very fruity of course). Mr Frossard proposed the toast Absent Friends, but few comments. I think we felt it better to say little and keep the party bright, as all had missing relatives.

In the afternoon we walked to Coloma where Stafford has an office. He (and many others) is looking after the evacuees' homes. Women ventilate and clean them each week. Then we went back to hear the King's speech. Mr Frossard had put the afternoon service half an hour later so that people could hear it. I did not go and told him he must give me a special dispensation. Of course, he said, Stay and enjoy yourself.

The curfew was extended to 1 o'clock for 3 nights. The Frossards left at midnight. I slept there.

DECEMBER 1941

Came back the next morning. Dr Jones called for 10 minutes. Then I ran as far as the Stubbs to wish them the compliments of the season. They are now living at Grandes Maison. They gave me 1 oz of tobacco.

I had an early dinner and set off for St Andrew's. I had not been out for nearly 3 months. We had tea at Miss Lihou's, *Real Tea,* and before we left to go to Belle Vue with Mrs Godfray, Miss Lihou added to my Xmas present. At Mrs Godfray's I saw the fowls and rabbits. I had a glass of lovely Cherry Brandy (German) with some nice cake. I had to leave early as it is dark at 7. I heard the Churchill broadcast from the White House again.

Sunday, Dec. 28. A SE gale, heavy rain and terribly cold. Only 15 at church, collection 12/6. Had dinner at the Doctor's. He opened a bottle of Champagne and although 23 years old it was very good. Then I had a liqueur.

I went to Mr Pattimore to try to get a few cigarettes for the Doctor who has only 10 left. I went there again after the 4 o'clock service. Finished the Champagne, then a nip of rum. Got home 2 minutes after curfew (first time late).

Tuesday, Dec. 30. At 1.30 there was a terrible bombardment of gun fire. I got up and watched, then took cover. It lasted only 10 minutes. I heard that it was German guns. Planes were passing but nobody heard them. A heavy white frost, but a lovely moon.

I cooked my fowl and Xmas ration of pork. I got a little suet and a skin for the chicken. It was lovely with swedes and sprouts. I am sending the breast for Mrs Godfray and Miss Lihou. Elsie is coming down tomorrow for the usual and a rabbit I am killing for Miss Lihou.

As regards Xmas fare, I *saw* 1 orange. My grocer sent up 6 walnuts, 2 oz Guernsey sweets, an extra oz flour (some flour!). Still I won't grumble. I have a good shelter, wood and coal, a few tins of fruit left, some wine and whisky, and have not yet bottled the sloe gin. Do you remember Kit, the sloes we picked at St Martin's?

I swopped a fowl with the Pattimores for a bottle of whisky and some tins of fruit. They worried me for one, and I could not very well refuse Mrs Carré as she made my cigarettes for a long time. But now our ration is so small I smoke the tobacco in my pipe.

Everything is so scarce that it's all barter for foodstuffs. The only shops are vegetable and exchange ones. It's amusing what people put in for exchange. I cannot enumerate these, it would fill a book.

Uncle Ned called to say he had news from Marjorie. He is looking as fresh as a rose but very thin now. Tom is sick. He's had dysentry since Xmas Eve so must have had a poor Xmas.

JANUARY 1942

Wednesday, Dec. 31. I went around Brock Road looking for my white Leghorn that ran away on Xmas Day. I didn't find it. Someone has put it in the pot by now. I can count that lost. I have only 3 fowls and 8 rabbits left.

Reflecting on the past 12 months I cannot say hardships have been too bad, much better than I expected. Food has been scarce but we have lived and not been too hungry. Now we must look forward with hope to 1942. Viewing things generally I have great hope of things in East Europe cracking up, and Japan left alone to carry on if she wishes.

Dr Jones has been in bed for a few days. He came downstairs for a few hours today and seems much better. I had walnuts, a nice square of pressed figs and drank some Or-lem, very flat. I left early. Now at 11.30 there is a lot of rifle fire. I expect it's the Germans firing out the old year, a bit early. I am listening to Exchange Greetings from the A.B.C.D. Powers, London calling America etc. Freedom's Front.

Thursday, January 1. I went out to the front gate just to see New Year's morning in the New Road. Well, it was very quiet when a German, who I think is the Sergeant Major (I often see him at the Schools) came by. He said, Good morning, and gave me such a salute that I thought I must be the civil Governor of the New Road.

I must say the Germans have been very quiet all the holidays. They had their jollifications accompanied with the usual spirits (they could be seen carrying in the bottles). The roads have been remarkably quiet and I saw nothing for complaint.

After my little dinner of stewed up chicken I decided to go for a cycle ride and call on Miss Lihou where I knew Mrs Godfray would be and wish them the compliments of the season.

On the way out it was amusing to see the couples and little families along the Banques, all carrying their bags. They have to take their food when visiting. In Brock Road (St Peter Port) at almost every house there were Germans going in and out or smoking cigars on the doorsteps, as though they were in their own homes. Then in Queen's Road were Germans carrying parcels in their arms wrapped in Presses or some printed papers, and from the way the parcel was raised it was not difficult to see it held a bottle.

I left the Vauquiedor at 6 and in Amherst I passed somebody who shouted, Come back. It was Kitty Head and Peter with their new baby boy, a fine chap. We chatted about you all. They get news occasionally from her family in England.

Ned called, but I had to pack off soon as I was due at the Doctor's for dinner. So now holidays are over, very satisfactorily spent, and I am ready to start the New Year, and if as financially successful as last year under these difficult conditions, I will not complain.

JANUARY 1942

Friday, Jan. 2. I did little work except pay the men, Messervy and Martel. They telephoned to say that Simon had influenza and boils, a funny complication. I forgot to tell you the following.

Uncle Ned called about 2 days before Xmas to see if I could spare him a bottle of whisky. I had none to spare but during the night I had an idea. The Doctor, during my illness, said he could give me a certificate. I called at Newington next morning and asked for it, then went to Town, got the necessary and when Ned called I was able to present him with the needful. He was delighted and went away as happy as a lark, and said I was a damned good schemer. But it is not that. It is energy and how to do it. With most people I have met in my life, their policy is how not to do it, and it's astonishing how they can conjure up excuses, and make themselves believe they are real. I could write a chapter on this mentality.

Tom returned to work today and seems much better. I am keeping all the Evening Presses but probably you will never want to wade through all of them. Still, if you get a glimpse, you will know how it is being occupied. I often say, our camp is not barbed wire, but surrounded by water, and it's too far to swim the Channel, and these days too cold!

At 8.30 (really 7.30) the firing was terrific for 5 minutes, and the heavens lit up. It startled me, yet I had to run and watch. I could hear the planes. They generally pass here going to Brest.

Tuesday, Jan 6. My German came back from Berlin last night. I did not see him arrive, but when I came back from the Doctor (who is now rather ill) he opened the dining-room door and asked me in. The usual New Year greetings, and from his description of the sea voyage it was not pleasant, using his hands for he cannot speak 6 words of English, I think he was seasick. He presented me with ¼ lb of pipe tobacco. I thanked him very much.

He had been to Berlin to see his firm, but he does not live there. I made a mistake, his home is in Mosel. I said, Where the wine comes from. He told me he had brought me a bottle, but it was at Morningside. I hope he doesn't forget.

Wednesday, Jan. 7. I came down just in time to let the Dutchman in. He is the clerk. He lives in Nocq Road and is engaged to the daughter of Mrs Roberts who used to work for Mrs Le Poidevin. She is a telephone operator at the Brock Road exchange.

In the afternoon I went to Delancey, called on the Mahy's, Pointues Rocques, and managed to cadge a box of early seed potatoes. There are none about and this is serious.

I went to choir practice. We have to have it in the vestry now the schools are occupied, crowded as you can imagine. During practice there was a terrific bombardment and on the way back it started

JANUARY 1942

again. I ran and kept near the wall, as several pieces of shrapnel have dropped about here.

When I reached home a man was trying to get in for shelter. Then a German threw his bicycle on the cement path and rushed in. The poor chap looked terrified, he was pale and panting. After a few minutes I asked him if he could speak English, French a little? My chance to show off! So we chatted a little, very little, as you know I soon get tangled up. He said he was from Frankfurt, had been here 4 months but was soon going back. He had a very weak and frightened face and I should say very little heart. Of course he may have been through a lot and have reason to be frightened.

At 10 it started again worse than ever. I looked out for a time but then took cover.

Thursday, Jan. 8. Lorry drivers were banging at the front door at 9 o'clock. I ran down in my pyjamas and let them in. When they found the dining-room door locked they came upstairs in their big boots on my nice stair carpet and went into Erwin's room.

More bombardment and machine gunning today.

Friday, Jan. 9. Scarcely daylight and another bombardment. I came downstairs and Mrs Rowe was already there as we have another arrangement now. The girl who worked for the Germans here has been unsatisfactory I believe and has now left. I suggested that Mrs Rowe should come in the mornings, do out the dining-room and lay the fire. Then, when she comes in the afternoons to attend to my requirements, make his bed. This has been agreed to and of course they will pay me. A far better arrangement as I will not have strangers in the kitchen. It's proving a grand plan for when I got down this morning Mrs Rowe had a nice fire for me in the study.

I went to Town this afternoon for my coffee ration (which was acorn coffee, horrible stuff) and anything else I could find. I fared better elsewhere! I paid a few bills for Dr Jones who is pretty ill now. He had Dr Wilson to see him this afternoon. I managed to get 2 eggs for him. They are priceless and practically unobtainable, but Elsie spared me them.

I get 4 lbs of bread one week, 5 lbs the next. This is my short week and I am stranded tonight. I have just a small crust left. It's amusing when you have to look at a loaf and wonder if it will allow another slice. I got short because feeling peckish last night, I toasted a slice to eat with a little dripping I had. I cut it rather thick and now I must fast a little.

The next 2 months will be difficult as there are no potatoes. They are going to release the dried beans next week, but even if there were tons they would not last long. And I hear the Germans have to be supplied with 30 tons of vegetables each week, which in

JANUARY 1942

the end must put us short. Up to now I am not worrying. We still get our ration of meat, I have a few rabbits as a standby, and hope for better days.

Saturday, Jan. 10. Very cold. I have a funeral. Jim Ellis, Lily Ellis' brother dropped dead on his way home from work last night. He's the father of Reg who you will remember learnt his trade with me. He's in England. There are so many funerals this week that I cannot get the hearse or coaches. I have very little material left for undertaking now.

Mary came tonight. Weather almost too bad for the journey along the front. I could spare only 1 slice of bread. I expect she could manage 6 this cold weather. She took the answer to Jack's RX letter. It was stamped Canterbury, near the coast. I wonder if he has joined up. I sent the monthly letter to Kit. I think it's her turn.

There were 3 huge steam boats in the Town harbour bringing tons more timber, huts, oil, etc. The place will be a fortress by the time they have finished.

Sunday, Jan. 11. Very cold again. A lovely fire when I came down. Mrs Rowe told me there was 1" of ice. I am sure she does too much, washes for about 20 people, looks after me, and now the dining-room, that fire and mine and the German's bedroom.

As we came out of church it was snowing a little. I went to the Salt Pans to see Mrs Ellis, was there only 1/2 hour, and when I came out there was more than 1" of snow. It seemed strange riding through the snow, so beautiful and white. All the Germans were in the doorways of the Grosse Hougue Dorey's Cottages (they now occupy the 26) looking surprised to see snow in Guernsey. It stayed on the ground.

Monday, Jan. 12. Again came down to a marvellous fire. The snow still on the ground and 1" of ice. I dug some carrots and parsnips for my dinner and the ground was frozen for 2".

Tuesday, Jan. 13. We had an awful gale last night. My back was so cold and creepy when I woke up several times. When I came down the house was, as Mum would say, as cold as a tomb, but there was a nice fire in the study. Then I went outside to look at the weather. There was a SE gale (the coldest wind we get in Guernsey), it was raining, sleeting, hailing and the cold was unbearable. I had some coffee, no breakfast, and went with the van to the Salt Pans. Even the Germans had not turned out building their huts at Grosse Hougue. Then to the church.

By the time I got home Mrs Rowe had fetched my loaf which I soon put out of shape! I could not face going to the Greffe for the

JANUARY 1942

burial permit so sent Martel, being so much younger than I am.

Mr Frossard took the service at 3. He was dressed for the occasion in leggings, coat, mac, and his surplice over everything. Luckily the heaviest sleet and rain fell when we were in church. There were 18 wreaths. I sent one and included the Employees as Reg had always worked for me until he evacuated. I just perished at the graveside. (Fancy me complaining of the cold!)

Mr Matthews' funeral was after mine (Miss Matthews' uncle) but I told Mr Frossard I was too cold to stay. He said I was wise to go home. If this weather continues I am sure a lot of people will not stick it. The food is not good enough to resist the cold, and there is little fuel.

Thursday, Jan. 15. Had an awful gale last night and it's terribly cold. There are flocks of Lapwings passing over, generally a sign of snow.

Luckily the weather moderated. I had to go to the Capelles in the afternoon for a Préciput, Mr Thorn deceased. We later found we had valued the wrong place! The Germans living there had looked surprised to see us walking around the greenhouses. But it turned into a blessing in disguise for me, as Stafford asked me to return for tea with him.

After feeding the fowls I consulted Mrs Rowe who said it would be a change for me. She said she would lock up and just leave the front door open for my lodgers. So I went and Mrs Rowe is now concurrent with the management of the house.

We had real tea. It went down 'lovely'. It's now months that I have not had real tea during the week. Madam was not there (she visits her mother on Thursdays). We had a large dish of pork to dive into. I don't think I've had such a tea for years. I laughed when Stafford said, Let's make the best of things while she is away, and he fetched another 'dodger'. We had another go and laid it on lavishly. I don't know what Mrs Ogier thought when she saw the dish. His son and wife had left for a dance in the Central Halls (Red Cross). They were mad to go, a SE gale had sprung up.

We had supper when they returned, bread and butter and vegetable marrow jam and coffee. Then later a nip of cognac, and after the news a nightcap.

I could not have waltzed around the bedroom much, as it is loaded with their drawing-room furniture. The Germans have taken Coloma where Stafford had his office, so he is obliged to use his drawing-room.

Pork fat for breakfast again. They had killed two pigs, and the States allow a quarter to be kept by the owner. So they had half of one which they salted.

This is a good joke. At first the States allowed farmers to keep half of each pig. One farmer cut his across the back and sent them the fore part and kept the hind quarters. I hear they made a little fuss, but he said he had kept half and this they could not dispute. Now the order is, cut down the centre of the spine. (Trust a Guernsey farmer to be cute.)

I left the Ogiers in a gale, head wind and a deluge. I was soaked, have never been so cold, and my fingers were numb when I arrived home to find a lovely fire and hot coffee ready. I nearly cried as my fingers began to warm up. But it was worth it to get such an extra good meal these starvation days.

Saturday, Jan. 17. At about 7 I heard the telephone, jumped out of bed to rush downstairs, but when on the landing there was no phone ringing. It was an alarm clock, Erwin's, the Boss's, here in Flo's bedroom. You bet I rushed back to bed.

At 11 I heard planes, very low, then bombs banging. It was 3 English planes that dived out of the blue, passed over St Sampson's harbour and released the bombs over the Town harbour and machine gunned it. I hear one bomb dropped right in the hold of a big steamer. Tucker, a local man, the crane driver was killed, also another man and some Frenchmen, and a fire started. But I have no definite details, just that they came over the ships' masts and were gone like a shot out of a gun.

Sunday, Jan 18. Many happy returns of the day Darling Flo. Sorry I cannot send a present. Dr Jones (who seems a little better) asked me your age tonight. It's so long ago, that eventful morning when Mum presented you to me saying, There's your darling baby girl. I am sorry it's not your wish, a boy. But then nothing mattered. It was all over and a bonny baby girl with black hair. It took some time counting before I could tell him I made it 37.

We have now winnowed our greenhouse beans. They were so late it was a bother to dry them. We had 11 baskets, 165 lbs. Not a lot but a catch crop after the potatoes. Tom is now swamping, getting ready for the next crop.

After church I went out with Stafford to make out our Churchwardens' budget. I had to walk as I have no lamp. There was a new moon so I could see a little. A mild, clear sky and starting to freeze.

Monday, Jan. 19. Had a quick brekker of baked pork fat and coffee. Beautiful and clear riding home, but freezing and I perished. I heard the overseas news at ten. What booty the Russians have captured.

I have to attend to my feet. I am limping, my feet have got thinner and my shoes must slop causing my heels to be tender. All my shoes are worn so thin that the least little stone you tread on gives you the jihops. I cannot get them soled, no leather, only

JANUARY 1942

rubber motor tyres.

The tank over the bathroom is frozen hard. Mrs Rowe said she had a mind to have a good skate!

I see by the paper that Tucker's funeral (the crane driver who was killed in Saturday's raid) was well attended, including German officials who took wreaths.

Wednesday, Jan. 21. I have a Douzaine Meeting this afternoon for the parish budget. The Germans are dissatisfied with the labour cost for the amount of food produced. I hear they want to remove 800 men and allow no women labour in the greenhouses. I don't know how they intend to occupy the men. They must have work and be fed. We should be able to produce sufficient foodstuffs except for flour, which of course they are importing for us, and for which the States pay.

Friday, Jan. 23. Down in time for the 9 o'clock news. Mrs Rowe had fires in the dining-room for our visitors and in the study for me, with the kettle boiling for my coffee. Had a good brekker. My sister had given me a 2 lbs dodger as she knew I was short, and luckily for me, Mrs Godfray had a loaf given her, so they also sent me a 2 lbs dodger. Not that they knew I was short, but perhaps because when Elsie comes down on Tuesdays I generally give her a snack. So I gave Mrs Rowe and Tom some and they were very pleased.

It's a wicked night. The rain is lashing against the windows, and I am thankful to be so cosy here, and to have a nice bread and butter supper with some of that beautiful sloe and apple jelly from the attic. The jelly had settled down in the pots, they were little more than half full. Fancy keeping so well since 1938. There is only 1 left, worse luck, but I have been most thankful to have them.

This afternoon it was so cold and wet when Erwin (the German boss here) came in and the house was reeking with the smell of coffee, that I took him in a breakfast cup full. When he brought back the cup he gave me a packet of German tobacco, very nice of him. I was delighted as I had nothing to smoke.

I think the food problem will be critical before long. I cannot imagine how some people get on these cold mornings. There is stealing everywhere now. Some have had as many as 17 rabbits stolen, Le Maitres had their bakehouse on the Bridge broken into and 20 loaves and 4 lbs of yeast taken. The Ogiers, the Hermitage, had ducks and fowls stolen, and some weeks ago Le Riche had all their tobacco and cigarettes taken. Last week Phillips, Fountain Street had about £15 worth stolen. If people cannot get food, I can see they will break in, and they do it on these rainy, windy nights when they can't be seen or heard.

Fuel is a problem. The Germans have stopped the cutting down

JANUARY 1942

of trees, and now we are allowed only 1 cwt of logs per month. Consumption of gas is restricted. Last week when my meter was read I was 1,200 feet to the good. I boil all water on the study fire, and Uncle Ned made me an iron saucepan for my vegetables, as I know you would not allow aluminium saucepans on the fire!

Saturday, Jan. 24. I had to go to Town, messages for Dr Jones, etc. I first went to the Waterworks, South Esplanade. Then I thought I would look at the large steam boat damaged last Saturday by bombs, berthed opposite the plantation. There was a large hole in her bows, and from a big barge moored nearby they seemed to be taking a lot of wood on board in slings. I think they are making a shield, will concrete the hole and take her to France for repairs. She is about 5,000 tons.

The other boat, sunk by the jetty, is about 8,000 tons, and is sinking all the time on the sandy bottom. She floats aft and rises above the jetty.

Next I went to the Savings Bank, then for my coffee ration. Was lucky, got real coffee, not acorn. Then to Bachmann to get a gold jewel valued for Dr Jones. I think he will sell it. Mr Brice said it's value is approx. £3. Next I bought some seeds for the garden. They are very scarce, especially onions and leeks. Paid several bills. Back to dinner which consisted of boiled potatoes and red beetroots *only.*

A gale sprang up. I was glad to see Mary but she was soaked. She brought me an RX letter from Kit, sent Oct. 22 which said about your nice summer holiday and receiving my Swiss message. Fried spuds again for tea to save bread, but very nice, and a tin of grapefruit and coffee. The gale continued all night.

Sunday, Jan 25. I was up early but Erwin was up before me and gone by 9, unusual for him on Sunday. We had our usual services, only 24 in the morning. The 4 o'clock was well attended. It's funny what the collectors bring up, it's mostly notes, 6d. States notes, 1/0½ and 2/1 German marks, and metal coins 2½d and 1¼d.

I treated myself to a cup of tea and had a little marmalade to put on my bread. Last week, Elsie brought down some oranges and sugar and Mrs Rowe made the marmalade for Mrs Godfray. I think Elsie found the job too complicated. It made 5 lbs, tasty but a bit sweet, I think.

There were 3 oranges over which they made me keep. Mrs Rowe has made me a few more pots. I don't know where the oranges came from nor where Mrs Rowe got the sugar, but she says I will owe it (some hope).

Uncle Ned has just called in. I gave him a nip of whisky. Stafford Ogier had a nip at dinner time so now the bottle is empty. But I got

JANUARY 1942

a bottle of Hine's Cognac last night, so won't be without a drop of hot for a few evenings yet. Up to now I have managed to fall on my feet and my friends say I am damned lucky. But what I have had I have shared fairly well around.

The spirit of the Guernsey people in the shops is wonderful, in spite of short rations and difficulties getting vegetables. Even now they still make jokes and laugh over their fate. I listen to the remarks and quaint sayings, and find their optimism is never daunted, they never lose faith.

Monday, Jan. 26. I went to Mr Despointes, Rue-à-Chien, to try to get a rabbit for Dr Jones, but more especially to try to get early seed potatoes to plant in Allendale greenhouse. I really thought it a hopeless journey. No rabbit, but to my surprise, he said he would spare me 2 boxes of Early, and then, after my talking nicely to him, spared me 6 boxes of Late, all at 2/6 per box. He could have got 7/6 he remarked. I sent for them this afternoon.

I sent my doe out in the hand cart as I wanted to have a cross with a very large Flemish Giant. He has a fine stock, has made £36 this year, and has a stock of 10 large breeding rabbits in hand. I could get £6 for my lot, but I want them for food.

I tried elsewhere for a rabbit for Dr Jones. Mahy, Fig Tree will let me have 2 at 25/- each. The Doctor is mad if he pays that amount. But this afternoon I managed to get him one for 10/-, not a very large one. I killed, skinned it and took it up. *He* was pleased. *I* was pleased and excited when my seed potatoes arrived. I had been rather worrying about late seed potatoes. Now I have those 6 boxes I can eat the few I had intended to save.

It's awful about seed potatoes. Some are supposed to have come from Jersey but have not. The Potato Board (States) tells me I *might* have some, but I must wait till all the States Control are supplied. So you can guess how excited I am over my day's work. What a blessing I tried to get a rabbit for Dr Jones.

Tuesday, Jan. 27. Another gale, much rain and very cold. I went to Mr Bird's store to try to arrange with 6 men to work in the New Cemetery. The Douzaine asked me to take charge and superintend the work. Now the men hold a pistol to my head saying they would work for me, but will not take orders from the Sexton. To this I would certainly not agree, so you can guess there was an altercation. So I told them they were free agents, but for my part I accepted no conditions. One or two of the bulldogs looked and snarled, but that didn't frighten me.

I am going to see the foreman after dinner, and if they would rather not send them, I will not carry on with the job unless the Controlling Committee send me other men. I am not being dictated

JANUARY 1942

to. The cheek, when I am looking after them for no pay, just to give them work.

Mrs King who used to live at Allendale, has died in her 83rd year, and I had to go out to the Tertre, Vale, between the showers, and now I have a rush again.

Thursday, Jan. 29. Again terrible squalls of wind and rain. I went to the cemetery early to start the men. They were all there waiting for me! I paired them off and they started getting out the roots of those enormous elms. [*See illustration 18.*] Remember them? There will be just flower beds instead of the old elms which seemed to blend so well with the old church. Still, the world is always changing and we must submit to the rule.

In the afternoon I went to the Camp-du-Roi. The gale was then at full force. I have never ridden in such weather. At Grand Fort I don't know how I kept on the machine, and decided not to go any further than the Fig Tree for another rabbit for Dr Jones. But when I inclined left along the Camp-du-Roi the wind was on a beam, in nautical terms on the quarter bow. I bought the rabbit, not very enormous, but 22/-. As it was not for me I paid!

I decided to continue my journey up past the Câstel Church, then on to Mrs Godfray. She is in bed with a bad cold. I enjoyed 3 cups of tea and much bread and butter. I did not mind eating a little extra as Elsie said their officer had given them a white loaf. Then I went upstairs to see Mrs Godfray who was glad to see me but said I should not have come out in that weather.

Not a bad run home although I had to pedal *down* Amherst Hill, so you can guess the wind was strong. Elsie gave me half a loaf and 3 eggs, so I had a nice supper.

I forgot to tell you that last week I gave Elsie an old alarm clock we used when sterilizing the ground. Their German officer's batman wanted to buy one, but they are unobtainable. I would not sell it for money, only for tobacco. So I came back with 2 oz of tobacco and got 80 cigarettes too. Elsie had 20, I gave Tom 20 and I had 40 for myself. Not a bad barter.

Friday, Jan. 30. We have had a rough month and thank God it ends tomorrow. I still have fuel but most people are without. I don't know how poor people will get through February and March.

Bel Air Hotel in Sark was burnt down last night. Poor old Bel Air, where I have had many a good lobster lunch washed down with lovely English ale or sparkling wine. And all this with plenty of bread and pats of Sark butter for 2/6 plus a tip for the waiter. I fancy I can hear the waiters in their foreign tongue saying ham, beef or tongue. Good old days those were, probably never to return. Still it's nice to have known those days.

FEBRUARY 1942

I forget if I told you that 3 weeks ago Houmet du Nord Hotel, L'Islet, was also burnt down.

I have just returned from the Doctor. He is still on the couch in pyjamas and dressing-gown, but is I think much better. When I left (and I must admit I had had a slight decoction of Johnny de Kuyper) it was 1 minute to curfew time, the gale was still raging, and I was blown to my quarters in less time. I write this only to let you know what a hell of a night it was. Now I am going to enjoy a chapter of Oliver Twist before twisting myself under the bedclothes.

Sunday, February 1. Last night another awful bombardment. It broke out several times. We now get lots of shrapnel dropping on our greenhouses. I have had several panes broken.

Today being the first of the month we had Choral Communion. Only 11 people plus the choir who were in fairly full strength.

I had a fairly good lunch at the Doctor's. I take my potatoes and bread and have no bother cooking on Sundays.

Lots of things happen here which I don't care about mentioning now, as I never know if these books will get into your hands or not. Times change in many ways, but (as I remember on a Christmas card we sent) not in the ways of friendship.

Tuesday, Feb. 3. Stan de la Motte called at about 11 and brought the wine as usual. I gave him coffee. Went to see the men at the cemetery. Then heard that Mr Lawton had met with an accident in Nocq Road yesterday, so I called to see Miss Lawton. I had not been there or spoken to them for some months, not for any reason, but as Mary has started coming on Saturday afternoons, I could not have them on our short rations.

Miss Lawton explained that Willie was passing opposite the Anchor Laundry when the Germans were coming out with their wagon and pair. The horses being restless, it appears the pole struck him and he fell unconscious. The ambulance took him to hospital where they say he is comfortable. We will hear more tomorrow. I am lending him a pair of my pyjamas. He is short and you cannot buy any.

This afternoon I went to Town for Miss Lawton with the insurance card, then on to St Martin's about a small job for Miss Mauger, but they were out. So I went on to Miss Houstoun where I had some awful bramble tea which they seem to like, some nice bread with butter (Guernsey) out of their ration, and jam. After telling her all your news I went back to Miss Mauger, and luckily they were now in. It's a pull cycling to St Martin's.

The Town was crowded, Frenchmen by the hundreds, some only lads, half clad and looking miserable and cold. People tell me they call from house to house begging for bread. I don't know why they

FEBRUARY 1942

bring them here.

In Market Square I saw 2 or 3 groups with knapsacks on their backs or under their arms, some with overcoats, outsizes and boys wearing them. I thought that only a writer like Dickens could describe the scene. I saw it well enough, but my hand is not the hand of a ready writer, so I must leave it to your imagination.

I saw them in Fountain Street eating their dinner. They had a sort of brown enamel dish and spoon, went into Mde. Pomier and came out and sat on window ledges and doorsteps in the cold. I passed close to one and it seemed just like cut up carrots. I don't know how they can work on such food.

I went to Blicq for onion seed and we were 30 in the queue. We were each supplied with a 1/6 packet. I sent my men and managed 3 packets, 1 for Tom. I am planting them in boxes in the greenhouse, then I can supply the neighbourhood I hope.

Wednesday, Feb. 4. I fixed my men, had an early lunch and took the usual provisions out to St Andrew's. Mrs Godfray has a cold and it is not convenient for Elsie to fetch them. It's a good pull going out, cycling all uphill.

Mrs Godfray was downstairs but still not well. I saw Elsie's fowls, the only ones in Guernsey now laying I think. Had a nice tea with marmalade.

Mrs Godfray introduced me to the German officer staying there. He could not have thought much of my French, but being a polite officer said I was quite fluent. He gave me a cigarette, and when I showed him what I smoked in my pipe (Lipton's tea with bramble) he immediately went upstairs and got me a 2 oz packet, and said when I came again, if I were without, I must tell him. (Very kind.) I left loaded with parsnips, a swede and a 1 lb loaf, very acceptable and two eggs.

Thursday, Feb. 5. Very cold and sleet falling. I again had an early lunch as I went to a show at the Central Hall, my first outing for 12 months, Guernsey Co-Optimists present Tit Bits. Jackie Ogier sang the Cobblers' Song from Chu Chin Chow. You will all remember the song, in the first show you ever saw in London. I thought it a wonderful show, didn't you? Then they had selections from the Geisha, not bad. The place was crowded. There were a lot of Frenchmen and other foreigners there. I don't suppose the poor devils had anywhere else to go.

Tonight was very dark. Jim Ogier told me that one night he left the Club, Commercial Road, at 9.20 but missed the turning by the church and must have got into Bulwer Avenue. He managed to call at a house, they lent him a bicycle lamp, and he got home 3 minutes before 10 curfew.

FEBRUARY 1942

Friday, Feb. 6. A very cold morning with blizzards of very fine snow. I wish it was raining down manna as when it is so cold I find 4 lbs bread for a week is not sufficient. But we have to manage. I got in plenty of wood as I expect a fall of snow.

Well, the weather was rough today, but part of the night was rougher at New Road. It started at 4 o'clock, then I got up and dressed for some little time. I will not relate my experience but some day I may remember to tell you, I am not likely to forget, and the details I can always remember.

Sunday, Feb. 8. Again very cold. Went to church at 10.45, only 15 people and I did not blame them staying away. Had lunch at the Doctor's. He opened a bottle of sparkling Burgundy, very nice. He is turning out all these bottles which have been there for some time. Miss Matthews and I drink the greater part.

We had our last 4 o'clock service today and next Sunday we go back to 6.30. Mr Frossard asked me to tea, but I did not go as I had to feed the animals. Tom did not come, I think his wife is ill.

The telephone rang and it was for Erwin. He happened to be in the dining-room, his office, so I called him. He asked if I wanted English cigarettes. Of course I accepted, and he gave me 2 packets of Guards Parade. I was bucked as our ration is only 10 per week.

This has been a black week as far as the war is concerned, but rather uneventful as far as Guernsey is affected, except for the frosty weather. Riding a cycle your hands get numbed. I went to Mrs Godfray on Thursday as Elsie could not come.

So far I am managing to keep on my men. I am working at Commander Giffard's, Braye-du-Val. All drains are again choked. You would not know the place. I wish Rosy could see it now. The tennis court is covered with a very long hut, and all the lovely gravel paths are covered with siftings.

I have just listened to the Prime Minister's talk. Then came a very heavy bombardment.

On Saturday Mary brought me a nice chancre, not very large but very full, 4/4. I was glad of the change from the food we are getting. I had the remainder for my breakfast.

The Germans would not pass the States Budget, and they have to discharge something like 1,500 men from the Glasshouse Board, and 35 of the Forestry men. A lot have to report to Saumarez Park and I understand they will be given employment. We must produce more food with less labour.

There is that awful bombardment again. I expect there will be a lot of glass broken with the shrapnel. I have been a little depressed the last 2 days and now Mr Churchill says we must be prepared for a long war. Some hope of seeing any of you yet. Still I won't dwell on these matters too long.

FEBRUARY 1942

Undated - Feb. It's now a week since I added anything to this chapter and temperatures have been down to freezing all the time. I went to Mrs Godfray on Friday. It's too cold for Elsie to come, and was very cold returning along the Front. I can generally keep my body warm but my hands get numb. They gave me 3 eggs and something to smoke.

Mary came on Saturday, but it was almost too cold for her. Still she is young. I forgot her birthday on the 15th, but will give her a little present.

What traffic in the Town harbour and opposite Woolworths. There were about a dozen little vedettes, river boats. They reminded me of when I went to France with Mum and up the Rance. What miles of truck rails, tons of cement, timber and even empty packing cases. There's a stream of lorries flying about all the time.

I have had to get rid of my two chicks. They scarcely grew on the food available. I have two fowls left which I will, no doubt, have to kill soon. Then I will have only eight rabbits to worry about. I am expecting a litter on Monday. I have put her in the greenhouse, but even there it is almost too cold. Still I have given her plenty of hay.

There was a very large fire in Cornet Street on Friday night, the Clarence, next to Bucktrouts, which also would have been burnt but for the NE wind, which certainly saved it. I was doubly glad in that it's our tobacco factory on which we depend for smokes.

It's while I think of these things I must jot them down. Mrs Frossard gave a small Whist Drive at the Rectory, four tables, no refreshments. It was terribly dark returning, I was obliged to lend the Malletts my torch. They were worried about getting back and I could not go with them because there was not time before curfew. Mrs de la Motte came from Town on her bicycle. Returning she was run into and the ambulance had to take her home. It is not worth the risk of going out at night.

The last few days have been colder than ever. All day long showers of sleet fly about the air like fine sawdust. I am longing for this weather to change. It is now five weeks that the temperature has been down to freezing point, and you know how cutting the NE wind can be in Guernsey.

My men at the cemetery could not stand the cold today. Their hands are covered with great chaps. I did not like even looking at them, I know how painful they can be. So I got them a bit of shelter and set them to cutting up those enormous elm roots. Some people are asking for the roots, but it was decided to give them to the poor.

Dr Jones has no fuel and is breaking up old sofas, stretchers and all the rubbish in his outside sheds.

I went down to Miss Lawton yesterday with a gardener who is going to plant her garden, under my supervision. She asked my

FEBRUARY 1942

advice, but I knew if left to her now Willie is in hospital for 12 weeks, she would never manage it. I told her she must expect to spend about £10 and get only £3 in return, but she realizes our position. £10 in your pocket is no good if you have no food. After I had started the man, I was glad to get out of the biting cold.

I can assure you Kit, I have found my Guernsey Frock most comforting these cold days, although Mrs Rowe and others say it is not becoming to me and doesn't suit me at all. They say I look like a fisherman. But Foster, when I wore it for the first time shouted out, *One of the good Old Timers!* which I thought a good expression.

Two funerals from the Asylum this week. They told me at the Greffe that there were 182 deaths in January and February. When I am at the Foulon tomorrow, I will go on to Mrs Godfray to save Elsie coming down. It's really too cold for her to make the journey.

Dr Jones came down here this afternoon, the first time he's ventured out for 6 weeks.

I hear that 1,200 tons of coal has arrived. It's time. Mr Bird had just 1 ton left. Our ration is now ½ cwt coal, ½ cwt coke per month. People with no gas get a little more.

I have just been listening in. What a lot of divided opinions in the House of Commons. I cannot understand what it all means. Some want ships, others heavy bombers, others dive bombers, others more fighters. It's all very bewildering. Now they say the construction of our wonderfully advertised battleships cannot stand up to the shelling that the Bismarck took. I am wondering if we will ever get it right. It sounds awful to outsiders listening. People here say the first 5 years will be the worse, so we have some hope!

I had been wearing the thin flannel shirts Flo and Ted sent me, then early in February I put on the thick flannel ones Kit had made for me while she was here. It was then I started wearing my Guernsey. I wear it with a stiff white collar and people say I look like a parson. I think I must, as a man in our choir who came to the door looked me up and down and then said, What are you going to read, the Lesson I suppose.

There are eight very large boats in the Town harbour with mast gear, derricks, wireless and what not, bridges and gun turrets. At St Paul's Church [now demolished] (by the Royal Court) there were crowds of men stacking wood, hard wood and tree stumps, high around it. You could hardly see the windows. I saw about 6 wagons and lorries taking rolls of barbed wire out of Dorey's coal store.

Sunday, March 8. I went to church as usual but we had a funny experience. During the singing of the first hymn, George Budge came up to the Rector. The Rector then said we would have to

MARCH 1942

curtail the service as the Germans were outside waiting to come in. He pronounced the Blessing and said the collection would be taken at the door.

Then about 50 Germans marched in. Mr Frossard introduced us (Churchwardens) to the Chaplain who spoke French well. Mr Frossard was in his element with his fluent French. The German organist played a voluntary while they put the red flag, the Swastika and the crucifix on the altar. The men had their prayer books and sang a hymn, to the tune, Sun of my soul. They sit down to sing.

There was some mistake. They had spoken of having a service once a month and were to give notice but this was not done.

I went to the Vale church yesterday. Inside the Common gates it's fenced off for hundreds of yards, and they have tons of wood and sections of huts all covered with material to represent grass.

This evening a German officer knocked on the study door and asked if I could supply a conveyance to take a body from Victoria Hospital (which they have been using as a Red Cross Hospital for months now) to Fort George at 12 noon tomorrow. He wanted only me and the hearse, they had the coffin, but asked if I would supply side handles. I said I had none to spare. It was like a dream why they should come to me. I immediately telephoned and was lucky to fix up the hearse.

Undated. I arrived at the hospital at 11.30 and found no one there. They had moved all their patients to the Vauquiedor Hospital. We waited till nearly 12. Then a nurse, an officer and others appeared, and they talked about Camarades. Then they asked me about wreaths. I said I had arranged with the officer yesterday that we would pick them up at the Caledonian Nursery. He looked relieved. Then the officer I saw last night came and apologised for being late. (He spoke fluent English.) I presented my bill and he paid me.

We collected eight wreaths, one a large and special one with a wide sash, at one end it had a white ground and a cross, at the other a white ground with the swastika.

At the Fort they brought out three stools and draped them to the ground with black material. Then they placed the coffin and covered it with a large red pall which looked more like a flag with the swastika in the middle. The big wreath was placed at the foot with the sash and ribbons well spread out and the emblems to the front. This was under a high wall facing S and was done, I think, for a photograph to be taken. (Some ceremony). I expect he was some big pot. The officer then gave me 3/- for the driver and we were discharged.

Undated. There are eight in my litter of rabbits. They are lovely. I wish Rosemary and Jane could see them.

MARCH 1942

I had my monthly letter to Jack back with his reply. I was glad to see his handwriting. Mary brought two RX messages, one from my brother Willie and his wife Winnie, and one from Rosemary. Mary took the answers. She brings the forms for me to sign (a great help). Rosemary must be tall, 41" at her age.

I took my old watches to Town this morning for repairs (if possible). I will then exchange them for tobacco. People here are almost selling their souls for smokes!

I hear there is a big German 'lot' here today. Planes are flying around. It's a long time since we have seen many. They are making this a proper fortress. Barbed wire is now to go around the Bridge railway and Church Lane. Dozens of coils are lying in the gateways. The Grandes Maisons quarry is a busy place. They are tunnelling all night and the blasting wakes me up.

Sunday, March 15. After lunch at the Doctor's I went to Mrs Godfray. Her German officer came in. He talks French well and that suits her. He had been up in his room entertaining three of his officers. He told me it was their big Remembrance Day of the fallen in the last war.

Monday, March 16. Today I had to go to Elizabeth College to see Inspector Hannibal for a permit for coffin material. I rang the front entrance bell twice. Then an officer just going to his car beckoned with his hand for me to go in the lobby door. Another chap made me go outside again and pointed to the bell. I said I was told to go in and pointed to the car which had not gone away, and the officer confirmed that. So I went in again and marched upstairs.

A girl interpreter informed me that the officer was not in and wanted me to return tomorrow, but I managed to fix it for the afternoon. I went and there were 2 other small builders there, and while waiting I saw a small picture of Napoleon on the deck of a ship, and over the desk a picture of Hitler.

The first man had no bother as it was for work for the Germans at Old Government House. The second man was told by the interpreter that she could not understand. He only wrote, to put up a fence between 2 gardens, no mention of what he wanted. Then she went on to my application and said, *That's the way* to write out a form. I thought, one up for J.C.S.! Then he took my form and signed it, and I went away happy till I got to the Piette, to find they were out of stock of most of what I wanted. Still, it's all in a day's work.

I lost my way coming out and found myself in the basement. It's unbelievable down there. Still, I got out without being challenged. It's distressing to see Elizabeth College occupied, especially remembering Speech Days of the past.

MARCH 1942

Tuesday, March 17. A lovely mild morning. Very pleasant dressing by daylight. For years now I've gone to bed in the dark. I generally listen to the 10 o'clock news, read till I'm tired, then pack off nice and warm.

An enormous anti-aircraft gun was being towed down New Road this morning. They have a 200 ton floating crane in St Sampson's harbour landing some very large engine from a barge. I mention these things as I think of them.

When in Town besides answering Kit's RX letter to Tom, I brought down a copy of one to Dr Jones from Flo. By the messages arriving you seem to understand our situation, which reminds me of the song, Sad, Oh sad, our situation. [I have been unable to trace this song.] But I hope not for many years.

We are now getting the outside ground planted with late potatoes, and I cut the dead wood from my loganberries.

Friday, March 20. A beautiful morning with a very heavy dew. The States men came to dig their half of my field.

Saturday, March 21. The first day of spring, the wind has gone to the NE again, and it's perishingly cold after a mild week.

Dean Giffard's wife has died and I went to the funeral at the Town Church. I know Kit would have liked me to go, because she knew the son in Toronto when she taught there [at the Bishop Strachan School] and she talked to Mrs Giffard about Canada. Not a lot of people there. I would have expected all the clergy and church-wardens of the island to have attended, but times have changed.

I wrote a letter of sympathy to the Dean and included you children in it.

Mary brought three RX letters from Flo, Rosemary and Mr Phelps [his tomato agent]. He says he hears from you occasionally. A very large number of letters has come this week.

Thursday, March 26. After a brilliant moonlight and calm night it was such a lovely spring morning that I was down before 8. Had an early breakfast of radishes and bread and scrape.

I now have most of the ground planted. We will need good crops this year, otherwise it will mean starvation.

There are now more orders in the Press. We have to take down the card at the door (THIS HOUSE OCCUPIED), and two other forms will be sent for us to fill in stating what rooms we do not occupy, and pinned as near as possible to the front door, so anybody calling can see what rooms are available. This is most unfortunate as I was rather well fixed up, my dining-room an office and one civil servant sleeping which does not inconvenience me too much, especially as Mrs Rowe does their cleaning, so the

APRIL 1942

kitchen and scullery are free for my use.

I have a Douzaine Meeting at 4 pm about the Budget, April 16. As I write this a heavy bombardment is going on in the upper parishes, planes passing over, I expect. I had to rush home from the Doctor's as it's dangerous with splinters of shrapnel dropping. I don't mention events of the war as you hear the same news on the wireless.

Wednesday, April 1. When we fix the new order forms with the list of rooms not used, I suppose if the rooms are wanted for billeting they will simply open the door and take what they want. All this is very trying, as at any moment we may have the house full.

I have not been to any of the special Lent and Passion Week services, just the choir practices. We have a nice anthem.

I bought Flowers for the altar in Town, and a nice bunch for Mrs Frossard (an Easter Egg). She was pleased.

Maundy Thursday, April 2. What a different atmosphere compared with the old days preparing for Church decorations. Mum would never miss primrosing on Good Friday, even if spring was late. Now all is changed.

Good Friday, April 3. It was a mild morning, cold air (the usual for Good Friday). I went to the 10.45 service, a fair number at church. I had the inevitable veg. and bean stew from the big saucepan. Still it went down well, but not *so* well. I expect I missed the fish and sauces that dear Mum prepared and the lovely boiled spuds, now unobtainable. It's two years now that I've missed Hot X Buns. We have made quite a lot of jokes about it.

Just as I was leaving for the afternoon service we had an April shower, consequently very few there. Made a difference of over 30/- to our collection. A costly shower for us.

I thought a lot about Mum today and primrosing. There are plenty this year. Now I am glad the day has passed. It's decorating in the morning, not the afternoon as arranged, because the Germans are holding a service at 2.30 instead of on Sunday, in order not to upset our arrangements.

I have killed the last fowl. I sold it to Major Hill for 20/-. Even that was cheap compared with ruling prices. The Press advertised fowls trussed and delivered ready for the table, 35/-.

Saturday, April 4. A nice April showery morning, but a warm sun. I went to Town, Savings Bank, tea ration and to see if my silver watches were ready. The Town looked awful except for lovely displays of flowers.

APRIL 1942

Shop windows were full of goods offered in exchange, mostly for food or tobacco. Some were even offering £4 for sovereigns, £3 for half sovereigns.

As I was passing down Trinity Square I heard a person (it was Miss Lamiot, you may remember her at the Post Office) saying, I cannot believe this is Guernsey. When I compare it with beautiful Guernsey of only a few years ago, it's really heart breaking.

I cycled between showers but Mary came down drenched.

Easter Sunday, April 5. I went to the 8.30 service, 65 attended. Then home to the empty house except for one German quietly sleeping upstairs. To compare it with the old days made me quite sad. No going through the hot greenhouses to see how the tomatoes were doing, then breakfast with Easter Eggs, and a nice breakfast.

I walked to morning service with Lily and Floss Mallett. They were somewhat gloomy and depressed. There was no Easter Sunday morning finery, nobody with new dresses and spring hats.

But I must say the church looked nice. My flowers looked lovely on the altar, and I thought of dear old Mum and how she used to worry if she had fixed them in good order. But there it is, the world still goes on, so I suppose we must not dwell on these past events too much.

They have a wireless now in the dining-room and have just turned it on. They are always in and out but don't bother me at all. So I don't complain, trusting they will not turn me out.

Easter Tuesday, April 7. A telephone message. Another death at the Asylum. What a lot die out there. I had to go to Mr Corbet, Hermon, as the relatives are in England and he was friendly with the family. I am getting a lot of running about as he knows so precious little about the people, but he doesn't want the States to bury her. I will probably arrange that the States pays the bill and the money will be recovered from the family when this awful war is over.

What upset me when I got home was that my telephone had been taken away, and I was informed they were fixing a military telephone in the dining-room. I managed to telephone all day, but tonight I am cut off and I don't know what this means. It will be impossible for me to carry on my business without the phone.

Saturday, April 11. Again bad luck. Two German officers and a civilian knocked at the door. The interpreter, who spoke English very well, introduced me to the officer, then said that according to the paper inside the lobby, I was the only person living in the house. I said, There is my housekeeper. But does she live here altogether, they asked. I said, No. He informed me they wanted 2 offices and I think they said a bedroom.

APRIL 1942

We went upstairs, looked in Jack's room. I opened the door of the dressing room, and the officer the door of the big bedroom. Then the spokesman asked, It's attics up there. I said, Yes, and downstairs we marched. In the hall they had a little discussion, then turned to me and said, We are afraid it won't suit (too small). Oh, what a reprieve! Then I began to imagine they would return later and tell me they would want the study and drawing-room for these new civil contractors.

I don't know if all this upset had anything to do with my little mishap, but on Friday morning I went to the Bridge feeling well. I chatted to Turner and W. Bird, they could have noticed nothing wrong, but when I got to Dredge he said, Good heavens, who's been hitting you in the eye! I took no notice, went on to the National Provincial Bank. When Frank Dorey saw me he said, Good heavens, what's the matter with your eye. He said it was so badly bloodshot that he could not see the eye at all.

I went home, looked in the glass. Well, it looked awful, so I went straight to Dr Jones who said I had broken a blood vessel, and one much larger than he had usually seen, and wrote me a prescription for a lotion.

Monday, April 13. I rested a little on Saturday and stayed at home on Sunday. Today Mr Frossard called, and when he saw it he was alarmed and insisted on getting a Doctor. My phone having gone he went across to the Manse to telephone.

Dr Fox came, and he also said it was a big vessel, and a blessing it was not over the brain. He took my blood pressure which was just above normal and he said nothing to worry about, and a sample of urine. He thinks the heavy weights I had lifted the day before, or cycling along the Banques in a gale helped to cause it. He said at my age I should not cycle up hills or ride in bad head winds.

Wednesday, April 15. I went to the Douzaine Room for a Parish Meeting at seven, passed my Churchwarden's Trésor a/cs before the Very Rev. the Dean. The parish accepted same, then a new Constable was elected, a Douzenier and other business. Mr Frossard walked home with me through the Robergerie because it was more sheltered for my eye in the cold E wind. When I go out I wear a shade over it.

Saturday, April 18. This week my men have been planting more of my late potatoes. Food is very scarce now. I don't know how some people manage. I am feeling fairly well but it is very difficult for me to manage without a telephone.

Mr Browell called. He helps at the Red Cross and Mary had told him about my eye. He was so hungry he asked for a couple of

APRIL 1942

potatoes. I had some freshly boiled ready to fry when Mary comes. I gave him a little meal on a tray, spuds, red beetroots and some of Kit's pickled onions. He did enjoy it and I also spared him a slice of bread and butter and a nice glass of special port, 1818 Vintage. I have been drinking a little lately to try to build myself up.

Mary came and we did the grave with white Tulips, Ornatus I bought in Town, lovely little Arum Lilies John Mahy brought me and Wallflowers, Forget-me-nots (beautiful) and Pansies from our garden. Mary took home a load of cabbages I got for her on the Bridge, and three nice broccoli from the field.

Tom came in last night and said he was starving. I gave him parsnips, leeks and turnips from my small stock, and a 1 lb loaf as I had a little to spare.

The Germans are tunnelling in Grandes Maisons Quarry, driving under Delancey Park, and carting all the stone on rails through Manuelles' fields, crossing the road through Carisbrook Vinery, then to Manuelles' cracking machine. The blasting is awful. Several tiles on the roofs of the Rectory and Dr Fox's house have been smashed already. It's dangerous passing along the road when they are blasting. They are also working the quarries at Bordeaux.

I had two messages again this week making four in two weeks. I am wondering how far Kit is from Flo. Not very far I think as she gives Rosemary lessons. It seems Jack is in Canterbury, but I don't know if in the Bank or Army. Will hear some day I suppose.

Sunday, April 19. Up at 8.30 after a sleep of nearly 9 hours. It's a lovely mild morning. Mrs Rowe was already cleaning the dining-room office and had my breakfast on a tray. Everything now is as silent as though we were in Sark. Erwin is dead to the world in Flo's room.

As I look out of the window I see the beech tree starting to unfold its long, pointed leaves. It seems only a few weeks ago I was writing to you about the same thing. I can't realize a twelvemonth has flown by already.

I can hear a company of Germans on the march singing. When I compare this with old times it seems we are in prison. I won't go to church though Mrs Rowe says my eye is clearer and I feel a little fresher. I had not intended to lunch at the Doctor's but he has just called and says Miss Matthews expects me.

In the afternoon I went to see Miss Lihou (it was so mild and fine and so lonely down here). I was glad I called as she wanted me to do some business for her. Then I went on to Mrs Godfray who was glad about the business as it will ease her sister's mind so much. I had a nice tea with fig jam and German sausage. Her officer has left for Granville in connection with Red Cross ambulances.

APRIL 1942

Monday, April 20. I have just been to the Bridge. I have never seen such a queue, from Hart's, the Chemist, they were 3 deep to Nocq Road. Along the pavement were hundreds of bicycles lying in piles, six and eight deep. The people were so anxious to join the queue that they just threw them anywhere, and all this for about 6d worth of egg powder.

The potatoes at Allendale are coming on, and I see the robin has got her young, three, one egg was not fertile.

I am now staying in, hoping the telephone people are coming to connect me up again. I have been two weeks without it.

I went out again to Miss Lihou about that business. I called to see Miss Houstoun. I am having the inscription on the gravestone for Auntie Edie and can then get the cross fixed up again. I wondered if Miss Houstoun could suggest some short epitaph, or one of Edie's short quotations. I took her some broad bean seeds. She has had her little lawn dug up and is planting haricots, etc.

Undated. I heard the Primate of all England, Archbishop Thomas Charles Temple, recorded from Canterbury Cathedral.

I don't think I told you about our police having stolen food from the German store. 18 were arrested including two sergeants. They have gone through their trial this week. (Papers April 20 - 24, 1942). Sentences vary from 4½ years to 1 month. Sergt Pill was acquitted. Steve Duquemin got 4 months for buying from them. It's an awful disgrace for the island and this game has been going on since 1939, before the German Occupation. They have lost their jobs, pensions, some had 20 years service. What fools!

Saturday, April 25. Since breaking the blood vessel in my eye the bloodshot has nearly gone. Mr Frossard called to see how I was.

Mary came down as usual. She suggested she ought to board here in case I might get an attack in the night. I think she is much better off staying with her boy friend's sister who, for his sake, will take a mother's interest in her. It would be most difficult as I am situated with the German billeted. I would be more tied as I could not leave her too much alone. Then I could not guarantee her regular meals as Mrs Rowe does not come till the afternoon. Then there is the distance travelling to Town in all weathers. Of course she offered to come for my good.

I spoke to Miss Houstoun about it and she thought it would add to my already strained anxieties. So I have agreed to stay alone for the present.

I am getting a fair amount of food. Had a lovely tea this afternoon, stewed rhubarb sweetened with sweetener and honey. Luckily I have a 1 lb jar. We get no sugar ration now, just occasionally a box of 200 pastilles of saccharine.

APRIL 1942

Sunday, April 26. It's 7 o'clock Sunday evening and lovely here with the sun pouring in. The beech tree is again unfurling its leaves and again there are dozens of sparrows picking something out of the leaves as they open.

I have had a nice quiet day. The house has been very still. Mrs Rowe made me a little cake and a milk pudding, quite a luxury these times. Only half ration of meat this week. I may kill a rabbit. I have 2 lovely nests, one litter I believe of 10 and one of 4. I've sold 4 at 2/6 each. Too cheap I am told, but I have too many now and at only 7 weeks old I think a good price.

Most people are now living only on green vegetables, cabbage, lettuce, radishes, no roots about yet. I don't know how people can live on such poor food.

I heard on the wireless this week, they are sending medical supplies via the Red Cross, and England is not forgetting the Channel Islands. I trust they will leave us alone for some little time yet. I also heard Sir Donald Banks' talk. Very nice. We can manage this summer. It's the winter that's the strain, so I am not worrying till it comes.

Sunday, May 3. It's about a week since I added anything to this noble work! And much has happened since.

Frank Mallett has been arrested by the Germans at his works on the Banques. He has been working for them, building and repairing all sorts of lorries. I hear he had a few words with one of them and showed his fists, hence the arrest. The girls are in a state.

Then a German doctor has been killed in Sark. Some say shot, some say with a coal hammer, some say by a Sarkee and others say suicide. I say I don't know! My father used to say, Don't believe anything you hear and only half of what you see, and the way reports go about here, it's about true.

I have been trying to prepare for next winter and have bought 3 huge stone carts condemned. They are made mostly of ash and elm, weigh 16 cwt mostly of iron of course, the axle about 2 cwt 20/- each. We towed them across the Bridge behind a trolley van. I also fetched 2 for Dr Jones and was given one over the bargain. I will be busy next week smashing them up on the Alliance path. The 6' wheels will take some smashing up.

It was Erwin's birthday on Thursday, April 30. I knew only when a German officer called at 8 in the evening with a bunch of tulips. Nobody was here and he asked me for a vase and water. He unlocked the dining-room door, waited a little, but nobody arrived so he left.

When Erwin arrived at 8.45 I told him about his caller, and he asked me in to drink his health. We had 2 glasses each of Peach Brandy, and he gave me 2 cigars. A lucky day for me as in the

MAY 1942

morning when we were doing his telephone, he gave me a 2 oz packet of tobacco.

It's lovely here in the hot sun and the quietest Sunday for weeks. Yesterday Mary brought me a RX message from Ted, Nov. 4. I am now reading The Pickwick Papers, C.D. very enjoyable.

The new potatoes have started, 1 lb per person per week at 3d per lb. Thank God I have a garden and had stored a little. I managed to get 2 of my men to help me in the garden one day. I throw all the weeds to the rabbits and they get rid of the lot.

Tuesday, May 5. We broke up one of the stone carts. Dr Jones came on the scene and helped us (I mean by giving instructions!) He advised me not to stoop too much. He noticed my veins were rather swollen as I worked. Don't stoop, they say. Then I say, you can't do anything. I cannot retire and have servants to wait on the ring-ting-ting!

In the afternoon I went to Mr Despointes and managed to get 3 pints of bean seed (lucky). I went through a lovely lane Mum and I passed down dozens of times in the old Ford. The heat rising from the ground, the lovely ivy-green hedges, the perfume, the coloured tulips in a field, the sound of hundreds of birds singing, with the lovely silence broken only by the bird sound and the humming of my bicycle as it went down the hill, all this filled me with sadness and happy recollections of the pleasure Mum and I took in such lovely Guernsey lanes. Then minutes after I was in the troubled world again.

Wednesday, May 6. It's a most wonderful still day, calm and burning sun. We are now worried at not getting any rain. Too dry to sow seeds. There seems to be no end to difficulties.

I managed to get 3 pints of bean seeds from my sister. It's all scrounging now. At the shops I got Tom Roberts 5 lbs peas 5/2 cabbages 1/5 and he was lucky to get these. I also managed to exchange for him a 2 lb loaf for a packet of cigarettes which cost 1/3.

Sunday, May 10. It's again a few days since I have written, and in that short time many things have happened, including Frank Mallett's trial. He is sentenced to 12 months' imprisonment. It seems to me very stiff. I believe he can appeal and if successful the sentence might be reduced to 3 months and a fine of £500.

Yesterday I went to Mrs Godfray with my carpenter to cut down a clothes chest by 7" for her German officer. He was very pleased we did not damage the chest. He gave us a nice soup lunch and kept us going with cigarettes. I charged him 3/- and he gave me 5/3.

Mary brought me another RX message from Ted in which he

MAY 1942

invites me to La Hougue. I have told him it's difficult to transplant old trees. I think I must finish up my course here.

On the whole I have had a very good innings, good health, worked hard, and except for Mum dying so soon I would not complain at all. All things being considered I feel I must bow to the inevitable and leave my bones here with Mum. After all I have lived my life and must be content. I see others around me who have not been nearly so fortunate. I would like to have been with all of you, but this war has made it impossible.

Poor Tom Roberts has herpes (shingles) on his face. He looks awful and it's very painful. Over 50% of the people here have had an attack on some part of their body, due I suppose to poor food. I gave my 1 lb. potato ration to Tom with a few parsnips and onions.

I have just had another picnic in the garden, five of the baby rabbits and the mother out. A blessing there were no cats about. It was amusing to see the little devils let me get quite near, then scamper away jumping sky high, and then look around to see if I was after them. I managed to catch some in a barrel with tempting food. In they went, I lifted up the barrel and they were trapped. The mother was easy to catch she is so tame. What bothered me was the quiet rain falling, but I did not curse it as it is wanted badly.

A meagre feed at the Doctor's today, just a few new spuds and 2 fried eggs between the three of us. I will listen to the Prime Minister's talk tonight. I hope he has heartening news for us. People now seem a little impatient, but they all find time flies like smoke. I think it's getting the news four times a day makes it pass quickly.

Monday, May 11. I have lent your cousin, Vernon Le Maitre, the following music, Hora Novissima, Last Judgment, King Olaf, Flag of England, Israel in Egypt and Songs of Hiawatha. I have taken the piano down to Cliffdale.

Sunday, May 17. I have had a rather upsetting week. Three of my large does have been stolen, one in kindle due next week, my old favourite whose litter of eight I had about eight months ago and now in kindle due in 2½ weeks, and another nice doe. They left only two mothers with nine and seven young, and two babies about 10 weeks old. It is very upsetting.

It will be impossible to keep anything in the big garden now. They even go into the greenhouses and rake up the potatoes before they are come. I feel almost certain I will lose the lot in the Greenhouse at Allendale. I should dig them in 3 week's time, but people advise me to dig them now. But what's the use. They are not half come.

It's easy to see how they climbed over the wall from the Alliance Vinery. The ground is trodden and it looks like sabot marks. We

MAY 1942

have a terrible lot of Frenchmen living on Delancey. We are not allowed out after curfew, nor are our police.

It's impossible to find out and there's no way of tracing the thieves. Then they are devilish hungry. Only yesterday I saw 2 foreigners coming from the Bridge with lettuce, and they were eating all the outside leaves, brownish and not even washed, and I often meet them along the road eating cabbage leaves. We will soon be nearly as bad!

I am now just finishing my old potatoes. I managed to eke them out well, and I still have a few parsnips. I gave away a dozen last week, Tom etc., and I still have a large swede that cost 1/-.

Mrs Rowe made me my usual barley cake mixed with all sorts, chocolate beans (at least the husks) ground, she stewed me rhubarb with sweetener, and made a rhubarb tart and a little milk pudding. I just mention these things that you might know that I am not among the worse fed, (poor devils).

The police came and took all particulars, meansurements of foot marks, value of lost rabbits, but there is no hope of ever tracing the culprits. I notified them only so that they may know what robberies are taking place.

Monday, May 18. This morning I went to tell Walter Lake to be careful. He told me to look into his rabbit hutch. It was empty. His were only nine weeks old.

Today Tom started cutting down Miss Lihou's trees in Vauquiedor Hill. On my way there I took a huge bunch of Lilac to Mrs Le Poidevin at the Hunkins. They insisted on my staying to tea and made me eat 2½ slices of bread and butter, a rock bun, and I drank 3½ cups of *Real Tea*. What a treat, and they made me take home 2 buns. I did not like eating their ration till they assured me they had plenty, so I enjoyed a good fill.

Miss Naftel was at Miss Lihou's. Her brother's loss was far worse than mine. He has had 20 fowls stolen in three months at different times. I then popped in to see Mrs Godfray. I am glad I did for her German officer gave me a packet of 20 Virginia cigs, La Surfine de Qualité, and I am enjoying them as I write this.

I am sparing him ½ lb of best coffee, 1 tin Lyons coffee, 1 small tin of concentrated coffee in exchange for sugar. He said he would give me cigarettes as well. I can spare it as the coffee we now get I like as much, but he is a faddist.

Yesterday on the Bridge I noticed everyone gazing. It was a bull harnessed to a van with a yoke, as in the old days. I don't think such a thing has been seen there for over 50 years.

It's a sight sometimes to see the Germans carting furniture from place to place. I saw a huge lorry going up the Vauquiedor with a lovely drawing-room suite, upholstered easy chairs, and 4 Germans

MAY 1942

sitting one in each. They looked so comfortable. They waved and laughed at me as they flew past.

May, undated. It's pouring with rain again this morning. I think we have had enough now.

The Essential Commodities Board have thought fit to give us a double ration of tobacco for Whitsun week, 5/8½d. Not much if you say it quickly! I must lock half up for next week, otherwise I will puff it all before Whit Monday. There is little else to do but smoke, wonder, sleep and a little work. Still, we are all keeping up fairly well. We are getting 2½ lbs potatoes per person this week.

June 5 nearly round again, three years poor Mum has been dead and I have been alone practically the whole time. Being the war period I think has made it easier to bear, with no outings, and I have been better by myself. Out of kindness people ask me out, but I am better alone, except of course for our family circle which you must know I have missed very much.

I think it was all for the best that Kit went off. I have been able to manage quite well. Mrs Rowe keeps my table linen, such as I use, and my bed linen nice and clean. My manners will be lost. Sometimes I compare my meals with the way they were served by dear Mum. All that I have missed very much, especially the quality of the food. Still, all here are determined to try to stick it out till we meet again, which I hope won't be too long coming.

Tom has just called. He looks a sorry sight with shingles all over his chin and lips, but it is clearing very quickly. At least 30% of people have had a dose. My man Martel, is laid up, weak. The doctor says malnutrition. The food, mostly cabbage, does not suit him.

I am going into another enterprise. I have taken Mrs Winterflood's shop on the corner of New Road and Brock Road, a cheap rent and perhaps I was silly, but Lily Ellis wanted a job. We call it her shop and it will sell vegetables, second-hand clothing or anything else. I think I will try and sell lots of things I have here.

This afternoon I heard that Erwin, the chief, is going away tonight for about four weeks. His lady clerk, in hospital for two months, came out for two hours (special) this afternoon as it's her 21st birthday. She lives in Brock Road and came and told Mrs Rowe. The new man, who speaks a little English, will not sleep here, so I will be quiet and can lock the house at 11 pm.

I don't know why Erwin is going. Mrs Rowe says his clothes are left in his bedroom as usual. I thought something was strange, for he and another man were in the dining-room till 2 am and there were lots of movements this morning. The fireplace was piled with rubbish and papers, and the sideboard and drawers cleaned up.

The sun is shining beautifully as I write this. There are lots of

MAY 1942

details I don't care about mentioning now, as we never know if these books will get straight into your hands.

My ration this week was pork which I boiled with the usual 7 vegetables. I had the fat on my bread which saved my butter. I enjoyed it but very likely I would have refused it a few years ago.

Tom has just been to a funeral. The wife of his district foreman, Brimage, had twins at the Emergency Hospital and died 8 hours afterwards. (Lack of nourishment I suppose). The babies are alive.

Saturday, May 23. I went to see Ted Ogier, Duvaux about a job he wants done. Mary came and brought three RX messages from Flo, Kit and Jack. I understand by Kit's message that Jack must be in the army (Looking very smart). Mary had a nice tea, fried potatoes (the last old ones), stewed rhubarb and (an extra treat this week) rice pudding.

Whit Sunday, May 24. I went to my sister's this afternoon and inspected their allotments. They are also working a lot of ground over at Bill's brother's greenhouses. The boys only bake 3 days a week, and by working this land and the greenhouses they are able to keep their two men employed all the week and sell their surplus vegetables in the baker's shop.

They made me stay to tea, an invitation I did not refuse! They have more bread than I have. Minnie fried some Ray fish, and we finished up with rhubarb cake.

I got to church just in time, a rush after a heavy meal. Still, I did not have to sing the solo in the anthem! The church was crowded, £4.12.0 collection, and a really nice Whitsunday service. Mr Frossard made special prayers for absent relatives and friends, at which you know he always excels.

There is quite a noise with buses at the Schools and hundreds of Germans with their packs. They are leaving here tonight.

Whit Monday, May 25. Came down at 9 o'clock to unlock in case the German who is taking over might have to come today. He did not. It's blowing half a gale from the Southard, dull and cold. I think I will stay in and do a little office work.

I will get my dinner of new spuds, new peas, a 1/- tin of lobster and some rice pudding. I don't think anybody's got rice (I have).

It poured with rain all the afternoon, and now at 6 o'clock the rain is driving under the fan lights, the wildest Whit Monday I have ever known. I have just finished a lovely tea with half a dozen cups of *Real* tea, (Typhoo which Kit left in the kitchen cupboard mixed with China I found on the mantle shelf.) I get this treat about once a month.

I didn't eat lobster for dinner. I'll keep it in case I get shorter

MAY 1942

of food. I look at each tin about half a dozen times before I open it, then often put it back in the cupboard. Not that I deprive myself of food, but I had a good day yesterday feeding at my sister's, so thought it wise not to be extravagant.

It's now beautifully silent. Not having anybody in and out is like old times. Since October I've had company here, which of course I'd rather have done without. The States pay me £3 17s.6d. per month for my lodger and the dining-room, but I'd rather do without it if I could.

I have had a most enjoyable Whit Monday (under the condition we are living in). When I reflect back to 3 years ago I just say, Now the day is over, Night is drawing nigh, Shadows of the evening steal across the sky. I say, thank God those years have passed, and perhaps better days are before me. Mr Frossard always preaches that the darkest shadows are just before the dawn.

I had Grandma West's stone cross fixed up and Edith's inscription cut in the stone. I couldn't think of a suitable epitaph, and the lines Miss Houston suggested that Edith quoted were too long. So I just put, *At Rest,* as the poor girl never was the last years of her life. The job cost £3 5s.0d. and now I think my duty is completed.

Mrs Frossard told me she had had a RX message from Flo and was very pleased. I hear the machine running where the Germans are tunnelling both ends of Bisset's quarry, Grandes Maisons. They work day and night, Sundays and all.

Tuesday, May 26. As I slept on the couch this afternoon heavy rain woke me up. After it had steadied Mrs Rowe arrived and found my bedroom flooded. I had forgotten to close the windows. She had to bring down sheets, bolster, pillow. I think she was cross, but I soon got a blaze going. She wanted me to sleep in Erwin's bed, but I declined.

Thursday, May 27. Rain on Wednesday too, and still blowing half a gale though the sun is shining. The broad beans, potatoes etc. in the field are weather-beaten. I hope the apple trees haven't suffered too much. I can hear the buglers on the Park (practising, I think).

I had two RC messages today by post, Flo, 24 Jan. 1942. I rang Violet to order a present for Kitty Head's baby, but she has no material and her eyes are bad, so she cannot help. Kit's, 10 Feb. 1942, Jack lucky, she writes, no need for anxiety.

S. Ogier has just telephoned. He is bringing me some new spuds, lucky again. I cannot complain, something always turns up for me. And I got 4½ lbs granulated sugar in exchange for my coffee, not bad I suppose.

MAY 1942

Saturday, May 30. The May tree in the field is only now opening its bloom.

Mr Frossard came in last night to tell me to be early for church in the morning as the Germans would be having a service at 11.30. He told me that the Rev. Greenhow who is ill has just received a RX message to say that his only son was killed in action. He was in the Air Service and only 21.

I met Angelo Clarke in Town and he told me that Jackie had been wounded in Crete. He has had no news since. He also said he was running a sweep for the Derby, June 13th, and as I always like a flutter I got a ticket, 1 mark (2/-) to win £50. My number is 1301. 13 is lucky for me (sometimes).

I have written a letter of sympathy to the Rev. E.H. Greenhow. I've had a lot to do with him this winter as he is the Chaplain of the Vauquiedor Mental Home.

Sunday, May 31. I managed to get a lobster yesterday, 2/- not very full. A fair sized one costs 10/- The cocoa we get is gritty and takes a lot of sugar, but as we say here, Better than nothing. Mary told me that ladies' stockings (French) were 10/- per pair 6 months ago and today 18/-. Most women (and some pretty old) go without.

I saw two ladies struggling up Amherst with their loads in black bags. They had evidently been in the country lanes breaking up branches of trees for kindling. It was obvious they were people not accustomed to that work. All day long you see women struggling with their packs of vegetables, and struggling it is. Some have to rest on the road.

I got 6 lbs of extra spuds for Mary, 6 lbs for Tom. I will send a few to Mr Browell. Mary says he is half starved. He buys peas in the Town and eats shucks and all. People in boarding houses were badly off enough before the war, with the damned old grabbers. Now it's much worse.

There should have been a law to imprison hotel keepers who overcharged and underfed their boarders, and then prevent them from opening again for 10 years. It's the only cure. I've been to picnic houses with just 4 people and had a nice reasonable tea. Then when I went later with double the number, they tried to get away with the same amount of milk, bread and butter, etc.

Monday, June 1. What exciting news on the wireless all day yesterday. Now it's June, all I dread is that soon the days will shorten. Still, I won't bother till they do. It's been a real June day, mild with sunshine, all that could be desired.

I got an early telephone call from the Constables calling us to the Douzaine Room this afternoon, because it's Mr P.J. Ogier's Golden Wedding. Being the Dean of the Douzaine, we had decided

JUNE 1942

to give him a cheque for £20.

So we met, two Constables and 11 Douzeniers and all trailed into the Muriaux (as you know his house is next to the Douzaine Room). His daughters and only son were there. It was 4 o'clock and they had callers, Mrs Mimmie Ogier, Mrs A.A. Upham, Mr and Mrs Romeril from the Manse next door to me and others I did not know.

The Constable made a little speech and presented the cheque. Mr F. Higgs also spoke, then Mr Ogier tried to thank us but broke down. We had some wartime biscuits made with barley flour and wartime minerals, awful stuff.

That job over I went to the Vauquiedor. Tom was just leaving work. The trees are down and have to be cut into smaller pieces. It's tons of timber and such heavy wood, evergreens, oak and beech. I am hoping to have a little.

On my return Lily Ellis was waiting for me. We expect to open the shop on Friday. It will be difficult to collect vegetables at first, but things will regulate themselves.

Stafford rang up to say he's had a message from Flo. They were delighted especially as Flo mentioned that I'd spent Xmas there. You seem to be worrying about our welfare.

We are comfortable, have enough food, but not enough good milk or sufficient fats. I still managed to eat vegetables, I suppose being hungry, although I cannot say I ever feel *very* hungry. We are losing weight, I have lost 20 lbs and feel tired with little exertion, and cycling is tiring.

Tuesday, June 2. It is early morning, lovely and still with blue skies and a golden rising sun. I am writing this by the open windows.

I have a Douzaine Meeting this afternoon to discuss the Budget Report in the Billet d'Etat from June to December 1940, 6 months Occupation Expenses.

Airport	£11,946	13s.	1d.
Food	£18,511	7s.	1d.
Quarter's Upkeep	£13,141	11s.	6½d.
Refreshments	£ 8,614	15s.	1d.
Transport	£30,081	6s.	5d.
Hotel Expenses	£ 6,506	16s.	4d.
TOTAL ON ALL ITEMS	£108,266	2s.	7½d.

I think I would have left out the ½d.

I don't know how Guernsey will pay. We have the Sales Tax which brings in 1/8 in the £1. Rationed food is not taxed.

JUNE 1942

Wednesday, June 3. Mary called for the new potatoes I had promised her. Unfortunately, the man had not yet brought them (Gigands) so I spared her some of mine. She enjoyed a little snack of dry bread and stewed rhubarb.

I moved the rabbits from near the wash house (as liquid was leaking from the hutches staining the cement and would soon cause a smell) and put them against the back wall. They are more exposed for robbers there, but the best I can do.

I am writing this in the garden and the calm, the glorious sunshine and blue sky make one feel that perhaps life is worth living.

I have been to the Bridge to have my hair cut. It was getting long, especially for bathing which I hope to start soon. Gooseberries were priced 2/6 per lb. Just then the price shocked me, but I am recovering and I think I will get some to mix with rhubarb. I have a nice lot in the field, but will wait till they are fully grown.

Most of the Germans have gone from around here, I hope for ever. They are practically gone from the Church Schools and from Dr Jones' garage and stores, and I hear Mr Cross can have his house back after 12 months.

The red and white pinks (that sounds funny) are in bloom. I will put some on Mum's grave on Friday.

I noted in this account that most of our Police Force had been charged with stealing food from the Germans' food store, and were sentenced. Now the same Force has been charged with stealing from our civil stores ever since war began. The Bailiff, when passing sentence, gave them a good dressing down. See Star June 2, 1942.

Thursday, June 4. Again a most beautiful morning. Real June summer, a heat wave. I was up with the lark. Had a lot to arrange for the opening of the new vegetable shop tomorrow. Had to send scales, baskets, flower boxes, ledgers, books, pencils, ink, cash box and I gave Lily Ellis £25 in cash to start paying for goods, as it's all cash jobs. I always seem to start everything on the so-called unlucky Friday. Hence my luck perhaps.

A company of German soldiers passed going towards Town, singing as usual. Near Potter's corner they were on their side (right now), a very large lorry was turning the corner from Town when a small blue car going towards Town tried to cut in and went crash into the lorry. I saw a crowd and heard a lot of shouting but did not go up. (My policy, keep away). I don't know if anybody is hurt.

I have just been to my sister and managed to cadge 2 lbs of good flour and a loaf, something extra to carry on with.

Friday, June 5. It's Friday, the eventful June 5th. Three years ago

JUNE 1942

today, 1939, on a lovely morning such as we are having today, you will remember how we rushed out to St Martin's to hear the sad news. Well, they say we must look forward and not reflect on the past, but that's impossible.

I took lovely pink Roses with many Pinks and lovely blooms from our garden and put them on Mum's grave. They looked very nice with the white and purple Stock and Sweet William and Mignonette plants.

Saturday, June 6. Another perfect day. I bought a large lobster for Mrs Godfray, 8/9 cooked it and took it out this afternoon in the sweltering heat rising from the tarred roads. My face was quite burnt but I did not get too hot.

Mary came as usual. After tea and the news we went to the grave. Most of the roses had almost died, such is the heat under that high wall. We put more flowers, cut the grass and it looked well. I told Mary that 3 years ago tomorrow June 7th, the patch of grass around was a mass of wreaths and crosses.

Sunday, June 7. I heard in the vestry that we are to have our wirelesses taken away for good. It quite upset me to think that we won't know how the war is going.

Monday, June 8. Oh, what devilish news! It's only too true, we are to lose our wirelesses. The Constable rang me up. We have to meet tonight to make arrangements for receiving them. We have 3 depots, Fountain Lodge (where I am stationed), Braye du Val (Commander Giffard's house), and Glenbrook, Les Effards. Tom Roberts and his pal are night watchmen till the 17th. I am lucky, my initial is well down the alphabet, so I will have mine till the 16th. This was the only comfort.

Tuesday, June 9. Just back from Fountain Lodge, Vale Road, taking in wireless sets. Only 21 today. I expect people think they can keep them till the 17th, but they will have to come according to their initial. There is a notice in the Press about this, and that the Germans are calling them in purely for military reasons.

We are getting plenty of lovely peas now, and 5½ lbs of new potatoes per person per week. I have plenty and spared Mary 5 lbs and often oblige Tom. I had plain cooked peas and spuds mashed together and they were very nice.

Mary and Evelyn are coming to tea on Friday. Mary is on holiday and has been rather poorly this last week.

It's pathetic to watch the people bringing their wireless sets. Some are on little low trolley carts packed in sheets, shawls, curtains, old men carrying theirs, girls, all varieties of shaped

JUNE 1942

people in all manner of shabby dresses and suits, some sunburnt nearly brown working in the greenhouses with no shelter (as formerly) of tall tomatoes.

A German came into Fountain Lodge tonight wondering what we were doing there. They had evacuated the house some weeks ago but had kept the key and used to return for a bath. I expect he felt baulked tonight, but he did not give up the key. The lock has gone to have another fitted!

I am writing this on the couch in the study looking at the Orange Blossom tree against the ivy wall. It's a mass of bloom and the scent is lovely. The Pinks etc. are nice, the lawn awful, grass 12" high. My rabbits have a tempting view.

Wednesday, June 10. This morning I went to Fountain Lodge, but they were a bit quiet so I went on to St Andrew's with the necessary, and took them a few potatoes.

Miss Lawton called at 2 on her way to the doctor. Her brother is still in hospital but losing weight all the time since his accident. They are afraid he has a malignant growth. She feels certain he won't get better. They talk of an operation. I don't think he could stand it.

I am doing all the listening in I can before the 16th. After that we won't know how the war is going. I dread to think of it. I know the time will be dreadfully long.

Mrs Rowe made me a milk pudding and stewed some rhubarb with 1/2 pint of gooseberries I bought at the (my) shop, 2/- per pint. I had a spider crab and don't suppose I would have eaten one before the war. Now I suppose I would eat anything. Still we are a long way from starving yet.

I am listening to the enthronement of Bishop Garbeth, York Minster, as Lord Archbishop, the knocking, the Induction, the fanfares, then O be joyful in the Lord (a lovely setting). Inducted, Installed and Enthroned, I should say with that language he is well placed in the chair. In the sermon he mentions the Occupation of the Channel Islands. The BBC promised support in a nice wind up.

I had a fright this afternoon. Simon phoned from the shop that I must go down quickly, most important. When I got there 2 Germans were surveying Manuelles' stores, which are part of the block where my shop is. They asked to see upstairs, but I told them it was my workshop. They looked around and asked if I knew of any empty houses. I did not, and then to my relief they went off. I hope I don't get many of these shocks.

Friday, June 12. Yesterday was as cold as any winter's day, with wind and rain half the night. I was obliged to get up and put more clothes on the bed. I have nasty rheumaticy pains in my head this

JUNE 1942

morning, and it is so cold I have lit the fire, fancy, in mid June.

Mary and Evelyn came and I showed them round the vinery and field. I picked the rhubarb and when the gas came on at 5 o'clock, Mrs Rowe cooked it with the goosegogs, and as I had some milk actually made custard, a treat. The girls quite enjoyed their tea, brought their own bread and butter, and I supplied extra bread but little butter.

Mary left early as she has to work at Le Lacheur's tonight. Then Mr Frossard called for me to sign cheques, chatted with Nurse, and we all murmured about losing our wirelesses.

I was glad to hear the running commentary of the 2,000 guineas Royal Oaks, the King's horse first. I can hear the officer whistling in the dining-room.

Saturday, June 13. Everybody asks everybody else, What's the news.

Sunday, June 14. I was the only one in the vestry this morning still holding a wireless. My initial is not due till Tuesday. I dread to think how we shall get on then. We will get the German version of the news on the front pages of the Press and Star and we may judge from their reports.

I am having a quiet afternoon pottering in the garden. I think my rabbits like Sundays, they get about 20 feeds. As I roam about the garden I find tempting little snacks.

I see an advertisement in the paper for some sick person, 'Apple Fancy'. I think I will spare the poor devils 1 lb. whoever they are.

I have been listening to the march past of all the Services before the Kings and Queens, Ambassadors and Ministers of Europe to celebrate American and Empire Day, the United Nations in the name of the British Commonwealth. Very inspiring. There must have been thousands in the Mall.

Monday, June 15. Went to Fountain Lodge in the evening. Then called on a friend, had a chat and smoked some local tobacco, very nice. Brought home a 3 lb pot of jam (rhubarb, etc.) and some tobacco plants. Heard the news, not too good in Libya. I am nice and quiet here at present, all alone.

Tuesday, June 16. I got up with a heavy heart, the last day for my wireless. 8 o'clock news not good. Tobruk considered serious.

I went to the Rohais to pick a 40' spar for S.T. Ogier for a flagstaff. He seems to be getting ready! I dread to think of the days passing without any war news. Time will be very long now.

Wednesday, June 17. This afternoon the Rector brought me a letter he wished to read to the choir. There is a little friction, a lot of

JUNE 1942

piffle, a storm in a tea cup. At practice I managed to pacify them, but not in the way I would like to have. However for once I managed to bridle my tongue, only for the Rector's sake. I sent my wireless in tonight. That concerned me far more than these petty quarrels.

Thursday, June 18. Was down before 8. No wireless to turn on. It's just awful to feel that I cannot know what is happening. My only consolation this morning Messervy brought me a tobacco ration, 1 oz. tobacco, 1 packet cigarettes, 5/-. What a price. Still, I must have something to break the monotony.

Sunday, June 21. After Morning Service we ran over the anthem for tonight's Recital. The friction surfaced again. Mr Frossard got quite upset, and told them their attitude was not that of a Christian spirit, and made them kneel down and recite prayers after him. They all came in the evening and we had a successful Recital. (Collection £15) We decided to give it all to the Children's Fund.

The Star has collected over £1,000. Some people don't agree with it. They say the parents should have sent their children with the schools. Others complain that it helps the parents of these children to get what they otherwise could not have, and also ask if the children get it at all. Of course it's safe with boots and clothing, with foodstuffs it's another question. I am neutral because I don't know, but I think more of these children should have been evacuated with the schools.

Monday, June 22. A depressing day after the news of Libya. To think we held Tobruk for 8 months, and that last convoy fought their way down with the Fleet Air Arm, and then, through lack of something, the Army cannot hold these places. I cannot understand what's the matter. I was obliged to stay in most of the day and then our spirits seem to flag.

Wednesday, June 24. I went to bed as usual, then at about 12 o'clock, when I was dead asleep, I heard noises downstairs so I rushed on the landing and called out, Who's there. I could not see anybody but a German shouted something and I knew by the voice it was Erwin. He rushed upstairs, shook hands and said something I did not understand. So after exchanging a few words which he did not understand, I went back to bed.

Erwin went into the dining-room and woke me again when he came up to bed at 1 o'clock. I never shut my bedroom door so consequently hear every sound.

He was off before seven, came back later and gave me a 2 oz packet of tobacco, London Shag from Holland, so the packet stated, 50 grams. He came from Granville on the same boat as

JUNE 1942

Mrs Godfray's officer. He was away 32 days.

Oh, what a fright I have just had. A thrush has flown in my study window. I could see something coming over my head, bent down quickly and the blooming thing flew around and out again. The damned thing made me jump, my legs are still tingling. Nice news after I told you I had good nerves! It's just awful without our wirelesses.

I am amused to hear of RX messages sent. My Cossar gone, Nothing from Lydell or Belfrage lately. We miss Pye, not apple [Names of Newscasters and make of Wireless]. Dining-room window empty, hope you and the Yanks here for Christmas. No teeth left, stone deaf, nearly blind and crippled with rheumatism. Otherwise all merry and bright.

More choir trouble. I had decided to call a meeting here in the study, but after telling the Rector of my decision to try to clear this up, we decided it will be at the Rectory. I thought of this meeting in order to let them have full freedom to vomit up what's in their bellies, trusting it might choke one or two. If this doesn't clear the air they can all go to the devil and I trust never come back. I took more cheek for the Rector's sake than I intend to take again. Rule with the iron rod and take the consequences is the best way when commanding a ship. Sometimes they get wrecked, but you can always repair, and often they're then stronger. In other words, no damned nonsense.

End June - Beg. July. The meeting was well attended, and although there were faults on both sides, the choir heard some home truths, and I hope were not too thick-skinned to take it all in. I must say the Rector did not spare them. It's now arranged that the Senior Choir will receive an apology which in my estimation amounts to nothing.

Now to more sensible talk. Mary came on Saturday. I gave her some taters I am digging in the greenhouse at Allendale, a fair crop. Jehan, who lives next door, told me that someone pulled up all his outside potatoes planted only 2 months before, and Freeman next door had his stolen. So I expect to have all my outside lates stolen. If this game is not soon stopped we will have no lates for our winter store.

Wednesday, July 1. I went to Mrs Godfray with Messervy to ease her gates and alter a box for her German officer. The job was not half done when I was wishing I had told him it could not be done. It was an awkward job but we managed it and he was pleased. I took my lunch out.

Practice in the evening. All the choir turned up in force now the trouble is over.

JULY 1942

Mr Stubbs has had an operation for hernia at the Country Hospital. Tom Ozard is very ill with pleurisy.

I have been watering my vine in the ¾ span. It has its first grapes, a heavy crop of nice bunches which Mrs Rowe thinned.

Thursday, July 9. It's now some days since I have added anything. There have been many happenings, some I will not write about but will hope to tell you later.

They took Tom Ozard to the Emergency Hospital where he died on Monday. His funeral was today. I was a mourner being first cousin, but as he was a choir member I sat in the choir. There was a large attendance. The surpliced girls' choir met the cortège at the gate. As the hearse arrived German horse-drawn wagons were passing, a strange scene. A very impressive service. Mr Frossard gave a brief survey of his life as a church follower and always in the choir. There were 50 wreaths.

Mr Browell has just called. He is always half starved. I managed to give him a 1 lb. loaf. He said it was a godsend. Mrs Rowe fried him some potatoes and I gave him a few to take back. I have a big crop of earlies so could spare him some.

The Germans are fixing rails from the White Rock to St Sampson's. I went to Elizabeth College again yesterday for a permit for timber. It is heartbreaking to see the old College. I had to sign my name before I went in. The officer was out so I had to go again in the afternoon, and had to wait 1½ hours. I then went on to St Andrew's.

Poor Elsie's lovely spaniel, Goldie, was killed yesterday, run over by a car. They were terribly upset, did not sleep all night. Even the German Officer cried, he was so attached to him. He took Goldie out in his car every day and has always had the dog's meals sent ever since he lived there. He offered Elsie £20 but she would not sell him.

I hear most people have to give up their bicycles and sewing machines. Unless a man lives over 3 miles from his work, he will have to give up his bicycle.

Sunday, July 12. I had a hectic Sunday last week, July 5, which I won't forget in a hurry, full details of which I will explain to you if ever we meet again.

The Boss brought a joint of meat which he asked me to cook, also salt and bread. They invited a few civilians and a soldier and officer to partake of a cooked meal at 7.30. Mrs Rowe agreed to cook it.

They brought a barrel of beer, fixed it on two of my stools in the garden, brought cigarettes, chocolate etc. and said at first for 5 people. But by 5 o'clock there were 8 and when I got back from church there were 12. The table was laid in the dining-room (their

JULY 1942

office). They wanted salad which I picked in my garden.

Then they fetched bottles of champagne. You never saw anything like it. They danced on the cement paths to music from a wireless they brought. This went on till dark when they took the barrel of beer into the drawing-room.

Then at 1 o'clock they were hungry and I had to cut the remainder of their bread. The officer plastered on the butter and slices of tomatoes on top, theirs and all mine, standing at the kitchen table. Although half asleep I was thinking what you would have thought if you could have popped in just then. They told me to take some beer if I wanted it so I had it next day, lovely Lager. I smoked all night, but although they tried, I did not drink anything but beer for my supper. Of course they wanted me to go to bed, but I was not leaving them the run of the house.

The civilians who came with their wives did not know where they were going and were annoyed to see the inconvenience to which I was put and apologised. I don't know what the Carpenters opposite thought of the noise, the singing and shouting. This went on till 2.30 when they decided to drive them home.

The car would not start and I guess Mr Romeril next door did not get much sleep. At last they got off only to be stopped on the Bridge, and the car taken from them. They came back here. The officer went down to see if he could put things right, but he could not as the chauffeur had no permit and, worst of all, was not allowed to have civilians in the car.

The ladies stayed with me in the study, the men in the drawing-room drinking until 5 o'clock when curfew allowed them to go. The others slept in the dining-room till 7.30, then went off.

After the 'Ball'! I wish you could have seen the broken glass outside. I don't know how many bottles of champagne they opened, but they let one fall on the cement and it smashed to atoms. They broke 6 or 8 glasses, 4 of mine. I showed them the state of the carpet and they said they would get me another, but that's as far as it will go. It had about 50 empty cigarette packets about the floor.

It's a good thing it takes a lot to frighten me or I would have gone mad. I did not feel very fit the next day having been up all night and smoking so much. I hope we will meet one day and I will give you the story in detail. Erwin tells me he is going to bring me a bit of beef in eight days (perhaps).

Now further developments. Erwin got up at 6.15 yesterday morning and went off at 8 o'clock. He came back with a soldier (who was at the party on Sunday) and asked Mrs Rowe for me. I was still in bed so he asked her if she could get a bed ready for their chief who had just come from Jersey and had been very ill during the crossing (it is blowing hard). She said he could have Jack's room and got it ready.

JULY 1942

I soon got up when I heard the talking. They went off before I got down, but he left me 3 cigars. He came later, very pale, and got up at 1.30. He came to sleep again tonight and I don't know how long he will stay.

Fancy me paying 1/3 per lb for tomatoes. Logans and raspberries are 6/- per lb, peaches 1 mark (2/-) cucumbers 1/6 peas and beans 1/- and cabbage 4d per lb including outside leaves and stump. Greenhouse grown carragean moss sells at 3d per oz. I have managed to get a small lobster, 2/10 and 3 mackerel. I have plenty of potatoes besides my ration at 3d per lb.

Monday, July 13. It looks as if we will have another long night. We have visitors in the dining-room and Erwin has just come to ask for a large dish of water to stand bottles in, I expect to cool the champagne. They have the wireless going and lots of talking. He gave me a packet of 5 cigarettes. I will stay in tonight! But it's awful with no wireless for news.

Thursday, July 16. Messervy came in at 8.30 this morning and said, Very bad news. He really startled me, he was so long before saying anything. I was obliged to say, Out with it. There has been a fishing boat accident.

Mr G. Bowditch, who lives at Eastdale, Church Rd., had struck a rock opposite Houmet Paradis, Bordeaux, and was drowned. His mate managed to swim to a nearby rock. The 2 young Lajoie boys were just following and went to their help. They struck a rock and had to beach their boat. Katwick, a Dutchman, was following just behind and went to their help. He managed to save the three, but poor Bowditch was drowned. His son, with other help, went out at low tide and picked him up. The son has just called to order the funeral. Inquest tomorrow.

Undated. The funeral went off well. The girls' and big choir attended and lots of people and crowds of fishermen. There were 41 wreaths, 6 were large floral anchors. Frossard gave an address and paid tribute to the brave Lajoie boys and Katwick.

I had an awful upset yesterday. I was not very well, a little stomach trouble. Then Mr Bird phoned to say the Germans were going to pull down his house (The Haven), and a large store I am renting from him (where I keep all my ladders, scaffolding and builders rubbish) so I must move out.

Tom Roberts and I went all over the place trying to find a store till I was dog tired. It will be an awful job to move this stuff. We started clearing some this morning, and took some boards down to the Carpenter's shop. While we were there 3 huge cars drove down with German officers. They walked around the place for some time.

JULY 1942

Now I hear the store might not have to come down. So we await orders. They want space for their railroad they are fixing from the Vardes quarry to the cracking machine. They are taking down the wall along Nocq Rd. (the side of my old Carpenter's shop) and taking part of the front gardens. When this is finished they will have a railroad from the Vardes quarry to St Sampson's and it will continue through Bulwer Avenue right to the White Rock.

I picked 13 lbs of rhubarb from the field for the new shop, 10d per lb and about 50 lbs of fallen apples, not much bigger than marbles from Mrs Le Poidevin's garden, which we sell for 8d to 10d per lb. It's unbelievable the high price of things, but people don't seem to mind. It's the only way to spend their money. Even poor people buy any sort of flowers. Carnations are 1½d and 2d each. We formerly gave them away.

I find it very depressing with no wireless.

Saturday, July 18. I was awakened at 4.45 am, such a knocking at the door. I rushed to the landing and heard Erwin talking through the front window of Flo's room. I don't know what was the matter. He dressed and went out. I heard the noise of cars, then I went to sleep again.

I did not wake till 9 o'clock and both Mr Frossard and Stafford had been trying to get me on the phone, so Stafford sent a man around. I had to be in Court at 11 as someone was buying a Rente due to the Cure and the Rector and Churchwardens had to be there to pass contracts. It was a rush but I was there. Rather a loss for the church, as we now lose 5% and at present cannot invest the £280.

Mary came down. No RX messages have come for 3 weeks. She took home some potatoes. I am digging a very good crop but am allowed to keep only three perches or 3 cwt, whichever the greater. Anything over I have to send to the Potato Board. They pay me 2½d per lb, little compensation for all our hard work, while others having no ground, could have all their evenings free.

It's rained every day since St Swithen's. It rained on that day, so they say 40 days of rain now (some hope). It's been an awful July. I told Mr Peek in Town this morning that I had never known a worse July. He said he had. I asked him when and he said, Last winter (laugh). He looks awfully thin.

It's distressing to see the men, all those robust men you knew, walking about Town, their clothes practically falling off them. You never saw such a change in people. Women on the whole don't seem so bad, but there are exceptions, Mrs Stubbs especially. Her husband is back from hospital after his operation (hernia). It's by the dozen the men have been in hospital for the same operation. The chief OT has gone back to Jersey after a three weeks' stay. Mrs Rowe usually gets 10/5 for looking after the rooms. While he was

JULY 1942

here they paid her 15/7½ (7½ marks).

Sunday, July 19. While I was going to church this morning there were three or four hundred Germans leaving the Church Schools each carrying a suit which looked new. Very few at church. Mr Frossard's text was a good one, In times of prosperity rejoice, in times of adversity *consider,* (Ecclesiastes Cp.7, v. 14). A good maxim and he made a rather good case of it.

Many robberies of potatoes. They rake them out of the ground or just pull up the stalks and take what comes with them. People are pulling up their onions only half come, as they are being stolen. There will be no onions this winter, and if they do the same with parsnips and carrots, vegetables will be scarce. So far I have had none stolen although I had quite expected to lose everything at Allendale as the place is empty.

Undated. I found 2 tons of cobbles tipped in the lane opposite the side gate. Erwin had left his car in the lane overnight and you can guess what it looked like covered in stone dust. When he came out he did create! A labourer was sent to wheel them in. I put them in the corner by the wash house and they are sending boxes to put them in. I was obliged to get the hose and wash down the cement paths.

Tuesday, July 28. I was enjoying my tub when I heard a dog howling terribly. The lady clerk rushed out, I could not with my face covered with lather. There was a lot of confusion outside, and when I got down I found her poor dog in the front garden with, I think, its back broken.

She telephoned for the vet who was not at home. Someone else phoned the police. They could do nothing. By then it was decided to get an officer from the Schools who came down and put the dog out of its pain. There was weeping and wailing.

A soldier was deputed to bury it. He wanted to make the grave in the front garden, but I made him go to the field by the old mill. I helped him to ensure the grave was deep enough

We have two large boats in St Sampson's harbour unloading coal. We now have hundreds of tons, and wood of all descriptions. You would never believe the amount. Imagine only the sleepers needed for a double rail from St Sampson's to Town and the Vardes, laid 18" apart.

Sunday, August 2. I went to the 8 o'clock service. Heavy thundering so not many there. Mr Peek came to the 10.45 in a landau from Hauteville. He is looking very frail after his operation.

It's been very lonesome here today and I don't like to go far. I miss my wireless very much. It's wonderful to hear a thrush singing

AUGUST 1942

in the lilac tree. He's been singing there for the last 10 days. I wish you could hear him. He doesn't know there is a war on!

I have answered four RX messages and sent a monthly to Jack. I was glad, Kit, you understood what I meant by my 'Little Mary'. Now they tell me my face is also much thinner. What can you expect on the grub we get. No meat this week and only a half ration of oil.

I had a real hectic week. Mr Bird rang me on Tuesday morning. He wanted me down at his coal store at once. He shouted, Very urgent, rush down! I was there in a few minutes. He was very agitated.

The Germans had put up a partition down the centre of the coal shed, had kept half for parking cars and lorries at night, the other half Bird used for his coal. He had piled coal dust against the partition and one end had collapsed. The German officer created an awful row and said he must clear out altogether. However, I came on the scene and set my men to work. He made me stay all the while. I was as black as a crow when I reached home. Mrs Rowe said I looked like a workman. My cream shirt was black.

The next day I had the partition strengthened to their satisfaction, and now the storm is over they might let him stay. Had the partition collapsed the other end, their 2 enormous cars would have been ruined.

It was like bedlam on the South Quay with the traffic this week. They have taken down the dwelling house, The Haven, also a store, to make room for their railway. It was a sight to see women, children and even men with trucks, wheelbarrows, go-carts and quite good prams, in fact any conveyance you can think of, picking up the wood. People of all classes were struggling with loads of wood. Some men could hardly handle their loads.

I am getting the fallen apples from Mrs Le Poidevin's garden, apples the size of marbles and including the maggots, that rubbish sells for 10d to 1/3 per lb. But people are hungry and there is nothing else to spend money on except eatables. Nectarines are 1/6 to 2/- each, grapes 4/6 to 5/- per lb. I bought nice large cooking apples from Mr Sebire (The Orchard). They sell for 1/6 per lb.

Sunday, August 9. A very fine Sunday and a quiet day here for me. Mrs Rowe and I picked up baskets of Quarenden apples from Mrs Le Poidevin's garden. Mary came down and took 6 lbs. Then we went to Mrs Rowe and had tea (real tea) quite a treat, and salmon and apple tart.

Then I went to church, lots of people. Frank Mallett was there. He looked fairly well. He came out of prison this morning after doing 3 months. His sentence was 12 months or 3 months and a fine of £540. They paid the fine, very wise I think.

1. From an original by Charles Coker
"I cannot describe the beauty of the sea from The Banques"

2. Mr & Mrs Sauvary

3. Flo with her daughter Rosemary

4. Jack with his daughter Jane

5. Jack in service uniform

6. Kit in nursing uniform

7. Flo's husband
"that grand lad Ted"

8. Mr Gervase Peek,
Guernsey's "Grand Old Man"

9. "New Road", built by Mr Sauvary in 1914 (with postwar attic windows) and the Manse next door

10. The Old Ford outside "New Road"

11. View down Church Lane from "1449", The Old Forge

12. "Pullman Car", the horse drawn bus

13. Tom and the "Skipper"

14. Mrs Rowe, owner of "1449"

15. Mary Ayres (née Sauvary) given in marriage by her uncle

16. Delancey Monument, demolished by the Germans in 1943
A memorial to Admiral Lord de Saumarez 1757-1836
Guernsey's most distinguished sailor

17. St Sampson's Church

18. St Sampson's Church "sheltering under the old elms"

19. The Channel Queen Memorial. The unknown man washed up on the beach was buried here

20. The grave in "the sunny jib patch"   Inscription on a boulow

21. *The cinema in St Julian's Avenue*

22. Smith Street – Queue for sweet ration at Collins – The Pollet

23. German Observation Tower at Fort Richmond

24. Machine gun position at Fermain

25. *German transporter, Weighbridge, St Peter Port*

26. *German light railway, Glategny Esplanade, St Peter Port*

27. SS Vega, Red Cross supply ship

28. Ships of the Royal Navy outside St Peter Port

29. *Memorial to air raid victims 28.6.40 and other war victims 1939-1945*

AUGUST 1942

I have sold 18 bunnies out of my 21 at 2/6 each. I let one of the mothers out in the garden during the day. She has got very poorly, 11 was too many for her to bring up, but I think I will bring her round. I have seven large ones in reserve for the winter.

I have a lovely lot of onions for this winter if I don't get them stolen, lots of runner beans for drying, a fine lot of shallots, about 75 lbs and plenty of potatoes. I have spared Mary quite a lot, also Tom Roberts and a few other friends to help them on their road.

I have had lots of my potatoes stolen. They pull up the stalks, take away the potatoes and replant the half dried stalks, so I decided I will dig them. They are lates and it's really too early, but I cannot afford to lose any more.

Thursday, August 13. I got up at 6 this morning and kept watch until the world was moving about. I know they take them in the early morning, as they leave the diseased ones in the furrows for me (very kind!). Later we dug them all and burnt the stalks. I had a bumper crop, over 350 lbs per perch. It was quite a business with people passing the wall in New Road and giving their opinion about size and quality.

Uncle Ned has just called with my old two quart can he made me when I got married. He has cut out the bottom part and replaced it with a new one. No tin now for new cans.

I note by the last messages from you that Jack must be Captain now, and that he is moving, you're saying goodbye. Of course he may not be leaving England. *[See p.290.]*

Sunday, August 16. Referring to August 13th when I dug my potatoes, I did not mention that a foreigner called me to the wall and put up 1 finger. I assumed he wanted 1 potato seeing such abundance. Although not allowed I gave him one, size about 1½ lbs. Then he put up one finger again. I explained that he had one, still that would not do, so I gave him another. Then he put up his finger again. The men roared with laughter, but still he persisted and pointed to the potatoes, so I gave him a very large round one. He did not want it but pointed to one quite as large but very flat. I told him to put them out of sight and clear off. After struggling to get them stowed away he took and pulled me by the hand, and kissed the sleeve of my coat. Shrieks of laughter. I said I did not mind the blessing but objected to the kiss.

Then a big Gestapo with an armlet and swastika looked over the wall chatting with a well-dressed German civilian. He called me and pointed to some beans and turnips I had planted on a heap of ground by the gate. He wanted a turnip. I pulled him one, then he put up one finger so I had to pull him another. He got out his purse to pay, I told him nothing, So he said, Cigarettes. Being completely

AUGUST 1942

out I said yes, so got 2. It was really fun, but sounds nothing when you write it.

I got up nice and early this morning and got ready for church. There was a knock at the front door. It was Edmunds, the people next door to tell me I had lost another lot of potatoes. I had left about ¾ perch near the house. They were not quite come. I wish I had dug them on Friday. What a fool I was! However it's what I have to give to the States, so they are the losers.

I have telephoned Gerald Martel and Tom Roberts and (although Sunday) I am having them down at 6 o'clock. They will pull up the stalks, just lift the ground and take the biggest spuds, and tomorrow we will re-dig and get the remainder. I am wondering when all our trials and troubles will be over.

I went to Minnie's and got a loaf yesterday. She gave me two nice squares of apple cake, very acceptable as I did not cook any dinner. I had dry bread, a small portion of cheese, apple and a cup of cocoa (skimmed milk). Mary came as usual and took five baby bunnies for one of her friends. I may not breed any more this summer. It's a lot of work to get food for so many.

Sunday, August 23. It's about eight days since I added anything to this long chapter of events, but there have been many happenings. The raid on Dieppe naturally made a great confusion among the Germans.

The whole telephone communication of the island was cut off. However by the next day all was connected again. The Germans stopped the whole of their work, closed the White Rock for any of their lorries. Of course no civilian is allowed there without a pass. They say that nearly every window from the Longstore to Town had a gun pointing out. Everybody in Town was sent home by 8 o'clock and the curfew fixed at 10, and fixed permanently for the winter.

I have had another hectic week here. I will explain that all to you later. Now the whole of the South Quay is torn up and the rails laid.

Mary came down yesterday and brought me a message from Flo, I think my 53rd. We had a lovely tea and she took her usual stores.

Lily Ellis is kept very busy in the shop and is doing well. Up to now I am rather glad I made the venture.

A good attendance at Church this morning. I am writing this in the study at 1 o'clock, not a sound anywhere. The leaves of the dear old beech are falling, rather early, I think because of the wind this week. I was glad of the rain as having dug my potatoes it may not be too late for the turnips and swedes I have sown.

I am going to the Doctor's for lunch as usual. I am glad I have nothing to prepare on Sundays. I had part of a lobster for breakfast and I had one last week (lucky again as there are very few about). Mrs Rowe made me an apple tart. So you see I manage with my food.

AUGUST 1942

This week has not been quite as good. One day I had plain hot potatoes for dinner, another day toms, onions and fried spuds, my way very burnt.

I have spent a nice Sunday. Had tea at Mrs Stubbs', bramble tea, slice of melon and a piece of choc. cake, but of course I took my bread and butter.

It's really awful not getting any news except what appears in the Press. The Germans called the Dieppe raid a fiasco and brave British lives sacrificed.

Monday, August 24. I picked up the remainder of Mrs Le Poidevin's apples for the shop. She will have made about £30 on them (not bad). Then I flew out to Miss Lihou with the money I drew for her from her bank and she paid my bill for cutting down the trees.

Back to a patched up dinner and rested till Mrs Le Poidevin arrived with Winnie who picked blackberries in their garden. They came in for tea which they brought (Real). Needless to say I drank most of it. I went with them as far as the Vale Road to help Winnie to wheel her mother in the pram. I gave them scarlet runners, lettuce and a cucumber. They brought their own bread and butter and gave me a pot of jam, three scones and a few rock cakes. I was quite tired after a hurried day.

Gussie has phoned to invite me to their Silver Wedding, Sept. 3rd, but I am not going owing to difficulties here.

Tuesday, August 25. I went to Gussie to try to fix up not to go to their Silver Wedding Party, but they would not hear of it. In the first place my evening trousers are eaten to pieces by moths, then it is difficult to get back by curfew. So I promised to try to go.

Wednesday, August 26. For their present I bought a silver sugar dredger for £3 Peter Bachmann is going to engrave it, Old English, VVC-GSC – 1917-1942. Peter spoke of Flo's message, also of a little woolly for Kit's baby. I am going to look for it.

It's pouring with rain and the gravel outside has 1" of water. I have never seen such a wet August. I have not even been to the beach yet. The house is very quiet for the moment, everybody gone. It's Peaceful. I wish it were always so.

Thursday, August 27. Again very dull, low clouds and has rained practically the whole night. Thunder from 5 to 7 am. Everything is flooded. Bird's office, which the Germans occupy, got swamped owing to a choked pipe, so I had to be on parade.

The sun came out, burning, during the day. I tried to dry my onions on the lawn (if you can call it a lawn now), and spread some hay to dry. Everything is drenched. I gave the rabbits some dry hay.

AUGUST 1942

I sent the van out to St Andrews with the last load of tiles for the roof at Miss Lihou's.

Willie Le Maitre is in bed very poorly. It's difficult even to get a doctor to see you, they have very little petrol allowance.

My whole pint of milk went sour. Mrs Rowe is making me some plain scones for tea.

The Constables have just telephoned. I have to go to Mont Morin tomorrow about a Bornement.

Friday, August 28. Put my onions in the attic to dry, about 125 lbs. I will sell some in the shop.

Went to Ted Ogier to see about a job. He gave me a nice bunch of grapes, Canon Hall. Later went to the Bridge which was packed with people, all waiting for fish. I had to wait 1 hour. Had 4 mackerel. Needless to say I won't eat all myself. Mrs Le Cheminant (Nurse) was there. We chatted and she inquired about all of you. I found the little woolly for Peter's and Kit's baby.

Saturday, August 29. Picked 10 lbs of runners for the shop. Went to Town. It was very exciting. There was a German mock battle going on, soldiers posted at every pillar and corner. On my way back, passing the Royal, I got into the thick of it. I got off my bicycle and watched for a bit. Big guns and small tanks were firing, and rifle shooting was going on.

I had just passed when they (I suppose) stormed and took the White Rock. They threw out a heavy smoke screen. They fire them, they roll along the road and then burst. In a minute the Pollet and Clock Tower roadway were obliterated. But it soon clears.

What a tragedy about the Duke of Kent. We saw the account in the Press. They say about 15 lives lost. I don't know the full account. We get very little real news now we have no wirelesses. It's very dull here especially now the autumn evenings are coming on. It's very dull at the Doctor's too. Miss Matthews gets very depressed and worried. They have cooking difficulties and very little gas allowed.

Mrs Rowe is frying the mackerel at her house. I am very tired of it, but there's very little else to eat. I hope to get another lobster this afternoon to eat with fried spuds when Mary comes later.

Wednesday, September 2. I took the present to the Cortvriends on Monday. They liked it very much and made me promise to go to the dinner tomorrow night. There will be 11 of us and they have champagne. But I don't feel much like going anywhere.

I went on in the rain to see the job at St Andrew's. I took them nice black grapes.

SEPTEMBER 1942

The Constables called me to the South Side this afternoon The Germans have to pass their rails over an underground flush cistern. I don't know how they will manage. They could easily have made a little detour and missed it, but that is not their way.

Saturday, Sept. 5. It's been an awful week, more rain and quite cold. I am sure, were it not for the leaves on the trees, you would not tell the season.

The States are legislating to stop barter to a great extent. People now steal anything and take it to these shops, and the police cannot find the owners. Last week two local men got 12 months prison. They stole about £20 worth of goods from a shop and bartered the goods.

My stomach hasn't been quite in order this week, but well again so I can now eat grapes.

Sunday, Sept. 6. I awoke early so thought I would go to early service, first Sunday in the month. I struck a match and thought my watch said 7.30. When I got downstairs it was 10 to 7. I was cross but thought I would rest on the couch and think I fell asleep.

I heard my lodger came rushing downstairs to answer the telephone. He has a through bell in his bedroom. He bellowed for 5 minutes then went back to bed. It was 10 to 8. The hour had slipped by nicely. There were 43 communicants, not bad.

At Morning Service Mr Frossard preached on the three years of war. He informed them at the 11 o'clock service on Sept. 3rd that war was declared. He said we had a lot to be thankful for and I think he is right, but I hope it's now coming to a close. It's awful here without news. Time is not long but it's the anxiety.

Monday, Sept. 7. A beautiful September day. I went out to Mrs Godfray and Miss Lihou and took them lovely Canon Hall grapes and an apple each weighing 1 lb. I left early to see the roof at Mrs Petruschke. I had a glass of lovely milk, full cream, the first for a very long time. She also gave me a nice little melon. It was a long cycle ride and hilly.

Tuesday, Sept. 8. Another lovely day. I went to St Andrew's again about a choked drain at Miss Lihou and a leak in the roof at Mrs Godfray. Got back for a nice baked dinner at 2.15, a tender piece of meat a little bigger than a fowl's egg when cooked, lovely floury potatoes, onions, toms and chopped parsley.

We are busy just now. Mr Bird's work is pressing. Mr Peek rang me about a job at the Press. I cannot understand why he bothers about this at his age, 86, especially after his operation in Jersey, 4 months ago.

SEPTEMBER 1942

It's lovely now sitting by the window writing this. It's dead silent except for the birds singing, real peace. I have just done the time sheets and the tally boards. I must try and make some bills this week. As I have told you before it is only when I am on the rocks that I think of making bills, and then I always start with the easy ones! Still there is no bother getting in the money. They seem only too pleased to get their jobs done.

Mary came down this afternoon for her usual. I gave her a huge apple, nearly 1 lb. Mrs Rowe said she would never get through it, but she did without trouble.

Undated. It's now a week since I have written anything, but what a terrible lot has happened during that week. First I will tell you that so far September has not been such a good month after all, very few really fine days. Now for our shocks.

On Tuesday, Sept. 15th there was an order in the Star. All British born men and their dependants (wives and children) must go to Germany. I called at the Gigands. The Ogiers were just reading the news. We telephoned Mr Frossard and they were in a state about it.

Stafford and I went to the Douzaine Meeting re our Budget. We are two million in debt. They did not bother much about that! The topic was this new order. Mr Higgs was in a state, he being the only British man on our Douzaine.

The next day's Presses had the forms to be filled in. Things moved rapidly. Ambulances were on the Bridge to take people for medical examination. It's awful the few exemptions. Mrs Clarke, over 75, has to go with her husband, E. Gerrish and family, Jack Hart, the Chemist, Mr Cross, Mr Bartlett, in short it's affecting about 3,000. I met Mrs Potter and they have to leave their shop and have already received their orders to meet outside St Sampson's Church, noon Friday.

We had our usual Sunday morning service. Mr Frossard made reference to these happenings and tonight we are having a farewell service. He is asking for blankets, etc. I will send some down. They each have to take a tin plate and mug, and will be supplied with 1 loaf, an egg, a portion of chocolate, and will be served with a bowl of soup before leaving.

It's now blowing a gale from the S West. If it's like this tomorrow it will be an awful crossing (I hear to St Malo, then on to Germany.)

This has cast an awful gloom over the island. People staying are worrying nearly as much as those going. Everybody now wonders what will be the next move. Perhaps men of military age. People who had property and many belongings stayed here, thinking to save their life's savings, yet those who evacuated and left everything behind may perhaps be better off. I am starting to feel that I won't

SEPTEMBER 1942

have gained anything by staying. It now looks like a gamble.

It's dreadful meeting people who have to go. They leave everything behind, and I suppose will have only one change of clothes. And will we ever see them again. I met Jock Wallace. He has to leave his hairdressing business to strangers to look after. This is much worse than the Evacuation.

We had a fine Evening Service and of course special prayers for the people going. The church was nearly packed. The processional was Fight the good fight, (Sankey tune), Sun of my soul, (A & M), then God be with you till we meet again, (to Sankey's tune) went with a swing by the whole congregation. There was plenty of weeping, a very sad scene.

Mr Frossard preached a very fine sermon, text, The Lord watch between me and thee when we are absent from one another, Genesis 32, verse 49. Recessional hymn, Abide with me.

While we were counting the collection several people came to the vestry to say goodbye. Mr Smith's daughter from Le Riche was one. She happened to marry an English boy.

Monday, Sept. 21. First day of autumn. It started with wind and rain. It cleared a little by 11.30.

All deportees from St Sampson's had to meet at the church at noon. I went down and took Mum's big black bag full of apples for the children. Mr and Mrs Warry came with a basket of apples. The people started to flock down. We had extra clothes and shoes given in case of need, but most people had everything they wanted. It was a sad sight and I little thought we would ever see such a scene outside St Sampson's Church.

There were three bus loads and a lorry for the luggage. I managed to dispose of my apples. We gave them a good send off and a great shout which they returned smiling. There were a few weeping, but funnily enough they were the women who were not going. See Presses Sept. 15 to 21st.

Tuesday, Sept. 22. Everybody has been pitying the travellers on the high seas to St Malo, but Mr Peek, when he phoned me up about work at the Press Office, said the boat did not go. The people were breakfasting at the Royal and being taken in batches to the hospital for a wash and brush up. It seems to me as if this delay will be worse than if they had gone straight off.

As I am writing this waiting for my baked dinner of 1/- of meat and nice Savoy cabbage, the rain is pouring down and it is still blowing hard, more like winter.

When I went to the road I saw the buses coming back with the deportees. They sent them home. I hear it's the weather, then that a boat has been sunk outside somewhere, it's impossible to get the

SEPTEMBER 1942

truth. All I know which is authentic is that they are back home again.

I have received a letter from Mr Browell who also has to go to Germany. Sept. 22nd. He writes, Dear Jack, I have no time to come to see you, so must write and shake hands by post. I hope you will keep well yourself, and continue to get good news from those across the water. The new future looks rotten, but I know it will soon change into a happy present. Chin, chin, Old Jack, Yours always W.M. Browell.

Wednesday, Sept. 23. It has been blowing and raining all night and no better now. I have been to the Bridge. The deportees were chatting in groups. They have to fall in for a second time at St Sampson's Church tomorrow at 3 pm. I spoke to one man who told me he was a prisoner of war in 1914 and had his Xmas dinner on a train, bread and water. Now he is captured again.

Thursday, Sept. 24. You might hardly believe it but it blew a gale again last night, and the rain lashed harder than ever at my back bedroom windows. The heavy showers continued all day, but with less wind. They telephoned from headquarters after dinner that the deportees would not have to report at the church at 3 p.m. The sailing had been put off till tomorrow, Friday. If they wanted a loaf they could get it at the Ladies' College, ¼ lb of butter at the French Halles and a feed (as they call it) at Stroobant [for details see F. Stroobant's *One Man's War,* pages 63-67] near the White Rock. I don't think many will accept the offers as it's too far and little chance of a conveyance.

I have done little today except make a few small bills and feed the animals. A lonesome day and I am without tobacco or cigarettes until Monday. I have been smoking bramble leaves (they sell it for making tea, 4d. per oz) and I mix it with tobacco leaves we grow, but it dries my lips too much, so I must slack it off a bit.

Friday, Sept. 25. Again a very squally morning with showers of rain. I went to the church to see our English deportees assemble at 3 pm. There was lots of joking and some of the men had miniature Union Jacks and were holding them out in the wind. One or two Germans were there, there were roars of laughter, but it was all taken in good part. As our people left they were in high spirits. I expect they will go this time. Some of them told me that the suspense, waiting since Monday and having to go back home (some of them had sold their homes), was much worse than if they had gone straight away on Monday.

SEPTEMBER 1942

Saturday, Sept. 26. I have just heard that our people arrived at St Malo between 6 and 7 this morning. They won't have had too bad a passage, the wind went North.

By the Press tonight all persons who were notified for Wednesday, Sept. 23rd, must now report at St Sampson's Church at noon, Sunday, Sept. 27th.

Sunday, Sept. 27. Mary came down for the Morning Service. Not a large congregation. After the service we waited to see the deportees off. I understand they are sailing tonight. I am not sure but I think there is another batch to go.

What a surprise I had yesterday when I saw three baby rabbits, quite big and with their eyes open, running about. I did not know the doe was in kindle. Some of them had got loose some weeks ago and they must have been flirting. However it's only three so I can soon dispose of them. What surprised me was that none of us noticed her nest.

Now this morning I had a greater surprise which upset me. All my lovely apples and pears had been stolen in the night. I left them on the trees as I intended storing them for the winter. It's impossible to keep anything.

Thursday, Sept. 29. My birthday, 66 years, quite an old man. I managed to get an extra loaf, Mrs Rowe made a nice apple tart for tea (and a small one for Mrs Godfray to share with Miss Lihou). Then I managed a bottle of sherry.

Mary came down to tea. She brought me three presents, the first a cherry wood cigarette holder, the second toothpaste in a nice container and a refill (German), the third a saddle cover for my bicycle, each with a card, Love from Flo, Love from Kit and Love from Jack. It was very thoughtful of her. She thought it would remind me of 3 presents from the children.

Elsie came down and brought me 2 eggs (they are 1/- now, but unobtainable). She brought her niece down for the run. We assembled in the study for tea. Mrs Rowe was there as well and was a great help. After tea we had grapes (Muscats), then later a glass of wine, with greetings for the absent ones. All very successful and in fact not expected or really planned.

Mary could not get a birthday card, so made one and sent it by post. Mrs Godfray sent a lovely card with a sheaf of Violets. I am keeping it to show you her wonderful handwriting – From Mrs Godfray and her sister E. Lihou. I am copying the words, they are so good.

> May joy and happiness be yours along life's busy way,
> May all the treasures of the past grow dearer day by day,
> For truly, it seems only right that you should have the best,
> You who have made the days so bright with joy for all the rest.

OCTOBER 1942

Saturday, October 3. Mary came down as usual. I got a lovely lot of Chrys. for the altar as it's Harvest Festival tomorrow, and some for Mum's grave, yellow and bronze, beautiful blooms. Mrs Frossard was quite pleased with them. People sent a few vegetables, grapes and flowers and a 1 lb loaf was on the altar.

Sunday, Oct. 4. I went to Early Communion. Mary came down for Choral Communion and although she has not been confirmed it was arranged that she could take the Sacrament. During the Occupation people cannot be confirmed, but they promise to be as soon as the Bishop can come over. The Harvest Festival services were very bright and the church packed in the evening. Collection for the day, £12.

Week Oct. 3-8. The States now have to be relieved of 500 vergees of the greenhouses they had taken over. The Germans say they are costing too much to work, and it's the 'capitalists' or owners of the land that must stand the loss. The loss to the States working them last year was £265,000. I have decided to take mine back. I gave them over to the States the first week of the German Occupation. The States have had them two years and three months. Of course they have paid no rent. I took the vinery back on Oct. 6th, 1942.

They came and valued the crop yesterday, carrots only just coming up badly, and two houses planted in cauliflower, value £1 17s.6d. (won't break me). So Tom starts back with me in the old firm, although I have been able to have him occasionally for special jobs the last two years. Although I was not paying him (the States were), he was always in the garden or field. Now, although I will be responsible for at least his £2 per week, it will be much better for me.

Of course I may lose £60 to £80 per year on the garden, I will stand to do better on the building work. Anyway lose or gain, that won't worry me. I will be more comfortable. Then now I have the Greengrocer's shop, I can always get my goods sold before I take from outsiders should there be a glut.

Oct. 5-10. This has been a terrible week for everybody in New Road living on the West side. Starting from Potter's corner, the Germans are taking every house including mine and the Manse, and up Brock Road as far as Lake's. They say they want to billet their men in blocks, in barbed wire areas. We have to clear our furniture and be out by Oct. 15th, Thursday. Billeting officers are trying to fix up houses suitable for each family. It is awful to have to move, especially at this time of the year. For the moment I am taking my furniture down to Allendale. I will board at Mrs Rowe. She is very

OCTOBER 1942

kind and most helpful, and is fitting in my desk and I will use the room as an office.

Sunday, Oct. 11. I am writing this in the study, probably the last time I will write in this study. Who can tell. Perhaps I will never come back here. Still, although I have been here for 28 years (ever since I built the house and we moved in when you were small children), I will not worry on that score.

I am rather relieved now we are going, as the last 12 months I have always been on tenterhooks, and felt sure our turn would come. It's hundreds of families that have had to move, some 3 times. I am afraid the furniture won't be up to much by the time the war is finished.

Dr Jones also has to move. He is the only unfortunate one the other side of the road. He is going to Collas' house, Hillside, the Cognon. I had taken it for myself, but at the last moment decided to give up housekeeping till this job is over, or I get back to New Road again. Mary is having a day off tomorrow to help us.

I was fairly busy last week with two funerals. It's wonderful how I can get enough work for the men. Timber is the difficulty, putty is unobtainable except French, and it's not much good.

Tomorrow New Road will be busy. I hope it's dry. Wind is now North and it's looking hard and cold. People are telephoning and offering their sympathy. I can sleep at Mr Frossard, S.T. Ogier, the Stubbs and others. I thank them all and say, Your turn will come.

I think I will be very comfortable at Mrs Rowe this winter. I think you know her house in Brock Road, first on the right going up, dated 1449. She is letting me keep my rabbits at her place.

I often wonder if I will want to relate my experiences of the last 2 years. Some have been difficult since I have been occupied. Having Germans in the house has not been altogether a bed of roses! Now this phase is over, or I'm hoping it will be after tonight. All being well I hope to sleep in Brock Road Monday, Oct. 12th.

Monday, Oct. 12. I had a very restless night, Sunday, Oct. 11th, sleeping and waking up, and downstairs our friends were actually playing the accordian at 2 in the morning. During my naps I dreamt and planned, packed and moved all my furniture and crockery etc. more than a dozen times. Still that was only dreaming.

Monday it was business in earnest. The New Road was a sight, a van at every house. I only wish you could have seen those vans stacked sky high. Mary came down and helped us and saved my legs quite a lot running up and down stairs.

OCTOBER 1942

Sat. Oct. 17. We only just finished in time. As we were clearing th study and kitchen the Germans were bringing in their beds and furniture. We had to leave lino, and I left all the stair carpets. I thought it better to save the stairs.

I am storing carpets, blankets and linen with Minnie at Cliffdale for the moment, also the oak grandfather clock, one or two chests of drawers and the big double bed which they are actually using. Non-perishable furniture and crockery are at Allendale where I will probably get it stolen, but I am not worrying. The big couches, chairs, oak suite and a few other things are at Martel's, L'Islet. Gerald Martel works for me. Saucepans and enamel are here. I took all the curtains.

I have a splendid office with my big desk, and the telephone was fitted on Tuesday. Mrs Rowe also took my safes and desk from the little room under the bathroom. She has been a brick in every way. In fact, everyone sympathised and did their best for me.

The Germans took all my gravel and put it all over the Manse paths. That I did not mind so much, but somebody stole all the runner beans that I left to dry for the winter.

Mary came as usual, to Mrs Rowe now.

Sunday, Oct. 18. As I was going to church I met Mr Bird coming to see me. He gave me quite a shock. The Germans are going to take down the buildings around Radford's Corner for another railroad. That will mean Mrs Kimber's shop, my Carpenter's shop, Manuelles' Blacksmith's shop and Hunkin's Sailmakers's. I don't know where I will go.

The billeting officer, Vernon Le Maitre suggests Mr Angel's Carpenter's shop, Braye Road. I wish I could find something nearer. It will be a job moving all my gear. Of course I can get plenty of help, and it need not be at my expense (although I had my own men to move my furniture.)

It's awful to think that I was cleared out of my house last week and now it falls to my lot to have to clear out from my shop. However, whatever happens I am now more comfortable at Mrs Rowe. She is a good cook, I have a very comfortable bedroom, my rabbits are in her little conservatory, so we are all much better fixed up than I was at New Road. So no regrets, Amen!

Thursday-Saturday, Oct. 22-24. New Road is transformed. It's just lovely to see my front and back windows covered on the outside with fowl-house wire (all houses along the road have it) and short curtains at the front windows fastened with blue ribbon! I see they have improvised a table against the beech tree. They have already cut down Dr Jones' eucalyptus tree in his front garden. As you know anything in their way is soon cleared.

NOVEMBER 1942

We are well guarded at night. I hear the thud of the sentry up and down every 10 minutes, and at 11 o'clock the bugle call at every third door, then we hear the whistle. I don't know what it all means.

Monday, Oct. 26. Sunday was a very rough day, scarcely anybody at church and I did not blame them. Today it was terribly squally. At 3 pm we had the worst squall I have ever experienced. We had one of the greenhouse lights blown away, and several greenhouses were blown down. I saw one in Duveau Lane, 150 ft laid flat. You will think I am always writing about the weather.

I went to see Dr Jones this morning (now a walk to the other side of the Bridge). He is not well. He said he had had a heart attack. I am not surprised after all the upset of moving house.

Monday, November 1. The telephone rang early. I sleep on the ground floor, cross through the dining-room to a nice drawing-room where I have my desk and use as an office. It was the Matron of the Vauquiedor Hospital, now occupied by the Germans. (The women of the asylum are at the old Town asylum, the men at the Câstel). A Hungarian girl had died and she wanted me in soon as she wanted a notice in the Star that morning. Other foreign girls used to visit her and she would like them to know.

I had awful rain riding into Town. The dead girl was Anna Gref, of Budapest, Hungary, aged 28 years. An RC funeral. She was mental, would not eat and had been fed by a tube for some months.

I went on to the Star office. By then I was soaked. I then sheltered underneath the Arcade by Clarkes. It poured in deluges for 1½ hours. Fountain Street was a river the full width, at least 6" deep. People told me that the High Street was a sight. You can imagine the water rushing down the Grange, into Smith Street and on to the High Street. In 1½ hours we had 2" of rain, and 4" in 24 hours. When I got home I had to change even my vest, but being in lodgings there was a nice fire and a hot dinner ready for me, much better than I have been accustomed to the last two years.

I have had some awful news. I *do* have to move from my Carpenter's shop Radford's Corner. The Germans are making South Side a barbed wire area and I think closing the South Quay. Miss Dyson, Mr Bird, Mr Johns the butcher and all others along there have to move out. I am hoping to take a Carpenter's shop at the bottom of Mont Morin. But what a devil of a job moving all my gear. I dread to think of it. To make matters worse Tom Roberts is laid up with inflamation of the kidneys, so I won't have his help. Still we will get through somehow. I am taking things as they come and don't intend to worry. But I am longing for all this to be over. I think by now we are on the last year.

NOVEMBER 1942

Tuesday, Nov. 3. It's been a nice day with a few hours of sunshine. I buried the Hungarian girl. Father Hickey officiated and about 20 Hungarian girls were there. Three of them carried wreaths, all were carrying large sheaves of flowers. There was also a wreath from Mr McCathie who was there. He was her first employer when she came to the island. He told me she was a very nice girl, stayed with them for 18 months, then went to Mr Thomas.

After Father Hickey had finished the burial all the girls knelt on the wet grass and recited aloud in their language some long prayers. Then they collected money among themselves and told me they wanted to put up a small stone. Most of them gave 5 marks (10/8). I bought the grave for her and she has money to pay for the funeral expenses. The Matron said she had about £50.

Thursday, Nov. 5. Yesterday it again rained like the devil. We have never known such a wet season. Today I am starting to move my Carpenter's shop to Mont Morin. It's awful the amount of stuff I have to move, benches, scaffolding and ladders, wood stock, paint gear, nails etc. and tons of useful lumber. They are leaving only Mr Bird's coal store as they have 700 tons of coal, too much to move.

I hear this afternoon that the Germans were at Mont Morin contemplating taking that area too. If so, I don't know where I can go. It's now getting beyond anything reasonable.

Saturday, Nov. 7. This is the second day moving my shop. Yesterday we moved five van loads, today four. It's unbelievable the amount of short ends of wood and rubbish that accumulates in the course of years. It's more than 20 years since I moved there from Nocq Road. I have another 4 days at least next week, and then will only just be finished in the time allowed. It must be cleared by November 12th.

I am dead beat tonight. I am writing this in a cosy room at Mrs Rowe by a lovely fire. Mary came as usual, we had the usual fare and she left soon after we returned from taking flowers to the grave.

I was so busy last Saturday, with the upset of having to move the Carpentry business, that I omitted to mention about Mum's birthday, but I know that October 31st was in all your minds as it was in mine. She would have been 69. I got a wreath, mauve double Dahlias and lovely dark bronze and yellow Chrys. Dahlias are not my favourite, but Mary said they looked nice.

Wednesday, Nov. 11. Armistice Day. There were services at 11 and 5. I could not go as I was too busy moving and I am not finished yet. The Germans told us only about a week ago. I have only tomorrow if they don't allow us to continue on Friday. If not I will have to leave some things behind. I have got about 20 loads away, the accumulation of years. Some things I'd forgotten I had. The

NOVEMBER 1942

trouble has been transport, few lorries, petrol is scarce, few horses and these cannot be worked too hard as they are on short rations. I was looking at them today and it's not difficult to count their ribs.

We have had a week of marvellous fine weather for the move, and I am beginning to think it is perhaps not a bad thing I have had to move. Now I have had a spring clean.

Elsie came down for the usual provisions. I could not go out, too busy. Mrs Godfray is in bed with Herpes, otherwise Shingles. I gave her a small tin of lobster and a few apples. It will tempt her appetite, though Elsie says she eats well for a woman of 91 years.

We have the Mont Morin shop filled and they have allowed me to put the remainder in the greenhouse at the side. A shady place and not much use for growing. I am lucky to have it. I had to give the underneath shop to Foster, the wheelwright, as it has a forge and the only one available here.

The news about tonight is that the Germans are perhaps taking all the houses on the North coast. I hope it's not true. It will mean that my furniture stored at Gerald Martel's Tea Rooms, L'Islet, will have to be moved again. I think the American landing in Africa has brought this about. I will be glad when this job is over, although up to now our hardships have not been too bad.

We are having our choir practices at 5 pm, earlier because of black out restrictions. We now have a new organist at church, Stanley Keyho.

They say the news is very good this week, and everybody seems a bit bucked up.

Saturday, Nov. 14. I think I will remember Sat. the 14th for a long time to come, in fact the whole week. Talk about moving stores from a builder's shop after 30 years or more. The accumulation of materials, registers, ranges, hearths, curbs, spars, battens, mixed timbers, short ends, etc. etc! I have about 6 loads I am going to sell off. I know it's too good for firewood but it must go.

It's years since I worked like this and did so much lifting. We had a roll of lead about 7 cwt and about 1 ton of lead. However our shop and store at South Quay is cleared. We were supposed to finish on Thursday but nobody interfered so we carried on till Saturday night, and if possible I will go and scrounge around on Monday.

Now I have moved I think it's a good job it happened, especially if they leave me there for 6 months, during which time I will reduce my stock and generally put things straight.

As I told you we are well guarded at night in Brock Road and New Road. At times a man cycles around with a whistle and shouts something, and they rush off somewhere, sometimes to the schools for their grub.

Then just before daylight, at about 6.30, you hear the tramping

NOVEMBER 1942

of about 100 foreigners marching down chattering away. Sometimes it's pouring with rain and the noise of their sabots! I think they include every nationality. Many wear sacks over their head and tied with a cord around their neck, like a bonnet, and they work all day like that.

One thing is certain, they will never stand our winter clad as they are. I am sure hundreds will die. I am told they have a hospital full of them. They have a proper camp at the top of Brock Road with all the States houses and three large huts built in the field in front of Mr Peek's Rink. The stores below are used as kitchens.

The Bridge is now a network of rails, and with the puffing billies (I mean the engines) running and whistling, it's getting more like London (Victoria) stations every day!

Mrs Blight is ill, and I hear very low in a coma. I think she's in her 92nd year.

I must stop now and be thankful that this week is over, and will trust that I won't be moved again too soon. But my men told me the Germans had been looking at other houses in Mont Morin. Up to now they have taken from Frank Dorey's top right, to half way down, and from Gaudion's the same down the other side. They seem to be having a game with us.

Mary came down as usual, but in future she is coming on Fridays. Her boy friend has to work late during the week and Saturday is the only day left for them to go to a show.

Mid Nov. I have had an awful rush as I'd only just moved into my new shop and we had 4 funerals in the first week. A good start! Mrs Blight's was one of them. We had to work on Sunday.

When Tom was in Town going to the Greffe for me he saw seven coffins carried out from Lovell's for the Germans. I will tell you some day what happened.

I am well fixed in the Mont Morin shop. We are busy cutting up all my old rubbish of wood. There is a good sale for it, and it's no use keeping so much especially as they may move me at any time, and I have loads to dispose of. I am selling everything I can to reduce my stock.

Monday, Nov. 23. I have taken over Mr Lake's greenhouses today and will work them with mine. It's a risk as we get so much stolen. I had a lot of my dry tobacco leaves stolen last night. We caught a large rat but it was not the culprit!

We are expecting Diva down tomorrow. She is living with her two old aunts in Mont Durand, both over eighty and one bedridden and now going blind. I help them a little with food and sent them a large bag of chopped kindling wood. It's just awful here for old folk. We can manage. Fish, etc. is difficult to get unless you can

NOVEMBER 1942

be about at the opportune time, and old people cannot.

It's the Frossards' Silver Wedding on Dec. 27th and I am calling a meeting of about 20 of the congregation at Mrs Leale's, Antigua, on Thursday, at 3.30, to decide if they are in favour of making them a presentation. I don't mind as the ladies will have to do the collecting! Just like the men you will say!

Thursday, Nov. 26. Well, we had our meeting today. Most of the people asked turned up. It was raining and very cold so two or three from long distances did not come. I had to preside unfortunately. I hate the job. I have a good flow of language when I am alone! Still it went off exceedingly well, and one person came into the shop and said he had never enjoyed a meeting so much, but I think mostly because he was one of the few asked.

Had it not been my duty to preside I would not have gone, I had such a bad cold, most unusual for me. I knew I was not wise to go out, but men never are.

Friday, Nov. 27. I have not been so well today, but had to carry on as it is pay day. Mary came down and did the flowers on the grave without me. We had our usual tea and a little more bread than usual.

Stafford rang to say that the big wall of the new cemetery, about sixty feet, had collapsed right in front of my old shop. Since the Germans moved me, they have been digging a deep trench in the roadway close to the wall, and of course it's all re-claimed land there, and the wall collapsed.

I went down and they had just dug out a Frenchman who was buried. He was dead. Two others had been taken to hospital. It was sad to see the poor chap lying there. The OT official, a very nice refined Frenchman, told me he was from Paris, married with three children. The irony of it was that the man killed was going back to France tonight. I don't know how, when or where they bury these people. George Austin, the Sanitary Inspector, told me on Sunday at church that the average death rate of these foreigners is fifteen per month.

Saturday, Nov. 28. I had a rather bad night with my unusual cold. I did not get up until 1 pm had no breakfast and a small dinner. Tonight I am much better and ate a good tea. Will later have some boiled skimmed milk with rum. I am on my last bottle so must go carefully. I have had some promised for Xmas, so quite expect to be in luck's way.

You cannot buy spirits of any kind, no matter what you are prepared to pay. A little Burgundy comes to the island, Créme du Menthe and Benni. It's about 15/- per bottle, out of my reach

NOVEMBER 1942

altogether. Still I don't complain. I have fared fairly well considering. I am by a lovely fire, cosy and warm.

Sunday, Nov. 29. Few people at church now as the mornings are keen and there is no heating. Mr Frossard asked the congregation if they could spare anything of their meagre rations for the children, a few raisins, two or three prunes, fruit, or even half lumps of sugar, anything would help. They are tying to give the children a little extra at Xmas, a little dinner on Dec. 21st and a party in the afternoon. There will be a retiring collection at both services next Sunday, and at all other churches, chapels and RC churches. Then he read, Mark XII, v. 41, the Widow's Mite. In many ways it's difficult to give even one lump of sugar from a 3 oz weekly allowance. And there is no such thing as buying sweets now.

The only extra for sweetening is boiling down sugar beet. Mrs Rowe boiled down 25 lbs this week and got 2 lbs of syrup. It's very nice and we have it in our coffee and on our bread.

I had a nice box of Camembert this week 1/2, the best I have had yet. Some boxes are putrid and stink something awful, yet we manage to scrape and eat part of it! Sometimes we get only a portion, 3d.

My man Simon has been working at the Press Office for the last 2 months. To oblige Mr Peek the last 2 weeks he has worked a lot of extra time at the Town Harbour trying to salvage Mr Peek's boat, the Rambler. They managed to lift her by the 20 ton crane, but when she left the water the wire broke and down she went. That night a barge came and grounded partly on her. They lifted her again and took her to Helman's Brickfied, Vrangue. He says she is practically matchwood.

You will remember the Rambler which took Flo and Ted to Sark for their honeymoon. I reminded Mr Peek about it and we had a laugh. He is looking very poorly. At 86 it's wonderful how he gets about.

I met him at the Press Office this morning and he stood me a glass of lovely port. He seems to get on with everybody. The German Harbourmaster let him use their crane and their big lorries to cart the remnants of the old Rambler. He takes everything in good part as it comes along. He was moved from his house at Delancey, then again from Hauterville, and I expect most of his furniture is gone. Still he carries on, but I'm afraid it won't be for long.

Sunday, Dec. 13. Vegetables cost a lot of money these days. Through the Potato Control Board I got down from St Saviour's 2 tons of mixed roots, for the shop. The account was £48. Not much if you say it quickly.

DECEMBER 1942

The week has been very mild. I had to go to Grange Court, opposite the Ladies' College, to see the Police about a permit to open the road at Cognon, Vale. They agreed to meet me on the Monday in front of Electric Station at 10.30. Tom and I waited in the blasted cold East wind till 11.30, but they did not arrive so we packed off.

I went to see them again on Saturday, told them the story again and they said, We have been and saw the road closed and it's quite all right. I told them that the road was not closed, we had not started. But why? Because we have no permit. But you can have a permit, so you must carry on. I rubbed it in that we were there as agreed and waited an hour. But he said, We have been at 9.30. So what the devil can you make of it! I did not bother to explain any further, but intend starting on Monday.

While in the Grange I went into the Ladies' College to get a permit for paraffin. Again red tape. But I was more concerned to see the poor old College turned into offices, Coal Board Control, Electric, Gas and a dozen other Controls and Controllers. While there I changed my address for all my ration books, about six weeks late. I have not yet received my fuel ration for Oct. or Nov. Still I will see that I get it.

Saturday afternoon I went to St Andrew's. It was my first chance for three weeks. I took Miss Lihou a bottle of Port and some Sloe Gin. Kit will remember where we got the large sloes. After a snack of tea I went on to Mrs Godfray. I took her Sloe Gin and a small, sample bottle of Apricot Brandy. (You may remember it was in the sideboard cupboard for years.) I gave each of them a nice Chaumental pear. She is still in bed but much better and the doctor says she can get up on Monday.

More bad news. My large pieces of furniture stored at Gerald Martel's place, the Tea Rooms, L'Islet, must be moved again. The Germans are turning out people along the coast road, 21 houses at L'Islet alone. All you see all day long now are vans, trolleys and trucks of furniture.

On the Bridge we now have four large concrete gate pillars opposite Johns, the butcher's shop. I suppose for double gates. The whole of the North and South Quays are closed to the public, with penalties and punishments if found there without a permit.

6,000 RX messages came this week. I had one from Marjorie and one from Kit about Miss Myres. I was glad to hear she is still alive. 2 for me out of 6,000. I say, What am I among so many. Mrs Rowe did not even get 1. Mary had 2.

I have counted the collection and divided the change. I have Mrs Warry, Lily Ellis, J. Ogier, Mr Frossard and G. Budge all after me for change. It's impossible to get it. Nobody knows where our copper goes and we have scarcely any silver now, it's all German marks and small coins, 2½d. and 1½d. in value.

DECEMBER 1942

Mrs Rowe is getting my hot skimmed milk which I have every evening with a small piece of cake. I must stop now. Gas is going out at 10. You see how we are restricted, but in spite of all, everyone is the same. They cannot understand how time flies.

Christmas Week. I have been busy trying to get a few presents together and making arrangements for the Rector's Silver Wedding presentation on Dec. 27th. It's on a Sunday so we have decided to have it in Church after the 4 o'clock Carol Service. I don't like the job of speaking but I will have to do it somehow. Mr Peek got the wallets made at the Press Office and we are putting ten £5 notes in each, and are having all the names printed in book form. All looks very nice.

Poor Mr Peek looks, and is now, very bad. He got the news through the RX of the death of his daughter Maud, Mrs Mauger, and this has also upset him.

I killed a rabbit for Mrs Rowe, and one for Diva and the two old aunts she is living with. I also took some potatoes, B. sprouts, flour and a loaf for their Xmas. Then I took Mrs Godfray and Miss Lihou each a bottle of wine, three apples, a bottle of liquor, ½ lb chocolate and a piece of the last of Mum's Christmas puddings, 1938, and it's fresh and beautiful.

Monday, Dec. 28. On Thursday evening, Christmas Eve, Stafford phoned me to go out then. I didn't feel much like it, but as we had to make final arrangements about the presentation I quickly changed into my Sunday best, took my shaving gear etc. and walked with my bicycle up Brock Road and through the Robergerie.

When I passed Mr Peek's Rink there were hundreds of foreigners lining up for their evening meal. I was almost afraid passing as they might have bagged me in the lane and taken my bicycle. It was as dark as a grave, but I got through the crowd all right. Talk about chatter. It was like a lot of ducks.

I had a nice evening there, brawn from the pig they'd killed. Then we chatted by a huge log fire, had a nightcap and went to bed at 1 am. Then what I had quite expected, nobody about in the morning, and of course we did not go to Early Service. But I went to the 10.45, a nice Xmas Service, very bright with anthem. We all thought and spoke of you all and all absent friends.

Then I cycled back, had a nice dinner of goose, pork, stuffing, B. sprouts, baked taters, plenty of wine, then a chat by a good fire and the King's speech. We had an early tea (Real tea) as Mrs Frossard and Monsieur were dining at Barrit-Hills, Village De Putron. She had to walk there and the Rector went after the 4 o'clock service. I did not go. I told the Rector I must have a special dispensation and he agreed.

DECEMBER 1942

We had a nice evening, chancre for supper, lovely, and again Real tea. Stafford's mother and father were the only other visitors. Drinks and a chat and plenty to smoke finished a nice Christmas Day. I slept there the two nights and came home Saturday morning.

Reported to Mrs Rowe, then went to wish Dr Jones greetings, and to my sister's. I had three RX messages, two from Kit, one from Rosemary, which reads as if Jack is in Africa (plenty sand).

Sunday we had the Carol Service, nine lessons, no sermon, then the presentation.

The church was packed. I wrote out my speech and read it from the Chancel steps. I was not nervous but think I read it too quickly. Stafford, the people's warden spoke, also Mr Lainé the Rector's warden of St Mary's Church, L'Islet, and Mr Peek for the congregation. See the Press, Dec. 28th and the Star, Dec. 31st (which cracks me up!)

The wardens went to the Rectory for supper. We drank their health.

Don Bisset's father died this morning. (He had promised to bring me some cough mixture, a big bottle of Demerara, but put it off till this afternoon.) They are making the coffin at his shop, but he wants me to superintend the funeral.

I don't intend to see the old year out, although very glad it's passing, and I jolly well hope it's the last one living under these conditions. Stafford has just phoned to tell me they've had four RX messages from Leslie, the first since March. They are delighted.

New Year's Day, 1943. I have spent a very quiet first day of the year without going outside the front door. It was pouring with rain and blowing a gale. I cleaned down my desk. It was in the state you often saw it!

At dinner time we had a slice of dear old Mum's last Xmas pudding, which was a very large one. Fancy made in 1938 and eating it in 1942. We eat it cold with our bread and butter. We must not lose the recipe. Mrs Rowe wants it. [*See Recipes.*]

After tea of salted herrings I have drunk half a bottle of Loupiac to try to quench my thirst. Mrs Rowe is on Ginger Beer. Still, it's worth it although I had to pay 10d. each for the six I bought in the market.

Tonight we are grading our runner beans, haricots, etc. some for seed, the remainder for eating. I have three or four baskets in case we get short of food, but it's not likely this winter.

Saturday, January 2. Weather nearly as bad as yesterday. I waited over half an hour for a bus on the Bridge, but had to go home for my bicycle as I had to be at the Ecclesiastical Court with Mary's

JANUARY 1943

intended by 3 o'clock. It was awful riding in. Now they have their licence. The Dean inquired about you all.

I went on to Diva's and took her and the old ladies a 2 lb loaf. They said it was a godsend. Got home all wet and cold, but none the worse.

Sunday, Jan. 3. I went to early service. Lovely morning but frosty. Went to St Andrew's and took Miss Lihou and Mrs Godfray an apple tart each and some rusks. Did not wait for tea, just had a liqueur.

When I got home Stafford had been ringing me up to go out there for tea. I jumped on my bicycle and rushed off there and then. Had a nice tea and supper, a chat by a lovely fire, a tot of rum and bed at 12.

Monday, Jan. 4. In the afternoon supervised Mr Bisset's funeral. The old chap was 92, a very good innings, I thought. Many friends there, 10 wreaths. I put a report in the paper for him and said J.C.S. supervised on behalf of Mr D. Bisset.

Things are now very dead here. We get no war news except what the Germans put in the papers.

It's amusing to see how people tow everything behind their bicycles. One milkman I saw had 2 big cans on the front, two on the carrier and six large ones in a trailer. Most women get their root vegetables etc. in prams. The ladies in Town all market that way.

I am just back from Mrs Stubbs, Grandes Maisons. I went for a chat and a tobacco ration I had bartered for. I had a job to get back it was so dark. When I passed my house, New Road, I thought, Fancy, shut out of your own house. They have broken one of the large panes in the dining-room window. It's patched up with a piece of cardboard. I bet the place will be in a state when they give it up.

Mrs Rowe is finishing shelling my beans. I have a fine lot so will probably sell some in the shop. The fixed price is 2/6 per lb. Black market you would probably get 5/- or do even better bartering.

I took my tomato seed to Mr Poat this morning. He is raising my plants from the seed I saved in 1940, the year we could not even give tomatoes away.

Tuesday, Jan. 5. I went to the Old Rectory to see Uncle Ned. He sleeps there alone now he has no Germans billeted on him. I took him a bottle of white wine we can now buy for 5/-. He would like me to keep him company some evenings, but it's so devilish dark coming back that I hate going. He had a nice fire in Marjorie's sewing room. I will spend a few evenings with him next moon. New moon tomorrow.

JANUARY 1943

Wednesday, Jan. 6. After 4.45 practice (by daylight as we have no blackout in the church) I went to see Uncle Ned. I managed to find my way to the front door. I knocked hard then heard the tramping along the passage, the drawing of the great bolt. It seemed we were the only people in St Sampson's. I walked along the dark old passage that I had seen in all its glory as you knew it in Auntie Kate's time. I looked at the dismal place and thought about the contrast, and poor Uncle Ned sleeping in that big barrack (that's how it appeared to me).

We chatted, listened to the wind howling, read RX messages and then it was time to leave. How to get out of that blooming garden! It was quite a puzzle to find the gate, but once in the road I crept down Church Lane and was damned glad when I got home. I won't venture there again on dark nights.

Friday, Jan. 8. Mrs Rowe has been spending her evenings boiling sugar beet. She puts about 12 lbs cut up in an iron boiler and lets it boil for 5 hours or more. Then it's a devil of a job to squeeze the pulp. She gets about 4 pints of liquid which has to be boiled till it thickens. That takes hours on the gas. The result is a 1 lb jam pot full. It's very sweet and like dark Golden Syrup. It's a lot of trouble but well worth doing as we get only 3 oz of sugar per week.

Mary came down on Friday. She was full of arrangements for her wedding next Friday. A carriage will fetch me, and we go to Belmont Road (where she is going to live with her mother-in-law) for a reception, just a glass of wine and if they can, a piece of plain cake. She wrote my RX messages in a book.

I went to see my old Carpenter's shop. Kimber's is down and the front of mine, which looks like a ruin. I don't know who will compensate me. They are laying the railway, and when the trains are passing and you meet your friends they shout out, next station Paddington or Victoria.

Lily Ellis has been sick all through the Xmas holidays. Eunice Falla and my man Martel had to look after the shop. It affected the business somewhat, but we had to manage. The shop would pay very well if we could get the right supplies, but the G.U.B. won't take us on. They already have enough shops to supply, so we have to depend on outside sources. We get enough but not always the things we want.

Wednesday, Jan. 13. The day opened rather fine after an awful gale which did a lot of damage. 17 boats were smashed up in the Old Town Harbour, many beyond repair they tell me. The Germans had moved a sort of pontoon there and they tell me it broke adrift and did the damage.

Being a fine morning I went to Miss Lihou as she wanted her bill

JANUARY 1943

which she paid. Then I went to see Mrs Godfray. She gets up only after dinner these weeks.

Mr P.G. Ogier came in at 6 o'clock, absolutely soaked, about his mother's funeral. She died in the Emergency Hospital this afternoon. You will remember Mr Ogier, Duval. I worked with him on the Cadastre for years. He is not very fit himself, although he recovered wonderfully from two strokes some time ago.

I am going to take some French medicine, which I got from the chemist, with my skimmed milk. I am well but my voice is nearly gone. It's an awful effort for me to speak. I am rather anxious about it. I will try this and if no better will stop smoking and go to the doctor. I don't know what causes this, no cold or cough or pain, just my voice weak. I must keep fit till after Mary's wedding on Friday, otherwise when the parson says, Who gives this woman away, he might not hear me say, I do!

Friday, Jan. 15. Well the wedding day arrived. I got up early as I had to go to Town.

After going to the Greffe I went to the market. It made me think of Covent Garden (but on a very much smaller scale) as I saw it many years ago, with the vans all backing in and unloading. People were beginning to flock in with their prams, push carts and all imaginable contraptions for carting their heavy loads.

Everybody was saying, Good morning, it's fine. Of course, we all knew that! Then I did think it was a little different, because at Covent Garden nobody looked at me. As Mr Tom Barnes used to say, Though you are of some importance over here, in London you are just a living speck of dust. I think he liked to feel, how are the mighty fallen into insignificance, when some of our celebrities got to such places. I met Angelo and we chatted.

I got back for an early dinner, ran to the bank as it's pay day, then got ready for the wedding. *I looked very nice?* in my striped trousers I had made for Jack's wedding, black coat and vest, white shirt and wedding tie and yellow gloves, what you call, well got up. I fancied I could hear poor old Mum say when I was careless about my dress and got ready in a minute or two, You rush and are like a carrot half scraped. I had to laugh to myself. Mrs Rowe said I looked posh, I don't know what that means, but I can tell you my boots shone like glass.

Anyway, the carriage came and I was ready. We drove up to the Canishers (Mary's digs). I was introduced to the landlady and the two bridesmaids. They thought it funny to ride in a horse coach. They had never been in one before. The usual perambulator crowd with their kiddies was outside St James' church, and dressed in all manner of apparel.

The Rev. James chatted with me for a few minutes inside the

JANUARY 1943

porch. There were about thirty people including Evelyn. It was a pretty little wedding. Bridesmaids were dressed in pale bluish flowered material, tiny blue forget-me-nots and little green leaves, very pretty. Mary wore a blouse of the same material and blue coat and skirt.

Then into the vestry to sign the articles. I told them that knot was tied easily and quickly enough, but it can't so easily be untied.

Then out we went, arm in arm, showers of confetti. I got my nice new 27/6 hat full. We drove to Gruts to be photographed, only the five of us. The best man was Ted's brother. [*See illustration 15.*]

On to Belmont Road. I stayed only long enough to have a glass of champagne and a piece of cake, as the carriage will not wait, and got home at 4.30. All that lot in less than two hours and that's over.

Mrs Rowe thinks the material of the bridesmaids' dresses is flowered georgette. Anyway it was a neat and pretty French material, which cost £3 for each dress. I could have put the lot in my pocket it was so thin. I gave Mary £2 for a wedding present, all I can afford now.

I am now going to bed. As evening comes on my voice has almost gone. I take Syrup Famel Créosole. It's like taking coal tar!

I don't know if the planes will come over tonight, but last night the Germans were firing at them part of the night. It was impossible to sleep for some time.

Monday, Jan. 18. Many happy returns Flo. I expect you have been guessing I was thinking of you today. If I remember rightly you are thirty eight today. How time slips by. I will, if spared, give you all one nice present to make up for all the birthdays and Xmases we have missed. One thing certain, we will all be very lucky if we get through this and all the family united. I often tell people here that when the ranks are reformed, there will be many gaps for the rear files to step into. Still, we are hoping for the best.

I had a funeral yesterday, Mrs Bowditch, Church Road. I buried her husband exactly six months ago. I told you he was drowned at Bordeaux going out to the fishing grounds.

Friday, Jan. 22. Mary came down this afternoon. We did the grave with Soleil d'Or and lovely Violets Mrs Rowe picked from her garden, very kind of her. Mary did not stay to tea. She wanted to be home for her husband's tea. I told her a new broom sweeps clean. She did not agree.

The winter is slipping along fine except for the tons of rain, and no really cold weather yet, thank God, as fuel is scarce. I can manage well this winter, the next we are hoping the war will be over.

JANUARY 1943

Saturday Jan. 23. For breakfast I had my usual lovely apple with ample bread but very little butter. I have a piece $3/8"$ left to last three meals. Mrs Rowe said I will.

It was a lovely morning, clear blue sky and quite warm, so I went out to St Andrew's. They were glad to see me. I took them each a bottle of sloe gin Kit and I made in 1939. They were delighted to have it. I had tea at Mrs Godfray's. Elsie had made a lovely cake. She said it was your recipe Kit, made with fresh butter, sugar and white flour she had been given. It was the best I had eaten since the war.

I got back at 6. Mrs Rowe was waiting so after feeding the rabbits I had another tea, plenty of bread, little butter, 3 oz of cheese, brawn and celery. Then I went to the Old Rectory and stayed with Ned. Got back in lovely moonlight 5 minutes before curfew.

I led my 2 rabbits today, so all being well by Feb. 23rd I should have 2 litters to increase my stock by about 18, most of which I will of course sell.

I am writing this by 1 candle power, hence the scribble. Our gas is cut off at 10. Mrs Rowe is busy boiling sugar beet to make Golden Syrup (I should say Black Syrup). The beet costs 2/6. We have to boil it on the fire as the gas ration won't run to it.

Wednesday, Jan. 27. Mr Brache from Les Français, Vale, pruned my apple trees, and we cut away part of the pear tree to give the trees behind more light.

After dinner I went to Priaulx's stables (where the Germans keep their horses) and asked for a load of manure. He said I had better see the Captain and directed me to the Manse. I rang and was ushered into the once nicely furnished drawing-room (now a plain room with bare boards and a deal table). I told the Captain my mission. He said he could hardly say anything for the moment, as probably on Friday they may all be gone. I said, Well somebody will be here. Oh no, it's not definite, but we may all be gone. (I hope it's true.)

I decided to go to Mr S.T. Ogier as we had some insurance matters to settle. I had tea there, lovely fried bread in deep fat with rashers of their freshly salted pig. I added pepper, then dark red beetroots. It was a real treat and the flavour delicious. (My voice is very weak still and after eating this fat it felt much easier.) Then we had rock buns, nice plain cake and finished up with pumpkin jam, not bad for wartime.

For supper three hours later we had bread and fat. This was accompanied by the news at 6 and 9, a real treat. I helped with the knitting machine by turning a handle, nice pastime. After a double nightcap, one of Rum the other Sloe Gin Kit and I made, we retired quite sober with a serious promise that Stafford would see that I

JANUARY 1943

was down by 8 o'clock.

Thursday, Jan. 28. Damp and chilly again. I got back from the Gigands at 9.30. Bryan is not at all well and I am going to take him some calomel for the liver today. My ordinary work is proceeding according to plan, in fact I think I will have to take on another carpenter.

But the news today is very distressing. All ex-officers and I think criminals, have had their papers from the Germans to report tomorrow to the Medical Board. They include Mr Frossard, Dr Jones, Mr Poat, Don Bisset, Capt. Falla and they tell me about 1,500 have to be transported to Germany. That's the latest. I have been telephoning about the matter. I think the churchwardens will have to apply for the Rector to be left here, also the Doctor.

It's also reported that it is possible that a lot of Freemasons will have to go. That will mean my turn next. Then I will at last say I wish I had gone with Kit. But up to now I cannot really say I regret being left here, *only*, as I have said before, for your sakes, as I know you must always be wondering how we are getting on.

Saturday, Jan. 30. I had an early telephone call from Dr Fox to say he could not see me to examine my throat as arranged, as he himself has to go to the Regal for a Medical examination by the Germans. I don't know what it all means. Mr and Mrs Frossard, Dr Jones and most ex-officers have to go up.

Sunday, Jan. 31. We had a terrible night of squalls of hail and rain, and the gale is still continuing this morning. Going to church it was almost impossible to walk with the high wind. You know how it can blow in Guernsey. There were only about 18 people there, and the noise of the wind made it difficult to hear the sermon.

Mr Frossard is rather depressed at the possibility of having to go to Germany. Mrs Frossard is also worried (the wives and families have to go as well). I think it will end that I, myself, will have to go. I will leave Tom and Gerald Martel in charge of the business and vinery. The only salvation is that summer is coming, and whatever the hardships it's nothing if the weather is warm.

I spoke to the Dean yesterday about asking for exemption for the Rector. He thinks that at present we cannot do anything, as they have not said what this call up is for.

The weather is so bad that I had thought of not going to the Doctor's for lunch today, but on second thoughts have decided to go. It might be the last time we will have lunch together should he be sent away. But I cannot think they will take him. He is very shaky and seventy four years old. I dread the walk across the Bridge.

The doctor has been to see Uncle Ned. He has to stay in bed for

FEBRUARY 1943

a week. He has a tired heart and a touch of pleurisy. I told him last week not to do any plumbing while the weather is so cold. But everyone is after him for saucepans, kettles and about leaking pots. He has shrivelled up but walks briskly. He cannot see along the road, and I tell him and Percy he will be run over. He is staying with them while he is ill. I say it is not prudent for him to sleep alone at the Old Rectory but he will not listen. The difficult part is that if the house is not occupied the Germans might take it over, and he would probably lose furniture and all. We are going through a critical time just now, and this is another Black Sunday.

Monday, February 1. This has been an awfully depressing week. On Sunday evening when the Rector gave the Blessing he just managed it without breaking down. I think he was wondering if it was the last time before going to Germany. Poor Mrs Frossard was weeping in her seat. All the parsons and doctors have been to the Regal to pass the doctor.

I went to see Dr Fox about my throat. He told me all the doctors had been exempt. He said that if the medicine he was trying had no effect I would have to go to Jersey. I suppose to see a specialist. I told him about a tooth that has caused me a lot of trouble over the years. He said, Better get it out, but it would not be the cause of my throat trouble. (I have my doubts.) I rang Mr Tanner and to my surprise he said, Come when you like. So I fixed for 11 tomorrow.

Tuesday, Feb. 2. I went on my bicycle. We had a long chat about old times and the war and all the trouble he had gone through moving furniture.

Then I explained about my tooth which he said would affect my throat. He said it should have been out months ago. I could not explain how tender my gums were, but he took great pains, in fact he was nearly an hour about it, deadening it with stuff no other dentist in the island has. He massaged both sides of the tooth, injected and then began the 'operation'. It gave me hell, but not where the tooth was but further back. I have never known anyone to be so patient and careful.

To my surprise he charged me only 3/6. I told him the job was worth £1. He said it would probably take months for the glands in my throat to get normal again. I am hoping that's what caused the trouble, in which case my voice should come back. If not I will get anxious. People on the phone now all ask me if I have a cold.

I went to see Mr Frossard on Monday. It was a pathetic sight. Mr Frossard was arranging with me what he would put in a safe I had taken to the vestry for his private papers etc., and poor Mrs Frossard was weeping and by the look of her eyes had been all night. It's really awful to be torn away from your home at a few days' notice.

FEBRUARY 1943

We had a nice rabbit pie today and a *special* milk pudding, and I had a bottle of Rum brought me as well. I had two RX messages from Kit today so must now start to answer seven.

Monday, Feb. 8. We have just passed through a very black, depressing week, everybody stopping everybody else to know who has to go, people coming to see me or telephoning to know if Mr Frossard had had his orders to go.

Yesterday I forgot it was the first Sunday in the month and missed the Early Service. I was sorry as it's possibly the last here for the Rector for some time.

When I got to the 10.45 service Miss Ross was waiting for me. She wanted to send a petition to the German General to try to get an exemption for the Rector. She assured me the Rector agreed and was informed officially that it might succeed.

This meant writing a Humble Petition and getting it translated into German, getting hundreds of signatures, and delivered to the German Chaplain by 10 the next morning. We did all this.

Mrs Frossard did not come to church. The Rector looked very upset but preached two good sermons and managed to get through the services, but very shaky on the, perhaps, last Blessing for some time. The appropriate Recessional hymn was, Holy Father cheer our way. Light at evening time. The whole thing has cast a gloom over the parish and it's impossible to feel bright.

We are putting a platform to raise the choir seats 7" level with the Chancel, and this morning I started my men on this. I managed to find enough wood. I left the Rector at 2. He was taking a funeral and had then heard nothing.

Mrs Warry had rung for me to go there to see biscuits they had made with half our rations we had spared, and about how to divide them. As I passed the Rectory a policeman went in. I could not pluck up the courage to call to hear the result, but when I got to Mrs Warry I got her to ring up. It was too true. Mrs Frossard told her they had received the final orders to leave Wednesday.

It's too awful to think of the parishes of St Sampson's and the Vale without Rectors, and already three others of our ten gone. I will go and see the Rector in the morning. It means I will have to be in charge and I don't feel up to it just now, as my voice is troubling me. I might feel a little better now the tooth is out. I am now thinking the Germans are preparing for a siege, in which case we would be better out of it.

Tuesday, Feb. 9. This has been a very exciting day. As I told you we are raising the choir stalls. While I was there Mr Frossard sent all his private papers to be put in that safe I had taken to the vestry. Later he was sent for to go to Grange Court, where he was informed that in consideration of all the good work he had done for the island and the schools since the Occupation, they would give him an exemption. Mrs Frossard rang me up very excitedly and said how delighted she was. But Stafford had already informed me. Then people called to see me to know if the report was true, and I telephoned a few.

There has been great excitement in St Sampson's this afternoon, but as you will know still disappointment for those who have to go. Warren Hardy is now added to the list.

The Rev. James has to go, so Mr Frossard will work both the Vale and St Sampson's churches. History repeats itself, for years ago both parishes were carried on by one parson.

Evenings, as darkness falls, we hear the dull, sickening thuds of the guards up Brock Road. Later the silence of the night is often broken, perhaps by a company coming home or the double horse wagons trotting up to Priaulx's stables. They would have been out carting ammunition which must be done in the dark. Some nights we hear a whole crowd marching and singing along New Road.

We seem to have a lot of heavy guns firing these nights. It's when our planes pass over. Quite a number of pieces of shrapnel dropped on Mr Lake's greenhouses and smashed the glass. It's unfortunate for me as my potatoes are now up in his big span.

Sunday, February 14. Valentine Day. We are not sending out any! I don't think you children lived in the days when we sent them. Poetry, also quite insulting pictures used to be posted.

Well it was a very happy Sunday morning today. It was quite fine and we talked outside the church of how lucky St Sampson's was that Mr Frossard had an exemption and had not gone with the 120 who left on Friday night with their wives and children. (It was blowing a gale.) All our congregation were jubilant that Mr Frossard and his wife are staying with us.

It's a terrible tragedy for all those deported, and I believe that when they got on the boat they were told that some were for France and some for Germany, and only wives over 65 would be allowed with their husbands. I just mention a few who went, Lt Col Randall and his family, Major Langlois, Mr Bartlett, Joe Eveson, Tom Wyatt, the Rev. James, Major Falla and his brother Jack, and others.

I had a very busy week and the choir stalls are now raised to the level of the chancel, only 7" but what a difference. The choir are now above the level of the congregation. I schemed and managed to get enough wood for the floor joists.

The Miss Malletts and others were quite surprised to find they were elevated. It's a great improvement. Now they want me to fix book boards. I don't know if I can find the material.

I am still rather worried about my voice. I cannot think what is

FEBRUARY 1943

the cause. I can put up with it provided it is not a malignant growth. That's the only thing that makes me anxious. It's such a delicate spot that delay might be dangerous. For a job of that sort I would like to be examined in London (not now possible).

The prayers of the church were asked for Mrs Romeril who is at the Emergency Hospital seriously ill, and they say she cannot get better. It's sad for those children.

I hope to start planting my outside potatoes tomorrow. I am spending £4 4s.0d. per week on labour in garden and both vineries. Quite a risk if we are to get most of the stuff stolen as last year. Still I am risking it. Money is no use here, it's food we want. I have enough potatoes to last me till the next crop. That's the advantage even if I lose money.

The people in Church Lane had about 15 rabbits stolen, and Pollard about 50 loaves, but the culprits were caught, the Frenchmen from Delancey Cottages. It's all the more serious as they are interned owing to typhus in the camp. The OT and the police found the rabbits skinned. They offered to return them but of course this could not be risked owing to the epidemic. I expect they will take mine next. Each morning when I go out I expect to find them gone. Locking up is no use, they break open anything. But I do feel safer now this gang is caught.

Saturday, Feb 20. Today we hear the news that Mr Cross and others who were taken with hundreds of Englishmen to Germany last summer, are being invalided home again.

This has been another black week. Mrs Romeril died and was buried today. The service was at the Chapel. Mr and Mrs Frossard and Stafford and I as Parish Churchwardens went. We sent a wreath from the Rector and Churchwardens, Deepest respect, sincere sympathy. The Rev. Ord and the Rev. J. Leale officiated.

Kit will feel sorry especially for the children. John helped her so much in the garden and field the summer of 1940. It was very young for her to die, only in her forties.

Only 4 oz of meat per head this week and for the next few weeks. We had a nice rabbit pie today, the pastry was lovely. I have four rabbits in kindle, two due the 23rd.

I have a funeral at the Foulon on Monday so I will call on Mrs Petruschke when I pass near and take her bill. I have carried it in my pocket for two months waiting for a chance. It pays me to take it, I get treated well!

I went to Town in the bus, owing to the E wind. The Fish Market had only one stall and that with limpets. Spring flowers plentiful, 1d a dozen blooms. Ira Ozanne was in the bus on my return, but when he saw me he put a bottle on my lap and asked if I would leave it at Turners on the Bridge, as this would save him one hour. I later

FEBRUARY 1943

found he had paid my fare, 8d.

Sunday, Feb 21. It's 9 pm. The 'chariots' are just passing up the road. I hear the Germans chatting as they pass going to Priaulx' stables. It's a lovely mild night but frosty air.

I have just been inhaling steam with eucalyptus and other ingredients in a basin, with a towel over my head. I don't know if it's much use for my trouble.

I went to both services today, but did not sing at all. In fact I couldn't if I tried. The collections today were for the deportees in Germany. We had £17, very good I thought.

Friday, Feb 26. It's some days since I have added to these lines. The last two days have been beautiful with sunshine, and we are all wondering if the winter is really over. As I sit here in my new study making up the men's money, I see everything passing at the bottom of Brock Road, and right up Church Lane. [*See illustration 11.*] The brougham has just passed with the Bank men. They all come in the same trap, Midland, Westminster, etc. We have bank days, Mondays and Fridays.

I am seeing the doctor this afternoon. If he finds no change I expect he will send me to Jersey to see a specialist. Mr Frossard found my voice better recently, and I seemed to be a little better today. But at times I fancy it's going to be a long job. Still I am hoping for the best.

I see the postman coming in. Oh, it's a RX message for Mrs Rowe and two for me. One from the Rev. Dickens who says they have had Flo for lunch. One from Mr Lazenby who cannot have had my message for he says he has heard of me from Flo.

I had two nice nests of rabbits on Feb 23rd. I don't know how many yet.

Mr Cross and five others arrived back from Germany this week. They had a bad 10 day journey coming back. Mr Cross came straight home, but I hear the others went to hospital. Mr Cross told me the first camp was awful, but after they were moved and with a Red Cross parcel each week added to their meagre rations, they were not badly off.

We dug and planted Mrs Rowe's garden, put in four boxes of early potatoes. A delightful day, lovely hot sun, but as usual in early spring, very cold in the shade.

Saturday, Feb 27. After dinner I went around the greenhouses looking for rabbit food, I saw that the Germans had taken down the hedge between Lakes and Priaulx, and now all the greenhouse border is a cartway, and it quite upset me. All that lovely rhubarb is ruined. I had luckily dug out half a dozen crowns.

FEBRUARY 1943

They are turning the big Alliance patch into an air raid shelter. They have dug a big trench about 12 ft wide and 180 ft long, and up to now it's 10 ft deep. Yesterday they blasted a boulow. The explosion blew splinters of stone which broke at least 12 panes in my big span. I don't quite know what to do about making a complaint. I may perhaps see the officer on Monday.

I hear all the French and other foreigners will be out of quarantine tomorrow. For three weeks the OT have been on guard with loaded rifles, because of that attack of typhus. Most of their works closed down.

I went to see Dr Jones this afternoon and again took 10 lbs of potatoes. They are always without. They get their ration of 5 lbs each but cannot make it last. I still go there to lunch on Sundays. As I told you they live at the Cognon, Vale now. The place looked miserable, no fire, no wood or coal to burn. The kerb and hearth were covered with tar.

People now mix tar (8d per gallon) with rubbish of coal dust, let it clug [Unable to trace this verb – could possibly be 'clog' or 'clag', *Ox Dic Vol 2*] and get a nice fire for some time, but it's not wise to poke it, something Dr Jones is doing all the time. Hence the mess, and you can guess how it shows up on a cream tiled hearth and kerb.

Miss Matthews had her cats in the back garden in lounge chairs on cushions! She has only three left, and one won't live much longer. They cannot get enough food, just limpets and skimmed milk and bread which must come out of their rations. She has been mad to keep them so long.

It's quite a game to see people up and down Brock Road with baking tins and jars tied in white cloths going to the bakchouse. I think they must take only potatoes, as the meat ration is too small, 6d worth per head this week. They also take grated carrots to be baked for making tea. So little gas is allowed that they mostly have to use the bakehouse.

I see Mr Romeril has to take the dinner down now, and the children fetch it returning from school. It must be awful at Maison-de-Haut now with no mother.

Mr Ted Ogier rang on Sunday morning to say his sister, Eunice, had just died, 70 years old. The funeral is to be on Wednesday from the Chapel, the interment in the select corner (so called) jib patch. It's nearly filled now.

Saturday, March 13. I have not written for some few days. Miss Matthews was not very amiable when I was last there. She had just telephoned the vet to come and put her (I think favourite) ginger cat to sleep. So the house was in a sad mood.

The Chapel was nearly full for the funeral of Miss Ogier, with all the celebrities, many from Town including Jurats. The Dean was ill

MARCH 1943

so sent his son and wife to represent him. Mr Peek could not attend, was taken ill suddenly. Mr Frossard gave the short address by request of the family. There were 73 wreaths, an awful lot to manage when so far from the cemetery. The Star (March 6, I think) has a nice account of it. It was a lovely sunny afternoon. I was glad when it was over.

We have had a quiet time in Brock Road, but now the foreigners are out of quarantine they started marching down just before 7 o'clock, hardly daylight. It's tramp, tramp, and the chatter of about 300. So you can imagine it in the early morning. But still everyone seems safe, even the children run about everywhere, and nobody seems to take notice of anybody else. To me it seems strange.

There was an order out this week about Artillery Shooting from 8 to 1 o'clock. Many roads would be closed, typewritten orders with particulars for our district at Collas' shop on the Bridge. So Thursday morning my men could not come to work.

My gardeners did not want to lose time so decided to get to the vinery before 8. They were the only lucky two as, for some unknown reason, nothing happened. I took a chance and went out at 10.45 and found people about the Bridge, some saying it was cancelled. Anyway up to now we know nothing except that they did not shoot. We had to leave all doors, windows and lights open and were expecting terrible rumblings.

Yesterday I went to the cemetery with the Stone Mason and Tom and we fixed a kerb around Mum's grave. It looks very nice. I am not bothering about the Headstone till you all come over (if ever) and we will choose it and decide on the inscription.

I have four nests of rabbits, one litter of 10, one of only one, the other two not counted yet.

Last week Stafford called one evening at 6 on his motor cycle and would insist on my going out for tea. He said he would fry a slice of bacon (home cured) each and I would sleep the night. I could not resist the temptation, so there and then I went on the back of his motor cycle. I did not let him go too fast!

Stafford and I got the tea ready. I fried while he warmed up a tin of beans. Real tea. We had all ready when his wife got home from visiting her mother. We chatted till supper time, then lovely pork fat. Oh, what a treat. It seemed to do my throat good. Plenty of bread and nice cocoa to drink.

Next morning Bryan brought me back on the motor cycle, not too cold and I felt all the better for the change. They are very kind to me, and it was a real treat to get a bit of pork. It's now over 18 months since I had any from my butcher. The meat ration is very small and then half bone. Still under the conditions I don't complain. It's the lack of butter and milk that's getting me down.

My tomato plants came on Friday and we began planting

MARCH 1943

immediately. I know they say it's an unlucky day, but I cannot put things off for superstition, and if I had Saturday is the 13th! So there you are. I had to chance the luck either way. Mr Poat raised the plants from seed I saved that awful season, 1940, when I gave at least £650 worth to the pigs and cows, and what they could not eat I threw into the quarry. (That's history now.)

My plants are a lovely sample. I have just telephoned Mr Poat to say how pleased I am with them and to tell him I wanted 1,000 more. But Mr Higgs saw the balance of mine and bought them. Of course it's not Mr Poat's fault as when I gave him the seed I said I wanted only 2,500. However I will have some of his sort. It won't matter much.

Monday, March 15. On Saturday I took Dr Jones a few potatoes. They cannot manage on their ration. They were again without fuel. I sent Tom down with a large elm limb and part of a box cart. They could burn the devil down there. It must be awful to be without coal.

I now have 30 baby rabbits and nearly all sold.

Yesterday after lunch at the doctor's I took my Trésor accounts to Stafford for the auditors, then went to see the old people. Stafford insisted on my staying to tea. His wife and I cycled to Evening Service. Stafford stayed to look after the house. (It's not safe to leave a place alone.) We played bridge, my first hand for over four years. We played for the benefit of Mrs Ogier, Junior, who wants to learn.

I rose with the lark, (Oh no, it was seagulls calling.) After breakfast I went straight to the shop. I expect the men wondered why I was in my Sunday best. Then I changed into my old togs, not that I do any work, in fact I have no energy now.

I am sitting by a cosy fire. I have steamed once and I have to inhale once more for at least 15 minutes. It's now six weeks I've been at this game and my voice is not back yet. The doctor is taking a blood test on Wednesday. It seems to be the same game as with Mother, looking for something that shows no symptoms. I don't understand doctors.

Friday, March 19. I went to the doctor on Wednesday. He examined my throat again, saw little change, but said my voice was clearer, as clear as I usually spoke. I soon told him differently. He wanted to say I never did speak clearly. Then I told him some facts, my digestion works well, I sleep nine hours every night waking only once, my weight has been $9^{1}/_{2}$ stone for the last 18 months, the hardest work I do lately is feeding the rabbits, and I could not understand why I did not improve. He said, Remember you are not a young man. I told him 66. He said he would change my medicine.

MARCH 1943

He took the blood for testing, right arm since I am left-handed. He applied the tourniquet and pushed the needle in. My skin was devilish tough. I enjoyed seeing the blood being pumped into a little bottle.

We have had a lovely month so far. In two days the winter will be over, the mildest winter I have ever known.

What a mess of clay, etc where the Germans are making that dug-out on the Alliance patch. They have been taking my stones stacked around the May tree, and making a gap in the long masoned wall, all without asking. So we went into the Manse and told the officer. He made a fuss about the gap, but instead of paying for the stone I had a fine load of horse manure, and I think they will pay me for the 16 panes of glass they broke in blasting.

I had another 15 broccoli stolen from Allendale. I rang the police who told me I was lucky, for every one of mine the country people lose 50. They also took a lock off Lake's greenhouse. I must try and get that back.

I went to see Mrs Godfray and Miss Lihou yesterday, the first time since my voice is bad. They were glad to see me. I took Miss Lihou a bottle of wine and Mrs Godfray some voice tablets and some lovely Easter Lilies. (I will put some on Mum's grave.)

Elsie was working like a man in the field in front of Belle Vue. She is working 20 perches of ground. Mrs Godfray is a little cross about it. They gave me one egg (they are worth 1/- each).

Sunday, March 21. I cycled to Town, fine sunshine, cold NE air. I had to get a permit for twine for peas. Most people are excited as the Germans are calling up a lot of our men to work for them, people in shops or on non-essential work. Land workers are not to be called up. I hope they won't take any of my men.

Miss Matthews phoned this morning to say that Dr Wilson had called to see the Doctor again. She has to make up a bed downstairs and he must not have visitors, so I won't be going there to lunch today. I find him failing a lot.

It's getting very depressing here now we get so little war news. We are all hoping it will finish this year, otherwise people will not be able to stick it much longer. Lack of essential foods begins to tell on us. Still I don't think there is any need for real anxiety till next autumn.

George Austin (the MOH) told me in the vestry this morning that he sent my blood sample to the Germans to be tested. They no longer have material for the work at Lukis House. The Germans would be sure to have a good medical staff. I am longing to hear the result, but I think it was the best next move.

MARCH 1943

Wednesday, March 24. I went to Fred Fuzzey's funeral at Bordage Hall this morning, there were quite a lot of people but I did not go to Candie for the interment.

We have had a rather funny week. German orders were to the effect that there would be Artillery Practice, heavy guns, on Thursday, 7.30 to 3 pm and Friday, 5 to 7 pm. Most of the Town people had to clear out of their houses, Hospital and Asylum cases had to be moved, and dozens of roads closed. I hear there were over 90 ambulance cases. The evacuation was from South Esplanade to Longstore, mostly along the Front, but all the Town and Post Office, also Delancey Lane and the Park. Most of the shooting was towards South and East. Everybody was wondering if the vibration was going to crumble half the Town and most of our greenhouses. The orders were to leave all windows and lights open.

Stafford rang me on Wednesday evening and suggested that since I would have to stay in all day, why not go there early in the morning, and have a baked pork dinner. I decided to go.

It meant getting up at 6 am which I did not relish, but I soon got washed and shaved, and flew to the garden and opened the lights of Lake's and my vineries as I thought the men had arranged not to do it. Then I took food to the rabbits and packed off on my bicycle for the Gigands. Men who wanted to put in their day's work were rushing about.

I got there at 7.30, nobody up, so I wandered about. We had breakfast. We waited, but it was a fiasco, a few heavy shots were fired but nothing to shake a town.

My men went to work at Allendale which was not a closed area, but found it wet on the greenhouses so decided to try their luck at getting to the shop. They went up two closed roads and nobody stopped them. Tom also worked. They got their day's work in. Messervy did not risk it so was wild to have lost a day's work. You can imagine the inconvenience it put people to. I hear there were some who left their houses in the country and had their fowls and rabbits stolen.

After a baked dinner at the Ogiers, Lionel, who was on holiday, took me to his house, (Mr Henry's, the Hermitage, Vale). While he was having his dinner I looked around, saw the cow, pig and rabbits, etc.

Then I went on the Common and chatted with a young man who was tethering his goats. He was so chatty I said, You seem to know me. Of course I do, I have carried for you often. I did not remember, but he said it was gratis, for the Army. I concluded the Salvation Army.

Then I had the history of the crippled old goat. It was given to them, gives little milk, but for sentimental reasons they cannot kill it, and it won't die. So you see life is funny and his story interested me.

MARCH 1943

Then I walked over the Common to Bunker Hill. Well, you could not imagine the goings on there, dug-outs, excavations, with concrete machines and gantries. You would not know the place.

Then I turned for the Hermitage where Lionel and his wife were picking watercress. They gave me a bunch. Then we got on his motor cycle (he is allowed one being a billeting officer) and were back at the Gigands by 3.

So much for the shooting. I chatted to Mr Ogier, Snr. in his greenhouses, and came home at 6 o'clock. I enjoyed myself, but for a lot of people a wasted day.

Saturday, March 27. Dr Wilson saw Dr Jones on Wednesday and said he had better go to hospital. He could not be looked after at home. They have no coal, no gas after 10 pm, no candles, no paraffin, so they took him there the same day. I saw Miss Matthews this morning. She said he was a shade better, but I doubt if he can get better, his heart is bad and his legs are swelling. He has so often told me that this is the beginning of the end.

Wednesday, March 31. This has been another eventful week. Tuesday Stafford called about our making up the Churchwardens' Budget for the Constables which we could have done in about 10 minutes. But he would insist that it was better for me to go out that evening and sleep there which I did.

When I got home on Wednesday morning Mr Frossard rang to say Mr Peek had died and Mrs Peek wanted me to do the funeral. So I went to Doyle Road and made all arrangements. For the convenience of Town people and owing to lack of transport, the service is to be at St James Church. The interment is at St Sampson's cemetery in the family vault on Saturday. Mrs Peek was naturally very upset.

You can guess I was busy, a special job. In the afternoon Mrs Holmes from Brock Road came to say her husband had died at King Edward Sanatorium. That job I will do on Monday.

Saturday, April 3. Mr Peek's funeral at St James' Church. The Rev. Davis and the Rev. Frossard officiated. Press Staff, Le Riche's and De La Mare's etc formed a guard of honour outside the church. What a display of flowers in front of the church, about 150 wreaths. Printed form of service, three hymns, usual lessons, a packed church. Mr Frossard gave an address.

I managed to get Mr Smith, Civil Transport, to let me have a huge lorry with crates, and they took most of the flowers.

They managed to get them to St Sampson's before we arrived and placed them each side of the path from the main gate right to the vestry, a really huge display. Some people met at the cemetery

APRIL 1943

instead of going in to Town. Mr Peek is a man who will be much missed.

I think this will be my biggest funeral for wreaths. I feel relieved tonight that job is over and went without a hitch.

Sunday, April 4. Another glorious and wonderful morning. I went to the 8 o'clock service, then had breakfast of porridge with milk and sugar. I am having it to try and pick up again, as lately I seem to have fallen back somewhat. My voice has improved a little with the fine weather. It seems more of a weakness than anything. The blood tests from the Germans proved negative, so I don't know what the doctor will try next. But I intend trying to get to the bottom of this in its early stages.

Miss Matthews has just rung up. She would like me to go to see Dr Jones this afternoon. Mrs Rowe has been making a rhubarb tart with the first from the garden. It's 3/- per lb. I am being well looked after. Mary and her husband are coming to tea.

Sunday, April 11. A really lovely morning. I was up early. Went to Morning Service. Tried to get any news going, but little. What there was was good. Had an early dinner and went to see Dr Jones at the Emergency Hospital. When I asked him how he was he said, Very very weak. I can assure you he was. He slept most of the time I stayed with him. He thanked me for coming out. I felt it was the last time I would see him alive and told Miss Matthews so. She said Dr Wilson found him a little better. I told her that in my opinion he would not live 48 hours.

I went to church in the evening, sat in the choir, but of course could not sing.

Monday, April 12. Again a glorious morning. Miss Matthews has just telephoned to say the Doctor died at about 9.30 this morning. I was not far out with what I told her yesterday. I have to do the funeral. We will have the organ and perhaps the girls' choir. All the old landmarks now seem to be dropping out.

Undated. The weather is still marvellous, sunshine from daybreak to dark, and not a breath of wind. We have decided to bury Dr Jones on Saturday to give his sister, Mrs Willett, the chance of coming up from Jersey for the funeral.

I went to the doctor. He, as well as myself, sees little change in my voice, and suggests going to hospital for the day for an examination. He says they would give me an anaesthetic, not chloroform, but a local, an injection into my arm.

Saturday, April 17. We had Dr Jones' funeral this afternoon, quite

APRIL 1943

a lot of people, 43 wreaths. Mr Frossard gave a nice address about his being Dr in the parish for 50 years. We had the organ, girls' and big choir, three doctors pall-bearers, Mrs Honey (Emily), Miss Matthews, Mr Honey and Jack Lainé being the main mourners. Now that's another chapter closed. I sent a nice wreath from myself and family, also the same for Mr Peek.

Monday, April 19. Another wonderful day. I got my chest terribly sunburnt yesterday, and now I can scarcely bear anything against it. I did it to try and cure my throat, it should be as good as radium treatment.

I went down to see Miss Matthews tonight and to take her a paper of the funeral, but she had already had one given her. We chatted about poor old Dr Jones, about the good and bad times we had had together, and I did not get home until 9.30 (curfew at 10 now).

I woke up rather early this morning, pulled up the blind, lovely cool air came in and it was glorious moonlight, like day at 5.30. Then the foreigners came tramping down in twos and threes, then in bigger numbers. I thought that Brock Road had never known times like these. The French that were at Delancey when the typhus was on have gone I think. These that pass up and down now look much better class, are better dressed and most of them wear ordinary boots. But what a clatter it was when we had the crowd with sabots.

I feel I must talk about the weather. It's as fine as any August. Jim Ogier from the shop tells me we are going to have a ration of tobacco for our Easter Egg, two pkts cigs, 2 oz tobacco, three cigars, total 8/6 Not a bad slice out of a working man's pocket in one week. Nothing for the women except flowers. There will be letters in the Press again about it all.

People pass loaded with their heavy root vegetables, and also flowers. They laugh and joke and say, If we can't have nice food on the table, we will have nice flowers. You see even the poorest carrying home their flowers, and they must even have a little fern. They think nothing of paying 3/- or 4/- for flowers. It would surprise you the amount of flowers Lily Ellis sells in a week in our little shop.

My men now say the wages are too low to pay the prices asked for vegetables. I am giving them a rise of 1½d which means an increase of 6/- per week. I don't know where it will all finish. Still if I get the work and get paid for it, then it's not out of my pocket. I only wish my voice would come back.

Thursday, April 22. The men are coming up the road for their money. I have it packed in envelopes as usual. Good Friday tomorrow. We all joke about our Hot Cross Buns we have ordered, but we know there will be none.

APRIL 1943

I have finished the Choir Stalls, so we will be in great style at St Sampson's Church for Easter Sunday. Mrs Le Picq was sweeping and putting the finishing touches when I left. The poor old girl is looking very old. She was proud to say this is her 26th Easter that she has kept the old church clean.

I find Uncle Ned failing fast, stooping, and looking very old and thin. I hope he can hang out till Marjorie comes back.

Good Friday, April 23. A lovely bright promising day. I went to the 10.45 service, quite enjoyed it, but could not give vent to my feelings. I miss not being able to sing. I still sit in the choir and take up the collection.

I spent over an hour picking the spider crab for tea. I went to the evening service. What a pleasing change when we came out. It was pouring with rain, a blessing as we had had a drought and it seemed serious for seed sowing. I had to run all the way home. As usual I had no mack, but I did not get very wet.

Saturday, April 24. Lovely weather after pouring all night. I took down the flowers for the altar, beautiful blue Iris, white and red Tulips and a huge bunch of Lilies-of-the-Valley from my garden. Mrs Frossard had never seen such a beautiful bunch. I am sending her a big bunch, her Easter gift. Mum used to like to send her flowers from our garden. I do wish you were here to see and enjoy them.

All the little girls were at church helping to decorate. They were bright and happy, and longing for Easter Sunday tomorrow to wear their surplices. The 16 girls in the choir all had 2/6 yesterday.

Tom has just come in. He is always very funny. I hear him telling Mrs Rowe that he got sick over the Hot Cross Buns, too much saffron, too yellow, and the currants baked too hard. Still we are hoping that next Good Friday we will have some. We said that last year, but I think the time has come.

Easter Sunday, April 25. It was dull last night and it started raining. I went to the 7 o'clock Easter morning Communion. It was still drizzling but not enough for me to wear a mack, although I took it. It was only just daylight as by summer time it would have been 5 o'clock. A nice lot of people, 60.

For the Morning Service I took down several surplices which Mrs Rowe had washed. They were lovely and white. She put a little starch with mine and the men noticed it had a special touch!

We had quite a procession. We started from the vestry door, Foster carrying the Cross, walked outside to the big west door and entered singing, and processed up and down the aisles. The service was choral. The weather is still dull, but the rain has been a

APRIL 1943

blessing to us.

Don Bisset has just brought me a bottle of wine. I am very lucky to get it, as I know he could easily have got 20/- or more for it. I drink it lately to try and pick up strength, as I fancy that's part of my throat trouble. It's disappointing for me not to be able to sing in the Easter Services after over 50 years singing in the choir, but I think I might be able to again. We always live in hope, they say, If you die in the stairs, never despair.

Mary came down yesterday and brought some yellow Tulips for Mum's grave. I had yellow and red ones, and a huge bunch of Lilies of the Valley from our garden. The grave looked very nice now I have a granite kerb fixed. I put a bunch of my Tulips on Dr Jones' grave as there were no flowers on it. How soon are the dead forgotten. I miss him a good bit as he was always calling, and I have had lunch there every Sunday since the Occupation.

I told you that about a year ago all our police were locked up for stealing from the German and our local food stores. A man, Smith, from the North Side got one year. He was only 36 years old, but I suppose he could not stick solitary confinement for I see in the Press yesterday, he has died in France. His wife was taken to France with the last batch that left here only two months ago. A quotation from a book on Commonsense Thoughts on a Life Beyond, about long solitary confinement without occupation being the profoundest death in life, is proved in this policeman's case.

Tuesday, April 27. It's a lovely bright and sunny day but with a very high wind, and perhaps that's why my voice is not too good today. I went to Dr Fox this afternoon and he arranged for my throat examination on Thursday morning, the 29th. I have to take pyjamas, dressing gown and slippers, shaving tackle, towel etc. He wants me to go Wednesday evening, have a good night's rest there before having my dope. I hope I don't feel queer when I come round. It's my first stay in hospital, so am hoping for the best.

Wednesday, April 28. I am now getting ready for my hospital visit. Have made all arrangements with Tom. I have given him a cheque and he can pay the men if I don't get back for Friday.

Elsie has just come down. She has bartered two of her fowls for 12 lbs of sugar with Mr Symons. I gave her a few of my new potatoes from Allendale. I am digging them before they are come. The foreigners broke in again last night, that's the fourth time, so I am digging them before I lose the lot.

I have had a tiring day and to make matters worse a drain is again blocked at Mr Giffard's. Still I am leaving all this to Tom to see about. All I hope is that my throat business is not serious and I can get back by Friday afternoon. But the doctor said that if he is

APRIL 1943

not satisfied he will get the other doctors to see my throat while I am there. Unfortunately it's now blowing from the West which means head wind all the way out.

For my tea I had part of a nice spider crab, plenty of bread, little butter and a nice rhubarb tart. I packed my things in an attaché case and the overflow in a little soft bag mum used for shopping. I went via Robergerie, Braye Road, Capelles Hill, but who should I meet but Kitty Head coming down. She stopped to ask me the way to L'Ancresse, surprised to see me. I was surprised she did not know the way.

We chatted and she told me her Father and Audrey were dead. I was struck that I did not see it in the paper. Then she spoke about my throat, found my voice weaker. Of course she was sorry and wished me the best of luck. She was first turned out from L'Ancresse by the Germans, went to live in her father's house, Amherst, now they are turned out again and gone to L'Ancresse. After my directions we both went on our way rejoicing.

I arrived at the hospital at 7.45 pm. I was struck to find I had a bed mate on my left I knew very well, Mr Sebire, our celebrated flautist. He said as I entered, My hope was right. They told him a Mr Sauvary was coming, but he did not think it could be me because he had seen by the papers I was busy undertaking. He told me about his accident, knocked down by a lorry, and a badly fractured arm. His daughter was there and the nurse came to tell him he could go home tomorrow.

Then in the next bed on my left is Mr De Lisle Carey, an old gentleman of 82. On his constitutional to St Sampson's, a walk he often took, he had fallen on the footpath where the Germans had cut a railway across the path and road, and being near sighted this 8" drop gave him a nasty shaking up.

After our talk and answering a hundred questions from the nurse, my age, where born, then I said to her, Where died, Emergency Hospital, she laughed, (I don't think she could make me out) my religion. I got into bed, chatted a little, then went to sleep till 8 bells, which was 20 to 5.

April 29-May 8. They started on Sebire, then Mr Carey, then my turn. I said I could go to the bathroom, but no hot water till 7. I got out while they made my bed. I had my breakfast (I had had nothing since 5.30 the evening before) which consisted of one piece of bread two fingers wide and 2" long. There was butter but difficult to see! I had a lovely deep, hot bath, the first for months, a nice shave, then back to bed.

We are only three in this private ward, and it seems funny to think that Dr Jones died in the bed in front of me only three weeks ago. After my meagre breakfast all I had to do was wait my turn for the theatre.

MAY 1943

At 9.45 the nurse came in wheeling the stretcher and said, Now Mr Sauvary, I must get you ready. I jumped on this contraption, stretched out and they tucked me in with a sheet after putting on long white wool stockings. Then she said, I am going to stab you but it won't hurt, just to make you feel drowsy. I said, not in the heart I hope. She laughed and said, By your manner you seem cheerful.

Then she wheeled me into the big ward and put me by the fireplace with a huge screen around me. There I lay for one hour and had the greatest difficulty in keeping awake. Once some clumsy fool came along and knocked the screen over me, and after a scramble they asked if I was all right. However I determined not to sleep. I told the nurse I wanted to see fair play when I went in. At last a man, Hubert, said, Your turn and wheeled this perambulator in.

Dr Dick Gibson was the first to greet me with, Ah, here's a familiar face. I told him the last time I spoke to him was in Sark where, one night it was blowing a gale and thick fog, when they all decided to walk to the Coupée. I know I turned back. He said, Good God, that's over 20 years ago! We laughed. He looked at my teeth and passed a remark I didn't catch. Then after a short chat he said, now we'd better start.

He rubbed my arm and said, Dr Fox will stab you here, you count 10. I counted I think up to nine and then like a flash was gone, and did not know anything till some noise the nurses were making at Sebire's bed. (He had gone home.) I asked her the time. It was 3.30.

I felt lovely, no headache, no pain and was comfortable, just a sting in my tongue. I asked the sister why, and she said they put a stitch in it to pull it out. Fancy pulling out my tongue with a cable! Later they brought me a cup of beef tea.

Dr Fox came in the next morning and said Dr Dick would examine me in a dark room then I would perhaps have to go on the table again, but not to be put off.

I waited four days but no Dr Dick came to see me. Still I said nothing as I was enjoying the rest and a lovely bath every morning. So for five days I slept, read, ate and slept again, enjoying it all. Then I thought it was time to enquire from the matron if I had been forgotten altogether. So she asked the doctor if he would come the next day, but he did not.

At last he came. We went into the bathroom blacked out. He pulled my tongue a mile out, stuck a little mirror with a bright light down my throat, turned it upside down, inside out, back to front, and I stuck it without coughing. He did this a second time, and said there was no need to worry, there was nothing malignant. He advised me not to sing any more, rest and in time I would be well. I asked about my teeth. He said they were jolly good, there was just one I might show to the dentist, and tapping my shoulder said I

MAY 1943

looked very fit and well for a man of 66 years.

The next day the ordeal was repeated and Dr Fox assured me they were both satisfied that there was nothing seriously wrong. On Saturday I told the nurse I wanted to see the doctor to get my discharge. Dr Fox came and said he thought I was staying six months, but I could go, but as it was blowing a gale I had better go home in the ambulance.

But at 3 I got up and went round the ward and said goodbye, and after tea got my bicycle. Terribly rough weather but I was blown home. Mrs Rowe found me looking washed out and said they must have starved me. I found the food enough but for certain I would not have eaten it before the war. Still I enjoyed the 10 days rest.

I saw Sebire yesterday. He told me they brought me back soon after 12 (so I must have been on the table for an hour), and I had not come round when he left at 3.

I did not think it possible for anyone to go through that experience without even a little shrinking. I enjoyed it all, but the only advancement made towards my cure is that Dr Fox has allowed me one pint of pure milk for two weeks. It's really nourishment I want. I have more than enough to eat but not the right food for me. I am now taking two or three weeks' rest.

On Thursday night the nurses had a dance. It was quite an exciting time, nurses passing backwards and forwards with their smart dresses. Four of the doctors came and some of the men visitors slept in our ward. To my astonishment when they got up at 5, one of them was Bartlett from Jack's bank. He was surprised to see me.

I am sure Mr De Lisle Carey will miss me. He is nearly blind and I often used to feed him. I think if I had stayed much longer he would have converted me to his way of thinking. He was like Auntie Edith, always quoting, in his case the Scriptures not Poetry. He was so grateful for what I did. He was always saying I was to have one of his watches in the top drawer. His son was to have his father's gold watch and chain and I the other, and I must pick out any books I want from his library.

When his wife and sister-in-law came he told them I was good to him, so his wife came across and thanked me and enquired about my health, and then the sister-in-law. The next time they came I was dressed, and when the old lady left she said she hoped I would have a favourable report from the examination and would soon be better. She said she envied me my complexion, but she is I think over 80, and must be near sighted!

Wednesday, May 12. This afternoon I took Mr Pattimore a nice bunch of Blue Iris for his birthday. He was very pleased. Mrs Rowe sent him a big bunch of Lilies of the Valley and Forget-me-nots. He

MAY 1943

is, of course, ageing, but *is* still among the living. Who would have thought he would have outlived Dr Jones?

The war seems to be getting on. Tunis seems to be finished. Here we are longing for it to be over. This week they have made another cut in our bread allowance, to $3^{3}/4$ lbs per head per week. It is not enough.

At church on Sunday morning I told Mr Frossard that the doctor had advised me not to sing, so I thought it best to leave the choir. They wanted me to come that evening and after that take my place in the churchwarden's seat and collect.

In the evening he kept the men's choir back and there was quite a little farewell. He told them that on medical advice I was leaving the choir, but I was not going far. He, and he was sure they, were all sorry to lose me. He asked how long I had been in the choir. I told him 50 years this Easter and they agreed it was a fine record.

He said there must be a change. I had always carried the Alms Plate because of my office as Churchwarden. Now each of the men would take a Sunday, starting with the youngest, George Symons. It was quite a little ordeal when they all expressed regret. Of course it's a great break for me, but the old have to make way for the young, and I don't really mind if only I could get my voice back.

May 10-15. The week passed very quietly for me. I got up late and am very much enjoying the pint of full cream milk allowed me for two weeks. I have had an egg or two given me, so am trying to pick up a little strength.

We are getting fine weather after a week of terrible gales. I am afraid we will get little fruit. The leaves of the apple and pear treees are quite black. I am lucky mine are fairly sheltered. Some of the potato patches are half rooted up and quite black.

Sunday, May 16. I was up with the lark. Very fine morning but few in church. For the first time I sat in my Churchwarden's pew. It seemed strange, especially when the hymns were announced. I nearly stood up with the choir. After 50 years it would not have been surprising if I had. Then of course I followed the choir with Stafford to the vestry to count the collection.

After dinner Stafford rang me to go there to tea. I went which meant no evening church, but I did not mind. The country was so lovely and the smell of the May trees going through the Robergerie was a real tonic. One tree was so lovely, shapely and white, I had to get off my bicycle to admire it. I am sure there is nothing so enjoyable and invigorating as the sweet smells in our country lanes.

I had a nice tea, went all over the estate, called at Choisi and had a chat with the old people, then came home at 9.30. I did not sleep there.

MAY 1943

Monday, May 17. It's again fine and I feel a little brighter. I am going to Richmond Corner beach for two hours. I went on Saturday and bathed my feet. The wind is N and the air still cold out of the sun.

I led two of my rabbits, the last I intend to breed this year. A meatless week so we had a rabbit.

Mrs Messervy has just telephoned to ask me to tell her husband that his brother has died in Jersey. He is working with Tom at Miss Ozanne, Watville, so I will tell him on my way to the beach.

One of the States' men has just brought me two cheques for a lot of accounts, 20 in all. For German Occupation a/c, repairing glass, locks, drains, removal of furniture and carpenter's shop, etc about £65 in all. Some date back to last September. I am glad to be able to cross them off my books. Now I have another lot to make and send off.

I had two hours on the beach and when I got back Guilbert Simon had called to say Aunt Mary Jane, his mother, has died. She was 89. I don't know if you knew her. After tea I went to Town, 29, Paris Street, to make arrangements. It seems to me these books will give most news about funerals. I certainly get quite a lot.

I went to Mr Tanner about my two lower front teeth. Luckily they don't have to come out. For ³/₄ hr he scraped, then he examined one which has been giving me trouble, and he will fill it next time.

Tuesday, May 18. It's so lovely again I think I will go on the beach after dinner. I have just received two RX replies from Kit, the first for a long time. One I sent Sept 29th, 1942, Kit replied Dec 8th, 1942. I received both May 18th, 1943. I am feeling a little better but my voice is certainly not improving.

I saw Mrs Cortvriend yesterday returning from Mr Tanner. Their fine goat had two kids, and two weeks after someone broke in and disembowelled it in the shed and carted it away. Just when they were expecting to have two quarts of milk per day for Gussie. He now seems no worse. They also had their rabbits stolen.

What a catastrophe about the breaking of that dam in Germany. There must have been hundreds of people drowned.

Sunday, May 30. Last Sunday, May 23rd, was very exciting for those lucky enough to see from the Front. At 8 o'clock we heard a lot of machine-gun firing and bombing. It appears that about a dozen of our planes met a small convoy off the Ferriers. As they started to come round the Lower Head buoy the planes swept over them, sank one steam boat of about 700 tons, and damaged several others, very noisy and exciting they said.

It seems the Germans are starting to cut off the number of boats coming here. It's weeks since we had any meat ration. I had mackerel for Sunday dinner and we have had two or three spider crabs this week. They were tasty and full. My brother Tom brought me a lovely lobster, so full and tender. I suppose they thought that since I had been sick and in hospital I needed something extra.

I am feeling much better in myself this week, very much sunburnt. I go to the beach, bathe my feet and sunbathe in my bathing suit. But yesterday I had to dress quickly when two or three hundred planes were passing over. One can never tell if they will do any machine-gunning.

I am digging Lake's big span of potatoes tomorrow and I think I will get a good crop. I had only £3 18s from the States for the Allendale crop, but I had a quarter of them stolen and had to dig before they were come.

Saturday, June 5. Mary came down on Friday and we did the grave as usual, and today I put some extra flowers, the anniversary, Mum died four years ago. Time has slipped away. I got a nice wreath made up of single Rambler Roses, pale yellow Daisies and white Lupins, the inside circle of dark and light Pinks with fern, and Love-in-a-Mist dotted around. The colours blended beautifully. I was really pleased with it. Mrs Rowe gave me a bunch of flesh coloured Sweet Peas. The perfume tout ensemble was most pleasing.

Most people now seem to be getting a little depressed. I suppose lack of good food and the war dragging on is getting on their nerves. I am not feeling very well, I get tired so soon and don't even enjoy smoking now. As Dr Fox tried to make me believe, I am not a young man. But 66 is no age. I see Mrs Godfray, 91, active and can see and has a good appetite.

Wednesday, June 9. Another sad accident. Quinain and his brother and two others were pulling in their trawl this afternoon when they noticed they were hooked into some corks and ropes. They thought it was some lost net when suddenly they saw a black object which exploded immediately. It was a mine. It blew the boat to pieces and two men were drowned. Quinain and his brother (or son) managed to hold on to some floating wreckage. Men in another boat about a mile away noticed an empty petrol can in their boat jump up, which made them look round, otherwise nothing might have been known about the accident. They went to the rescue and saved the two. They were taken to hospital, injured, but not seriously.

I am told that the boat that saved them, strangely, would not have been there, but being late on their tide could not get to their pots, otherwise all would have been drowned. It affects us badly for, besides the tragic loss of life, the good big boat has gone, and

JUNE 1943

they were good fishermen, so that's less fish for us.

Then on Thursday, and I think also on Saturday, the Germans were firing their big guns and the boats were not allowed out. Things are all against us just now. Four weeks without meat and the boats not allowed out. When will this devilish war be over.

I have now had potatoes stolen from the field and have telephoned the police. Mr Poat has had a lot of his taken too, also onions. I am paying 1/- per hour to have my grapes thinned, and quite expect to have them all stolen. We must grow food, only to have it stolen before it's half matured, such is life.

The Germans have pumped the water out of the quarry behind the Old Rectory and are working it. It's blasting like the devil. They use the blondin [cable way] and the cracking machine. All they do is make thousands of tons of concrete. They have a concrete complex!

Sunday, June 20. A subscription list has been opened by the Press and Star for the families of the fishermen drowned. They now have over £600 We had the collection for the Fund at church today, Trinity Sunday, and are sending a cheque for £34 I thought very good for our little church.

We have had rain and wind all this month, and tomorrow's the longest day. It will be awful if we have to put up with another winter. With all the rain the potatoes are getting diseased, which will be another set back for us.

We are picking tomatoes freely. I am getting 7d per lb in the shop, but I am afraid there may be a glut. The Germans are supposed to take our surplus, 4/5 per 12 lbs packed.

Mrs Rowe is telling me to tell you we had no meat again this week. Coming out of church this morning I went to Mrs Joule and the boat had just come in with 250 mackerel. I got two nice ones. We have had spider crabs for tea every day this week. Mrs Rowe says we will soon be looking like them! The great thing is they save butter.

Sunday, June 27. This week passed off quietly, although it made me very sad that the days will be shortening and winter will soon be on us. We have very little to look forward to.

We now have no coal in the island and very little wood. In fact people have been bothering me for more kindling wood which we have been selling in the shop at 4d per lb. The States have now fixed the price at 3d. It's really an awful price but people will give anything. Food (rationed) is getting very scarce, but we hope for the best and trust the war will be over soon.

The Fishermen's Fund has closed, over £1,300, a very good effort. See Presses up to 25th June. But I say it's all wrong. Mr

JULY 1943

Tucker was killed last summer driving a crane on the jetty when the English dropped bombs. For that case the public did not even ask his wife if they could pay for the funeral, a case just as sad.

I did a little work this week without feeling too tired, the first time since Christmas. I am taking special treament to get strong to face the winter. Mrs Rowe is very good to me. We had a lovely rhubarb and b. currant tart for tea.

Uncle Ned has been very poorly this week, a bad attack of diarrhoea. I boiled him some rice twice to try to stop it.

It was quite exciting just now at the bottom of Brock Road. About 15 foreigners, quite respectable and well dressed, from 20 to 30 years of age, started arguing. Some had been out for a walk, being Sunday, and gathered there at 9 pm. They suddenly took off their boots and shoes, others were in their vests only, no shirts, and lined up and started a walking match up the road. They are a more respectable lot than the last we had up there.

Mrs Rowe has just returned from Miss Lawton. I am going to feed the rabbits. I have a nest of 12.

Sunday, July 18. It's quite a few weeks since I added anything to these lines as I am afraid this reading will become boring. But as this Sunday is a special Sunday for our St Sampson's Church, I wanted to let you know what is happening.

I told you previously about the girls' supliced choir, a bigger men's choir, and with our new organist, Mr Stan Keyho, the alterations to the choir platform and stalls. The next thing was to robe the ladies which started this morning, about 20 of them, making 50 in all. Some ladies I could hardly recognise decked up in their cassocks, surplices, ruffles around their necks and mortarboards.

Tonight we will have a shortened service, then solos, duets, and a small orchestra. I am not much in favour of this for a small country church, it's very nice for a cathedral, but if it pleases the many I don't mind. But some tell me it's overdone. Of course you will alway find some die-hards and I expect this enthusiasm will soon die down.

The vestry is small, the men now robe in the organ loft, and we are like herrings in a box. On a warm evening like this I told some of the ladies they will have to take off their waistcoats. I am taking one of our red decanters (all I could find) in case of any fainting. The church will be packed to overflowing for sure.

Things seem to be normal here. The Germans work all day Sunday, lorries about, the trains carting wood, iron, cement. I cannot understand what they do with it all. You would not know the country. They tell me Cobo is quite transformed. They pull down houses, greenhouses, and make narrow gauge railways all over the

JULY 1943

place, and the country hills are a network of tunnels. They have one through the Park from Grandes Maisons quarry to Delancey Lane quarry.

I am picking tomatoes in full swing now. I expect 100 baskets tomorrow. I will send about 80 to the depot for shipment to Jersey, France and Germany.

Tuesday, July 20. We had a packed church on Sunday evening for our shortened service followed by Vocal Recital, very enjoyable. Collection £11 2s.9d. not bad.

On Monday morning I had to go to Blanchelande, St Martin's about a funeral for a French lady who lived in Church Lane. It appears that she left orders that I had to bury her. I remember her as a very reserved person who always dressed in black. I got soaked going out. It's now 12 and pouring a deluge. We have not seen the sun for three days. It's a real bad July. The roads are flooded and I can scarcely see to write. It will do good.

Uncle Ned has just telephoned from the Old Rectory. He wanted a few potatoes to cook for his breakfast. It is too wet to go to Percy's. He wanted to fetch them, but the rain was so heavy I said I would take them. I also took him some toms and half a bottle of white wine. It's poor stuff and I paid 6/6 a bottle for it.

Thursday, July 22. I had the funeral for Mrs Cohu today, a RC one. Father Kirk took the service. The person who came from Blancheland told me she kept watch, garde toute seule, she said, being French. I told her it was not prudent to stay alone in a building away from any houses, but she said it was her duty. What faith. Still it affected her nerves because when she tried to write her name (as I am making a report for the daughter who is in Canada to see) she was shaking so terribly I could hardly make out her writing.

Staff Ogier rang to say it was his mother's birthday and they wanted me to go for tea, a nice spread same as last month for his Dad. I went and before I left at 10.30 we had a goût of Crème De Menthe, Glacials Freezomint, lovely stuff, and a nice piece of cake. I arrived home at curfew, 11 pm and slept well.

I am picking and packing tomatoes freely now, and up to my eyes in work. There's a lot of booking including my carpentry work. I am now feeling a little better, but get very tired getting about, but I must stick it till peace comes.

Fancy Marshal Benito Mussolini, the Great I Am, resigning office. Something strange I think. I am hoping this will mean the collapse of Italy, then things will move. I notice the Proclamation is in a very mild form.

Things are extra quiet here now. We never see a plane, and most

JULY 1943

of the work seems stopped. We are all hoping we won't have to go through another winter as fuel is scarce, and rations low.

It's a great game now, night time stealing, and worst of all milking cows. Farmers have been five pots short some mornings. The cows are out all night and the thieves have the chance. Police watch and have caught some. But there have been stabbing cases. Harry Marley from the Penny Saving Bank got knocked about catching a foreigner.

I am just back from Dredge and managed to get two spider crabs. There were at least 60 people waiting for fish. Coupons two and three were in demand. Mine was No. 5. It was 9 o'clock when the boats came in, the catches were small, so many will not get fish tonight. A meatless week again, but I will have the other half of the rabbit I left in Mr Symons cold store two weeks ago.

Lily Ellis kept my shop open tonight. We sold quite a lot of tomatoes to the Germans as they returned from the North Cinema. She will have got rid of over 3½ cwt this week. I get a better price than sending them to the Depot.

We had an extra tobacco ration this week for August Bank Holiday, three pkts cigs, 2 oz tobacco, 10/1½ burning money I think. We are all getting restless now.

I have a bottle of Cognac ordered. If it comes it will cost 20 marks, 42/8½ and I could resell it for double, but I will keep it for my friends and myself. Money is not what's wanted, it's food.

October. It's now months since I've written more to these lines. I begin to feel it's the same thing, on and on, but I will just mention the few things I remember.

First, and this is strange. Poor Jack Lainé, Dr Jones' chauffeur, was killed at Richmond Corner on the 12th August, four months to the day after Dr Jones' death. A lorry knocked him over and he died soon after arriving in hospital. He did not get the chance to enjoy the £500 the doctor left him in his will. Hard luck.

Everyone here was shocked and up to now, over two months later, it's not known who did it. The lorry did not stop but it's understood it was a German. He had a large funeral which, of course, I had to carry out.

Sunday, October 31. I may have to retrace my steps, but I will start from yesterday, Saturday. It was a lovely morning so I took the day off. I tried to get a bottle of Bénédictine in Town in the morning, no luck, not that it's cheap at 20/3 per bottle. Still we must have something and I drink it with my milk *when* I can get it.

In the afternoon I went to the Lyric to see a play, Laburnum Grove. Messervy wanted me to go as his daughter had the star part with Reg Warley. She was the daughter, Elsie Redfern. I must say

OCTOBER 1943

she was exceptionally good, and I can safely say that I have never seen any amateur, or perhaps even a professional, to please me more. Messervy will be pleased when I tell him on Monday.

When I got back a nice wreath of bronze and yellow Chrysanths I had ordered for Mum's grave had arrived, so I took it down. I put bronze and white Chrysanths in the pots.

Today we had a great festival day in the church, All Saints, with a procession, the choir, Mr Frossard and we carrying our wands. Mr Warry had to walk with me as the other warden, Ogier, did not turn up. I felt rather sad, it being Mum's birthday, and Mr Frossard preaching about those gone before, and the hymns all about saints. It revives everything especially the many years Dear Mum and I had in the old church. The altar looked lovely, six candles burning and flowers beautifully arranged. Although Mum did not do them I supplied them.

Tonight while I am writing this, Mrs Rowe is making a shammy leather bag for my gold watch. It's impossible to keep the dust out. I have twice had it cleaned this year. I have five watches and all have stopped. I took four for repairs, two with the main springs gone. I think the springs were second-hand when they were put in less than two years ago.

November 7. Today I took a ride out to Pleinheaume scrounging for roots for the shop. While there I heard a terrible explosion. The Germans had blown up Delancey Monument. [The memorial to Admiral Lord de Saumarez, 1756-1836, Guernsey's most distinguished sailor. *See illustration No 16.*] We were practically certain it was coming down, it being in the way (they said) of the big guns they are putting in the Park.

But what destruction! That beautiful monument and such a wonderful piece of work, all of Guernsey granite, and all done by Guernsey workmen. I always heard it was 99' high. It was a wonderful landmark, the pilots used it for their bearings on the East coast. Now it is no more. It was blown up at 4 pm on Nov 7, 1943.

The Germans had been around with orders for people in the neighbourhood to keep their windows open as it was being blown up at 3. They were one hour late for some unknown reason. I bet if you come to Guernsey by daylight you will miss it. Everybody here is very sad tonight. I feel very sorry especially as it won't in any way help them to win the war. Still this war is all destruction, so we must put up with it and try to smile.

On my way back from Pleinheaume I called at the Gigands to see how Mrs Ogier was, as Stafford had told me she was sick in bed. When I arrived they told me they had been telephoning all over the place for me. Mr Cross, Mr Roger, Mr Baker and others had all had their houses damaged by the explosion.

213

NOVEMBER 1943

Nov. 8. I was astir early as I expected many calls to replace glass in windows damaged by the monument crash, and I was right. I had answered two before breakfast, and to make matters worse it was raining like the devil and a cold wind. Just my luck.

Things went well during the day, but we cut our last pane of glass. Leale and other merchants have been out of glass for more than a year, but I had a good stock and kept it for our own customers. But alas, today, we had to do the same as others and put bast in some of the windows.

Charlie Rogers, Grandes Maisons, had a narrow miss with flying stones. One came through their attic window where six of them were taking a bird's eye view and the splintered glass cut his face.

In spite of the rain I took a walk up Mont Morin in the afternoon to see how the poor old needle fell. From near Mr Peek's house I could see the remains. It was very sad to see that noble monument a mere shambles with the Germans on the base breaking up the remains with pickaxes and crowbars.

Then I turned and looked at Mr Peek's house, windows flying open in the rain, a wireless screeching some German talk, and the tramp of heavy feet in the now practically empty house.

I returned down Mont Morin with a heavy heart, as I felt the job was real destruction. But I suppose they think the British are demolishing their towns and statues so they will do the same.

Wednesday, Nov 17. After the N gales last week there have up to now been 19 bodies washed up on our N coast, from the cruiser HMS Charybdis we lost in the Channel a month ago. The inquest was held yesterday and they were able to name all of them. One was brought from Sark. The doctor thought he had been in the water a month. One had £6 on him, another £18.

They were buried this afternoon at the Foulon cemetery, each in a separate grave. The public was invited. I was not going but after dinner the sun burst so beautifully through the cold clouds that I suddenly decided to go. I had a lively fair wind, passed hundreds walking. Of course all the best positions were taken but I had a fair view.

Ministers of the Church of England, the Roman Catholic Church and the Free Churches all took part in the service. The Bailiff and other island officials were there. The German funeral party consisted of naval and military forces who gave full naval honours. The first burial was taken by Father Hickey, RC, the second by the Dean, the next by The Rev. Romeril. For the committal prayers the Dean took one row, the Rev. Kilshaw the other, reciting the prayers and dropping the earth.

In spite of the thousands present there was dead silence. This was broken by the Marines (Germans) about 80, who fired three

NOVEMBER 1943

volleys. (No bugles.) Then came the laying of the wreaths, first the Bailiff for the island, then two Germans. The Harbour Commandant, Dr Greff, said that the men they were burying had fallen in battle near the Channel Islands when the cruiser Charybdis and one destroyer [HMS Limbourne] were sunk. We honour them as soldiers and we commit them to their graves. They did their duty for their country. Dr Kratzer also placed a wreath, In honour of gallant men. (At times like these the world seems to me a problem. I read such lines as, That in Death which follows and results from duty done, the heart knows no frontiers and mourning becomes international.) [A Ceremony of wreath-laying and Remembrance is held every year on Charybdis Day, a permanent link between the island and the Royal Navy.]

When the service was over I managed to get through the crowd and pass the graves (two coffins covered with Union Jacks remained on the ground) and the display of flowers, over 700 wreaths, one a huge anchor, about 9 feet.

When this was finished I went on to Mrs Petruschke's farm where my men are working this week. They often ask about all of you. Their daughter was sent to Germany with her husband Freddy Knight. I was quite cold by the time I got home at 5.30 and nearly dark.

Earlier in the month I went to Camp du Roi, Mr Carré, Four Cross, where we use to get such lovely Muscat of Alexandre grapes. Mrs Petruschke particularly wanted a young vine. He spared me one as a favour. I am hoping he won't find out it was not for me! I then took it to the Foulon, a very long way but it's always worth it as I get a glass of the Pure, straight from the cow. I never miss a chance.

I will have some stories to tell you if this war ever ends and we are alive to tell the tale.

We are still kept busy and try to keep our tails up. The hardships for the people are not as bad as other winters. We are getting a few extras such as 1/2 lb rice, and a few others are promised this Xmas. I am spending my money, when I can, on anything I can get. Better a poor man alive than a rich man dead, and the majority about here seem to feel as I do. Some of course won't pay the price. I say fools if you have the dough. Of course, 35/- per lb for butter, 14/- for sugar, 6/- flour, lard (if you can get it) 26/- eggs (unobtainable now) 2/- each, at these prices a week's wage is soon gone.

The vegetables, leeks 8d, toms 7d, beans 8d, potatoes rationed 4d, carrots 6d, haricots 2/6, unobtainable in the shops but most growers have them, onions 1/- per lb, cabbage 6d, broccoli 7d. All these I have not to buy.

We eat nearly 2 lbs of sugar beet syrup per week, but it's a devil of a lot of work to make. The squeezing is the hardest part, and it

NOVEMBER 1943

takes a lot of fuel. Last week out of 18 lbs of beet we got 4½ lbs of syrup, lovely and brown and sweet. If only we could get suet to make a dough. We have not see any for three years.

Thursday, Nov 25. You will be surprised that Mrs Lake is dead (Nov 19). She fell and broke her hip and would not have it set. But Mr Lake told me some months ago she had developed cancer, and this was the primary cause of death.

I am just back from the funeral, a private one at the Vale cemetery. Only the hearse, one coach and five mourners. There were 13 wreaths. I sent one from all of us. Jack was always so friendly with Wallie. It was very cold and raining a bit. Mr Romeril took the service and thank God did the greater part in the house. I was quite wet and cold enough when I got back.

It seems awful that poor Mrs Lake had to spend the last year of her life in a furnished house, and die there. They say it's the fortunes of war. It's sad to see Mr Lake, now alone down the Braye Road away from all his neighbours. He was very depressed today. I was there yesterday and stayed a good time, and he said it quite brightened him up. Wallie is in America, right on the Pacific coast, and Maidie is married in Jersey.

I have just finished the two reports for the Press and Star. Still the evenings are long and it keeps me out of mischief!

December. I have not written much about church lately. We have been through Stir-up Sunday (as Mum and Auntie Edith used to call it) and Advent. Now we have come to Xmas 1943.

The Autumn has been rather cold for Guernsey with plenty of rain, but Xmas week was very mild. I had the most beautiful Chrys for the altar, ½ R. Mark each, 1/0½ what a price. I got a few extra and sent ½ doz each to Mrs Frossard and Mrs Ogier. We took the truck to fetch them and bought others for the shop at 8/- per doz. Our little passage was full. We spend money here like water. Nobody values the RM.

We had lovely Xmas services. I went at 9 and 10.45. Our choir sang the anthem beautifully. We had no afternoon service as Mr Frossard had to carry out duties in the Vale. (I told you the Rev. James had been sent to Germany being an Englishman.)

After the 10.45 service I cycled out to the Ogiers. We had lovely goose and all the extras for dinner with wine, lovely tea (Real) and a tip-top supper. Mr and Mrs Frossard were there and Dr Fox came for tea. Lucky to hear the King's speech, etc.

I walked back with the Frossards at midnight and I can assure we had a happy but not a merry Xmas. We drank the health of absent friends at dinner and again at supper, and we all wondered if this would be the last Xmas apart. But we all agreed we were not

DECEMBER 1943

downhearted and time absolutely flies, nobody seems to know why. I think it's their hope that keeps them up, for not one single person ever doubts that England will always be on top.

I always end up with funerals. I had three this week. Joan Upham's father died rather suddenly, and two others, all Xmas week.

I had a nice holly wreath for Mum's grave and a bunch of large white Chrys. I sent a few Xmas cards and I had seven boxes of cigarettes given me by the ladies. They were allowed a ration, two boxes Xmas week. So I have plenty to smoke during the holidays.

I think everybody has had more food this Xmas, little extra rations, flour, cheese, sweets, chocolates for the ladies. But milk is very short, one noggin per head and skimmed at that.

I have started to put on weight. From Sept 19th to Dec 17th I put on 5½ lbs which I thought very good. I think another 5½ lbs and I will again be normal. It cost a bit to do it but I thought it time to study my health.

Personally I have been well off in every way this Xmas. I managed to get good wines, spirits and liqueurs. I got Uncle Ned to come up and have a nip. He got home all right as I have seen him since!

I thought a lot about Jack on Thursday the 23rd Dec and wondered where he was. I imagined all our thoughts were united, and disappointed we could not send our usual greetings. But we must cheer up and hope for better times next year.

January 1944. Early this year two American planes came down off Pleinmont. Some of the men managed to get to the rocks in their rubber boats, and I think one or two bailed out. The papers said the Germans brought ashore 13 men, and two others were washed ashore.

Last week they were buried at the Foulon by the Germans. No flowers were allowed and no flags on the coffins. Only six of our local people were allowed to attend but could take no official part. Mr Frossard was included. The Germans took the service and had a firing party but did not fire. I think they are dead set against the Americans for coming to our aid.

Then on Jan 7th, Friday afternoon, about 4 o'clock, there was a skirmish, three or four fighters came out of the clouds over Herm. It lasted only a minute or two, then one came tumbling down and pitched in the sea close to where one of our boats was fishing. But it came spinning down so fast it was impossible to see if English or German. Very sad all the same. The others flew off to the airport. We've seen very few planes here for the last few months. Now they are coming again, second front getting near I suppose, if ever?

Our Food Control are getting very short of potatoes. The ration's dropped from 5 to 3 lbs per head per week, but won't affect

JANUARY 1944

me. I have my supply and some to spare my men.

The seed potato for indoor planting arrived only this week (very late) and we have to put them to shoot before planting. I got a permit for 3 cwt at 32/- per cwt. It's getting time the war ended as the ground is getting played out, but personally I am not expecting it to last much longer.

It now seems people must pay for our good Xmas fare. Our rations for groceries this week came to 1/0½ so you can guess it was a fat lot! Now the butter ration is 3 oz, sugar 3 oz, salt ½ oz (dirty, more coal dust than salt) and ½ lb macaroni.

Sunday, Jan 9. No meat this week but I killed a lovely fat rabbit, 8½ lbs dead weight, without head and innards, 5½ lbs and rolling in fat, kidneys completely covered. I gave half to Mrs Frossard. She told me tonight coming from church it was beautiful. I have three more to eat between now and March, of course (touch wood) if I don't get them stolen. Some people have had as many as 25 stolen in one night. Two people in Roland Road had six and eight respectively stolen last week, so they are nearing us at the Old Forge 1449 dwelling, and my rabbits.

I am very comfortable here tonight, sitting by a lovely fire, just finished tea, 7 pm. We have a large boiler of sugar beet on the fire. We have to cook it for six hours before squeezing.

Mrs Rowe is mending my much worn flannel pyjamas. They can only last out this winter. Last winter she told me I might get through with them, now I have to wear them another winter.

Flossie Mallett told me tonight at church that she is going back to school teaching and seemed delighted. For some time she has been at Dr Sutcliffe's dispensary. Lily Mallett has been in hospital for six weeks. She had an operation. Unfortunately she caught a chill while there and got pleurisy. But I saw her out walking this week so she is on the mend.

I am now going to put my feet in hot water. I have scarcely been able to walk this week, my feet have been so tender. Perhaps there are many reasons. It may be thin soles as I can assure you we are well down at heel. Or it may be that I have several pairs of shoes all different sizes. (Miss Dyson gave me a pair of Fred's, nearly a size too large, but I had to wear them as mine took water.) Also my feet have got thinner. Added to all these discomforts not having walked a lot for the last 20 years, simply pressing the old Ford pedals with my feet, has caused one or two nails to grow inwards. All these items together seem to have played havoc with my feet and brought them to this climax.

But I am happy to say that my 'Little Mary' is coming back and I will soon have a 'corporation'.

I have now managed to get thick leather soles on a pair I was

JANUARY 1944

asked to sell years ago. I paid but perhaps fortunately for myself never did sell them. Cost of soles 10/8 not much if you say it quickly!

Then in all my distress I went to the Controlling Committee (Footwear) and got a pair of brown shoes, quite nice, 37/6.

Now with these two pairs and soaking my feet tonight and rubbing them with zinc and castor cream ought to let me have a more comfortable time next week. I want you to know, over and above all this, I wash my feet every morning in hot water Mrs Rowe brings for my tub. But I do miss my bathroom.

I am not doing anything else tonight, even reading, hence my writing all this nonsense. All the same it's awful not being able to step it out. I cycle long distances.

I have not told you much about my voice lately. It's now 12 months since it started to fade away. Up to now it's no better. I don't know what to do about it. If the war was over I would go to London and see a specialist who would probably put it right.

Monday, Jan 10. I rose this morning, but not with the lark, 10 o'clock when I got off the perch, and I had slept most of the 12 hours I was in bed. Still I had nothing pressing. A dull drizzling day.

Made a few small bills (as I always leave the big ones, I hate making them).

This afternoon I went to see Miss Matthews. She gave me a few cooked limpets for Mrs Rowe's cat. A stray was outside her door and when I bent down to put on my cycle clips the darned cat flew at me! She could smell the jug and tried to snatch it from me. It is so difficult to find food for cats that won't eat vegetables with a little bread.

Sunday, Jan 16. It's already the Second Sunday after Epiphany. I still have plenty of work but do nothing myself except feed the rabbits, boss the now seven men about, pay and make bills, eat and drink three meals per day and retire soon after 10 o'clock after reading by a nice comfortable fire all the evening. We have tea at 6, then I get a cup of milk (if any?) at 10, and since Xmas have been able to put a drop on top (as the soldiers used to say).

I get disturbed at about 8.15. Tom rolls in, finds me in bed and if it's raining I turn over till 9.30. Have toast for breakfast with plenty of butter, and milk when the cow comes round! Our ration of skimmed milk is now ¼ pt per person. That's the stuff to get fat on! Butter now 3 oz. Mrs Rowe says with that amount she has to cook, fry and put it on the table.

Our ration was pork this week, 4 oz. Mrs Rowe's came to 10d, mine 1/9 which included mince made with lights and guts by the

JANUARY 1944

look of it. Still we eat it and don't complain too much, as really if nothing turns out worse, we have been well served considering all things. I hope the second front, if ever it comes off, is not too close to Guernsey.

The last week the Germans have been in companies training very heavily. About 40 of them (merely boys) were marching up Brock Road, Delancey, down Delancey Lane, back past the Rectory, then up Brock Road again. It was pitiful to see them after they had been around a dozen times. They were exhausted and were dropping out on the road. Not more than 15 passed the last time. The women here were quite worried to see the poor chaps.

Tuesday, Jan 18. Flo Darling, it was your birthday and of course we could not exchange greetings, but we could still concentrate our thought on the happy birthdays you have had in times past when we were all together, and poor Mum racking her brains for almost weeks before wondering what you would like best. Those good times are gone now, nevertheless we can still hope for better times than these, being cut off.

I did not get much time to think and wonder how you were spending the day, at La Hougue for sure, and perhaps Kit could come down for the occasion. Poor Mr Bird's wife died yesterday and I have been busy getting on with the job. Ruby and her Dad are very cut up although they had expected the end soon. Mrs Bird was 84, and the funeral will be at the church on Thursday. They had come to our church the last three or four years, in fact I think since the war.

This is my first funeral since Xmas. I wonder if it will be the last of this devilish war. I myself am trusting so and believe it will crack up before the summer. Lots of the Germans have gone from here and most of the OT. There is not a quarter of the traffic on the roads, but they do have their steam engines and narrow gauge tracks running from Town to St Sampson's, Bordeaux, via Braye Road to L'Islet and thence to Cobo and Vazon. Then I don't know where, as I never go out there. People tell me I would not know Cobo or Vazon.

Thursday, Jan 20. It has been wet, misty, damp and cold, but today has been gloriously mild and with beautiful sunshine. Mrs Bird's funeral went well. Budge tolled the bell. Quite a full church. There were 58 wreaths. Mr Bird telephoned me this evening to go and see him. He was very pleased that everything went off so well. He gave my men a good tip each.

It was as dark as the grave returning (he is now at the Chalet, foot of Delancey Hill). I lost my way at the top of Delancey Lane for 10 minutes, was glad to get on the Front. It's terrible these dark nights.

JANUARY 1944

I write these things for you to know that we go on much the same except we lose our freedom at curfew, 10 pm.

Saturday, Jan 22. A German officer rang me this morning. He said, You're Mr J.C. Sauvary, New Road. I said, No, Brock Rd. He said, I want Mr Sauvary, New Rd. I told him I was at New Rd but the Germans turned me out of my house, and now I'm in Brock Rd. He said, I must live near you, as I live in Brock Rd, but I explained that I lived in St Sampson's and he is in St Peter Port.

He wants me to go to Rockmont, Delancey, Jurat A. Dorey's house, to repair a large hole in the roof, damaged when they blew up the Monument, that's over a month ago. Now they want it done at once. I went to see the job, and now Tom has to work on Saturday afternoon.

Then I got a telephone call that Police C. Bretel was found dead in bed this morning. (No inquest, heart failure.) We will have to work tomorrow, Sunday.

It's really difficult to get on with a job now, what with the waste of time finding materials etc, short daylight (electricity rationed), and the men with very little go, owing to lack of fats, etc. It really takes the spirit out of anyone, not that I bother a lot. I find it difficult to get out much before 11 o'clock. I just carry on and don't intend to worry.

Sunday, Jan 23. A boisterous day and night with squalls and thunder. Few people at church.

The German language must be wonderful if long words have anything to do with it. I received the Rockmont job order from, Nr 108 HEERESUNTERKUNFISHUERWALTUNG, [Office for army lodgings], St Peter Port, Guernsey, 27 letters, a mouthful and mine is too small to gulp the lot out! However I have done the job, now I have to send the bill to A.N. Die Firma, Delancey Column Account.

I have just received a message from Mrs Landgon, Rozel, Cobo. Her husband died at the Emergency Hospital and I have to do the funeral at the Câstel, rather a long way off. He was Chief Warder at the Men's Asylum and I did all the funerals for the States through him, hence I suppose my getting this out of the way job.

Monday, Jan 24. I went out to Cobo twice today and to the Câstel cemetery. While there a large plane came over, they said a Yankee bomber. There was a lot of firing. I kept inside. I am quite tired with all this cycling.

Thursday, Jan 27. We had the funeral this afternoon. The Rector, Mr Waterbury officiated, assisted by the Rev. E.L. Frossard who took part as President of the States Mental Board. A grand affair,

FEBRUARY 1944

the verger tolled the bell, Mr Frank Way was at the organ and Mr Frossard gave an address in which he paid high tribute to the deceased. Miss Marie Randall was there and asked me how you were all getting on.

I saw Mrs Hickey at the RX Bureau, who also inquired about your welfare and spoke of old times at College.

Sunday, Jan 30. Yesterday I had to go with Stafford, Custodian, to Les Mielles, Mrs Tooley's house. I have to repair roof and fasten windows and send the a/c to Advocate Langlois.

The Germans have been living there for the last 18 months. It's derelict now, most of the furniture gone, the library books all over the place, the front gate knocked in. I compared the place, Kit, with when I fetched you from tea there with Miss Mellish.

When they all come back and see their houses they will faint. I just don't bother about mine. The Germans keep rabbits in our large safe outside, they just have laths and hay on the slate slabs. If poor old Mum were here to see it all! But what's the use of bothering as long as we get through with our skins.

Sunday, February 20. I have just sent on six of your RX messages, also one received from Mr Dickens. I hardly know what to tell you.

I received a nice letter from Capt John Brooks who was with Jack in Egypt, and is now a prisoner in Germany. I wrote him a long letter. I hope he can let you have extracts from it.

Last Sunday we had a St John Ambulance service. 60 of the ambulance members attended, a crowded church, Dr Fox and Dr Cambridge read the lessons. They got £22 collection. Mr Frossard as usual rose to the occasion.

We have had a terribly cold week, showers of sleet often falling. Only 15 people at this morning's service, it was so cold. I managed to stick it, but had to wear my overcoat. People cannot stand the cold on the short rations.

Mr Poat has been taken to hospital for an operation. I think it's a serious case. Uncle Ned had the doctor yesterday, he has a cold and is very poorly. I am going to see him after dinner. Mrs Rowe has made him a loganberry tart and a few biscuits.

Judging by our weather you must be getting it cold in England. I expect a fall of snow. I have potatoes 18" high in Allendale greenhouse, am afraid I will lose them. It seems the irony of fate when we are so short of them. For three weeks now the people have had no ration of them. I don't know how they manage on roots only and vegs, and some have a few dried beans. It's next to starvation.

My men are working at Miss Mauger's, St Martin's, but it was so cold and windy I did not go out to see them. I went to L'Ancresse Lodge and it was bad enough that way. We are decorating the

FEBRUARY 1944

Dance Hall as dances are allowed again and they have cleared out of the hotel. What a state it was left in! Lav pans all smashed, baths taken away (Oh my), thank God the place is not mine. The owner, Pitcher, being an Englishman, was taken to Germany last year.

Tuesday, February 29. I am just back from an RC funeral at St Magloire, L'Islet. Perishing cold, NE gale along Grande Havre Rd going to the Vale cemetery.

I was told this morning it was the last time I could have the motor hearse, no petrol. Nurses' cars taken off the road. Only bakers and butchers and two or three doctors allowed them.

It's been down to freezing point for over two weeks now, with showers of sleet or snow, but it did not stay on the ground. There is a little sickness here now and lots of people dying. Certificates say cause of death malnutrition. But spring will soon be here.

I met Winnie Le Poidevin who says I am a devil. They have pleaded with me for two years to spend a day, so I settled on the spot to go next Sunday. Now I must ring up and say weather permitting. Her mother, about 86, is in bed today. Uncle Ned very frail when I called yesterday. Edith (Percy's wife) told me she finds him weak. I saw Mr Pattimore last night. He also is feeling the strain of winter. We are getting 2 oz extra of butter this week, total 5 oz, no fats.

My brother brought me six ormers. They were lovely in spite of having no fat to cook them in. I am lucky to get an extra occasionally.

Wednesday, March 1. The policeman has just come to say we must be out of the house tomorrow from 2 to 6 pm for artillery practice. They will be firing from Delancey Park, Frying Pan etc. Mrs Rowe says she won't go. It's at her risk.

I will go to a sale of greenhouse timber in the Vale. Last week I bought about a ton of elm logs, £12, at an auction sale, and greenhouse timber, £32. We cut it up for the shop, 3d per lb. People have to buy wood, they get gas for only three hours per day.

Yesterday I took Mrs Godfray a large bottle of Cherry Brandy and Miss Lihou a bottle of special brandy I managed to get. They were delighted. It's Mrs Godfray's birthday on Sunday, March 5th. I had promised to go, at last, to the Le Poidevins, but they put me off (as Mrs Le P has a cold) till the 12th. This suits me well as Mrs Godfray wanted me to go there to tea on her birthday. I also took out a nice sandwich cake Mrs Rowe made them and one hind leg of a large rabbit we are having (meatless week).

Sunday, March 5. A very cold, frosty morning. I went to the Early Service then to the 10.45 Choral Service, after which I showed Mr Frossard a notice I had received from Victor Carey, Controller

MARCH 1944

Electricity Board, to say we had exceeded our ration at the church by 10 units. We must reduce at once or be cut off altogether.

Now funerals again. I mention them to show you the conditions under which people live. Mr Holland died the other night. He was from the Stafford Light Infantry stationed here, a noted footballer in those days, married and settled here, now living at Cognon Vale.

Now to hard facts. Mr Holland was ill in bed. Suddenly at 10 pm after curfew, he collapsed and died. His wife was alone in the house, and thinking it had to be done at once she set to, washed and laid him out, and then had to sit there alone till morning and she could send for her people. I went at 9.30 and she said it was an awfully long night. I should say an ordeal for a woman.

I went to the Dean's office on Saturday afternoon for him to pass my churchwarden's a/c for the Trésor. It's our Parish Meeting tomorrow to pass the a/cs and for the election of churchwardens. Mr Frossard has asked me to stand again and I agreed. The Dean is getting very shaky. He has too much to do and cannot get outside help.

Mothering Sunday, March 19. We have had a lovely day. Quite a lot of people at church. We put the Evening Service at 5 and before it I went to see Uncle Ned. He is staying at Percy's. He is getting better but frail. He hopes to come down to the Old Rectory a little next week.

I managed to catch a cold this week, a wonder for me. I have no pain, just the bother of my nose. I cannot turn the tap off! I feel tired. Eating rather poorly which won't hurt. My voice is now weaker.

Yesterday I went with Stafford to be sworn in. The Dean is really very frail. He asked me how many times I had been elected churchwarden, it was my 9th, so when completed (if ever) would be 27 years. I said I ought to make room for someone younger. He thought it better left as it is for the present.

Sunday, March 26. A most glorious morning. No meat for anybody this week but I am lucky. My brother brought me a dozen ormers. A lovely feed and I did wish you had all been here to enjoy them, they were so tender.

I did pity most people today, they have no potatoes or roots of any kind. I don't know what they will live on next month. I had about 10 people here yesterday asking for even a dozen spuds. It's awful to have to refuse but what can I do. I spared Martel 10 lbs Tom Roberts 15 lbs Pattimore 8 lbs Miss Matthews 4 lbs, but I cannot continue at this rate.

The trouble is the island has no late seed potatoes. 20 tons came Saturday. Now another trouble, we are not getting any rain, and

MARCH 1944

the ground is parched with the last eight weeks of NE winds and freezing cold. I cannot tell how the people will live the next four months on the small rations (3 oz butter, no fats, 4½ lbs bread, ¼ pt milk per day and one or two small rationed goods). I see famine before us unless we get rain. The new moon yeterday so I don't expect rain the first quarter.

I have two nests of rabbits, 15 in all, and I have orders for 40. How can I split them up. Most people have had their breeding does stolen this winter, hence the scarcity. I have just been up Brock Rd picking food for the rabbits. That's the way I spend my Sunday afternoons now. There's even a famine in rabbit food, no roots, no peelings.

In the market in Town yesterday the stalls had just radishes, a few cabbage and plenty of flowers. These grow in the fields where the bulbs were ploughed in.

Undated. I went to St Martin's to try and finish Miss Mauger's job at the cottage. I started it four months ago, but with the bother of cement and wood permits and only a few men, it's impossible to please everybody.

I am finishing planting my tomatoes in three greenhouses. We are allowed to plant a third in Toms. I have two houses in potatoes but I really believe I will have Allendale's stolen. The only vegetables in the shops this morning were greens and a few broccoli. I am told that people get their roots stolen at night time, even from their houses. But what can people do, they cannot starve.

Good Friday, April 7. Church at 10.45, fed the rabbits and had dinner, not of course the usual fish dinner I had as a boy, dried cod fish. I well remember how salty it was. Today we had a tin of salmon and spuds.

In the afternoon I went to the Ogiers to take a woolly jacket for Mrs Bryan Ogier who is expecting a baby any day. Mrs Rowe had it knitted for me with the remainder of the wool left over from Mum making shawls. They insisted on my staying to tea. I was glad as I had real tea and nice cakes. Then we all came on to church for 7 pm. The choir sang The Crucifixion very well. It was a nice evening and we had £10 collection.

Easter Sunday, April 9. I sent the flowers for the altar as usual. Mrs Frossard was pleased with them and thought the white Tulips lovely. There are lots of lovely flowers about now, but Oh! the prices. Poor people think nothing of paying 4/- or 5/- for a small bunch. Either they don't value the R Mark or think since they cannot buy food the next best thing is to see flowers on the dining table.

APRIL 1944

Well it was a lovely mild morning and a lovely Easter Day. I went to the first service, there were 85. Mrs Le Poidevin and Belle Hunkin came down in a Chair with Miss Pearce to the 10.45 service.

After the service I brought Mrs Le P and Belle to dinner as arranged. Mrs Rowe had one of my lovely fat rabbits cooked to a turn. They shouted when opening the front door, Oh, what a lovely smell, and I can assure you it was. We had baked (browned) potatoes and broccoli, and a lovely milk pudding after, full cream. Oh, what a treat.

In the afternoon Winnie and Reg came down to fetch the old girl. Being a fine day I made them cancel the Chair and took them to the 5 o'clock service. Then home for tea, Real tea they had brought down. Mrs Rowe had a fine spread ready, rhubarb tart, tinned apricots, jam sandwich, etc etc.

They left at 8.30, only 6.30 summer time. They had the wheel chair for Mrs Le P. The old girl is 86, very game, and sticking it well. I took her around her garden, now enclosed in barbed wire. The Germans are in her house and they have lost nearly all their furniture. I am wondering what Nellie and Amy will say when they know.

Undated. Yesterday was the christening of Bryan's daugher, Jocelyn, at St Sampson's church and a reception at Les Gigands after. It was amusing to see the style, an old trap I should say came out of the ark, and Mr Peter Le Maitre's baker's cart. Talk about medieval times, we have gone back hundreds of years.

Mr Frossard and I cycled out after the service. A great reception, 29 in all. Egg sandwiches, cakes etc, a lovely christening cake. Real tea which I've no need to say I enjoyed very much. Then we walked around to see the garden. We drank the baby's health. Mr Ogier toasted the four great-grandparents. Four generations alive, very wonderful. Then the crowd dispersed.

I was in the road with my bicycle, leaving with the others, but they made me turn back. Stafford took my bicycle, but I did not mind as I had nothing to do. Later we had another spread, then drinks, a nice choice. Then I left, arriving at 1449 at 10, curfew 11 since May 1.

I sent out a large bunch of Lilies of the Valley for the table, and I put a crown in the kiddy's hand as they tell me it's usual, silver for luck, and it's difficult to buy anything. Dr Fox was there, he brought a silver tea spoon. I don't know where he got it. Mrs Frossard gave a knitted coat, pre-war wool as mine was.

Saturday, May 13. Friday night I had the burglars at Allendale, as Tuck my gardener discovered when he went down to open up as usual. I immediately telephoned the police. The Inspector had no one to send. He said there were queues in town half a mile long,

MAY 1944

waiting for the shops to open at 10. They had French shoes. The same at St Sampson's.

I would not wait being Saturday, a short working day. So I counted the stalks rooted up, 130. They had at least 80 lbs of lovely new spuds, 5d per lb. I expect they cost me 10d per lb to grow. I had that side dug by the time the Police came after dinner. He wanted to know how he could make a report. I told him to take my word, in any case I would get no compensation, so why worry.

Well, in the afternoon I decided, permit or not, to dig the others. Although they were not come I was determined not to lose them. But Oh! while digging, the man dug up a nest of young rabbits, four about a week old. I took them home and Mrs Rowe and I fed them with a spoon.

I don't know if the thieves are local or German. If local I don't blame them. For more than eight weeks many people have been without potatoes, living on roots and cabbage, and now there are no roots. I would do just the same.

Saturday, May 27. I rose with the lark this morning (and by the way, I have not seen one soaring into the sky in Guernsey the last years). It was a perfect morning, so I dressed in my Sunday best, managed my tub as well, and was ready for breakfast by 9 o'clock, 1½ hrs getting ready. Mrs Rowe thinks I broke the record. I had bread coated with dripping and ¾ pt of milk. Not faring badly lately.

After dinner collected my extra rations? and went to Pike's Corner to sunbathe and paddle my feet. At about 4.45 great excitement, our planes came over, 26 in all. The Germans did not fire at first so I certainly thought they were their planes. But when they reached Jerbourg they suddenly twisted and bombed the airport, then machine gunned the White Rock and Brehon Tower. They came quite low, skimmed the water at times, dozens of them firing the shrapnel bursting. It was exciting. Then I decided to run for shelter, with dozens of women and children.

I have not heard what damage was done, and we will know very little. How the planes missed being hit I cannot understand. However they seemed to sail off for Jersey quite safely.

I lost my fountain pen (the one you all gave me). Tom found it in the greenhouse amongst the peas. Lucky again.

The wild rabbits dug up in Allendale greenhouse now have their eyes open and can drink and eat by themselves, so they will live.

We have had a very busy week here, planes coming over from England at least four times a day, mostly bombing the Fort and machine gunning. They say they are after detectors at the citadel. The Fort has a few pot holes from machine guns, but no civilians killed as yet. It's a case of taking shelter now with all the shrapnel falling.

JUNE 1944

Tuesday, June 6. I went to Mrs Le Poidevin and Winnie and Ed Hunkins for the day on Sunday, June 4th. Had a good time. Lovely dinner, beef, new spuds, green peas, plenty of gravy, then milk pudding. Mrs Le P. poorly. She hopes to live till the girls come back.

Went for a walk through the Nursery after a sleep. Miss Pierce came to tea. We had pre-war Beaune wine, cocktails and Irish Whisky, Dr Jameson, to finish up.

I left at 9.30, all downhill with a following wind. I did it in about eight minutes. I don't think my cycle ever travelled faster.

Mrs Rowe looked after my wild baby rabbits that we dug up with the potato stalks. They are four weeks old and I give them milk only once a day now.

I thought about you all a lot all day yesterday. I knew what was in all our thoughts, poor Mum died five years ago, Monday, June 5th, and it was again Monday, June 5th. I put a nice wreath of mixed garden flowers on the grave from all of us.

The weather is very windy and we cannot get rain. There will be no potato crop, and if the rain doesn't come soon, root and bean crops will be a failure too. People are getting very worried. The greenhouse crops might save us a bit, but the waterworks people keep warning us to conserve water as much as possible.

Now, the news this morning. The invasion has started. Thousands of planes passed over during the night. People around the coast could not sleep. It did not disturb me much. Unfortunately one man was killed coming out of his lavatory at 7 am, Rue Flére, that's just at the back of Auntie Minnie's. A shell dropped short and knocked him out, very sad.

Noyon, the pilot, brought in an American airman, aged 28, from a plane they shot down over L'Ancresse. He was near the Humps in his rubber boat. He wanted Noyon to go on for England but this was impossible. He had little petrol, and even if he had they would probably have sent a faster boat to catch him.

For tea we had a nice dish of strawberries sent us by Mrs Rowe's sister, butter not on our ration but black market, 48 RM £5 2s.6½d per 1¼ lbs quite cheap!

It's now quite certain the much talked of Invasion has started. The Germans say it in the Press tonight, so we are all hoping to be relieved by September if all gocs well.

We hear quite a lot of things here, but as we have no wirelesses we can't always tell what's authentic. One of the Germans told my gardener that we had landed in four or five places. I'm sure it's on a gigantic scale and after the long preparations I don't think our people will make many mistakes.

I just went across the Bridge tonight to see Miss Matthews and

JUNE 1944

a person came in and said the police were on the Bridge warning people they must be in by 9 o'clock, so I soon packed off. I did not get home till 9.20 and did not meet a soul.

Wednesday, June 7. You have all been in my thoughts today. Five years ago today we buried dear old Mum, just such a day as today, except that it is blowing harder.

It's only really 7 o'clock and we have to be in. I am just back from visiting Mr Pattimore. He gets up every afternoon. He is very weak. His heart is so slow, 28 to the minute, the doctors cannot understand how he lives.

Our planes have been over all day. Bombed the Town harbour at 9 am and L'Ancresse several times this afternoon. It's risky to go out. I hear there were several casualties at the jetty this morning.

Our telephone is completely cut off. I am hoping they won't keep us too long without it. I am preparing for the winter although we are hoping against hope to be relieved before. I got a ton of logs in today, £15 and hope to get another tomorrow.

The potato ration is only 2 lbs this week I think. I don't know how people live. People like myself are lucky to have ground. I expect to pick toms soon. I had two ripe this week and gave them to Mrs Cumber (Ruby Bird). She has to diet. She has had most beautiful lettuce from my garden through my Greengrocery Dept. We have a very good trade at the corner shop.

Everything is dying for lack of rain. I believe it's too late now for some things to revive. Potatoes are flagging, beans turning yellow and roots at a standstill.

While I am writing this the Germans are up and down guarding the telephone exchange higher up the road. They look in as I write this. They little know what I am saying but I won't let them hear me!

I can hear some banging, I think from the Town. I hope they won't try to relieve us for two or three months. I know it will be much safer for us to wait a bit longer.

Friday, June 9. We have had a quiet night. Very few flares about, the weather windy, a small shower of rain about 5 am.

I had a nice nest of rabbits Sunday week.

They are now bombing the Town harbour where there are two steamers with four or six escort boats.

June 11-17. One evening a few planes came about 7.30. I had a good view of one especially, which dived from a terrible height, swooped over the Town Harbour and got a steam boat and set her on fire. We could see clouds of smoke. People saw the plane release the bombs right over the gas works and just manage the dead hit. It was a lovely dive. I cannot understand how they manage to clear the

JUNE 1944

dozens of bursting shells.

They came again the following morning. They are after a damaged submarine. They will get her.

One small shell burst in Mr Le Maitre's garden, Brownhill, wounded a rabbit and damaged the back door. It's not safe to be out when the planes are machine-gunning and the shells going up. We are in the front line now, but not how the Germans gave it out on the wireless, Fighting in the Guernsey streets, and Town harbour attacked by the English. The next day they said, All quiet now and harbour again in our hands.

I went to Town and saw the steamboat (in the Island Queen berth) still smoking away. She was struck aft.

I have a funny and dangerous job, to take down a large wooden tank from a 25 ft stand. The bottom fell out and about 20 tons of water swamped down. I have two dangers to contend with. First taking the tank to pieces, it cannot be lowered and anyhow we haven't the gear. Next, the Germans have an enormous gun in the next field, Coutanchez, and they say that when it fires everything lifts up.

The Germans have no planes here for defence. The aerodrome is covered with posts and all our large fertilizer boilers (on large wheels and easy to move if they wanted planes to land). They have every device yet cannot win.

We had a lovely sight on Wednesday morning, June 14th, from 8 to 11. Crowds of glider planes were passing NW of the island bound for Cherbourg. Right over our heads we could hear the hum of hundreds of fighters escorting them. The looked like large silver eagles being towed by large black monsters. They travel very slowly. It was an ideal day for them, little wind and a clear blue sky, hence their shining silvery appearance.

Sunday, June 18. 9.30 am. It's really the most beautiful day we have had this year. The planes came at 6.30 and the gun fire woke me up. So I decided to get up at 7.30, one of the few times in my life to be ready for church before time. Mrs Rowe quite expects something's going to happen today! But I told her it's never too late to mend your ways.

We have heard of all the happenings in France this week, and are hoping to be relieved or released (whichever word suits best), but I myself hope it won't be before they have a good footing in France. We can stand a siege for a couple of months. They cannot get many boats here now and I hear none from Jersey to France at the present.

That submarine the planes came after managed to get away last night I hear. This may not be true as the rumours are terrible. I ought to have written a book on them, but I doubt if I could have

JUNE 1944

found enough paper for all! It's dangerous to repeat anything. But people have little else to do with no English papers, no wireless and no conveyance to travel any distance.

I am now going to church for the 10.45 service. All places of amusement are now closed except churches (that sounds funny!), but it's forbidden to collect in great numbers anywhere.

Great excitement! News after the morning service, Cherbourg peninsula in our hands. Called on U. Ned after a good afternoon sleep. It is so lonely at the Old Rectory I brought him back here for tea which he enjoyed.

Sunday, June 18. Later. Great news tonight. I hear we have captured Carteret, only eight miles from Jersey. While I am writing this, after 9 pm curfew, we can hear the naval guns shelling the French coast. Not much sleep tonight with the rattling of our windows. I am now thinking we will be relieved sooner than expected. I am hoping the Germans will leave Guernsey. If they do I expect they will kill their horses, at least 200.

I have just given my three remaining wild rabbits their drink of milk. I think I told you Miss Poole's cat had one. They are now six weeks old, eat well and are quite as tame as our pigeon. Do you remember it?

I have just been inhaling steam steeped with sage, a new remedy for my voice. It's really worse although I have no pain or discomfort, just the voice nearly gone. I suppose I should rest it completely.

Monday, June 19. I got up early, a beautiful morning. The Germans are having heavy gun practice, and at the same time we can hear our navy banging at the French coast. It's heavy stuff as our windows are rattling so.

While I was writing that four planes came over and dropped bombs on the Town harbour. I've just called at Dr Cambridge's surgery where my man is working. The dispenser had been called to his Town surgery, High St. She says all glass and doors are blown in and the furniture dancing about the room. The Town Church's beautiful Rose window is caved in.

Later I met Jack Hart just back from Town. He said the Pollet and High Street are a shambles, about 90% of shop windows smashed. They have box carts picking up the glass. Woolworth's windows and Creasey's basement plate glass windows with their steel frames all caved in and smashed. Thousands of pounds worth of damage I believe. Only one man in Town was hurt.

They've just come to tell me that Guilmoto, our grave digger, St Sampson's cemetery, has been hit. Something burst the tyre of his cart then struck his left side.

Later. I've heard that Guilmoto had a piece of shrapnel taken

JUNE 1944

out of his side about 1" long and well bedded in.

Tuesday, June 20. I got up early again. Mrs Rowe cannot understand it, but I must start to be on the alert. We are in the front line of war this time.

I hear a boat managed to get into the Town harbour with flour for us and spuds for the Germans. I am glad for the German vans were at the Potato Depot, Union Hall, yesterday taking ours. I think they wanted 30 tons, hence our ration of only 3 lbs per person. Of course it does not affect me. I have taken Mrs Frossard a feed of my outside early potatoes. I would have had a lovely crop had I been able to leave them three weeks longer, but I was getting them stolen.

Mr Frossard tells me the Front is closed from the Red Lion. There are one or two mines dropped by a German plane which I think was damaged, and they had not exploded. So the people from the Royal, Stonelakes, the Canichers, etc had to leave their homes for three days. Mr Frossard says all the windows in the Town Church are blown out, the organ quite exposed to the elements.

I have just helped a man unload 200 cwt toms in the corner shop. We are selling them at 7d per lb and I quite expect we will be giving them away in two weeks. There will be no boats to take them to Jersey or France. Another good year for the cows. They love them.

I hear the Food Control Committee are offering £25 per 100 ft of greenhouse for people to pull up their tomatoes and plant potatoes. So I will pull up two of mine. Of course if we were soon relieved we would have a market for them.

I went to the Coutanchez to see my men about the tank. It was blowing like the devil. As I arrived we had an alarm, they ring a bell. They have this enormous gun in the next field, and have about 20 guns around the hill. Luckily for me it was a false alarm.

I hope the Germans won't fight for the island, for if so there would be a terrible lot of damage and casualties. Everything is so congested here. Our people in the Press say we need not worry. We have plenty of food and could stand a siege for two months. For report of Monday's air raid see Press, Wed June 21st, 1944. Save me writing more particulars.

It's been blowing half a gale today. Our people must be getting awful weather off the Cherbourg peninsula.

We are now pulling up peas in the greenhouse. We had a good crop 1/- per lb. Mrs Rowe picked them all. We have pulled 100 cwt of carrots from Mr Lake's Greenhouse, 6d per lb. This sounds a lot to pay, but I pay £5 per week to my two gardeners. I expect we will drop a lot on tomatoes if we cannot export to Jersey or France, but things are getting very hot for shipping.

JUNE 1944

I had a funeral today, a premature child, a boy, who lived only seven hours, the son of J. Simon from Le Riche's. He married Mr Smith's daughter, also from Le Riche, the Bridge. John, the French boy, was very friendly with him. My first funeral for over three months (trade bad!).

Thursday, June 22. I went to Town to see Mr Hubert about his tank stand, fetch canary seed for Mrs Rowe's canary, pay two or three bills, and perhaps most important of all, see the damaged shops, and trust not to get an air raid on my journey.

Well at the Longstore, the road was closed, so I had to go inland. I parked my cycle at the bottom of the Pollet, 2½d. The E window of the Town Church blown clean out, most shop windows boarded up in some fashion, but it's a real smash up. They say what caused such a concussion was that as a bomb struck the water it burst. I paid a bill at the Star office, their windows boarded up and quite dark inside, one small electric bulb.

Then I went to the Government Office, Ann's Place, saw Mr Hubert, met Mr Frossard and came home. Very tired and ready for a meatless dinner, quite content, no air raid. But Oh, the Town!

Monday, June 26. Very little air activity this week. We see by the papers that the British and Americans have got on wonderfully well to have captured Cherbourg in three weeks.

Friday, June 30th, 1944. Today it's four years to the day that the Germans landed 7.30, Sunday evening. I remember they came with three aeroplanes, and the next morning what an uproar at the Royal Hotel, everyone taking in their guns, rifles, pistols, swords, daggers and the devil knows what. We little knew it would be over four years before we could get our freedom again.

Still I have been through it and it has been quite an experience, and I feel tonight, as I write these lines, that although I did promise that I would not stay here to be occupied and in the end got trapped, I have not really regretted staying.

The hardships have not been great, the food problem has been the worse. I have had a quiet time in many ways. I have of course lost my voice which might not have happened had I always had good nourishing food. I have only had to eat dry bread twice, and once or twice been down to only one slice for tea, and could not have breakfast until I fetched the loaf.

I know some people have been hard put to be able to live, but my experience has been that it's not only the food that matters, it's the mental effect on most of the people. They are unconscious of it, but don't make good blood. I have studied the people about here. The light-hearted and little brained are satisfied with every

JUNE 1944

little piece of good news.

It's the old story. I have always claimed you can feed the body as much as you like, but the spirit wants feeding otherwise you go down. Things get on your nerves.

I have had a patch of potatoes stolen at the top of Allendale garden. We had dug one quarter and got 30 lbs, and thought to leave the rest a week or two longer to ripen. They dug the lot for me! In New Road field they have been scratching all over the big patch. It's very disappointing because they won't be fit to dig before September.

Then today their damned, infernal sheep came tramping down from the Park, ran over my beans, and ate the tops of my lettuce and potatoes. Had we not been there to drive them out it would have been disastrous. I managed to pick a quart of gooseberries and with logans am going to make jam. I've got some sugar at 18 RM per Kilo, 19/2 1/2 not bad if you say it quick! 1 lb of butter 28 RM, £2 19s.9 1/2d. Still it's food and we must have it somehow.

This is the second meatless week. I had one of my small rabbits last week. This week I killed my big Flemish. I tried three times this summer to breed from her but she was too fat. She weighed 12 lbs, when cleaned 8 lbs. I had 1 lb of solid fat from her. I cut her in two and took half to Mrs Frossard with some of my special spuds, carrots and peas, from all of which I have had splendid crops, and they are of excellent quality, so I am blessed with some special favours.

I have a nest of seven lovely rabbits. I am keeping only one for myself. Then today I have two more nests of young. When these young are gone I am hoping to be finished keeping rabbits. The devils can eat all day long.

I decided to see the doctor. It's months since I have called about my voice which is certainly worse the last two weeks. I have now to talk in a whisper otherwise I have to strain to make a sound. But the primary reason for going was to get my ears syringed. I have been deaf and last night put in eardrops.

Dr Fox said I was looking more than 50% better than when I last saw him. My throat was the same, simply the vocal chords gone wrong which I suppose is difficult to account for. Having put the mirror down my throat a few times and my saying, loo loo, la la, and so no, he thought the only thing for me was to stop talking. I told him impossible! I said I would continue not smoking which I had not done for two weeks now. Don't know how long I can keep it up. Then he syringed my ears, we had a little gas and I came home.

As usual had a rest, read and a sleep. I really ought to be well on my treatment. Little work, hardly enough for exercise, fairly good food this last year and little worry. What can I have more.

JULY 1944

Saturday, July 1. This afternoon I went to see Miss Lihou. Mrs Godfray was there. Miss Lihou was very bright and laughed over things. My voice was very bad and I could only speak in a whisper. I left the necessary and she was glad I came.

I went with Mrs Godfray to Belle Vue. She insisted on my having some tea. I tried some nice logan jelly she had been given. I took her a loaf and some salad cream. She was very pleased. Also 2 lbs flour, 6 RM per lb 12/9½ what a price!

Mrs Godfray told me Elsie's niece had gone to the sanatorium with TB. I understand she is very bad.

I luckily took my mac, but even so I got a drenching coming home, had to change everything. And then I had another tea with lovely new jam Mrs Rowe made this morning with logans and gooseberries from the field. I then shut down the greenhouses, brought milk thistles for the rabbits. It's still too wet for me to take the lovely carnations from my vinery garden down to the grave.

Sunday, July 2. A very dull morning, again drizzling. Everybody was praying for rain and now we have it with a vengeance. I went to the 8.30 service. My voice is very weak and I am trying to talk only in a whisper and I think it's answering well. I have no need to force to make a sound.

I came home to a nice breakfast, an egg. What a treat. People will give anything from 2/- to 5/- for one.

Wednesday, July 5. It now seems it's one trouble on top of another. We were advised to plant one third of our greenhouses in tomatoes, although I admit the Germans did not guarantee transport. Well, we are faced with the 1940 trouble. I believe the States have a shipload waiting with thousands of packages and if no boat by Monday they will have to dump them. The best samples in the shops are 2d per lb and next week we will be giving them to the cows. It's a terrible loss for the island.

I had a circular today advising people to pull up half their crops and plant beans. I have a nice crop but if no boats arrive by the middle of next week I will pull up two houses, and leave one for the shop. Even that might be too much.

I am just back from the Banques seeing our sexton. Guilmoto is out of hospital and getting on now. He had a narrow shave. The shrapnel was quite near the lung.

I went to Town to try to collect payment of a bill from the Germans, nearly £7 for repairs to damage caused when blowing up the Monument. I could not see the right officer so must go again on Monday. I don't feel like losing the cash, and I sent it three months ago.

This is the third meatless week, but the men can go fishing again. I managed four mackerel this week. I also got 4 lbs black currants, 2 lbs raspberries and Mrs Rowe made jam again. She is bottling logans, all stores for next winter if required.

We have a circular today, the States are preparing for communal cooking as it's possible we will be without gas before long. It will be awful for those who have to give up all their rations and draw their cooked food from distribution centres. Even so I cannot understand how they can take it home for the family to have a hot meal. We seem to be getting into a pretty plight here, but the people seem to take everything quite calmly.

Saturday, July 8. I went to Town to see the States' engineer about a job at L'Ancresse Lodge. It's now months I've put it off hoping not to have to do it, but the place was flooded last week. They have moved the States offices right up to De Beauvoir Terrace, Ivy Gates, top Rohais.

While in Town I fetched my gold watch at Collivet, then went to Mackay. (Managed to get a bottle of brandy.) John Dyson seems to be boss.

After tea went to my sister's, Summerville Road for my bread ration. She gave me two eggs. I think she found my voice much worse. It has quite gone and I have to talk in a whisper. I have been doing too much chatting lately owing, I suppose, to the excitement about the Invasion. Otherwise I am keeping very fit.

Sunday, July 9. I like it when Sunday falls on the 9th, I like the evening Psalm 49, tune and words, although I could not sing tonight, which I miss very much.

Fancy, rain again this morning, and of course followed by a devilish wind. We were glad of the rain, but the evenings are so cold. We have not had one good summer since 1940, the year the Germans came. Mrs Frossard said coming from church she wanted a fire, she was perished with cold.

However, wonderfully good news today about Caen, La Haye du Puits, Russia, etc.

We are now worrying about you all when we read and hear about the V 1 "comets" the Germans are sending over. You must be getting an awful time in London. I wonder from time to time if we, I mean our family, will ever see it through.

We had a double quartette during the service tonight. It was rendered beautifully from the hymn, A & M 630. Gwen Pill took the solo. The choir men take the first part of the service and read the lessons to ease Mr Frossard who has to carry on for both Vale and St Sampson's. I cannot help as my voice has flopped out.

The Germans are leaving here little by little and we hope soon to be relieved, but we don't want the English here too soon. We can manage till the winter sets in when I hope they will come along,

JULY 1944

and we must then chance our skins. It's all a game.

On the 3rd July the Germans issued an order that all grass had to be moved before the 5th. Of course that was impossible. The farmers could not have found sufficient mowing machines. So the Germans sent their men and mowed fields down and took the grass away. Tuck, my gardener, told me the Germans cut two of his father's fields, I think they took away about 11 loads. Now I suppose Mr Tuck will have to get rid of his cows, for he won't have any hay for the winter.

They seem to be up to all sorts of dodges. Had they wanted the grass cut for any reason, why not give reasonable time. It looks to me all part of a plan. Their transport now is just about cut off and they have about 200 horses to feed.

The OT are practically gone from here, the quarries are all closed, most of the railway lines have been taken up.

A great patch of the top part of the White Rock was blown out Friday evening. It's quite plain to be seen from the Banques, about 40 ft of the top walk. I heard the explosion at about 11 pm. Just then there was a plane over, but some say it was a mine. So many rumours are about one cannot tell which is the right report.

Monday, July 10. It's really heart-rending to see the shops full of lovely red tomatoes, and all the vineries are giving them away now. I hear the Fruit Export Co have 250 tons and no prospect of shipping them. Up to now we have managed to get rid of mine at the corner shop. I don't know what price she manages to get.

I have been to L'Ancresse this morning with the States engineer about that tank job at L'Ancresse Lodge. The Germans left the hotel in a terrible state. Most of the windows are smashed.

Mr Cumber, Chemist, has brought me, as a great favour, a bottle of glycerin (pure) to gargle with. I am trying this remedy with Port wine (if I can get it) I am also promised. I must try something now as I can only talk in a whisper.

Tuesday, July 11. It was such a cold evening that after tea and closing the greenhouses I took a constitutional around the lanes and over Delancey. Oh! the destruction. You could hardly imagine it. I did not meet a soul except a young German boy on guard and well armoured, who spoke to me, and after a bit I understood he wanted to know the time. It was 9.30 and he was on till 12 o'clock. He looked bored, cold and miserable.

Very little news. 10 boats came up from Jersey this afternoon. If our planes happen to fly around there will be some excitement tonight.

Wednesday-Saturday, July 12-15. I have just been as far as Bisset's. He

JULY 1944

spared me a bottle of special Port. I am trying an old doctor's remedy, gargle with Old Port and glycerin. I tried with glycerin alone today and I am really much better.

Mr Cumber told me about one of his tenants who, three months ago, could speak only in a whisper. Two weeks ago he could talk quite clearly and shout. He met him today and his voice has completely gone again. His doctor cannot understand it. He has tried him with tonics and special medicines. It does seem strange.

I met a lady at Mr Langmead's yesterday (she getting cabbage plants, I peaches). I asked her to excuse my whispering. She told me of a friend of hers who lost his voice for two months, and it was worse than mine. It was something to do with what we drink and eat which dries up the throat and affects the larynx.

I change from one topic to another. It's all very humorous here at times. At a farm at St Peter's the old lady won't let her husband smoke. She says they must barter for something they can both share, but the old man is cute. They keep fowls, so he steals the eggs when he gets the chance and barters them for cigarettes. Someone at St Sampson's gets the eggs brought from St Peter's by her son-in-law.

You can get as much as 12/6 per packet. I am not smoking now, but I give them away or exchange one packet cigs for 1 lb salt, two packets for 1 lb sugar.

It's pathetic for some of us growers to see the women with their loads of huge, blood ripe tomatoes in various contrivances on wheels, and each person munching an enormous one. You can hardly see their faces for tomato! I have a bottom bunch with at least 10 tomatoes, all dead ripe waiting to drop off. I begrudge the time to pick them, only to throw them away or give them to the cows.

I went to Miss Lihou on Friday to fetch the raspberries and logans. I had quite a load, at least 10 lbs raspberries and 3 lbs of logans. Mary and her husband happened to be calling when I got home. They had two helpings each, without sugar. I think it was a special treat for them.

I have to go out on Wednesday for another lot. It's very kind of them to give me so many, but unfortunately now I cannot get sugar. I have ordered 4 kilos from one depot, but doubt if we will get luck. However we are bottling them for the present.

Sunday, July 16. I have just been to see Mr Pattimore. He is now very frail, can scarcely walk, but interested in everything. I must always tell him where all my men are working and which are the next jobs. But now, at times, he gets depressed and says he doesn't want to live to see the war over. It's too long and the food very poor for old people.

JULY 1944

Monday, July 17. Tom tells me we are going to have a meat ration. It would have been the fifth week without. The funny part is that he was told the meat was coming from Herm. He said we were all right for kangaroo steaks! He says funny things.

I have been working today for a change, a lovely summer's day which started with thick fog. We dug 3 cwt of carrots from one of Lake's greenhouses. I am planting one GH in potatoes again, in case of a scarcity. It's sickening about our tomatoes. Some bunches have 12 ripe tomatoes. I bet you would all have a good feed, especially Ted, if an aeroplane dropped you all here in the morning.

Wednesday, July 19. Fair weather. I managed to get my breakfast over by 10 o'clock. After dinner went to St Andrew's. On the way called at St Jacques and got a few peaches from Mr Longmead, 1/2 RM each. Took them to Mrs Godfray and Miss Lihou and a few buns. Ada, Miss Lihou's maid had picked quite 6 lbs of raspberries and 2 lbs of logans, so I was again loaded on my return.

This morning providence came my way. A friend came in to know if I wanted 2 kilos of sugar at 18 RM per kilo. or in English, 19/2½.

I got 1 lb of black currants and Mrs Rowe has just finished making the jam. Then I managed to get 2 lbs of flour at 6 RM per lb. or 12/9½ which I might spare to Mrs Godfray, but it's the only way to keep up your strength.

We have done well this week, had whiting twice for dinner and today three longnose. They were lovely, so beautifully fried. It's dull again. It rained on St Swithin's Day and has rained every day since. We picked 40 baskets of beautiful tomatoes to send to the cows. People now won't give even 1d per lb for them.

Friday, July 21. Rain again, not daylight till nearly 7 and as cold as a January morning. Still good news for us according to reports. I hear they threw a bomb at Adolf Hitler.

I was just having my tub when I had to answer the door (Mrs Rowe gone for her Friday half-day). Someone wanted to know if I could make her a seat for a commode. I was annoyed at her bothering me about a job of that sort.

It's 6 o'clock, and it's rained the whole day. If it clears I will go out to Miss Lihou with her bottle, as I think she is out of the necessary which, she says, is the only thing that keeps her up.

Monday, July 24. This morning started dull with plenty of air activity. I expected that as several boats were in the Town harbour. The planes paid us several visits, but at 7.30 they came along from towards Jersey and met five or six boats just coming out of the harbour.

JULY 1944

Talk about shell fire. One of the planes dropped a stick of bombs and nothing was seen of the biggest boat but a cloud of smoke and fire. When that cleared there was nothing but jetsam, I suppose I should say flotsam, and the poor men shouting in the water. People along the Banques could hear them crying for help. One of the escort boats saved those they could. A smaller craft just had her stern damaged and I believe she managed to get back into the harbour. It was all over in five minutes.

We had orders to pick and send tomatoes to the depot for Jersey. I sent 36 baskets. Now I expect it's all up for getting any away to Jersey, and they are crying out for them. A Jersey doctor has written an article in the Press saying they are better than any other food. See Presses from July 16-22.

Saturday, July 29. High winds and heavy showers this week. Thursday, July 27th was Miss Lihou's birthday and Mrs Godfray made me promise I would go to tea. Mrs Rowe made a birthday cake and a rhubarb and logan tart, but as the tart would not keep I took both out on Tuesday and for another reason too. Had I arrived late on Thursday tea might have been over when the cake arrived.

I put congratulations in the Press. She was pleased. Fancy, 89 years and still has all her faculties.

When I arrived tea was over. I was in the second relay, Miss Dorey did not turn up. She was ill. Miss Naftel, Miss Allez (both in their late sixties) and Mrs Godfray in her 93rd year were there, so it was Jack among the maidens. Then Elsie came in with her mother. So we started and had hot milk, full cream thanks to Mrs Godfray, and enjoyed it. After a chat we had a liqueur to drink Miss Lihou's health. She had half a dozen bouquets, and they said mine was the best and I think it was the finest.

It's a lovely evening. Being Saturday I've done nothing today except put flowers on Mum's grave, Glads from the garden, and I picked a sack of food for the rabbits. I have 22 now, but will dispose of 12 of the young ones next week.

I have very little inclination to do anything. My voice has completely gone and I am longing for the war to be over to consult a specialist. I don't go to the doctor much. I am afraid they might want to meddle with it or perhaps operate, and as I am normal otherwise think it better to see a proper specialist.

Sunday, July 30. A lovely Sunday morning. Everyone bright at church. A Mr Le Page preached well and very fluently. I believe he was to have been ordained but war broke out and he could not get across to the mainland.

After the service Stafford Ogier came back with me. He was stranded and borrowed a packet of cigarettes till Tuesday ration

AUGUST 1944

day. I had one to spare as I have not smoked for about two months owing to losing my voice. But I broke out today.

He got me to go out there after dinner and I was glad to go for many reasons which I will explain later. (I came back very bucked.) I had a nice tea but did not chat much. I am trying a rest cure, although nothing seems to make any difference. I just cannot speak and that's all about it, but if I only whisper I don't get so tired.

Monday, July 31. Winnie Hunkin telephoned to ask if she, her mother and Reg Hunkin could come down in the afternoon. Mrs Rowe agreed although it was a big washing week.

A real summer's day. They went to the cemetery and then I took them to see her garden. The Germans are still in her house. The old lady was very bright and cheerful.

They brought down real tea and I drank five cups. We had lovely tomatoes from my vinery, black currant jam and a grand apple and logan tart Mrs Rowe made.

They left at 7.30 with the old wheel chair. They wheel her in turns but it's a good push over Amherst. Soon after they left our planes came, but I expect they took shelter at the Rectory or Mr Poat's. Their visit lasted only a few minutes and the only danger is shrapnel.

Tuesday, August 1. I had a strenuous day. After dinner I went to St Martin's, first to Miss Mauger's cottages at Les Cornu where a part of a ceiling had fallen.

From there I went to see Miss Houstoun. She has swollen glands in her neck. You cannot notice anything, she wears a high collar. Jack, her brother, is looking very well. She insisted on my having tea.

Then I went on to Miss Mauger to report about the ceiling. Her tenant, Miss Gallienne, would rather not have it repaired and I don't blame her, as with all the gun fire, more might fall. I went round the garden.

Then I went to Miss Lihou with her bottle then to Mrs Godfray. Had tea there which I had taken because people cannot spare their bread and butter. I took a nice apple tart which was halved for Miss Lihou and her sister. We chatted. I got home at 9 o'clock, much tired with so much cycling.

Wednesday, August 2. I was tired after yesterday and rested most of the day. Luckily for me I can go and come when I like.

Friday, August 4. News all very good and everybody raising high hopes of being relieved by September at the latest. Another meatless

AUGUST 1944

week so we are having a rabbit. We have plenty of food now of a sort. I have all I want but am afraid there will be a scarcity of carrots and parsnips soon. We have a German order now to plant one tenth of our greenhouses in swedes.

I have made up the money for the men so am taking another rest. I think I do that mostly. Mrs Rowe has gone to the garden to pick the runners. She has picked about six baskets this week. I have a good crop and they sell at 10d per lb.

What a disaster about our tomato crop. Tom Roberts buried 50 baskets yesterday. Last year at this time I was getting in £10 to £14 per week at our shop, this year about £1.

Saturday, August 5. Real wonderful Guernsey summer weather at last. Tom went to Town for me but no luck. We are cut off now so won't get much of anything. Liqueurs, wines and spirits finished I think till we are relieved which, by the good news, will be this side of a month. Still we have waited long so hope they will not hurry over it, in order to save as much life as possible.

I am just back from my sister's getting my ration and she gave me three eggs. I am getting pity now my voice has gone.

Elsie, from Mrs Godfray, telephoned to say her niece has just died of TB at the San. Very sad and only 21 years old. I went out there at 5 o'clock and met her Grandpa who cared for her since her mother, father and family evacuated in 1940. They met me at Mrs Godfray's and I made all arrangements from there, burying at St Martin's on Thursday. I had my tea with Mrs Godfray, had a chat and arrived home 5 mts before curfew.

Sunday, August 6. Another most wonderful morning. I went to the 8 o'clock service, 55 people, all excited with the war news. Nice Choral service at 10.45. Had a rabbit dinner then a hot ride to the Câstel. On the way back it was so boiling hot and I was getting a bit saddle sore, I decided to rest at Stafford's, Gigands, for an hour. But as usual they insisted on my having tea there, and promised to have real tea to drink and that I could not resist. After tea we heard the news and came on to church, 7 pm. It was a glorious evening and all the good news seemed to brighten every one up.

Monday, August 7. Bank Holiday morning was a scorcher. I got in rabbit food and rested in the morning.

Left soon after dinner to make arrangements for the funeral at St Martin's church, first about buying a grave, then saw the Rev. Coulthard, then the grave digger, then the bell ringer. They all live in different places. The Germans are now billeting a lot in St Martin's. Next rang up the organist.

Everything then being fixed, being so near, I went to see Miss

AUGUST 1944

Houstoun, but she was out. Jack kept me chatting some time. Then I went to see Mrs Godfray. Got there at 7, fairly tired. She was expecting me and got the tea. Home at 10 pm, cut it rather fine.

Thursday, August 10. Another fine day, but cloudy after dinner with a hot, heavy wind. The ride to St Martin's church was trying, all uphill. I took my gear for the funeral in a parcel, also took Gerald Martel to help me and bring it back, as I was returning to Mrs Godfray to tea, and also taking Miss Lihou's allowance which I am afraid is coming to a stop now.

A very nice service, many people. There were 56 wreaths. I was glad to have Martel to help me.

Friday, August 11. It's taken me part of the day to write out the funeral report for the papers as I cannot talk a lot on the phone. I have now to make up the men's money being Friday, and I hope I am then finished for the day.

It's such grand weather I wish we were allowed on the beach. I suppose I must give up hope of the beach and bathing again this year.

Sometimes I get fits of worrying about your safety with these devils of robots, or V 1s as William Joyce calls them. I imagine Flo and Rosemary have gone down to Horsham, Kit evacuated with her school, Ted in the thick of it in London, and Jack, I cannot imagine where he is. I sometimes think Persia.

Saturday, August 12. Darling Kit, I did not write you anything on your birthday but my thoughts were with you, and I wondered how you were spending the day, being the 11th.

I had hoped we would have been together this year, and now it's getting late for me to see you even by my birthday, Sept 29th. Still we can be together in spirit. Fancy, I will be 68 years old, and it's people of my age to whom the war has made most difference. Five years off a man of 25 is nothing compared with a man over 60.

I have just been outside watching about 19 large planes going back to England. They passed down about an hour ago, they must have gone to Brest or somewhere in the bay. They did not fire at them, they were too high.

Sunday, August 13. Mrs Le Poidevin and the Hunkins came down to tea. We had rhubarb and B. currant tart sweetened with real sugar, a pound cake with sultanas, our own drying, lovely coffee buns, a tin of pre-war apricots, lovely, and best of all Winnie brought down real tea.

They went to church at 7. I am sparing Reg some moulded sash bass for repairs to Town shop windows. It's a barter exchange.

AUGUST 1944

Sunday, August 20. A lovely morning and lots of reassuring news. I went to the morning service then to the Hunkins to dinner. The old lady was really glad to see me again so soon.

We had a nice dinner, my potatoes (as the rations are poor), baked or fried corned beef with onions and vegetables, full cream milk pudding and a nice cocktail.

Mrs Rowe came up in the afternoon. Reg and I went to the bottom of Amherst to meet her, she not being sure of the way. We had a nice tea, apple and plum tart and a sandwich which Mrs Rowe brought, fruit salad, and best of all, real tea. What a treat. I managed four large cups.

After tea Reg and I went as far as Mr Wheadon's, saw Uncle Bert, chatted and came back for another yarn. Had a glass of hot milk with a drop of the right spirit in it before we left.

Then I wheeled my bicycle and walked home with Mrs Rowe. Along the Banques many people were sitting on the grass, no one allowed on the beaches. Two steam boats were making their way to Alderney. The end of a perfect day.

End of August. We are all saying, Now it's not for long. I am longing for it to be over, as I want to get to London to see a specialist about my voice which has now completely gone.

The weeks pass by and now little change except good news about the progress of the war. Our people dropped leaflets on three nights this week. I saw them, about the size of our Press with pictures of men holding up the white flag, maps of France and Russia showing American and English advances, and other matters, all in German. I suppose it's to encourage them to give up without resistance, which I, and all of us, are hoping they will. They are getting very short of food, in fact we all are now.

I'm sorry you won't be able to see how we were closed in all around New and Brock Roads with barbed wire, and fowl house wire on all the outside windows. They are taking it all down now. It seems to me they don't intend to put up much of a fight.

We have had a gale for two days and all the lovely apples are blown down, another difficulty if we have to go through another winter. They were always something to fall back on in winter time.

I have had the police down again about the Germans stealing my potatoes in the field. They cannot do anything except adjust my allowance. I will now be responsible for 1 perch less to the States. We will have some stories to tell you if we remember them or if I am alive to tell the tale.

Monday, September 4. Yesterday, Sept 3rd (by the way five years since the war began) Mrs Rowe and I arranged to spend the day at Mrs Godfray. We started at 10.30 (I had been to the 8 o'clock service)

SEPTEMBER 1944

with a basket each of provisions, a tongue in glass, a tin of gelatine, tomatoes, bread, etc. I was dreading the long walk to St Andrew's when around Potter's Corner a nice little pony with small wagonette stopped and the driver asked where I was going. I did not wait to tell him but dumped the two baskets and pushed Mrs Rowe in, then I said St Andrew's. We had a lovely drive along the front and he dropped us at the end of Mount Row. I have never known anything more lucky. I was glad mostly for Mrs Rowe's sake as she always works so hard.

We arrived at Belle Vue nice and early. Madam showed her the house and all the photographs (the first time they had met) and then all round the garden while I sat down.

Then Elsie called me to open the tins of meat which I had kept for a rainy day, but now, as things are going, I am getting reckless. We had a nice lunch with vegetables, gravy, then milk pudding and peaches, nectarines, figs and grapes which I had sent Tom out with the night before.

After a rest we took Mrs Rowe to see Miss Lihou. She was very impressed with Mrs Rowe and thanked her for the many nice cakes and tarts sent out at various times. The maid, Ada, then took Mrs Rowe to see the house and garden. Then we wended our way back for tea of baked apples, bread and butter, and our nice sandwich cake, buns and biscuits, all of Mrs Rowe's make.

Then a liqueur, Cointreau, before we left at 8 pm. I had a rather heavy basket as we picked up some chestnuts at the Vauquiedor blown down by the gale, and Mrs Godfray would insist on my bringing a few rusty-coat apples. All downhill and a strong following wind, we arrived home at 9 pm, one hour, not bad going. I stayed in bed till 10 this morning.

If fine tomorrow Mrs Godfray is coming down for the day. I am sending a Chair for her.

Tuesday, Sept 5. It's still blowing but the sun is shining between banks of clouds. Mrs Rowe can cater well and is very capable and I have seen that no provisions are lacking. All the good war news again this morning makes us feel we can delve deep into our very scanty stores. I am expecting my Tuesday man. I hope there is luck.

Sept 10-16. The day passed very well. Mrs Godfray looked in the pink of health, one can scarcely believe her to be in her 93rd year. We had a lovely dinner of rabbit stew, baked potatoes and runner beans, rice pudding then figs and grapes. We made her have a rest after dinner.

Mrs Rowe took her to the Bridge to see how the Germans had fortified the harbour. Then I took her to see the vinery. There was nice sunshine but a nasty wind blowing. She thought my late potato

SEPTEMBER 1944

crop very fine. But when she saw my tomato crop wasting it made her nearly cry to see such abundance of large tomatoes on the ground and hanging down the stalks. Well, she said, And yet you are smiling. Crying and worrying won't make it any better, I replied.

We had a nice tea, with tart and jam sandwich, and we gave her a snack for her sister, who is really frail but I think, with a little exertion, could have come. The trap took her back at 6 o'clock.

I went out on Saturday with the necessary rations for Miss Lihou, had tea with Mrs Godfray, and had a cold ride home, wind unfortunately East. Mrs Godfray enjoyed herself so much that I arranged for her to come again on the 12th. They charge 4 RM each way, making 17/4 but of course Madam can well afford it.

It was a finer day. We had the same bill of fare and in the afternoon Mrs Rowe took her to see the church and they sat in the cemetery. We have some nice seats there now.

I have a funeral this week, right from Blanchelande, but we are having it from St Sampson's Chapel, thence to St Sampson's cemetery. I am not doing much of the running about. I don't feel equal to it lately. My throat and voice seem worse.

I have started going to the doctor again. He suggested trying electrical treatment, but I am afraid to risk such a delicate part of the throat to amateurs, so he thought since I was not keen, wait a bit, and I might soon be able to get to London to a throat specialist.

Thursday, Sept 21. We get those leaflets every night now. Last week they must have dropped the cylinders when they were too low or they did not explode in time, for one broke through a greenhouse and burst the 4" hot water pipes. The other went through Mr Poole's van shed and smashed the pulper. They must explode with great force.

We are getting a very fine September now. It's the 21st and dear summer has ended and we start the autumn.

I had a rather poor night, slept only 2½ hours. My breathing is now getting bad. I have a wheezing on the chest, earache and bad headaches this week, so have telephoned Dr Fox to come and see me this morning. Something will have to be done. It would be very difficult to breathe if it gets worse.

I was banking on the war being over to get to London and go into the case properly. It seems so funny to me, no swelling, no pain, just the voice completely gone, but now this trouble of breathing starts.

Friday, Sept 22. The doctor called. He sounded my chest and said he thinks there cannot be a malignant growth. I told him I was very uncomfortable with my breathing during the night. He said if it

SEPTEMBER 1944

gets worse I will have to go to hospital again, be put under and have a further examination. If the worse comes to the worse he will insert a small tube in my throat to make breathing easier till he can get me to London, which he thinks won't be long now. I have to inhale again and he is changing my medicine. The next day I felt much better and had a lovely night's sleep.

Unfortunately I had to go to Collins Road about a job we hope to start on Monday, about £100 job. I suppose people were surprised to see me about at 10 o'clock, for the first friend I met, Mrs Stubbs, said, You're about early! Tom Roberts, who was with me said it was a pity I came out so early as I frightened people!

It's been a lovely day. My men are just coming up the road for their wages. They are excited with the report of an American boat about four miles out, flying a white flag, and the German boat also flying a white flag has gone out to her. We are all wondering what it means, perhaps an ultimatum. To avoid fighting I hope the Americans won't be in too much of a hurry. The Germans are very short of medicines for hospitals, etc. That might make them want to surrender sooner.

I think the civil population could hold out another two months, but gas and electricity are short, no coal or wood, bakehouses closed down this week for cooking dinners. I really don't know how people will manage to keep fires going, for even if they could get the logs they did cost 8/6 per cwt, and now 14/6.

I've just split up a pitch pine log about 14" square and 2'6" long. It weighed 180 lbs and Miss Matthews paid me £2 5s. for it, dear, but had I told people I could have got more.

Saturday, Sept 23. I did not do much today. I am not really well. I helped Tom in the morning to take logs to the shop from the Forge. Then after dinner fetched my ration of bread from Minnie, picked a nice lot of single asters all colours from the vinery garden, and put them on the grave. I stayed down in the cemetery in the lovely sun by Mum's grave. The air was autumnal but quite warm.

On the way back I went to see Uncle Ned at the Old Rectory. I am sure you would hardly know him. He is very thin, about a foot shorter, but has all his faculties as keen as ever. It's wonderful what people get repaired now, old pots and pans discarded years ago are again in use. He wanted me to stay a little but with a touch of earache and awful pains in the head, I came home and rested on the couch.

Then I inhaled steam, my head packed in a dozen towels (looked very funny), then had full cream milk and some brandy. Don Bisset came with a much overdue promise. I paid him 32/- but had he sold it on the black market he could have got 80/-.

SEPTEMBER 1944

Sunday, Sept 24. Last night I went on my perch to roost, as I thought for an all night sleep, but woke up and the old clock struck 12. I stayed awake three hours, but not in much pain except for my breathing a bit difficult. I took a dose of my physic and then slept till 9. Got up at 12.30.

Stafford came in from church to see how I was. I gave him two cigarettes. He had not smoked since Tuesday (and it's our very last ration till we are relieved). My gardener came in with my "morning paper" dropped from the plane last night. He shouted out, Here's your Daily Mail landed last night at 9.30. It's funny, they've dropped these German papers every night for the last three weeks. We cannot read them but I am keeping them in case you can read German (some hope I say).

We had a nice dinner, meat this week. It's months since our last issue, and it's only veal, but as we say, better than nothing. I was lucky this week, three dinners of longnose.

Tom Ozanne, (you might know him, one of our Deputies, a good Labour man), died this week. I went to the funeral at Bordeaux Mission Hall. A lot of Court Officials were there and I met Charlie Corbet, we sat together. In chatting I told him to bring me along a fish dinner when he could. To my surprise, at 8 next morning, who did I see outside but Charlie. He had six longnose, not large, but made two dinners. I was glad that I had gone to the funeral!

Now to go back to ordinary doings. I stayed in today. Had a nice dinner and a good tea. Lovely raspberries from my garden, can't have anything better.

Thursday, Sept 28. Got up early, a glorious autumn morning, as Mrs Godfray was coming down in the brougham. It's my birthday tomorrow but no conveyance available then. She brought me a green liqueur decanter with two small glasses, very nice. She said her mother brought them from Paris over 50 years ago. As she could not buy me anything nice she gave me 10 RM, £1 1s.4d. very kind. She also brought a narrow hat brush, silver backed, for Mrs Rowe. We had the usual dinner with figs and grapes for dessert.

After a rest I took her down to Allendale. She saw all my large furniture mucked up with dust and piled up anyhow, as the burglars had upset everything, and books from the little room thrown all over the place. She said it almost made her cry.

I showed her the greenhouse and all the grapes nearly ripe. Mrs Rowe picked her a basket. Then I took her through the lanes and over Delancey then home. By that time it was prepare for the next repast. The usual nice sandwich cake, etc and real Camp coffee. What a treat! We gave her goodies for Miss Lihou. The old lady said she had had a really enjoyable day, and hoped I would have many

OCTOBER 1944

more birthdays yet.

Saturday, Sept 30. Friday afternoon I went with Mrs Rowe to cut a few baskets of grapes and would you believe it, they had nearly all been stolen. We could cut only six baskets. I told them to cut all but they would leave three large bunches which they did not find ripe enough, and this morning they are gone. I must have had about 1 cwt taken, £7 10s. It's most disheartening. Mrs Rowe said, Something more for you to worry about on your birthday. However I'm glad to say that I don't worry a lot over these things. For certain it can't last much longer.

It's been a lovely day again. It's our Harvest Festival tomorrow. I took a nice lot of Belladonna Lilies and Michaelmas Daisies and put flowers on Mum's grave and I also sent a sack of potatoes. On returning from the cemetery I called in at the old Rectory. Uncle Ned was still tinkering.

I went for my bread and Minnie gave me two eggs, and Uncle Tom has just called in with three small longnose and a pilchard, always something extra.

Sunday, October 1. I went to the Early Service at 8.30. The church looked very nice, Chrys on the altar and lots of other lovely flowers, apples and pears, grapes green and black, a lovely round cake which smelt good, lots of potatoes, etc. It was rather chilly and such little light now our electric supply is cut down. There were 80 communicants.

Mrs Le Poidevin and the Hunkin family came to the 10.45 service, a large congregation, about 90 communicants, £10 collection. They came to dinner and we had the other half of the rabbit from cold storage.

After dinner some had a sleep (I did not), others read or chatted. A good tea with real tea that Winnie brought (I have none). Then it was time for them to tramp home wheeling the old lady.

The church was crowded for the evening service, the aisles filled with chairs, the gallery stairs filled, even the vestry, and then some had to go away. Nice Harvest hymns and anthem. Collection £18.10.0.

Monday, October 2. We gave out the fruit etc to the (no poor these days but) needy.

I went to St Andrew's and took Mrs Godfray and Miss Lihou a little of our tart, a little bread I had to spare and some grapes. They were glad to see me but a little depressed about the war. They are longing for it to finish.

The weather is very chilly, really too cold for such old people to

OCTOBER 1944

have to do without fires. They feel, especially Miss Lihou, that they won't pass through this winter if we are not relieved.

Tuesday, Oct 3. I had a very good night and have had good meals all day. All very nice except that I don't feel too well. I get tired when I have to speak in a whisper.

The evenings are awful now. It's quite cold but we are afraid to start fires too soon as we might get a severe winter and will want all the wood fuel as there is no coal. I really don't know what poor people will do. It's bad enough for us who have a little wood in reserve.

I am hoping to get my sweet corn ground next week. Electricity will soon be cut off altogether. They are without diesel oil. The climax will soon have to come, in spite of the Germans saying they can hang out till Jan 31st 1945. We all expected to be relieved before Xmas, but it's looking doubtful now.

Mrs Rowe is again patching my winter pyjamas. She said last year they couldn't possibly do for another winter! I hear the Jersey people are much worse off than we are for clothes.

Mr Frossard has just called. He wants me to take 18 2/6 for the girls' choir. They get a little pay after Festivals and I forgot. He had just been to see Mr Pattimore and found him looking very well. We had sent him some nice apples from the Harvest, they were pleased. Not that they are poor, but money cannot buy fruit here today, it must be in exchange for anything possible.

Saturday, Oct 7. When Messervy called for the shop key I heard him say he had had to walk along the whole of the Banques in the NE gale and pouring rain, and he was soaked. Nice for me too! I have to be in Town at Court at 10.25.

Some old Johnny wants to buy a Rente which he owes to the Trésor of St Sampson's. The interest is only 6s, 3d. per year, one bushel, three denerel. One thing it was a fair wind. I sailed in in about 10 mts. Stafford Ogier was waiting for me.

Oh, what a difference in the Court Officials. Their clothes are falling off them, and Victor Carey, the Bailiff, seems to have lost the most weight of all.

After going through all that weather the Rente only gave us a cheque of £7 10s. which I deposited in the Penny Saving Bank till we see the time to invest it again. The Trésor is dwindling away now, and it might be better to have the lot together, perhaps in War Loans.

Coming back I could not face the gale along the Banques, my breathing is getting difficult, so I went inland through the Canichers, behind the gas works, then Pitronnerie Rd, Coutanchez, Marette Lane, Baubigny, Sauvages Lanes, Robergerie, Delancey

OCTOBER 1944

then Brock Road home, with very little wind and no rain.

I bought stock and Guernsey Lilies for Mum's grave and the wind did not damage them.

In the afternoon I went to Minnie's as usual for my bread ration. She again spared me two eggs. Her milk had not come unfortunately for me, as she intended sparing me a bottle of full cream milk. On my return I did Mum's grave.

Mrs Frossard was just leaving the church. We had a chat over war news. She is always full of hope. I am going with them and the Menthas from the Royal to Winnie Hunkin's on the 17th Oct to supper, walking there and back with them. It is Belle's birthday. I will find her a bunch of Chrys or other flowers.

I also met Peter Bachmann. They would like me to go out to tea. I will perhaps go one Thursday, but it's such an outlandish place to get back from in the dark, and it can be dark these days.

I ate nearly all my 6d worth of cheese for my tea. It was strong, dry and tasty and I enjoyed it very much, but am certain neither you nor I would have looked at it before the war.

Our Camp coffee won't last much longer. But what a treat after acorn coffee, bramble or carrot tea, and the devil knows what other sorts. I myself had fared very well the last year or two as far as beverages have been concerned.

Sunday, Oct 8. Oh, what a beautiful morning after a week of gales. All good news this morning and a nice service. At our evening service, now at 3.30, Harold Brache, a Lay Reader, preached very well. Syd Mallett said the prayers and Reg Cann read the Lessons.

Mr Frossard can only be at our church once a fortnight now, as owing to no electric light, the services have to be in the afternoon, and he has to preach one Sunday at the Vale. This is the first Sunday and the church was quite full. £5 5s. collection.

I am going to have tea now. It will be a long evening as we cannot light up too early.

People can now use the bakehouse only on bread days. It is most difficult for people without gas. We are all right here so far. We have 135 ft each of gas each week, and for lighting I have my ration of electric light, I think 1½ units per week. We have not started fires yet. We want to save our logs for cold weather.

Tuesday, Oct 10. It's a most lovely day. I was about a little earlier than usual after a lovely night's sleep. My nose bled slightly while I was dressing.

I got my gardener to clean the rabbits. Tom put an old pot on the kitchen trépieds (trois pieds) for warming water for Mrs Rowe's washing. With the gales last week she was nearly smoked out. Then he carried logs from the Forge to the shop. We sold two

OCTOBER 1944

tons last week. Of course it's all by coupons.

I am giving Messervy 50 lbs of small spuds, really pig spuds, but people are glad to have them as an extra.

The only chimney I see working is at the top of Church Lane, a man making salt. Those who have the fuel can make a lot of money boiling down sea water. 3½ RM per lb 7/6. Many people now have no salt.

I hear no sugar after this week. I have a few lbs £1 per lb. I know someone who paid 25/- per lb. Matches are 2/1½ per box, but no more issued.

People now have only local tobacco, dried by themselves. I have not smoked it the last two years on account of my throat, in fact I don't smoke much. Anyway the ration was only 20 cigarettes and 1 oz tobacco per two weeks, so there could be no excessive smoking.

Monday-Friday, Oct 16-20. It's a few days since I added anything so will start with my week's events. As I told you we have had gales, real equinoctial gales from the East which have been extra severe, with terrible squalls of rain, thunder and lightning. Glass blown out everywhere. My greenhouses have not fared too badly, but Lake's little span had about 50 ft of lights blown right over.

Tuesday, the 17th, was Belle Hunkin's birthday party with the Frossards, Mr and Mrs Menthas and daughter and Miss Pierce from the Royal, Mr McCathie and Jack Sauvary, making 11 in all. Now I had occasion to call on Mr Frossard about selling a Rente from the Glebeland, (and by the way everybody seems to be redeeming their Rentes) and he was in bed with a cold. So he could not go to the party, but said Mrs Frossard would go and I must look after her.

I called for her at 6 thinking she would back out owing to the southerly gale (or I should say hurricane) blowing. However we set off and met only one solitary soul along the Banques. It took us 10 mts to get around the Red Lion which we hoped would be sheltered. Not a bit, it was bad till we turned for Amherst.

Oh, the shouts about our bravery facing such a storm. We were soaked, but Mrs Frossard had a change of stockings. We settled down to talking and a double cocktail which nearly set me going (as I would not let Mrs Rowe make me any tea and it was then 7.30).

We went in to dinner. Oh, what a spread! Lobster, tomatoes, lettuce, then rabbit casserole, lovely browned potatoes, broccoli and sauce (which I did not take), champagne, red wine, then apple tart. By this time I did not care for anybody. I told them I thought they were swimming, they only laughed, and what with Winnie and Mrs Frossard and the shrieks of laughter I began to think there was no war on.

It was really a pre-war turn out, smokes and all thrown in, but of course, Mr McCathie being there from Bucktrouts there was a

OCTOBER 1944

chance to get the gargle. Or perhaps they had got it in some time ago, for you cannot now get a bottle of anything for £10.

After coffee with a brandy liqueur thrown in and an hour's chat we had to pack off. Mrs Frossard carried the lantern, I the basket, and we had a lovely fair wind. I reached home at 10.15, 15 mts late for curfew, but I was lucky and met no one. Mrs Rowe was getting anxious and ringing up the Hunkins as I arrived. Had a lovely night's sleep.

Another gale sprang up next day. I went to the Douzaine Meeting and got a grant of £10 for Tom Roberts from the Fond Falla. His wife has been laid up three winters in succession, and it is impossible for him to pay doctor's bills. He was very pleased. After the meeting we had to wait ½ hour while a squall of rain, thunder and lightning passed.

Then, silly boy that I was, but I always like to keep my promises, I went back with Stafford to tea. It was very nice with a boiled apple pudding. But the weather did not moderate. There was a fair wind, but I had to wheel my bicycle. I met nothing and in the Robergerie I could not even see the hedges. I have never been out on a worse night.

When I got in Mrs Rowe was just going upstairs. She could hardly believe I had got home on such a night. I smiled and told her it was not at all bad!

Next day I had to go to the country, to Blampied's, then to Collings Rd where we are working. Then on to the Foulon to try to get swedes and parsnips, no roots in St Sampson's. Then to St Andrew's to Best's Brickfield and so to Mrs Godfray. Very tired after such a busy day.

I went to see Mr Pattimore. He told me he was 87 years, 5 months and 18 days old. It's wonderful how he sticks it.

Saturday, Oct 21. Went to the Manse with my gardener and got the German officer to come to Lake's greenhouses where his men had stolen my potatoes and beans (not many), but I thought he might try to stop it.

Brache, at the Cognon, Vale, had his grapes stolen a few nights ago, so they watched the next night with a policeman. The robbers came and they tackled them, but one robber threw a big stone. It struck Brache in the stomach then fell and smashed his foot. Next day the ambulance took him to hospital, and I hear he is in a critical state. It's very galling, but better let them take the lot than get killed.

This afternoon I had to go with a German officer to Dorey's Cottages. They want 14 of them got ready next week. They are bringing the navy back from Alderney. I expect they are evacuating the island.

OCTOBER 1944

The German army has occupied the cottages for two years and there is scarcely a pane of glass left. We have only narrow glass now so we have to put bars in. The officer said I must find men to get it done and I must pay them well and they must be ready. So I am in for a busy week.

We are still hoping the war in Europe will be finished before they have to fight for these islands. But the robberies are just awful. They steal sugar beet from the fields, break into everybody's greenhouses, steal the dried beans, potatoes and anything eatable. We won't be able to go on like this much longer. And I hear the Germans complain they have not enough food.

Sunday, Oct 22. A nice bright day showing sun, but heavy clouds about. The service at 10.45 was taken by laymen, Austin preached, and I must say he did it very well. Mrs Frossard told me the Rector is a little better.

I have interviewed a carpenter who is coming to help us prepare the cottages, and I hope Gerald Martel is finding me another from L'Islet. This I think will relieve my difficulties. It's a devil of a job for materials, but the German officer has promised to find them in this case.

Dinner, beans, potatoes and a Blenheim apple again, but very nice. It's now time for our evening service at 3.30, then a long evening with little light and no fire yet. I don't want to start too soon, we will want all our fuel later. People are already complaining about the damp and cold. I am longing for this war to finish so that I can get to London to see about my voice.

Monday, Oct 23. I was about early for a wonder, but I had to start my men on the German job at Grosse Hougue Cottages. I have five men on the job so hope to have them made habitable by Saturday night. The glass smashed is appalling, and people have even taken the coppers from the wash houses to make sugar beet syrup or to boil down sea water for salt, which they sell for 3 RM per lb 6/4½ syrup the same price.

It's quite a paying game if you can get the fuel. Most people who do it are those that can manage to steal. Each week they have half a dozen for prison. It's laughable because they give them their sentences and then send them home till there is room in the prison.

It's lovely weather again. On Wednesday I went to the Boot Department at the Ladies' College, and by luck managed to get a pair of galoshes.

In the afternoon went to the churchyard with the Cemetery Committee about some chalk. After we had gossiped there (it was so lovely and fine) we cycled to the Douzaine Room for a Douzaine

OCTOBER 1944

Meeting, mostly about the Câstel Douzaine wanting to make a complaint to the Controlling Committee about the butchers. They give 4d to 6d for the cows and charge the public 2/4 for the meat. There seems to be something wrong but it's very late in the day to start complaining.

I then fed my rabbits (they eat a cartload per day), had tea by gaslight and went to see old Pattimore to read him the news. Now I am going to inhale steam. They say my voice is a bit stronger, but I don't think so.

On Saturday I had to go to Court about passing a contract for Glebe land. Mr Frossard could not go (in bed with a cold) so it was arranged that Jurat Leale would go to his house, and just Stafford and I would go to Court and get it over. Then Saturday Stafford was down with a cold, but I chanced it and went. The Jurats agreed to take my consent (which is funny for should we object they can buy the Rente just the same), so I won't have to go again.

I went through the Town. It was awful to see the queues in the Market, 40 or 50 at each stall for 1 lb of carrots or parsnips. Messervy's wife stood for three hours to get only 3 lbs of sugar beet. I am going to spare him 30 lbs this week.

I bought a bunch of 6 yellow and 6 bronze Chrys for Mum's grave, 3 RM 6/4½. Mrs Rowe could scarcely believe I had paid such a price. After doing the grave I went to see Uncle Ned tinkering. It's funny to see the old saucepans and kettles, long discarded, having handles and patches. People say they will never waste or throw things away again as they did in the good old days.

Sunday, Oct 29. What a day, squalls and hail. At the 10.45 Choral service we could scarcely see, and at the afternoon service it was impossible to see. The preacher, a layman from St John's church, had a lighted candle on the pulpit. We are afraid to use much light, and anyway could not have at that time of the day. It comes on only from 7 to 11.

Monday, Oct 30. Wind still very high. They tell me that at 7.30 we had a shower of hail stones as big as marbles. I did not see or hear anything. I don't think I could hear a cyclone where I sleep.

I am going to Mr Ogier, Duvaux, to fetch the Chrys for a wreath or cross I am having made for Mum's grave tomorrow, her birthday. How times flies. I can hardly believe it's now over five years since Mum died, and what we have been through since. Mrs Frossard and others tell me it's a good job Auntie Kate and Mum missed all this, but I don't think the same. If I suddenly asked them if they wished Mr Frossard and others had died before the war, they would soon think otherwise.

I am waiting for 5 cwt of sugar beet I bought from Mr Wheadon

OCTOBER 1944

some months ago. I don't want it for myself. I grow more than I can use, but I know my men and others will be shouting for some. I hear the Germans are buying it where they can (although this is prohibited), paying over £100 per ton, controlled price £26.

But you can believe me, some people here would sell their own relations or country for money. It's almost unbelievable. There will be some tales to unfold after this damnable war is over. I would never have believed it. One time we used to excuse people and say it was for a little food they kept friendly, but it's money, the great curse. And it makes no difference what the Germans pay. It's only printed paper which costs them nothing.

Tuesday, Oct 31. Mum's birthday. A lovely cold morning, NE breeze blowing. I was up very early. I had three loads of vraic brought into the field (New Rd) by 9.30.

Later went with my man, Haysom, to dig the grave over. Mr Peters made the cross of mixed coloured Chrys. I did not have them wired, but laid flat with nice fern. There were more yellow than other colours. Mum was very fond of yellow. I am hoping and trusting that we will all be together for Mum's next birthday and this war ended.

I have just bought as a great favour ¼ lb of Guernsey tobacco. Our own growing is all we have to depend on now. I will probably not smoke it all as people are always cadging. It cost me 2 RM per oz or 17/- per ¼ lb and that's very cheap as things are going. Most people charge anything.

I have just bought 5 cwt of sugar beet, sold 3 cwt to my men and friends and not made a penny extra. In fact I lose breaking it into small weights.

I just came to my senses yesterday about 1 cwt of potatoes I sold, (it's illegal but I did it) for 28/-. Now I get my return from the States for my crop, 28/- and 2/- bonus, so I am 2/- out of pocket! I know I am silly because I was offered £5 for the cwt.

Mr Pattimore had a fall yesterday coming from the outside lav. He had a few bruises and scratches, but is none the worse today. I went to read him the news. I hear the news is very good today.

Mr Romeril who had to leave the Manse (next door to me) two years ago (when I also was turned out), and went to Maison de Haut, has now been moved again. I hear he is very angry. He has to go to Mr Falla's house, the Hauteur, Vale. They took Major Falla and his brother to Germany two years ago.

I finished my job for the German Naval Officer on Monday, only one day late. I have not seen him since. I expect I will have to go and patch some of the floors.

Things are tightening up here now, especially food and fuel. Some old people have no fires. Dr Jones' sister called this after-

NOVEMBER 1944

noon and brought me a nice egg. She told me that Mrs Dr Leale was quite without fuel. I will call and see her tomorrow. I might manage to spare her 1 cwt. I am a fuel retailer, as well as my thousand other jobs, so will scheme it somehow. Everyone has coupons for fuel, but now there is a shortage of wood, people with gas stoves cannot get an issue.

I bought two damned old roots from the cemetery, including ground and stones the old roots had managed to curl around. The devils will take some splitting up. I gave the Douzaine 10/- each root. Of course the labour to split them will cost something. In any case, cost or no cost, it's fuel.

Now this day has ended and it's been a bit of a sad day for me. I imagined all of you wondering how I was getting on here in this siege. I know all our minds were fixed on Mum and other birthdays. But sweet memories will always remain, so good night and we must trust this will be the last year of this infernal war. I am still banking on being finished and having a real Xmas.

Wednesday, November 1. I had such a jolly good night's sleep and would have slept on but for the sham invasion fight at 6.30. Down Brock Road they came firing their rifles every minute. When I got down I found Mrs Rowe very disappointed. She really thought the Americans had landed. Dozens were hiding in our front garden. I told her that when the Americans or English come it will not be so pleasant if they have to fight for the island. I did not bother to look, the firing and noise were damnable, but when it was over I had another good sleep.

Tom Roberts could not come up Victoria Avenue, a great girder was closed across the road.

I understand we have sufficient food of a sort till Xmas. I hope our people don't come too soon. I fancy, from the news of the progress we are making, the war may collapse and save fighting for the island.

I have a Douzaine Meeting next Thursday and I believe Mr R.H. Johns from the Controlling Committee is coming to tell us something about the German decision about these islands. Some are saying that by International Law they are not bound to feed us. I had always understood that if they could not feed the civilian population they should put up the white flag. Oh, let it be soon, not so much for my sake but for some of the poor devils.

Saturday, Nov 4. A most lovely morning like spring. I hear that Pilot Fred Noyon and Endicott have slipped off to England in their pilot boat, so you might hear of their arrival. Noyon lives at the end of the Bridge and has been fishing during the war. He was for many years Captain of the London Queen trading from London to

NOVEMBER 1944

Guernsey twice weekly. [See C. Cruickshank's *Official History*, pages 272/3.]

People here are very excited about it. He can give first hand news about conditions here and the time we can last out with fuel, etc.

After getting my bread and milk rations from my sister and putting more Chrys. on the grave, (the birthday ones were still nice and fresh) I went out to St Andrew's.

Miss Lihou was very miserable and cold, no fire, and distressed because they had taken away her gas meter for over burning their ration. Mrs Godfray says she won't have a fire till Xmas. They go to bed at six and rise at 11.30. That's the only thing old people can do now.

On the way back I called at my Collings Road job to pick up a cheque for £30. I am now going to write out a few cheques to get out of debt, and then shell some devilish soya beans they have talked so much about. They are a good food, very oily, taste like chestnuts. I am by a nice fire in a cosy room.

Monday, Nov 6. It was Jack Ozard's funeral this afternoon. He was a first cousin. His mother, Elizabeth Sauvary, and my father were sister and brother. Some of the Sauvarys were pall bearers. Quite a lot of people there, a full choir. There were 30 wreaths. I sent one from myself and family. Mr Fossard paid high tribute to him as a churchman and social worker, boys' clubs, institutes etc. He said his mind had been clouded over owing to the Occupation and lack of good food (he had been in the asylum for a few months), but had been quite normal of late.

Thursday, Nov 9. I have been busy getting in my potatoes to send to States, a very bad sample, all shapes and sizes, and a very poor crop, from French seed. It's impossible for people to peel them. They must be boiled in their jackets.

At the Douzaine Meeting, Deputy R.H. Johns read all the correspondence from the German General stationed here and that sent from the Bailiff and Jurat Leale, president of the Controlling Committee. The Germans are now taking 200 tons of our wheat, want 500 tons of our potatoes, 60 tons dried beans and we have to give them (weekly I think) about 40 tons of vegetables. That is besides what the German privates buy in our shops. Although it is forbidden to sell them anything except tomatoes and melons, I am sorry to say that some of our people will do anything for shady money.

Mr Ogier, Duvaux, had a lovely two year old heifer stolen from his stable last night, and it's nothing for pigs of 2 cwt to be stolen, and rabbits by the dozen according to the letters in the papers. If

NOVEMBER 1944

the war continues we are in for a very bad time. Our bread will give out on Dec. 15th, the potato ration is going down, there is no wood fuel, and gas and electricity finish in five weeks' time. I was glad to hear the news first hand, but it will be wise to keep it from the women.

After the meeting I went back to Stafford Ogier's house with him. It was his 54th birthday. Mr and Mrs Frossard came and we sat down to a nice high tea, pork from their pig, baked potatoes and beans, then a nice Xmas pudding made with carrots, potatoes, sweet corn, sugar beet and home cured raisins. Cider as beverage, and coffee with home baked biscuits.

I walked home with Mr and Mrs Frossard, nice and dry, fair wind and not too dark. I got in just by curfew, 10 pm. Mrs Rowe was waiting up. She gets very anxious, it's so devilish dark usually.

Friday, Nov 10th. While I was at the Douzaine Room yesterday Tom phoned to say a young man had called about a funeral. I said I would go to his house next morning at 9. I was sorry about my rash promise but jumped out of bed, sponged my face in devilish cold water, and had my breakfast while Tom got my bicycle out, which meant unlocking about three doors. They said, Take your coat, Take your gloves, it's freezing. A real February morning in November. They told me No. 4 in Salt Pans, and I, who always make the wrong shots, tried the third No. 4 last!

Saturday, November 11. Armistice Day 26 years ago, and we are still fighting the same nation. I hope and trust that I won't have to fill this book with my doings before the war finishes. The news is very good today.

But now we get news of their No 2 Secret Weapon which I understand goes 60 to 70 miles into the stratosphere and travels faster than sound. England must be faring very badly now. We often wonder how you are all getting on. It's very worrying for all of us here.

I am wondering if you have heard of our wireless SOS sent out last Sunday. The German authorities allowed the Bailiff to send a radio message to the Red Cross (International) at Geneva stating the present serious shortages of many essentials in the island, and asking for immediate help and a visit from a Red Cross representative without delay.

In the Press tonight the Bailiff says he was informed that the message was dispatched on Monday. The Germans say it was not in code so that any place or ship, English or otherwise, could pick it up. We have heard nothing yet.

I am not myself in such a shortage, but there are many in a serious plight. In the market today some people had to go away

NOVEMBER 1944

without any vegs, others had very little. At our corner shop Miss Ellis had only 2 cwt of carrots, 1 cwt of swedes and some parsnips to share amongst about 100 customers. I did not envy her the job. It's not surprising there's such a lot of stealing.

We had a ration of pork, the first pork for a year. Both our pieces are under 1/2 lb. Still we are pleased and baked them, they will flavour the potatoes.

One of my rabbits died today, not full grown, but would have made a good meal by Xmas. Mrs Rowe had half for her cat, and I took the other half for Miss Matthews' cats (just two now). Cats, dogs, horses, cows, in fact any animals feel the pinch. The German horses are falling away since the summer when they were in wonderful condition. The war affects even the birds. They steal our peas and lettuce and are half starved.

Sunday, Nov 12. A very squally, wet, dull and miserable day. Mr Frossard spoke of Armistice Day, and said there would be one for this war. I said, Oh, let it be soon. We had a poor congregation in the afternoon, and it was so dark at 4.45 we did not sing a recessional. There was very little news of any sort.

Huelin is selling bundles of veneer, £2 for firewood. I had 24. People flock for it. They have no kindling, just elm logs (nearly double the recent price) and green, and they have nothing else to burn. I don't know how they will light their fires when the veneer runs out.

We have been getting one box of matches per month, but I hear that's exhausted. I have only two boxes left.

The Germans have taken 500 tons of our potatoes. Of course all growers and people with land must have their winter stock, but will they come and take some of ours. I think that in the next month things will come to a climax.

I went to see Pattimore tonight. He is in bed and poorly. I doubt if he will go through this winter. Last night in the paper there were three sudden deaths, and the winter has not yet started.

The Germans were on the Front this morning getting sea water to make salt. Our bread is made with sea water and we cook our potatoes in it. I have a little salt left, enough till Xmas. Oh, what a story some will have to tell if only they survive.

Sunday, Nov 19. It blew great guns and rained in squalls so I did not put the lovely Chry I had picked from my greenhouse on Mum's grave.

A pint of milk my sister gave me turned sour, so Mrs Rowe is making curds for herself. (I don't eat them.)

I went out to Mr N. Blampied to get a few sweet apples he is giving me, I think because he is pleased I am repairing his green-

NOVEMBER 1944

house. Baked, they eke out the butter.

I had a funeral, Jas Cann, arranged for Tuesday when Reg Cann came to tell me his aunt had died, just 48 hours after his uncle. I had to get to work quickly and change the uncle's funeral, and will now have a double one. It's the first double funeral I have ever had.

Monday, Nov 20. The wind blew at hurricane force from 6 last night and has lasted all day.

Last week the Germans took all our stock of potatoes from the depots. I hear the States now have to come to the growers and take our stock to provide a ration for those who have none. I am told they will leave us only 90 lbs. Very vexing.

I have my supply (of lovely late Field Marshalls) to last till June, now I have to give them up. I feel like hiding a few, but that would be difficult when you feel your neighbour would be without. It would be impossible to eat spuds with them starving. There was an ample supply for a good ration for the whole island till next June had the Germans not taken away our 1,000 tons.

We had all hoped for a real Xmas this year, but now I think it's too late. Still I don't think it will last much longer, judging by reports. I am getting a bit worried about those V1s and V2s. I often wonder where you all are and how you are getting on.

I went to see Mr Poat, the weather was very bad, it was dark and I got in an awful tangle. Like a silly I would not let Mrs Honey see me to the gate from the back garden, and I missed the way. I was quite 20 mts wandering about his garden before I eventually pushed through a hedge and got to the gate. My hat blew away but I found it. I was so much afraid of falling into the boiler pits. I was soaked and just reached home by curfew.

Tuesday, Nov 21. There was great excitement here tonight. Mr Frossard phoned to tell me the German General told Jurat Leale (our President of the Essential Commodities) and the Bailiff that he had received a reply from the Red Cross, and they were sending medical supplies, soap and parcels to us soon. I immediately phoned up a few of my friends who were so glad to hear the good news. But some people are wondering if ever these things will come. I say, Don't worry, live in hope.

My double funeral went off very well. It was a dreadful afternoon, a thick drizzle and cold wind, and a heavy rain coming back from the Vale church. The only redeeming factors were that I had a fair wind and I had an aide-de-camp, so did not have to carry my gear.

Today the news in the Press is very disquieting. We do have to give up our stocks of potatoes (and I had enough to last till June) and keep only 90 lbs.

I've just had a Jerry call, it's the second time this evening. They are always on the barter and it's impossible to push them off entirely. He wanted a few beans and two onions and I managed to make a deal which suited him. I wanted brandy but accepted tobacco.

He speaks English very well and it's difficult to believe that he is German. He thought Mrs Rowe was my wife, but I told him I was turned out of my house and lodge here. He laughed and said, By the damned old Jerries! He thinks the war might go on till next summer, but believes that Guernsey will be relieved by the end of January. He said he had just had his bath and had to go on duty tonight.

Friday, Nov 24. I have been very busy getting in hard wood blocks for the shop as I am a wood retailer and was out of stock. And last night without any warning they stopped all electric supply for power. Now all this hard wood will have to be cut by hand. I had to chase about for a van, almost an impossibility to get. However I got in 4½ tons.

It's a fight here for your existence now. Tar wood, hard wood, kindling, packing paper, in fact anything you can think of is wanted.

I met a friend this evening who said he would let me have a bit of tobacco. You can guess I was soon up there! It's local and a very good quality. He thinks he is doing me a great favour, and I suppose he is. He spared me ½ lb at 4/3 per oz. Fancy my paying 34/- for ½ lb of tobacco, and I expect he could have got nearly double from the Germans.

Saturday, Nov 25. This has been a day of days. Wind again with heavy squalls and everybody in a bad temper about having to send in our potatoes. And I had such special Field Marshalls and such a size. I had also selected about 2 cwt seed in boxes. I have to give them all up for eating as they are not green and not much shooted. Still it must be if we want everybody to have a little.

The Germans have taken 500 tons (and say they won't take any more) so the States are collecting from us growers to feed those who have none. Then we hear they want a cow from every farm. Even now we get only ½ pt skimmed milk per day and 3 oz butter per week.

My rations last week, butter, sugar and flour cost 1/0½. Something to be getting on with! Next week only butter and sugar, and the bread ration is going down to 3 lbs per head per week. People who have no small store of sweet corn and sugar beet syrup must eventually starve before Xmas.

It's the first time I have seen the people depressed and bad tempered and say they wish they had gone away. For myself, up till now, I cannot really say I have regretted staying.

NOVEMBER 1944

It's a lovely moonlight night, cold and very heavy clouds, and I am by a cosy fire. It's 9 o'clock. I will shell a few beans and then inhale steam for my throat or voice, which never get a dashed bit better. But I suppose I go about in the cold and no doubt never rest enough. I am thinking of trying to see a German doctor at the Vauquiedor Hospital who did a slight operation on one of our local men who had not spoken, except in a whisper, for 6 months. Mine has been going on for two years.

I went to see old Pattimore tonight. He seems to be failing fast. I don't think he will see the war out.

Sunday, Nov 26. Stir Up Sunday, as dear old Mum and Auntie Edith used to call it, the last Sunday of the Christian year. Mr Frossard read the lesson from the old writers in Ecclesiastes, [Chaper 7, v 14.] and he preached for the third time in this war on the text, In prosperity rejoice, in adversity consider. Of course in these times he can make a very good case.

Everybody was very excited at the prospect of the Red Cross ship coming. It will be a wonderful relief for a lot of people. Austin, the chief of the MOH and one of our choir members, said that this week they had had two very bad cases. One family had not had soap for a year and the material to form their mattresses was cement bags.

I asked Mrs Rowe to see if she could find a couple of blankets to send for them. They are all at my sister's somewhere. She said they are all new Whitney ones and not suitable for dirty houses. But they must have something. I would like to buy them some army blankets but that's impossible now.

It was a hellish day with awful squalls of rain and hail and as cold as the devil. I was glad when the afternoon service was finished. At 4 o'clock you could not see in the church and I had to get a candle from the altar to count the collection.

I really thought we would have been relieved before Dec 25th but I don't think it's possible now. Tomorrow we start on our 3 lbs of bread per week. It won't affect me much for a month or so, as we have sweet corn flour, beans (dried), sugar beet syrup and such extras. But how the devil some people will manage I don't know.

I am now going to shell a few beans by a nice fire until it's time for bed. I am wondering (if you are still in existence) what you are all doing tonight.

Undated. The war news seems very good today. I have had a very heavy day carting in logs and breaking up veneer for the shop. I have £60.0.0 worth. How the people can afford it I don't know. It burns like the devil and they get only 28 lbs for 5/-. It takes about 1/- worth of veneer to start the fire. Logs are pretty wet and heavy.

NOVEMBER 1944

I had three loads in today, now about finished. (Now all must be cut by hand, electricity from 6 to 10 pm for lighting only.)

They rang me up from Mrs Godfray tonight, thought I must be ill as I haven't been out for three weeks. But it's not the weather to go, gales and rain have been the order of the day. For a change it's been a beautiful sunny day, a slight bit sharp, otherwise good, but by the look of the sun and the moon tonight, I expect rain tomorrow.

All water is cut off from the greenhouses. I hear the Germans say we must unglaze in order to be able to grow our crops. What a pretty plight we are in and yet cheerful, and it's only lately people are not smiling.

I told you about the German who said the damned old Jerries put me out of my house. Well he passed me on his bicycle this afternoon and called out, Mr Sauvary, I am going to live in your house. I called out, Look after it, don't knock it about. He laughed. They are always shifting them about. He was in Mr Lake's house in Brock Rd. I think it's just to give them a change and keep them quiet.

Monday, Nov 27. Oh, what a glorious morning, sunshine, no wind, but very cold air. Spent part of my morning going over roofs, and trying to get my men to patch a few leaks these gales have managed to find. I did not hang about very long!

Earlier, Mr Guilbert, architect, came for me. I was having breakfast. I told him I was getting independent, I did not work for anyone before 10, except for dead people, as these jobs could not wait. He laughed.

Tuesday, Nov 28. Oh, what a change since yesterday. It blew a gale all night (*they say*). I slept through the lot. I took all my potatoes and part of my seed down to the Depot. It almost broke my heart to have to part with such a sample, but it must be and I have to submit, and if I take an unbiased view I think it's the best arrangement for everybody. I took 5 cwt and hope that the few seed I kept back I might be able to retain for inside planting.

Wednesday, Nov 29. Great excitement this afternoon. The Germans had been searching houses round about the Bouêt and Victoria Avenue and as the story goes (but mind I cannot vouch for it) they found that about 10 houses had some of this coal dust, either from the Gas Works or from a dump the Germans have near Mile Stone Terrace.

While on a search of Thorn's house they found a keg of diesel oil and enquired where he worked. They immediately went to St Sampson's Electric Station, got the names and addresses of the men who worked there, and fetched our local police. He with the

NOVEMBER 1944

Gestapo started the second house search.

They made the first *find* at Eddie (who is our Cross Bearer), a wireless, which was not the object of the search. This will give him about three months in jail, I expect. (I tell people here that unless we can say we went to prison we won't be heroes!) Then they found a can of oil. They went around and found oil in five other places using it for lamps and stoves. They are all up for trial. *My brother Tom, being a Sauvary, and either honest or afraid, had none!*

Now we hear seven Germans died and three are dying, having dug up Crocus bulbs and (I suppose cooked and) eaten them. They are getting hungry too. Next news, the grave digger came down tonight and said he had to dig a grave for a German who shot himself. It is said he tried to shoot the Chief of Naval Staff. Maybe true.

I hear the Germans are taking 50 head of cattle this week. I am told they are going to take one fourth according to International Law, so we will soon be skinned out. Things are changing now. We are getting surprises every day.

People came yesterday to tell me Allendale had been broken into yet again. I went down and again secured the lock, but could not see anything gone, but it's impossible to tell. We had not missed anything last time, but when Mrs Rowe went down later to fetch some crocks and a Jersey jar she found them gone, and then noticed that Kit's sewing machine had only the stand left, the machine and parts from the drawers had departed.

We are told that our Red Cross ship will soon be here. Everybody seems to be expecting a parcel. I don't mind as long as they bring me some tea and a nice cigarette. I would like a change of ration, certainly, but I can wait.

Friday, December 1. This morning I went to the Cognon about a drain again. It was nasty raw, cold, dull weather. I was there all the morning which made a rush for me, being pay day.

I went to Town yesterday to see the young man, a Mr Rowe, who had lost his voice for about 6 months and can now speak quite plainly. He managed to get a German doctor to see him. He had an abscess in the larynx. Of course mine might not be a similar case, but I have asked him to mention my case to the doctor.

I am getting rather uneasy now, time is passing, it's just on two years it started, but lately it's affected my breathing. I get quite short of breath and especially when in bed, and now I could not hurry up hills or rush on my bicycle. Although changing very slowly it is getting worse, and I can see that getting very short of breath can be a nasty feeling. I am much afraid that if I have to wait till I can get to England it will be too late.

I spoke to Dr Fox about this three months ago. He said, Don't worry, I can put a tube till you get to London. But he can see

DECEMBER 1944

nothing and tell me nothing.

I am now reading about all kinds of historical excavations. What things they excavated in the city of Ram Shamra! I read all this in National Geographical magazines of 1933 etc. The port and city of Ugarit were very interesting and brought to light many biblical stories, Adam and Eve, the Ark, etc.

Saturday, Dec 2. Mr Rowe telephoned early this morning to tell me that the German doctor had agreed to see me and examine my throat. I had to go to Haviland Rd to give him all particulars, and I will meet him on Tuesday morning at 8.45. I am glad he is coming with me to the Vauquiedor Hospital. I don't suppose much will be done at the first sitting, but something will have to be done soon, for it is impossible for me to walk up hills except at a crawling pace and then I am panting for breath.

While I was in Town I decided to go on out to see Mrs Godfray and Miss Lihou. They were both in bed. Miss Lihou, as I told you, is without her gas stove having over-burnt her ration, and she has no fire. Mrs Godfray had now had hers taken for three weeks. So little is allowed that it is difficult not to overstep the mark.

I got back at 5, very cold. I then went to the cemetery with a large bunch of Chrys (mixed colours) they gave me. Then I fed the rabbits, had tea and am now writing this while Mrs Rowe is again patching my vests which she thinks I will have to wear this winter in spite of the patches.

Robberies here are awful. The grave digger has just rung up to tell me the grave planks were all stolen from the cemetery last night. And in the empty houses near the church people are taking down doors, mantlepieces and even pulling up the floor boards.

Mrs Rowe went down to my sister, Minnie, to get a couple of blankets I am giving to George Austin for the MOH. They say the distress of the poorest people is very bad. I told you about sleeping on cement bags and having no soap. It must be true about having no soap on their bodies for over a year, because the French soap the States have been able to get over is as good as nothing.

Sunday, Dec 3. I was up with the lark this morning. Mrs Rowe brought in my water at 8, otherwise I would probably have turned over and had another 40 winks. I was ready for early Communion at 9. A gale of wind and nasty drizzle. Mr Frossard said there would be no more early services until further notice. People had no candle light, so we must find other times for Communion Services.

Everything here has now to change, and I am afraid people, especially the poor, are in for a very bad few winter months. I hope the people who got my good blankets know how to look after them. But I didn't like leaving them in the drawers when there are such

DECEMBER 1944

needy cases. They say, if you have two coats give one to those in want, but I have not become so generous yet. I think it out but it is a tall order. Cast thy bread upon the water and thou shalt find it after many days.

Monday, Dec 4. I did not start early as I have a Parish Meeting this afternoon. A finer outlook today.

Making sugar beet syrup and salt is all the go now. People have all kinds of contraptions for carrying sea water. The drain on the South Quay empties at the bottom of the harbour just below low tide mark, and the incoming tide is bound to bring in the sewage. At high tide everybody flocks down there to get salt water in baths, barrels on trucks, pots and pans, and use this water for cooking vegetables. Those with the former make salt and sell it for 4 or 5 RM per lb. Of course the fuel they must steal.

Our Parish Meeting went off well and I managed to get my man back on the Douzaine. We then held a little Douzaine Meeting on an important subject which I will not record, except to say that to save the situation I took my courage in both hands and undertook an unpleasant job. So now I must not mind but go through with it.

I had been promised if I went back with Stafford, a high tea with pork, and you can bet I went. Had a nice time but came back early as I had to go the next morning to see the German doctor.

Tuesday, Dec 5. Had a lovely night's sleep till 5. Got up at 7.30, hot water all ready, by candlelight (no gas yet), shaved, had a good scrub down, had breakfast and was at the top of the Grange *on the tick*, 8.45, so you see I can do it!

We were at the Vauquiedor Hospital at 9. Waited standing in the corridor with others, Germans. Dr Wanner came at 10. He had first to go through the hospital and see the patients. Then he came back, took four German cases and I was called in.

It was a nicely fitted up consulting room with four German attendants. He shook hands with me and said, You're Mr Sauvary. I bowed. He said, Sit down. He wrote a few papers, I think sending them to those outside. He asked where I lived. I told him and he said, I know, I came in and telephoned, do you remember. I said, Yes. I thought when he saw me he knew me.

Then he asked my age. I laughed and pulled a long face and said 68. He tapped me on the shoulder and said, Very well preserved (I think was the word he used). Then he popped an instrument up my nostrils, said a lot to his German orderly writing it down. Then he poked another instrument in each ear and said, Good. By the way, he spoke English very well.

Then (as Mum would have said) came the fancy stitch. He said, I am going to hold your tongue and you will say, He, He, Ja, Ha, etc.

DECEMBER 1944

Then he said, Take out your teeth. I laughed and was saying I couldn't, when Rowe said, He's got no false teeth. I think the doctor was surprised.

After putting the mirror down my throat a few times he said, Thank you, and jumped up (excited I thought) and said I have found the trouble already, but I can't treat it here and I don't think in the island. I can't operate there, but after a chat with Rowe he said he would see Miss Alcock and should she have the apparatus they will ring me at 10 in the morning. I hope he can put me right although I am not quite easy in my mind yet.

Wednesday, Dec 6. Mr Rowe rang up as arranged and said he had seen Dr Wanner, who had seen Miss Alcock from the Grange, but was sorry to say she had nothing suitable for my treatment. So now I am done and no further ahead until I can get to England, then perhaps it will be too late.
I have one hope left. Perhaps they could do something for me in Jersey. The German doctor said should my breathing get worse to see him and he might do something to ease me. I will see him and ask about Jersey.

Thursday, Dec 7. I went to spend a couple of hours with Miss Matthews tonight. She is very lonely in that big house alone. She has a person to sleep there who often doesn't come till 10 o'clock, and you can guess that with no light after 7.30 and very little fire, things are getting difficult in every way.

It happened to be good weather coming back, but very dark. You don't meet a soul, but you hear the tramp of a German soldier passing, and they walk in the middle of the road. I don't, although it would be much easier, but the devils riding on cycles with no lamps would knock you over. I often hear one swish past. I don't know how they can see to ride.

We hear officially that the Red Cross boat left Portugal today, the 7th, bound for Guernsey with relief. People here are very excited. I expect it will bring medicine, soap, candles, etc, but it's reported there will be parcels as well. This will be a great relief for those unfortunates who depend on their rations. They cannot carry on much longer.

I spared some of my men 6 lbs of dried beans this week. It's not profitable for me as if the States got them they give me 4/- per pint, and I let the men have them at the shop price of 2/6 and lose the 1/6 subsidy. Not a paying job. Still they say, All's fair in love and war.

Sunday, Dec 10. The Second Sunday in Advent. A boisterous day. Very few people at church in the morning, in the afternoon a little

DECEMBER 1944

better, but so dark in the church. The Rector spoke on Watching. At the giving at the Intermediate School, the Bailiff gave the children a holiday on Monday, to watch out for the Red Cross boat due with 700 tons of food stuffs etc.

The Rector paid tribute to the wonderful work they do and the sacrifice of those people. He said that while we were in church a boat was battling though the Bay of Biscay from Lisbon. We sang Eternal Father strong to save. It was very real and topical. I thought this happening would make history, as there has never before been such a relief of need for the island.

Monday, Dec 11. Well the old boat has not done her 800 miles yet. I did not expect her till Tuesday or Wednesday. I hope nothing happens to her. Most people here are very anxious. I am waiting for news.

The weather is fairly mild now, although we are getting heavy showers, but what a joy to see the sun today.

Tuesday, Dec 12. Cold but dry at last. By the paper last night we need only 1 inch more rain to make our average for the year, 32". The last two years we were 7" and 10" respectively short of the average.

Well, our Red Cross boat has not yet arrived. But I heard it was given out on the English news that we were to have a ship in a few days. So now we are satisfied, we know that we are going to be looked after, although you, not knowing our exact condition, will naturally wonder. By tomorrow we can begin to expect our ship.

I often see the pilot, Old Barlow. Kit knows him, she has seen him pull up many crab pots around Herm, when we went out with Henry Bisson. I often see him too. He has to fish from the Town harbour, and is still using the same boat. I often wonder if Kit and I will get a few days fishing with him again.

No other startling news tonight. I wish this infernal war was over. Mrs Rowe and I are sitting by a nice fire. She is boiling down sugar beet syrup and I am in and out squeezing the pulp in the machine I made. It's much easier now. We have a stock which can carry us well into the summer if the war lasts.

Friday, Dec 15. Friday again, it's always pay day! Thick drizzle and a cold wind.

My sister Minnie rang up to say she had sold my piano. I stored it at her house two years ago when I left New Road. I'm glad it's gone. We got £35.

We have been cutting and selling logs all day. The coupons were released last night and what a rush for wood these damp, cold days.

I don't intend getting about too much these days. My breathing is getting worse, it's very noticeable now, and people can hear me

DECEMBER 1944

wheezing. I am wondering what will happen if it gets much worse. I was supposed to see the German doctor this week, but have not had an appointment made.

I got my half rabbit I left in George Symons' refrigerator last pure fat. The other half made five good dinners each, this half will do the same. The cat had the head. I have seven left fit to kill.

I ordered some Chrys for the church, 10/8 per dozen blooms. Then I went to Dr Jones' garden (with Miss Matthews' permission) and picked some nice, well berried holly for a cross for Mum's grave for Xmas.

Today we hear that the Red Cross boat leaves Lisbon tomorrow. If that is correct she will arrive on Xmas day. I am sorry for the people who are in utter need of this food. Of course we are all longing for this boat to arrive, but the huge mail supposed to be on board will certainly bring a lot of sadness for some. It's months since we received any RX letters.

Our gas is to be cut off on Thursday at 9 am. I don't know what people will do for cooking. No coal and very few logs.

I am doing a funeral for W. Machon. I served my apprenticeship with him in the same shop. His wife died at Blancheland. On the same day I am burying an unidentified man found on Richmond Corner beach.

Mrs Honey came in for a few minutes this afternoon. I gave her a little curry. She was delighted. Mrs Rowe cut her a nice piece of cake and gave her a few apples.

The war is not going in our favour these days.

Wednesday, Dec 20. It's a lovely morning, bright sunshine but the air very frosty.

I am afraid this place will become difficult to live in. My first news was that someone had stolen swedes and turnips from my greenhouse. Then I went on the Bridge only to hear that George Symons' butcher's shop had been broken into and three sides of pork stolen, our ¼ ration for Xmas week. What they will do now I don't know. Fancy stealing other people's rations.

Next I hear a whole greenhouse of potatoes has been dug up in the night. Another place had eight rabbits stolen. That's how we live now.

Thursday, Dec 21. At last the shortest day has arrived. Now we can look forward to longer days coming. I was up with the lark. I had my water warmed on the gas, for the last time I suppose till the Germans put up the white flag. It was cut off for good at 9 am.

I had the first funeral at 11 am. There were only about 20 people besides the mourners. 12 wreaths. At 11.30 we buried the unknown man near the Channel Queen Memorial. [The Channel Queen was

DECEMBER 1944

wrecked in fog off the N coast of Guernsey Feb 1 1898. The Memorial was erected by public subscription. *See illustration 19.*] There were only the four carriers, the sexton, the Rev. Frossard and myself.

Friday, Dec 22. We took the truck to Mr E.H. Ogier to fetch the large, beautiful Chrys blooms, 2 doz for the altar and pulpit, 1 doz for Mrs Frossard, churchwardens' gift. I got a few extra for my friends, 1/0½ per bloom, but we spend marks like anything here. Nobody values them.

We had a Douzaine Meeting at 4 o'clock. Mr P. Ogier resigned after 36 years. He was Dean and everybody said kind parting words and called him Father of the Constables. He broke down completely and could only put out his hand and say thank you. It's a terrible break for him. He was Cadastre expert with me for 15 years.

Saturday, Dec 23. Tom Roberts came down with me to the grave. I put the lovely yellow and white Chrys blooms in a vase and the Holly cross in the centre. They looked very nice.

Then I thought about it being Jack's birthday. 37 years ago Jack came into the world, now poor old Mum is under the soil. How strange life seemed to me then, All you children away, a devilish war raging, and we in Guernsey (or at least many) on slow starvation diet, only half clothed and without fires.

I sent Tom out to Miss Lihou with a bottle of Port and to Mrs Godfray with Sherry. I had them spared me as I was ill with my throat. I sent half a rabbit to Miss Diva Baker, I gave all the men a good Xmas box, one to Mrs Rowe and Miss Ellis, so now I am ready for Xmas.

The Red Cross boat is to arrive on Xmas day, but they won't unload her till Tuesday.

The stealing and breaking into shops is awful. In addition to Symons having £60 worth of meat stolen, Mrs Hamley, Bickleigh, lost 20 fowls and several people six to eight rabbits. They say the navy crowd from Dorey's Cottages has been caught with lots of stolen goods. People cannot go out and leave their houses. Luckily for me Mrs Rowe never goes out.

Sunday, Dec 24. What a funny Christmas Eve compared with old time we went to Town and had tea. I guess you were remembering those times as I was, when you kiddies dragged us into every toy show room, and the struggle Mum and I had to hide your parcels for the stockings. Do you remember the excitement coming into our bedroom when we were hardly awake. Then church, then on to Auntie Kate for dinner. Oh! the turkey. Is it any wonder I say, What a difference.

DECEMBER 1944

Well, after tea on Saturday, I went to Miss Matthews for a couple of hours. We sat by the fire. I call it a fire but we had to continually put veneer wood to try to keep up a blaze, for what little wood she had was damp. The lamp was a bottle of oil (not paraffin) and the wick a shoelace. We remarked, Xmas in the workhouse. Nothing could have been more dismal. Still we try to keep bright.

I left there at 9.30 and came home by lovely moonlight. Not a soul about. Mrs Rowe had a nice fire for me and of course I (lucky) have electric light. She then got me a nice hot drink. I hung up my two socks but nothing doing! Miss Matthews gave me a lovely handkerchief and Mrs Honey a packet of cigarettes, my only presents.

Christmas Day, Monday. I was up with the lark and went to the early Celebration, 9.30. About 130 people there. I had only time to rush home for breakfast, then back for the 10.45. The collections were for the International Red Cross, £70 which I thought very good.

I came back, fed the rabbits, then a telephone call from Stafford, they were waiting for me for dinner. They had to cook it in the furze oven for about a dozen people. I was the only one outside the two families.

We had a nice dinner, tender sirloin, the first sirloin fat I had tasted for years, lovely browned potatoes, broccoli, B. sprouts, parsnips, stuffing and gravy, then Xmas pudding and a nice milk pudding instead of the usual tipsy. We drank cider, then had a smoke in the drawing-room.

The Frossards came for tea and supper. We had real tea and cakes. I forgot the King's speech, the first time I have missed it. I was sorry.

We had supper at 8, fried Guernsey bacon and potatoes, fruit salad and Xmas cake. The table was not lighted as other years owing to the shortage of light, still it was as much like Xmas as possible. We drank the health of absent friends, we hope for the last year of war, then adjourned to the drawing-room with a bumper fire as it was very frosty.

I walked home with the Frossards at 12. At Richmond Corner we looked for the Red Cross boat, but nowhere to be seen. It was full moon and like day, not a breath of wind. Mrs Rowe waited up for me. She always thinks something will happen to me or I will lose myself.

Boxing Day, Tuesday. I had a good night's rest. After dinner I walked as far as the Banques as there were rumours that the Red Cross boat was in sight. Sure enough it was! [*See illustration.*] The Banques were thronged with people to welcome her. I waited for some time to see her enter the harbour, then we got the news that she was waiting

DECEMBER 1944

for the high spring tide at 6. Another delay it seemed, after all the rumours of when she was due, day after day. Now, when actually in sight, she stayed outside all the afternoon. Still we could see her, although not very plainly. A German boat went out with the local representative. Dr Collings is the head here.

Wednesday, Dec 27. They say that when she came into the pier heads, after dark, she looked lovely on the high tide, "the full moon silhouetting her as she passed through the shining tide, which was then like a large lake, not a ripple on the water."

At last the Red Cross has come to our relief. What a wonderful organisation. Everyone is now awaiting a parcel which I don't think can be received before Sunday.

But now I get the most disappointing news, no mail from England as at Lisbon there was no censor, so mail was not allowed to come. Perhaps we will get it on the next boat if they continue to send parcels.

Friday, Dec 29. I hear that all our parcels are landed and safely stored at St George's Hall with a strong German guard, but I think it's our St John Ambulance guarding the Hall.

There are Canadian and New Zealand parcels. I had a typewritten list of the contents of the Canadian one. It has about four items more than the NZ one, but the NZ one had 2 oz more of tea and 4 oz more of cheese. They will be a real blessing for many.

I don't know where I will spend the New Year. I am not asked out yet and think, the way I feel these days, I would rather stay at home.

People made a great joke when the RX boat was so long coming. They said the captain could not find Guernsey because he could not see Jerbourg and Delancey Monuments, the Germans having blown them up. It must make a great difference when approaching the island to find these landmarks gone, especially for the local pilots.

Saturday, Dec 30. At last news tonight that people can have their parcels on Sunday morning. The Bailiff has asked people to avoid queues by going at the usual time as for their rations. It's quite exciting and everyone will remember this last day of the year as long as they live.

New Year's Eve, Sunday. When I got up people were already marching down to get their parcels, and as I was eating my breakfast they were travelling back with them. I went for mine after church. I think I was one of the last *as usual,* but remember I did go to church.

Mrs Frossard was at Le Riche's superintending the taking

JANUARY 1945

signatures. She told me in the evening she thought I had forgotten. I said, Not likely!

Oh, the excitement of opening them. I was lucky and had all I wanted, tea, orange marmalade, cheese, soap. Lots of parcels had no soap and coffee instead of tea. I gave Mrs Rowe my soap as she had none.

January. There were more tears shed on Sunday over a cup of real tea than there had been shed for years. Some had not tasted real tea for three years. People are crying with excitement at having such a luxury. The people I have visited have nearly brought tears to my eyes when I heard how thankful they were. Some told me that although they had not eaten a lot, the food was real, and their hungry feeling had gone. What a real blessing for the 23,000 people in the island.

Some had no idea that such a colossal undertaking could be carried out with nothing to pay, all given. What a world we could live in if selfishness and greed could die out of people's nature.

You must read the Press, Jan 3rd, 1945, How the people of Guernsey received the parcels.

Now I get news in the paper tonight that the Red Cross is arranging for the evacuation of invalids. My throat trouble cannot be treated here and I believe comes under treatment by Radium and Deep X-Ray, so I am hoping to get to Switzerland in a couple of weeks. I hope it's not been left too long.

Wednesday, January 3. I am now definitely resting (I suppose rather late in the day), hoping that my throat trouble will not develop too quickly and that our boat will come for us soon. My only bother is short breath especially when I am in bed. If I lie on my back propped up a bit it's not too bad.

Dr Fox rang me up tonight. I had telephoned him to know about going. He told me he had already sent in my name, but he wants to see me and examine me. It is now three months since I have seen him. He was cross that I had been out in these very cold and windy days, and said I must not smoke. I have been having two or three per day, that can't hurt much.

He thinks it might be a month before a ship will fetch us and then it's to take us to a neutral country. After that I don't know. Perhaps I won't be able to hang out so long, but he says if I get worse they will fix a tube in my throat. On enquiry I find it's a bit of a nuisance and has to be cleaned out every day. I must submit to the inevitable.

I am starting to let my men run the shop. I think they can manage for a couple of months.

JANUARY 1945

Saturday, Jan 6. I had a very poor night. My breathing was very bad, I could not drop off to sleep. I managed to get a nap from 4 to 7.30. So I got Mrs Rowe to telephone for Dr Fox. He came at 11 and said he was not at all comfortable about me being here. I should be in hospital with a doctor near at night in case they might have to put in a tube, but he has been trying to delay it till I could get away for proper treatment.

So I have been busy for the rest of the day fixing up my men, but I will not come back but go straight on to a neutral country if they come in time for me.

My sister Minnie has just called to wish me goodbye, Mr Frossard has now left, my brother Tom called and brought me two chancres. Mrs Rowe is cooking them and might send me a snack to the hospital. Dr Fox is calling for me about 8.30. I have said goodbye to most friends including Mr Pattimore.

What details I have had to fix up today. What a life! There I was telling Mrs Rowe to ring up Dr Fox to call and see me. Ten minutes after Mr Bird came to my bedroom and said James Le Cras had died and would I go down and make all arrangements about the funeral. (I buried his wife only 6 months ago.) I sent Gerald Martel, told him to fix everything up and not consult me at all. This will be his first entirely alone.

Mr Bird and Stafford have telephoned to say they will help if wanted about books and accounts, but I am leaving everything to the men.

Sunday, January 7. Darling Flo, Kit, Jack, babies etc.
In my ordinary book 10 I explained it was advisable to go to hospital to be near a doctor at night in case of a bad attack.

Well, as arranged, Dr Fox called for me at 9 o'clock. Mrs Rowe had my suitcase nicely packed, enough she said to go round the world! But I need so many things.

I had finished my nice tea (Real), marmalade and Canadian butter by 7 o'clock, so went to say goodbye to poor old Pattimore who is still going strong. I feel he will live us all out. They were surprised about my going. Then I popped down to see Miss Matthews, I wanted to speak to her, then came home and settled down.

Mrs Rowe said it was she on nerves and me quite cool. I could not say why. I think that hour waiting for the doctor was an eternity to her. At last I heard the car.

In came Dr Fox. Are you ready? I said, Will I take this rug? Yes, and a hot-water bottle. Mrs Rowe knew where it was, the lovely one Kit got for Mum.

Off we started, my first ride in a motor car for years. I could hardly believe myself going to hospital till the hospital boat takes me to a neutral country. Still I was very comfortable riding out but

JANUARY 1945

Oh! the dark and dimmed lights.

I thought I knew the hospital, but when I got out of the car, Dr Fox took hold of my arm and said, This way, now up one step then bold marching steps (he did not say how many), then two steps. I was glad when we arrived in the hall.

We went straight to the general ward where we met a nurse. Two patients called out, Hallo Mr Sauvary. I don't know who they were. Dr Fox then said, Here is your patient, and gave her my case. I had the rug, bottle and hat and she led the way to the private ward.

I am in the next bed to the one I had 18 months ago. I undressed and got into bed. There were three bottles in it, but they were brandy bottles. I was soon tucked up for the night. Only one patient, Dr Faulkener in my room. They brought me a cup of hot milk. I managed to get three hours sleep, but my breathing is laboured.

Dr Faulkener told me this morning he can't think I have much the matter, I mean serious. Still I told him it's very uncomfortable. I had a cup of good milk and dry bread for breakfast. I could not see and there was no butter. I have since found my ration in the locker.

All the light we have after 10 o'clock is a stable hurricane lamp which the nurses carry round the ward every half-hour. When they came in at 1 o'clock, two arm in arm swinging the lamp, I thought I would sing, While Shepherds Watched, but I thought O Come all ye Faithful was more appropriate, but I have no voice so said nothing.

We had a quiet Sunday. They tell me it's very cold outside, rain and sleeting. George Austin called in for half an hour to see me. Evelyn, Sister Monsell, has just sent up two nice hot sweet cakes, (Queen) for my tea. How kind of her.

Thursday, Jan. 11. In 7 days it will be Florence's birthday. I begin to wonder if we will still have the pleasure of celebrating any of our birthdays together again. I think Flo will be 40 this year. How I long to see you all. However in spirit and truth we will be together on Thursday, all wondering if each of us is still in the land of the living. After everything we hear we have to be prepared for anything.

For myself now, I think I must write to you all in quite a different strain. As you know my throat trouble has developed, and when I drop off to sleep my breathing is very laboured and strained. That is why I am in hospital, in case Dr Fox may suddenly have to insert a tube in my throat, not very nice to think about but I have to face facts. I get no pain, no swelling, no discomfort of any sort, just breathing is difficult. When I am up and about it's easy, but if I talk much it comes on. You know I have no voice now, just a whisper, but I could make myself heard across the room.

JANUARY 1945

The doctor is trying to avoid putting the tube if I can hang out till the Hospital Ship comes to take urgent cases to a neutral country for special treatment. I think it's deep X-ray I have to get. I am losing hope about getting away soon. You know what ships are. They say three weeks I am not sure if they even know the number to go yet. I can only hope and trust. The doctor feels that if the tube has to be put in, it's better for them to do it if the treatment fails.

I am well looked after here, good food, not amongst strangers. Miss Hall is Matron. On visiting day the Hunkins telephoned to say they were coming, but it's such awful weather, rain, snow, hail, sleet, cold and wind. Hardly fit for a dog outside. Nice here in bed writing this, if I could feel everything would end well. I hear little war news here.

Thursday, Jan. 18. Darling Flo, it's your birthday and all the family will be thinking about you and wishing you many happy returns of the day, but most of us only in spirit. I hope you will have a happy day and a real birthday party. For sure Rosemary will be excited about it and you getting all your presents. Of course I told Kit to arrange about the presents. However, I wish you all the best and I hope it will be the last separated. Fancy, who would have thought five years apart.

I have been in the Emergency Hospital 12 days and I must say I feel much better. I got my real normal sleep back again last night, no discomfort or distress in breathing. When I awoke my throat was not dry, I felt there had been no strain. This I think is a wonderful improvement in so short a time. I hear there are about 300 for the Red Cross boat. Sometimes I wonder if they can be here in time for me.

Although Dr Faulkener here in my ward has told me from the first time he spoke to me, that my trouble is purely functional, I am treated here for malignant growth. I know as all my dishes and cutlery are marked, so they think it is infectious. I know when in doubt take precautions.

As I am writing this in the ward the sun is shining through 2 lovely windows. It's a glorious afternoon. The outlook is a nice field rising to the south with 10 fine cows grazing. They belong to the hospital farm so I get full cream milk while I am here.

I had just started tea when Mr Frossard called to see me. He joined me with Red Cross tea and a nice piece of cake. I drank your health Flo, and wondered where and how you are, but could not imagine. One thing I do often wonder and wish is, that when you hear the wireless news you do not worry too much about me.

Although I miss you all very much, I don't allow it to upset me too much and I hope you take a long view, as all these casualties might be in our families as well as others, why not.

JANUARY 1945

Fancy, my first week out here my men had 5 funerals. I don't worry, they must get on as best as they can.

Saturday, Jan 27. I have not written much these weeks. Hospital life is much the same. It's 3 weeks tonight that I came in. Time seems to fly. I feel about the same, my voice does not improve *but my breathing* is much easier and I sleep well now.

On Thursday afternoon the nurse came with prayer sheets and hymn lists and said the Rev. Waterbury was coming in for a service in the big ward at 2.30. As I am the only one of the 4 in our ward who gets up, I thought I would dress and join them for the service.

Matron said I had better sit with her and nurse. The others were all in bed. They started off with a hymn, Jesus the very thought (one Mum liked), then prayers, then lesson, St John Chapter 14, then sermon, text, Cast thy burden upon the Lord, He will sustain thee. Very good sermon, something said to suit each case there. The hymn, Rock of Ages. Matron, Miss Hall, had to sing hard to keep it going, and the Rector started each verse, then Benediction.

My first service in hospital. It seemed strange for me to be disabled and not able to sing a note and perhaps never able to again. If only the war could soon finish or I could get away on the Red X Ship.

It's been very cold since I've been here and snow nearly all this week. I hear England had 25 degrees of frost. I could see a lot of Lapwings from the wing today.

Undated. Again I have not written for some days. Hospital life each day is the same. Rex Trouteaud came in our ward 2 days ago. He had his operation yesterday, hernia. He had just come round yesterday when his wife arrived. He was still talking strange things, he wanted to have his hair cut. Now we are Sauvary, Dr Faulkener, L. Warry in a row, then opposite side Trouteaud. I have a nice view of the fields and trees.

Seven of the nurses went to a dance at St Martin's. We teased them about it. They got back at 10 o'clock. The Sister of this ward is very nice, Sister Murphy. The night Sister is Miss Collas, confectioners, Bridge. Her father died last year.

Mrs Godfray sends her maid down every Tuesday, generally with an egg or two. They are very scarce. We had our second Red X parcel on Tuesday. Bad luck, I had coffee, wanted tea. I think I have made a swop. I had a Canadian parcel again. I like them better on account of the biscuits. Some people like the New Zealand parcels better, with 1 lb of cheese instead of 4 oz.

I am still anxious about my throat, afraid I will not get away in time for treatment. I suppose it's thickening in the lower part of the larynx which causes breathing to be very troublesome.

FEBRUARY 1945

It was awful to see the Press last night, Mr J.C. Sauvary is lying seriously ill at the Emergency Hospital, regrets etc., I had given a lot of work for the benefit of my parish. Everyone was ringing up Mrs Rowe to ask if I had suddenly been taken worse.

Mrs Cortvriend rang up the hospital next morning. She and Gussie had been talking over this sudden news part of the night. I told her rubbish and ought not be allowed unless the family report it. Miss Lihou did not sleep all night. Mrs Godfray knew differently, Elsie phoned up Mrs Rowe, but too late to let her sister know. I don't know how these devilish reports get about.

Tuesday, February 6. Three days later in the Press tonight, They are glad to say that I have considerably improved. William Vaudin, the Editor of the Press, is coming to see me. He will arrange some statement in the Press, for as it is this has affected my business and we have lost some jobs.

I am feeling about the same, and if the weather clears and the sun would come out, I would go home for a day or two to straighten out my desk and arrange a few papers and other things, Diaries etc., which I want to pack up and put in charge for you, in case I don't get back or perhaps not cured. I quite think, that should my trouble turn for the worse I would not last long and it's a vital spot. When the breath is affected you're done according to the view I take.

Mr Frossard came to see me again yesterday. I told him I might go home this week for a few days. I had a letter from Peter and Kitty and one from Mrs Stubbs. They want to come out to see me, but the weather is so damp and cold I tell them not to come.

Good news today. The Vega, our Red X boat has arrived with her second consignment. The two parcels we have had so far have been a Godsend, such lovely things. Our people have contributed £8,000 since January. Very good I think.

Mrs Rowe sent me out a lovely cake, corned beef, half a loaf, syrup, cheese, four apples and tea which she changed for my coffee. I was glad to get these things as we get no pudding here now. They have made a big cut in the skimmed milk at the hospital.

Sunday, Feb. 18. It's now some time since I added to this long Gospel. I call it that now as I think it is coming to an end.

Miss L. Trouteaud came here a few days ago to see her brother Rex, and she brought me two messages from Red X Bureau, Nov. 3rd and 5th. Flo says I won't get this. Well I did, about Jack in an office. I also got a photo of Flo, Kit and Rosemary from Major Langois in Germany. I was relieved to know that you were well up to Nov 5th.

Dr Fox took me to St Sampson's last Friday. We left the hospital

FEBRUARY 1945

at 10 am, went to see a patient at Cobo and Grande Rocque, saw places I had not seen for five years. Oh, what a change. Then he dropped me at Brock Road.

He had to go to an inquest on a man blown up by a land mine, crossing the danger area going ormering. He died in hospital soon after. The place was clearly marked, but they will risk it.

I had a nice day at home. Nice rabbit for dinner and nice tea, only too many visitors for the first time out after six weeks. I had a Chair to take me back at 5 o'clock. Dr Fox said it was too late for my throat at 8.30.

Rex Trouteaud is now packing to go home. He has been here only 18 days, I wish I were going back. I am quite comfortable, my breathing is much better and I now sleep the night through. I feel sure very little treatment would cure me now.

I asked the doctor when he would take me to St Sampson's again. He said, When this fog has gone. I am hoping again about Friday. Fancy the men have had nine funerals since I am out here.

It's now 7 o'clock, the electric light has just come on but it's very poor. I can hardly see to write. Mrs Godfray's maid and Diva came to see me. Elsie brought me an egg. It was very fine and there were lots of visitors. We are now only four in this ward.

Friday, Feb 23. Dr Fox came this morning to know if I was still in favour of going on a Red Cross ship. I said, Yes. The final list has to be in today. Now we only have to wait for the Hospital Ship. He told me that if I could fix up a return conveyance he would take me to St Sampson's again for the day.

We are now six in this ward. Advocate Martel's father came in today. I am hoping to be able to hang out till I can get across somewhere for treatment. My breath seems to get shorter each week.

What a lot of funny things happen with stealing everywhere. People have to take their provisions upstairs at night-time. One man, Hotton, had a telephone message to go and see the German police at Grange Court. Before going he went to the local police who knew nothing, neither did the Germans, but when he got home his house had been skinned.

End of February. I have not written much lately. Hospital life – people come in and go out. Our ward is very comfortable. Lloyd Warry and Mr Cumber, chemist, are going home on Saturday, then we will be only four. Now nobody much to talk to. I cannot talk much to Dr Faulkener, he is rather deaf. Advocate Martel's father is rather bad, also Mr Isler. It won't be quite so nice for me as the first two months have been.

I went to St Sampson's on Wednesday. Started late as Dr Fox had an operation. He went to visit a patient at the Câstel, then Hirzal

FEBRUARY 1945

House, Town, two calls on the Banques, got home at 12.30. A nice drive.

I did not do much at home, saw a few visitors and a man called about a funeral. My man had taken a day off so I had to deal with the first part of the order. I had tea, packed up a few provisions then my Chair came. A nice drive out, arrived at the hospital at 6 pm tired.

I've kept a bit quiet since and last night had a nasty turn. My breathing was very bad, it's such a nasty feeling and I could not sleep. Sister Murphy sat with me for some time, and later she and Nurse Leale. I am better this morning but feel dull.

Dr Fox came in but did not know of my bad night and only asked if I was none the worse for my outing. So I told him. He will get a report from Sister. They are trying to avoid putting in the tube till I get away, but I think it can't be delayed much longer. I will keep a bit quiet today.

It's Mrs Godfray's birthday on Monday, March 5th. I had arranged to have a Chair from the hospital and go to tea, but I will not risk it unless I improve.

It's awful in the island now, it's two weeks since people have had a loaf of bread. I think it's the awful Germans not feeding us. All being well our flour will come, Red X, and then we will get 5 lbs per head per week. I have not been without bread. We had a little flour. Mr Baker (Sark man) gave me a slice of bread this morning and Sark butter.

I had fried Roselet for breakfast that Tom, my brother, sent out, and I have a nice rice pudding from home for dinner. I have all I want to eat, thank God.

The war seems to be going well but it is now quite evident it won't be finished in time for me to get treatment, which I can only get if the Hospital Ship comes or the war finishes. In case anything should happen to me suddenly I am asking Mrs Rowe to look after your clothes and all your little treasures I got away from New Road, also my desk and private things and Jack's desk with lots of things in it. She will take charge of same until you get back.

I am doubting now if we will ever see one another again. I stayed here and have had a quiet time and tried to save everything but perhaps it is not to be. Therefore don't worry about anything. Lots of sheets, blankets etc., are at my sister Minnie. I will try to add a little each day in case I get worse.

Thursday, March 1. It is now three weeks the people of Guernsey have been without bread. Yesterday was my first day without. This morning I had to have a Canadian biscuit for my breakfast. Later we all had our 2 lb white loaf from the RX. What a Godsend to those poor people.

MARCH 1945

New potatoes are to be cut off after this week. It will be starvation diet for many. I still have potatoes. I ate very little of our nice white bread today as I was not too well. My breathing was rather bad.

Tom came out this afternoon for the wages cheque, and brought me a change of clothes and a few eatables and salt, chocolate etc. I am now in bed and I trust I will get a lovely sleep like last night. It's been a most glorious day of sunshine. I went out a lot.

Friday, March 9. The doctor took me to St Sampson's. Made a call or two around the Bouêt. What a wonderful view when we came out at the Red Lion. You know how the Front can look on a lovely clear morning. I have never seen it looking more beautiful. *[See illustration 1.]*

I got home at 11 am, arranged a few things and gave Mrs Rowe different particulars and instructions for all of you. I am now acting on the assumption that we will not ever see one another again. It's all very sad, but I must face what now looks as though must happen. I don't think Mrs Rowe quite liked my manner and did not realize what it meant.

I had a nice dinner. I never got to shop or garden, a thing of the past for me now.

Sunday, March 11. 4th Sunday in Lent. I decided to go to church. Last night I walked from the hospital to church to time myself. I did it slowly and had little breath uphill. I did it in fifteen minutes so went this morning.

Got there in good time, 10 am. I saw Mr Cox. One of the Malletts had a chat after the service. Miss Le Pelley, Beaucamp and Miss Naftel, Fauconnaires, St Andrew's, chatted with me, but found me, I think, worse than when they last saw me. They missed me at Mrs Godfray's birthday and were sorry. But I explained that I wanted to miss the party owing to my voice being bad.

I enjoyed the service very much. Jack Mahy, a schoolboy of my time, spoke to me over the next seat. Said a good sign seeing me there. As a matter of fact I was not so well but feel I must get out more, otherwise I won't want anything to eat before long.

During the service they had that nice anthem, God so loved the world (Stainer) unaccompanied, which is always much nicer. We also had the hymn, How sweet the name of Jesus sounds. There was only one lesson, Matthew the Prodigal son, lost sheep, etc. He must have read two chapters, I think, because it was all the parables.

Tuesday, March 13. Visiting day. Beautiful sunshine. I sat outside for 1½ hours then came in to bed as I was expecting Mrs Warry who was going to have a Chair if possible and bring Mrs Rowe with her. They did not come. It's awfully difficult to get a conveyance.

MARCH 1945

Elsie came from Mrs Godfray and brought me an egg for my breakfast. We get our white bread and I have it toasted. I would rather have our ordinary standard bread. I have to be careful. My breathing is not improving and now I get short of breath even talking.

I slept well last night. I am afraid the war is lasting too long for me to be able to get the benefit of any real treatment in England. It is just misfortune to be stuck here like this.

Father Collard from St Stephen's church called at the hospital. I met him outside and we discussed my position. I said the only alternative if no relief boat came was to stop here and die. He rather relieved me by saying he was not quite sure, perhaps my time had not come. If one could think that it's satisfaction, because relief or no relief, we must go. I cannot say I exactly believe it's so.

I think I will try to get a hot bath instead of going out again, and if I feel better tomorrow I will go to St Sampson's for the day. I can see I must go very slowly now.

Friday, March 16. I had my nice hot bath and when the doctor came around I told him I could not stick it out here much longer. I wanted a change. I was comfortable in a private ward, 9/- per day, generally five or six of us. (Warry and Cumber have gone, Dr Faulkener still there and not making much headway. Fire Brigade Officer, Mr Oliver there, good company, Mr Isler, and Advocate Martel's father.) So I told the doctor I must go back home for a change. He thought it was risky but I am chancing it.

I left with the ambulance at 3 pm. Settled very quickly and have been well since.

Saturday, March 17. Had a very good night, breathing about the same. Just had a good rabbit dinner, then a sleep, and have come down to Richmond Corner. I am writing this in the lovely sunshine on the big rock. Not a cloud in the sky, sea lovely, a few small boats about the rocks. It's a very low tide and the men are ormering. My brother, Tom, brought me three yesterday.

There has been nearly three weeks of sunshine. If my breathing keeps like this night times, I will not go to the hospital again. No sign of the Hospital Ship yet or of the war finishing. I am anxious to get treatment.

Sunday, March 18. I did not go to church. I thought I would rest and go for a quiet walk. I went to see Mr Pattimore. I had not seen him since the New Year, over ten weeks in hospital. Went to Richmond Corner, beautiful and sunny.

Had two ormers for my dinner, quite a small tea, but at 6.30 I began to feel ill and my breathing got a bit difficult. I could see the

MARCH 1945

night coming on, so I asked Mrs Rowe to ring Dr Fox and state my case. He thought it better for me to get back to the hospital at once and he sent a small ambulance car. I was back in the hospital by 8 o'clock. Bad luck, only three days out.

Monday, March 19. I had rather a poor night, and in fact last night was a little worse. I am very restless today. I am writing this in the scorching sun behind the hospital in a nice field. I have a nice seat and a back rest. I am now going in to shave. I don't expect to feel like it at 6 in the morning. I am eating little these days to try to avoid pressure.

Tuesday, March 20. I had a chat with the doctor this morning and told him I was getting a little worried about myself. I am much afraid I am not improving but I hope for the best. I am going in now, it's 6 o'clock, only four summer time. Elsie came from Mrs Godfray to see me and brought me an egg. I was glad she came late and could not stay long. The least thing makes me restless.

Wednesday, March 21. As expected I had a bad night. I saw Dr Fox this morning and said something must be done. He is getting Dr Gibson to see me today.

Gibson thinks I had better have a tube in my throat, otherwise it's wearing me down too much. He also told me if I go to London he thinks they will insert the tube before treating me. It's what they call tracheotomy. Dr Faulkener in the next bed to me says he has done many, and it's quite a simple job when you have done one or two.

Thursday, March 22. However, after another restless night Fox called and it's not finally settled to do it. Matron told me they were having another talk, so everything is still in the air.

I am writing this outside the stables in lovely sunshine. I am losing hope of the Hospital Ship or getting to England in time. I have nice company here with Captain Oliver, Town Fire Brigade, but he will leave this week I think.

Tuesday, March 27. Dr Fox has been very poorly these last three days. Nothing about my job yet. Oliver and I went out for two hours this afternoon. It was so lovely in the hot sun, but so cold in the wind. Had tea, then shaved and sat on the verandah till 7.30, then came into bed.

It's getting awful here, no paraffin. Last night we kept our four blinds up, the moon was like daylight. I don't know how the nurses will fare. They sat up all night in the dark. I slept very well.

Mr Frossard came in last night for a few minutes. He is very sorry

APRIL 1945

I won't be at church for Easter Sunday. They will miss me after 50 years. I think I missed only once when I had to go to Jersey about a job for the Sisters, Queen's Road. It's when you find yourself laid up in hospital you miss these Festivals. Still they say all things come to an end, and think my chances of a cure and getting away are not good.

All I would like to tell you if I could, would be to get your Easter Eggs and charge them to me and I hope you all have a happy Easter. It's Tuesday evening before Easter Sunday. It's difficult to see writing this. I feel I am not making progress this week. I do wish my health had lasted one year longer. But it's not left for me to choose.

Friday, March 30. Good Friday today and there's been lovely sunshine. Oliver and I walked to Saumarez Park this afternoon and sat in the Park for ³/4 hour. What lovely huge pines have been cut down, by the Germans I believe. Then we walked back through the lanes. He picked watercress. I was well winded when I got back. I had tea, rested and shaved and then turned in for the evening.

Saturday, March 31. Not too good a night. Did not sleep after 2.30. Easter Saturday, stayed in bed most of the morning. Then Oliver got up, packed his goods, he is going home today. He is so glad. He has been here a month under observation and no operation necessary, all indigestion pains.

My brother came with two eggs for my breakfast, being Easter and nothing else to send. I went out a little in the sun but it's not been a good day for me, breath more difficult if anything. It seems very strange for me to be spending Easter in hospital. I try to keep my pecker up. If only this war had finished in time it might have made all the difference for me.

Easter Sunday, April 1. Heavy wind, drizzling rain, cold, in fact not a promising day. Some of the nurses went to the 8 o'clock service, others went at 11. I had a poor night, just couldn't sleep after 1, no pain, just restless. No wishing Happy Easters this morning, all that pleasure happening outside hospitals. This is a very strange day to me and I hope it's the last I will ever have to spend if it's to be like this.

A Mr De Garis has just come into the bed next to me. He got his throat cut by a German soldier stealing and milking his cows, and I suppose there must have been an altercation. I don't think the gash is too serious.

We are getting into a fine state here. If the Red X boat does not arrive today, we have to go on a 3 lb ration of bread next week. It won't hurt me, I don't eat that amount. Don't take too much notice of this mixture, I am almost too fidgety to write it. I suppose that's

APRIL 1945

how Mum used to get.

Easter Monday, April 2. What a strange day to me. I had a fair night's sleep as usual till 1 o'clock and then slept in snatches till 5.30.

Matron sent to say there was a celebration in the women's ward and would I like to go. I went at 9 am, just a blanket over me. Only four women and myself, not many for Easter. It was very nice and I thought it would probably be my last Communion on a Festival week. I did not feel very great and not improved much as the day went by. It may be the weather, it's been a poor day.

We had three Germans taking down particulars about the milking affair. The soldier shot one of their own Gestapos said an interpreter who gave it to a typist. Quite a lot of clicking for half an hour.

The Diary ends here.

Mr Sauvary died three mornings later, on Thursday, April 5th.

Extracts from a letter sent by a family friend, Evelyn Monsell (the daughter of Kit's godmother) who was a Sister at the Emergency Hospital throughout the occupation.

21 June, 1945

He [Mr Sauvary] came into the hospital for examination under anaesthetic, nothing positive was seen, although suspected. We did not have the bougres and aesophageal outfit, and of course could not get hold of any. Not that they could have helped except by confirming diagnosis.

After a few days he went home and about his business and stayed much the same for a long time. Then shortly after last Christmas he began to feel choky and have difficulty in breathing, especially after falling asleep. So Dr Fox advised him to come into hospital in case it was advisable to perform a tracheotomy in a hurry. By the way Dr Fox slept in the hospital the whole time, so was on the spot.

He used to be up and about, eating well. He still said he had no pain, only uncomfortable breathing. I used to find time to visit his ward most days, and we used to chat, chiefly about the "children" and what you were doing as told by Red Cross Messages.

All this time he was slowly getting worse. Dr Fox thought it advisable to do the only thing left – tracheotomy – and it was fixed for the morning of April 5th. I was with him the previous night before going off duty. He seemed quite happy.

He had rather a breathless night, and early morning became unconscious and remained so to the end.

To me it was the kindest thing that could have happened, as life would have been increasingly uncomfortable, and even to see his children, I would not have wanted to see him linger. It would have been no happiness to you to see him like that, even for a short time.

Dr Fox took the greatest care of him, as luck would have it he is specially interested in throats, and Miss Hall, the Matron in charge of the surgical floor, saw that he had all that was available for his comfort.

VALEDICTION

OCCUPATION OF GUERNSEY: AN APPRECIATION BY A GERMAN CHAPLAIN.

On the evening of the Liberation of Guernsey two services were held in the parish church of St Sampson's, one of thanksgiving for ourselves, and one which the Germans were allowed to hold for themselves before they were taken prisoner.

At the end of the service the German chaplain left the following words on the Vestry table written by himself in German, of which this is the translation:

"I express my thanks for all the Love of Christ which has come to us in this House of God during our stay in Guernsey. I pray that the Lord may lead the world towards the eternal goal of His heavenly kingdom and establish a peace higher than all human understanding. Jesus Christ, the same yesterday and today and for ever."

Thus did the church, in this and many Channel Island parishes, minister to friend and foe alike in strange and troubled times, witnessing once more to the Apostle's words "There is neither bond nor free, Jew nor Greek, there is neither male nor female, for ye are all one in Jesus Christ."

May, 1945.

Deutsches Rotes Kreuz
Präsidium / Auslandsdienst
Berlin SW 61, Blücherplatz

R.C.B. GUERNSEY

5/1365

ANTRAG
an die Agence Centrale des Prisonniers de Guerre, Genf
— Internationales Komitee vom Roten Kreuz —
auf Nachrichtenvermittlung

REQUÊTE
de la Croix-Rouge Allemande, Présidence, Service Étranger
à l'Agence Centrale des Prisonniers de Guerre, Genève
— Comité International de la Croix-Rouge —
concernant la correspondance

Absender / Expéditeur: Mr. J.C. Sauvary, New Road, St. Sampsons GUERNSEY. C.I.

bittet, an
prie de bien vouloir faire parvenir à

Empfänger / Destinataire: Mrs. E. B. Griffiths, 15, West Drive, Burgh Heath, Tadworth, SURREY, ENGLAND

folgendes zu übermitteln / ce qui suit

(Höchstzahl 25 Worte!)
(25 mots au plus!)

Everyone well including Mrs. Le Poidevin. Very cold snap. Jack still Bank? Ted same job? Not too lonely, but longing see you all.

Love, Dad. 14 AVR. 1942

(Datum / Date) 4-2-42

Empfänger antwortet umseitig
Destinataire répond au verso

004324   31 JUIL 1942   (Unterschrift / Signature) Sauvary

Example of Red Cross message

4. Antwort des Empfängers :
Réponse du destinataire :

(Höchstzahl 25 Worte !)
(25 mots au plus !)

Jack left Bank Summer 1940.
Ted same job. Captain called
Say farewell. Josephine lonely.
Hoping news Jack about August.
Coldest resp. Robins in Garage.

(Datum / Date)

May 30th 1942.

(Unterschrift)
(Signature)

Florence S. W. Griffiths.

Sacred

To the memory of
THOMAS son of
JOHN SAUVARY and
BETSY ROUGET his wife
who drowned at
BARRANCA RIVER PUNTA ARENAS
on the 20 March 1896
aged 23 years.
Also such two daughters
who died when young.
In the midst of life we are in death.
Also HENRIETTA grandchild
of the above and daughter of
John who died Feb 26 1878
aged 6 weeks.
Also BETSY ROUGET wife of
the above died April 20 1890
aged 76 years.
Also JOHN SAUVARY
died April 24 1890
aged 73 years

The inscription on the tombstone in the lower left-hand corner of illustration 18. It was found to be a family tombstone after the publication of the first edition of the Diary.

ORDERS OF THE COMMANDANT OF THE GERMAN FORCES IN OCCUPATION OF THE ISLAND OF GUERNSEY

(1) – ALL INHABITANTS MUST BE INDOORS BY 11PM AND MUST NOT LEAVE THEIR HOMES BEFORE 6AM.

(2) – WE WILL RESPECT THE POPULATION IN GUERNSEY: BUT, SHOULD ANYONE ATTEMPT TO CAUSE THE LEAST TROUBLE, SERIOUS MEASURES WILL BE TAKEN AND THE TOWN WILL BE BOMBED.

(3) – ALL ORDERS GIVEN BY THE MILITARY AUTHORITY ARE TO BE STRICTLY OBEYED.

(4) – ALL SPIRITS MUST BE LOCKED UP IMMEDIATELY, AND NO SPIRITS MAY BE SUPPLIED, OBTAINED OR CONSUMED HENCEFORTH. THIS PROHIBITION DOES NOT APPLY TO STOCKS IN PRIVATE HOUSES.

(5) – NO PERSON SHALL ENTER THE AERODROME AT LA VILLIAZE.

(6) – ALL RIFLES, AIRGUNS, PISTOLS, REVOLVERS, DAGGERS, SPORTING GUNS, AND ALL OTHER WEAPONS WHATSOEVER, EXCEPT SOUVENIRS, MUST, TOGETHER WITH ALL AMMUNITION, BE DELIVERED AT THE ROYAL HOTEL BY 12 NOON TODAY, JULY 1.

(7) – ALL BRITISH SAILORS, AIRMEN AND SOLDIERS ON LEAVE IN THIS ISLAND MUST REPORT AT THE POLICESTATION AT 9AM TODAY, AND MUST THEN REPORT AT THE ROYAL HOTEL.

(8) – NO BOAT OR VESSEL OF ANY DESCRIPTION, INCLUDING ANY FISHING BOAT, SHALL LEAVE THE HARBOURS OR ANY OTHER PLACE WHERE THE SAME IS MOORED, WITHOUT AN ORDER FROM THE MILITARY AUTHORITY, TO BE OBTAINED AT THE ROYAL HOTEL. ALL BOATS ARRIVING FROM JERSEY, FROM SARK OR FROM HERM, OR ELSEWHERE, MUST REMAIN IN HARBOUR UNTIL PERMITTED BY THE MILITARY TO LEAVE.

THE CREWS WILL REMAIN ON BOARD. THE MASTER WILL REPORT TO THE HARBOURMASTER, ST PETER-PORT, AND WILL OBEY HIS INSTRUCTIONS.

(9) – THE SALE OF MOTOR SPIRIT IS PROHIBITED, EXCEPT FOR USE ON ESSENTIAL SERVICES, SUCH AS DOCTORS' VEHICLES, THE DELIVERY OF FOODSTUFFS, AND SANITARY SERVICES WHERE SUCH VEHICLES ARE IN POSSESSION OF A PERMIT FROM THE MILITARY AUTHORITY TO OBTAIN SUPPLIES.

THESE VEHICLES MUST BE BROUGHT TO THE ROYAL HOTEL BY 12 NOON TODAY TO RECEIVE THE NECESSARY PERMISSION.

THE USE OF CARS FOR PRIVATE PURPOSES IS FORBIDDEN.

(10) – THE BLACK-OUT REGULATIONS ALREADY IN FORCE MUST BE OBSERVED AS ABOVE.

(11) – BANKS AND SHOPS WILL BE OPEN AS USUAL.

(Signed) THE GERMAN COMMANDANT OF THE ISLAND OF GUERNSEY

Published on front page of the Guernsey Evening Press on Monday, July 1, 1940

RECIPES

Guernsey Biscuits

Guernsey Gâche

Christmas Pudding

RECIPES

GUERNSEY BISCUITS

1 lb plain flour
½ oz salt
½ lb margarine or lard

1 oz yeast
½ oz sugar
8 oz water, or milk and water

Mix flour and salt, rub in margarine.
Cream yeast and sugar and add warmed liquid. Leave for a few minutes.
Mix with flour to form a light dough, knead well. Cover with a cloth and leave in a warm place for 1½ hours to rise.
Turn on to a floured board, knead lightly, and form into balls.
Flatten or roll into biscuit shape.
Stand on a greased baking sheet in a warm place for 15-20 minutes.
Bake in a moderate oven for 20 minutes.
Eaten sliced in half and spread with Guernsey butter.
NB   Although known locally as a 'biscuit' it is more like a tea cake, but crisp.

GUERNSEY GÂCHE (pronounced gosh)

1½ lbs plain flour
1 lb margarine
1 teasp. salt
½ teasp. nutmeg
1 lb currants *or* sultanas

4 oz mixed peel
2 dessertsp. caster sugar
1 oz yeast
½ pt tepid water

Rub margarine into the flour, add salt, nutmeg, peel and fruit.
Cream yeast and sugar with hot water.
Make well in mixture, pour in yeast, cover with mixture, then add the hot water working around with a large knife, then knead till the mixture leaves the bowl and hands clean.
Cover with a thick cloth and leave in a warm place for 1½ hours to rise.
Place in well greased tins. Bake in a hot oven for 1 hour.

CHRISTMAS PUDDING – Family Recipe

2 lbs each of currants, raisins and sultanas
1 lb plain flour
1 lb breadcrumbs
2 lbs suet
2 lbs demerara sugar
½ lb mixed peel
Nutmeg to taste (1)
1-2 teasp. mixed spice
6 oz chopped almonds
8 eggs
2 lemons, rind & juice
1 tumbler brandy (or more!)

Mix the dry ingredients thoroughly, bind with well-beaten eggs, add lemons and lastly brandy.
Grease pudding bowls with lard, fill very full and cover with grease proof paper smeared with butter and pleated pudding cloths.
Place in boiling water and boil for 9-10 hours.
When cold, re-cover with fresh grease proof paper and cloths (scalded and dried).

These puddings can be kept for a year, and are known to have kept perfectly for four years, those made in 1938 having been eaten in 1942.

GLOSSARY

Allendale – The house which had been the home of Mr Sauvary's parents. Behind it was the greenhouse which Mr Sauvary built during his apprenticeship. The house is in La Mare, a little lane off Roland Road.

Alliance – A large vinery bordering on both New Road and Mr Lake's vineries.

Bailiff – The island's chief citizen and representative, the equivalent of Prime Minister. He is appointed by the sovereign and presides over the States, the island parliament. The present Bailiff, Sir Charles Frossard, is the son of the Rector of St Sampson's, so often referred to in the Diaries, who later became Dean of Guernsey.

Billet D'Etat – THE BLUE BOOK – The Bailiff issues to each member of the States a Billet d'Etat containing the proposals which are being put before the States at the next meeting by the various Committees, and also draft Resolutions which, if passed, will reflect the decisions which the States have taken. There is a continuous record of the Actes from 1605 to the present day.

Bornement – A form of permit required for alignments, i.e. road boundaries. Each Douzaine maintains a Register of Bornements under the 1840 Ordnance.

Boulow – A boulder.

Box Cart or *Stone Cart* – A great, heavy horse-drawn cart used for carting stone from the quarries to the yards or cracking machines before the advent of lorries. Also used for coal and on the farms.

Bridge, The – A cluster of shops bordering the south and east of St Sampson's Harbour. There was once a bridge linking L'Islet with the land to the south.

Cadastre – The description and valuation of property for purposes of taxation. As an experienced builder on the Douzaine Mr Sauvary was one of the experts for this assessment. It was in this capacity that he had to make a report for the Germans, giving details of greenhouses suitable for cultivation in part of his parish.

Chair – A light vehicle, drawn by one horse. The word is given as obsolete in the 12 Volume Oxford Dictionary, 1933 and 1970.

Chancre (pronounced shanker) – A crab, highly superior to the Spider Crab, Maia Squinado.

Conseiller – There are 12 elected by the States of Election. They are members of both the States of Election and the States of Deliberation.

Constables (Connétables) – Each of the ten Douzaines has two. The Parish Constables evolved in the Middle Ages as officials appointed by the parish assemblies for purposes of police. In 1574 they were required by the Royal Court to ensure that all Court Acts were observed by their parishioners. They had local importance and in the 16th century the Constables were the official means of communication between the Bailiff and Jurats of the Royal Court and the Douzaine and people of the various parishes. Between 1602 and 1844 they were members of the States of Deliberation until replaced by Deputies. They have become executive officers of the Parish Douzaines, although in 1920 they lost their powers of police to the Police Force.

Controlling Committee – of the States of Guernsey was set up on the 21st July, 1940 by the States of Deliberation, shortly before the Germans took over the island. It was given virtually all the powers of the States.

Delancey Monument – A 90 foot obelisk of Guernsey granite on Delancey Park, a memorial to Guernsey's most distinguished sailor, Admiral Lord de Saumarez, 1757-1836. Four bronze panels on the base recorded his exploits. The Germans blew it up on 7th November, 1943. To the lasting regret of many it was never rebuilt. The panels are now in the Museum at Castle Cornet.

Dodger – Slang for bread. In 1914 it was unconventional English in the army for a sandwich, because the meat dodges therein! By 1918 the word was used in Australia for bread, and also in the British army for bread only. *Dictionary of SLANG*, Eric Partridge, Routledge & Kegan Paul, 1937, 1984.

Douzaine – The equivalent of a parish council. Each of the ten parishes of Guernsey has its Douzaine of 12 members.

Douzenier – A member of the Douzaine. A representative of the Douzaine is nominated by the Douzaine to attend meetings of the States of Deliberation, and holds office for one year. Douzaine representatives also vote in the election of Jurats and Conseillers. Records of Mr Sauvary acting in both these capacities are in the Diaries.

Essential Commodities Committee – A department of the Controlling Committee.

Fond Falla – correctly Thomas Falla Trust. This was established in 1854 by the will of Thomas Falla and augmented later by four bequests. Grants were to be made to people of the parish who were not in receipt of Public Assistance and had the misfortune of losing cattle or other losses or temporary illness.

Forge, The Old. 1449 – until recently this date appeared over the door – The home of Mrs Rowe who took over the house-keeping for Mr Sauvary soon after the Occupation. He went to lodge there when the Germans turned him out of New Road.

French Halles – One section of the Market buildings originally used by French traders.

Front, The – The local name for the East coast from Richmond Corner to the Salerie.

G.U.B., Glasshouse Utilization Board – One of the three Boards set up soon after the Occupation in order to conserve food stocks and to take special measures to ensure fair shares for all. (The other Boards were Farm Produce and Potatoes.) The GUB were thought not to have done a good job (for a variety of reasons and not altogether their fault). Large numbers of people had been thrown out of work because tomatoes and flowers (the two main crops) could not be exported. Work had to be found for them, the glasshouses were over staffed and the Germans interfered too much. So, many of the greenhouses taken over by the Board were offered back to their owners, which was what happened with Mr Sauvary's vinery.

Guernsey Frock named incorrectly in Diary – The GUERNSEY (GANZEY, GERNZEY) is the traditional pullover commonly worn by the fishermen. It is similar to others knitted by the women of Lowestoft, Fleetwood and Morecombe. Mr Sauvary's daughter bought him one at Mourants, in the High Street, some years before the war for 25/-. They sold the yarn, a tough five ply worsted, Temple Brand, but no pattern. It was easy enough to copy except the casting on stitch, and was knitted on about thirteen needles. His daughter soon gave these up (stitches coming off fore and aft!) for a circular needle. The hurdle was to have the courage to knit straight to the shoulders without making an armhole! The sleeve was then sewn in and then an armhole cut! Now Guernseys are widely known and made in a variety of untraditional colours, and recently even as cardigans.

Kangaroo Steaks – Kangaroos – they were in fact Wallabies – were kept on the island of Herm during the tenancy of H.S.A. Prince Blütcher von Wahlstall. Hence, Tom's reference when a meat ration was expected from Herm.

Longnose. Garfish – A long, narrow, green-boned fish, fairly common in the waters surrounding Guernsey. It is very occasionally caught off the South coast of England.

New Road – Mr Sauvary never gave a name to the house he built and lived in from 1914 until the Germans turned him out on 12 October, 1942. He always referred to it as New Road, the road in which it is situated. It is now a guest house.

Organisation Todt. OT – Civil Contractors who built the immense fortifications and underground chambers. They had an office in Mr Sauvary's house and the "boss" of that area was billeted there (see Erwin). They first employed Frenchmen and then a motley crowd of European "slave labour" and gained an evil reputation for their harsh treatment of these political and war prisoners.

Ormer – Family Haliotidae, the European representative, H. Tuberculata, is distributed from the southern shores of the English Channel to West Africa. This uni-valve shell fish is a highly prized delicacy but the devil to clean. Hence Mr Sauvary's mention that his housekeeper "did not mind preparing them". Predatory skin divers caused the States to prohibit all takings for many years, and the collection of Ormers is still severely restricted. A pioneer sea farmer is now raising Ormers from 'seed'. (*Guernsey Weekly Press*, 20.2.87)

Préciput – This refers to the rights of an eldest son concerning his inheritance.

Press – The Guernsey Evening Press, one of the two local daily newspapers.

Red Cross Messages – 25 word messages with a space for a 25 word reply. The Red Cross Bureau was opened on January 29th, 1941 when the first messages arrived, seven months after the Occupation. Thereafter there was an irregular service until D-Day, June 6th, 1944, when the island became completely cut off from news of relatives and friends. The messages were first taken to the

Feldkommandantur, and then passed on to the Red Cross Bureau. The recipient was then notified by post card, and had to go to the Bureau to read the message, and could take a copy if they wished. The reply could be written then or later.

Sauvary – A Guernsey family name centred on St Peter Port and St Sampson's. There are records of both Sauvary and Sauvarin (completely distinct) conveyancing property in the early 15th century (1409 onwards), with Sauvary, (Sovary, Savari) quite common.

Star – One of the two local daily newspapers.

Sterilizer – A mobile boiler for steaming soil prior to its being used in the greenhouses. This method was investigated by Mr W.F. Poat on the mainland and in the U.S.A. He experimented and, by laborious trial and error, mastered the steaming of soil. Science had not then been applied to horticulture and Mr Poat's work stands out as the greatest achievement in the island's greenhouse industry. Information from Guernsey Tomato Centre Souvenir booklet, where a sterilizer is on view.

Sugar Beet Syrup – This was made by a lengthy and laborious process from the Mangel Wurzel, known in France as the "demi-sucré", and in the island commonly but erroneously as "sugar beet". It has an exceptionally sugary root, the average sugar content being as high as 15%. First it was boiled for about five hours, then the liquid was pressed out. This was boiled till it thickened. Mr Sauvary records that 12lb yielded four pints of liquid and 1lb of syrup; and 25 lbs of the root gave 2 lbs of syrup. In October it came on the market at 7/6 per lb.

Tally Boards – All materials used on a job were recorded on these pieces of wood. After they had been entered in the ledger the boards were planed ready for use again.

Town – The administrative and shopping centre of St Peter Port backing on the harbour.

Trépieds – Trivot or Tripod – on which anything (water, sugar beet, etc.) could be boiled in the open.

Trésor – The Trésor (Treasury) accounts maintained by the Churchwardens comprise monies, rentes and investments which have been bequeathed or acquired by the parish church for its endowment. During the 18th and 19th centuries there was much selling of pew building plots in the churches with some conveyancing in 'places' in pews as well. These monies and the occasional legacy and donation received comprise the present Trésor funds. The present day amounts are quite small and the interest received barely covers the cost of altar candles let alone altar frontal cloths. The monies received by the Churchwardens from the rates are held in separate accounts, and these are expended on the maintenance and building of the fabric, half the cleaning, and on the churchyard and rectory.

Vedette – A small patrol boat.

Vergée – Superficial measure. 1 perche = 441 English square feet or 49 square yards. 40 perches = 1 vergée (1960 square yards).

Vinery – A group of glasshouses. They were originally used for growing vines and were then accurately called vineries. The name persisted when most were changed to growing tomatoes. Glasshouses or greenhouses come in a variety of shapes and sizes, hence the names span, lean-to and three quarters which occur on the New Road property.

Vraic – Seaweed was once widely used as a fertilizer, and resource was made to it again during the Occupation.

White Rock – The northern arm of St Peter Port Harbour terminating in the Signal Station and Spur Lighthouse.

Readers wanting further information about:-

1. *The Occupation* are referred to the Official History
   Charles Cruickshank, *The German Occupation of the Channel Islands*, The Guernsey Press Co. Ltd, 1975

2. *The Constitution and Government of Guernsey* are referred to:-
   Sir John Loveridge, *The Constitution and Law of Guernsey*, La Société Guernesiaise, Candie Headquarters, Guernsey, 1975

3. *Guernsey-French words* are referred to:-
   Dictionnaire Angllais-Guernesiais, compiled by Marie de Garis, Phillimore, 1982

OCCUPATION YEARS 1940-45

1940

June
```
S  2  9 16 23 30
M  3 10 17 24
T  4 11 18 25
W  5 12 19 26
T  6 13 20 27
F  7 14 21 28
S  8 15 22 29
```

July
```
S     7 14 21 28
M  1  8 15 22 29
T  2  9 16 23 30
W  3 10 17 24 31
T  4 11 18 25
F  5 12 19 26
S  6 13 20 27
```

August
```
S     4 11 18 25
M     5 12 19 26
T     6 13 20 27
W     7 14 21 28
T  1  8 15 22 29
F  2  9 16 23 30
S  3 10 17 24 31
```

September
```
S  1  8 15 22 29
M  2  9 16 23 30
T  3 10 17 24
W  4 11 18 25
T  5 12 19 26
F  6 13 20 27
S  7 14 21 28
```

October
```
S     6 13 20 27
M     7 14 21 28
T  1  8 15 22 29
W  2  9 16 23 30
T  3 10 17 24 31
F  4 11 18 25
S  5 12 19 26
```

November
```
S     3 10 17 24
M     4 11 18 25
T     5 12 19 26
W     6 13 20 27
T     7 14 21 28
F  1  8 15 22 29
S  2  9 16 23 30
```

December
```
S  1  8 15 22 29
M  2  9 16 23 30
T  3 10 17 24 31
W  4 11 18 25
T  5 12 19 26
F  6 13 20 27
S  7 14 21 28
```

1941

January	
S	5 12 19 26
M	6 13 20 27
T	7 14 21 28
W	1 8 15 22 29
T	2 9 16 23 30
F	3 10 17 24 31
S	4 11 18 25

February	
S	2 9 16 23
M	3 10 17 24
T	4 11 18 25
W	5 12 19 26
T	6 13 20 27
F	7 14 21 28
S	1 8 15 22

March	
S	2 9 16 23 30
M	3 10 17 24 31
T	4 11 18 25
W	5 12 19 26
T	6 13 20 27
F	7 14 21 28
S	1 8 15 22 29

April	
S	6 13 20 27
M	7 14 21 28
T	1 8 15 22 29
W	2 9 16 23 30
T	3 10 17 24
F	4 11 18 25
S	5 12 19 26

May	
S	4 11 18 25
M	5 12 19 26
T	6 13 20 27
W	7 14 21 28
T	1 8 15 22 29
F	2 9 16 23 30
S	3 10 17 24 31

June	
S	1 8 15 22 29
M	2 9 16 23 30
T	3 10 17 24
W	4 11 18 25
T	5 12 19 26
F	6 13 20 27
S	7 14 21 28

July	
S	6 13 20 27
M	7 14 21 28
T	1 8 15 22 29
W	2 9 16 23 30
T	3 10 17 24 31
F	4 11 18 25
S	5 12 19 26

August	
S	3 10 17 24 31
M	4 11 18 25
T	5 12 19 26
W	6 13 20 27
T	7 14 21 28
F	1 8 15 22 29
S	2 9 16 23 30

September	
S	7 14 21 28
M	1 8 15 22 29
T	2 9 16 23 30
W	3 10 17 24
T	4 11 18 25
F	5 12 19 26
S	6 13 20 27

October	
S	5 12 19 26
M	6 13 20 27
T	7 14 21 28
W	1 8 15 22 29
T	2 9 16 23 30
F	3 10 17 24 31
S	4 11 18 25

November	
S	2 9 16 23 30
M	3 10 17 24
T	4 11 18 25
W	5 12 19 26
T	6 13 20 27
F	7 14 21 28
S	1 8 15 22 29

December	
S	7 14 21 28
M	1 8 15 22 29
T	2 9 16 23 30
W	3 10 17 24 31
T	4 11 18 25
F	5 12 19 26
S	6 13 20 27

1942

January
```
S      4 11 18 25
M      5 12 19 26
T      6 13 20 27
W      7 14 21 28
T   1  8 15 22 29
F   2  9 16 23 30
S   3 10 17 24 31
```

February
```
S   1  8 15 22
M   2  9 16 23
T   3 10 17 24
W   4 11 18 25
T   5 12 19 26
F   6 13 20 27
S   7 14 21 28
```

March
```
S   1  8 15 22 29
M   2  9 16 23 30
T   3 10 17 24 31
W   4 11 18 25
T   5 12 19 26
F   6 13 20 27
S   7 14 21 28
```

April
```
S      5 12 19 26
M      6 13 20 27
T      7 14 21 28
W   1  8 15 22 29
T   2  9 16 23 30
F   3 10 17 24
S   4 11 18 25
```

May
```
S      3 10 17 24 31
M      4 11 18 25
T      5 12 19 26
W      6 13 20 27
T      7 14 21 28
F   1  8 15 22 29
S   2  9 16 23 30
```

June
```
S      7 14 21 28
M   1  8 15 22 29
T   2  9 16 23 30
W   3 10 17 24
T   4 11 18 25
F   5 12 19 26
S   6 13 20 27
```

July
```
S      5 12 19 26
M      6 13 20 27
T      7 14 21 28
W   1  8 15 22 29
T   2  9 16 23 30
F   3 10 17 24 31
S   4 11 18 25
```

August
```
S      2  9 16 23 30
M      3 10 17 24 31
T      4 11 18 25
W      5 12 19 26
T      6 13 20 27
F      7 14 21 28
S   1  8 15 22 29
```

September
```
S      6 13 20 27
M      7 14 21 28
T   1  8 15 22 29
W   2  9 16 23 30
T   3 10 17 24
F   4 11 18 25
S   5 12 19 26
```

October
```
S      4 11 18 25
M      5 12 19 26
T      6 13 20 27
W      7 14 21 28
T   1  8 15 22 29
F   2  9 16 23 30
S   3 10 17 24 31
```

November
```
S   1  8 15 22 29
M   2  9 16 23 30
T   3 10 17 24
W   4 11 18 25
T   5 12 19 26
F   6 13 20 27
S   7 14 21 28
```

December
```
S      6 13 20 27
M      7 14 21 28
T   1  8 15 22 29
W   2  9 16 23 30
T   3 10 17 24 31
F   4 11 18 25
S   5 12 19 26
```

1943

January
```
S       3 10 17 24 31
M       4 11 18 25
T       5 12 19 26
W       6 13 20 27
T       7 14 21 28
F     1 8 15 22 29
S     2 9 16 23 30
```

February
```
S       7 14 21 28
M     1 8 15 22
T     2 9 16 23
W     3 10 17 24
T     4 11 18 25
F     5 12 19 26
S     6 13 20 27
```

March
```
S       7 14 21 28
M     1 8 15 22 29
T     2 9 16 23 30
W     3 10 17 24 31
T     4 11 18 25
F     5 12 19 26
S     6 13 20 27
```

April
```
S       4 11 18 25
M       5 12 19 26
T       6 13 20 27
W       7 14 21 28
T     1 8 15 22 29
F     2 9 16 23 30
S     3 10 17 24
```

May
```
S       2 9 16 23 30
M       3 10 17 24 31
T       4 11 18 25
W       5 12 19 26
T       6 13 20 27
F       7 14 21 28
S     1 8 15 22 29
```

June
```
S       6 13 20 27
M       7 14 21 28
T     1 8 15 22 29
W     2 9 16 23 30
T     3 10 17 24
F     4 11 18 25
S     5 12 19 26
```

July
```
S       4 11 18 25
M       5 12 19 26
T       6 13 20 27
W       7 14 21 28
T     1 8 15 22 29
F     2 9 16 23 30
S     3 10 17 24 31
```

August
```
S     1 8 15 22 29
M     2 9 16 23 30
T     3 10 17 24 31
W     4 11 18 25
T     5 12 19 26
F     6 13 20 27
S     7 14 21 28
```

September
```
S       5 12 19 26
M       6 13 20 27
T       7 14 21 28
W     1 8 15 22 29
T     2 9 16 23 30
F     3 10 17 24
S     4 11 18 25
```

October
```
S       3 10 17 24
M       4 11 18 25
T       5 12 19 26
W       6 13 20 27
T       7 14 21 28
F     1 8 15 22 29
S     2 9 16 23 30
```

November
```
S       7 14 21 28
M     1 8 15 22 29
T     2 9 16 23 30
W     3 10 17 24
T     4 11 18 25
F     5 12 19 26
S     6 13 20 27
```

December
```
S       5 12 19 26
M       6 13 20 27
T       7 14 21 28
W     1 8 15 22 29
T     2 9 16 23 30
F     3 10 17 24 31
S     4 11 18 25
```

1944

January
```
S     2  9 16 23 30
M     3 10 17 24 31
T     4 11 18 25
W     5 12 19 26
T     6 13 20 27
F     7 14 21 28
S   1 8 15 22 29
```

February
```
S     6 13 20 27
M     7 14 21 28
T   1 8 15 22 29
W   2 9 16 23
T     3 10 17 24
F     4 11 18 25
S     5 12 19 26
```

March
```
S     5 12 19 26
M     6 13 20 27
T     7 14 21 28
W   1 8 15 22 29
T   2 9 16 23 30
F   3 10 17 24 31
S   4 11 18 25
```

April
```
S     2  9 16 23 30
M     3 10 17 24
T     4 11 18 25
W     5 12 19 26
T     6 13 20 27
F     7 14 21 28
S   1 8 15 22 29
```

May
```
S     7 14 21 28
M   1 8 15 22 29
T   2 9 16 23 30
W   3 10 17 24 31
T   4 11 18 25
F   5 12 19 26
S   6 13 20 27
```

June
```
S     4 11 18 25
M     5 12 19 26
T     6 13 20 27
W     7 14 21 28
T   1 8 15 22 29
F   2 9 16 23 30
S   3 10 17 24
```

July
```
S     2  9 16 23 30
M     3 10 17 24 31
T     4 11 18 25
W     5 12 19 26
T     6 13 20 27
F     7 14 21 28
S   1 8 15 22 29
```

August
```
S     6 13 20 27
M     7 14 21 28
T   1 8 15 22 29
W   2 9 16 23 30
T   3 10 17 24 31
F   4 11 18 25
S   5 12 19 26
```

September
```
S     3 10 17 24
M     4 11 18 25
T     5 12 19 26
W     6 13 20 27
T     7 14 21 28
F   1 8 15 22 29
S   2 9 16 23 30
```

October
```
S   1 8 15 22 29
M   2 9 16 23 30
T   3 10 17 24 31
W   4 11 18 25
T   5 12 19 26
F   6 13 20 27
S   7 14 21 28
```

November
```
S     5 12 19 26
M     6 13 20 27
T     7 14 21 28
W   1 8 15 22 29
T   2 9 16 23 30
F   3 10 17 24
S   4 11 18 25
```

December
```
S     3 10 17 24 31
M     4 11 18 25
T     5 12 19 26
W     6 13 20 27
T     7 14 21 28
F   1 8 15 22 29
S   2 9 16 23 30
```

1945

January
```
S      7 14 21 28
M   1  8 15 22 29
T   2  9 16 23 30
W   3 10 17 24 31
T   4 11 18 25
F   5 12 19 26
S   6 13 20 27
```

February
```
S      4 11 18 25
M      5 12 19 26
T      6 13 20 27
W      7 14 21 28
T   1  8 15 22
F   2  9 16 23
S   3 10 17 24
```

March
```
S      4 11 18 25
M      5 12 19 26
T      6 13 20 27
W      7 14 21 28
T   1  8 15 22 29
F   2  9 16 23 30
S   3 10 17 24 31
```

April
```
S   1  8 15 22 29
M   2  9 16 23 30
T   3 10 17 24
W   4 11 18 25
T   5 12 19 26
F   6 13 20 27
S   7 14 21 28
```

May
```
S      6 13 20 27
M      7 14 21 28
T   1  8 15 22 29
W   2  9 16 23 30
T   3 10 17 24 31
F   4 11 18 25
S   5 12 19 26
```

INDEX

This index is designed as a general guide to specific events and personalities. It is not exhaustive and the editor apologies for any inadvertent omissions or mistakes.

Airmen
  American, 217, 228
  RAF, 70
Alderney, 26, 38, 74, 244, 253
Allendale, 59, *passim*
Allez, Miss, 240
Anderson, 41-2
Austin, George, MOH, 74, 177, 196, 254, 263, 266, 276

Bachmann, Peter & Kitty, 65, 90, 117, 124, 146, 163, 203, 251, 279
Baker, Miss Diva, 64, 98-9, 114, 176, 180, 182, 271, 280
Baker, Mr (Sark), 281
Beaugie, The Rev., 65
Beech Tree, 70, 73, 76, 101, 138, 140, 162, 172
Belle Hunkin, 225, 226, 251, 252
Best's Brickfields, 253
Bichard, Mrs, 85
Billet d'Etats (Blue Book), 37, 148
Bird, Mr Walter., 44
Bird, Mrs W., 85, 220
Bird, Ruby, *see Mrs Cumber*
Bird, Wilfred, (coal merchant), 44, 55, 78, 101, 125, 131, 137, 157, 160, 163, 165, 172-4, 275
Bisset, Don, 58, 88, 146, 181-2, 187, 202, 237, 247
Bisson, Henry, 40, 47, 55, 58, 96, 269
Blampied, Mr, 91, 253, 260
Blanchelande, 211, 246, 270
Blight, Mrs, 176
Bourne, Mr, 39
Bowditch, Mr & Mrs, 157, 185
Brache (Cognon), 253
Brache, Harold (lay reader), 254

Brache, Miss (Cognon), 50, 253
Brache, Harold, 251
Brache, Mr (Le Francois, Vale) 186
Braye du Val, 52, 111, 129, 150
Bretel, C. (Police Force), 221
Brimage, Mr, 145
Brooks Capt. John, 222
Brooks, Mrs, 62
Browell, Mr W.M., 43, 50, 67, 79, 137, 147, 155, 168
Burroughs, J., 47
Burton, Maurice (naturalist), 73

Cadastre, 54, 56, 86, 89-90, 184, 271
Caledonian Nursery, 48, 132
Cambridge, Dr, 71, 222, 231
Cann, Jas., 260
Cann, Reg. 251
Carey, Victor (Bailiff), 203, 223, 250
Carpenter, Mr, 64, 102
Carré, Elsie & her father, 41, *passim*
Carré, Mrs (Four Cross), 84, 215
Carré, Mrs, (Hougue Guillmine), 33, 52, 57, 63
Channel Queen Memorial, 270
Charybdis, HMS, 214-5
Churchwarden (swearing in), 224
City of Benares, 32
Clarke, Angelo, 43, 147, 184
Clarke, Jackie, 147
Clarke, Philip, 27
Clothing Coupons, 33
Cohu, Mrs, 93
Cohu, Mrs, 211
Collard, Father, 283

Collas, Mr, 61
Collas, Sister, 278
Collings, Dr, 273
Collivet, 236
Corbet, Barlow, 63, 269
Corbet, Charlie, 248
Corbet, Jack, ("Ginger"), 40, 55, 67
Cortvriend, Gussie & Violet, 25, *passim*
Cotîls, 71
Cross, Mr & Mrs, 104, 149, 166, 191-2, 213
Cumber, Mr, (Chemist), 237-8, 280, 283
Cumber, Mrs Ruby (neé Bird), 85, 220, 229

de Garis, Mr, 285
de la Motte, Stan & Mrs, 127, 130
de Lisle Carey, Mr, 203, 205
de Putron, Mr Lloyd, 30, 66, 76
Delancey Monument, 213, 273
Delancey Schools, 31, 37, 49, 61, 73, 103
Deportations, 1st, 166, *passim* 2nd, 187, *passim*
Despointes, Mr, 125, 141
Dickens, The Rev., 192, 222
Digby Roberts, Dr, 71
Doreen, 59, 96
Dorey Cottages, 108, 120, 253, 271
Dorey, Arthur (Jurat), 56, 81, 104, 110, 221
Dorey, Frank, 36, 61, 137, 176
Dorey, George, 110
Douzaine (Parish) Meetings, 34, 37, 42, 64, 123, 135, 148, 166, 253-4, 257-9, 267, 271
Douzenier (sworn in), 113, 224
Downing, Mr, 63
Duquemin, Mr, 77-8
Duquemin, Steve, 27, 35
Dyson, John, 236
Dyson, Miss, 44, 173, 218

Ecclesiastical Court, 181
Edmunds, 162
Elizabeth College, 76, 89, 133, 155
Ellis, Elsie, 36
Ellis, Jim, 120
Ellis, Miss Lily, 69, 89, 109, 120, 148, 162, 183, 200, 212, 242, 259, 271
Ellis, Mrs, 120
Ellis, Reg, 130
Elsie (Mrs Godfray's maid), 39, *passim*
Elsie, *see Carré*
Endicott, 257
Erwin, 119, 122-4, 129, 138, 140, 144, 146, 153, 156-9

Falla, Eunice, 183
Falla, Major, 187, 190, 256
Falla, Raymond, 34, 37
Faulkener, Dr, 276-8, 280, 283-4
Finey, The Rev., 33, 40, 48
Fond Falla, 253
Foster, Eddie, 131, 175, 201, 264
Fox, Dr, 46, 137-8, 187, 188, 202, 204-5, 208, 216, 222, 226, 234, 246, 265, 274-6, 279, 280-1 287, 283-4
Freeman, 154
French Halles, 43, 113, 168
Frossard, Charlie, 55, 91, 114
Frossard, Guy, 49
Frossard, Pansy, 55
Frossard, The Rev. & Mrs E.L., 27, *passim*
Fulford, 34
Fuzzey, Fred, 196

Gallienne, Miss, 241
Gibson, Dr Dick, 204, 284
Giffard, Comdr & Mrs Rosy, 52, 129, 134, 150, 202
Giffard, Dean of Guernsey, 134
Giffard, Sir Henry, 112

Glasshouse Utilisation Board
 (GUB), 86, 183
Godfray, Mrs, 33, *passim*
Greenhow, The Rev. E.H., 53,
 147
Gref, Anna, 173-4
Guernsey Frock, 37, 47, 50, 131
Guilbert, Oscar, 97-8, 207, 264
Guilmoto, 231, 235

Hall, Matron, 277-8, 287
Hamelin, Mr, 60
Hamley, Mrs, 271
Hart, Jack, 66, 107, 139, 166,
 231
Haysom, 256
Henry, *see Bisson*
Hickey, Mrs, 222
Higgs, F, (Dean of the
 Douzaine), 148, 166
Higgs, Mr, 104, 111, 195
Holland, Mr, 224
Hollies, The, 71, *passim*
Honey, Marjorie, 47, 62, 90,
 201
Honey, Mrs Emily ("Bim"),
 58, 68, 200, 261, 270, 272
Honey, Percy & Edith, 200, 223
Honey, Uncle Ned, 45, *passim*
Houstoun, Miss Mary & Jack,
 59, 64, 127, 139, 241-2
Hubert, 204, 233
Hunkin, Reg & Winnie, 51,
 70, 83, 143, 172, 226, 228,
 241, 243-4, 249, 251, 253, 277

Identity cards, 34-6, 38-9
Isler, Mr, 280, 283

Jack, 25, *passim*
James, The Rev., 47, 184, 190,
 216
Jane (granddaughter), 25,
 passim
Jehan, 154
Jo – Josephine, 25, *passim*
Johns, R.H., 103, 111, 173, 179,
 257-8
Jurat, Election of, 103, 112

Kangaroo steaks, 239
Kate, Auntie, 68, *passim*
Katwick, 157
Keyho, Stanley, 175
Kilshaw, The Rev., 79, 91, 214
King, Mrs, 126
Kit, 25, *passim*
Kitty "Head", *see Bachmann*
Knight, Freddie, 215

Ladies' College, 179
Lainé, Jack, 76, 200, 212
Lajoie (boys), 157
Lake, Mr & Mrs Walter, 29,
 143, 170, 176, 190, 192, 196-7,
 208, 216, 232, 239, 252-3, 264
Lamiot, Miss, 136
Langdon, Mr, 221
Langlois, Major (Advocate),
 104, 190, 222, 279
Langlois, Mr (Delancey
 Lane), 62
Langmead, Mr, 89, 238
Lapwings, 47, 121, 278
Lawton, Mr & Miss, 31, 33, 41,
 43-6, 62, 64, 66, 69, 72, 127,
 131, 151, 210
Le Gras, James, 275
Le Maitre, Bill, Billy, Willy
 & Minnie, 25, 55, *passim*
Le Maitre, Peter, 226
Le Maitre, R, 89, 95, 123
Le Maitre, Vernon, 104, 107,
 142, 172
Le Page, Mr, 240
Le Pelley, Miss, 103, 282
Le Poidevin, Mrs, 51, 70, 103,
 111, 118, 143, 158, 160, 163,
 225-6, 228, 243, 249
Le Poidevin, Winnie (Mrs
 Hunkin), 223
Le Quesne, Mrs, 62
Le Riche, 52, 75, 113, 123, 167,
 198, 232-3, 273
Leale, Enid, 108, 177
Leale, Mrs "Dr", 256
Leale, Nurse, 281
Leale, Shop, 82, 87, 110, 214
Leale, The Rev. Jack (Jurat),
 64, 255, 258, 261

Lihou, Miss E, 40, *passim*
Limbourne, HMS, 215

Mackay, 236
Mahy, Jack, 97, 110, 282
Mahy, John, 138
Mahy, Pointues Rocques, 118
Mallett (Vale Road), 94
Mallett, Floss, Flossie & Lily, 69, 92, 95, 98, 103, 130, 136, 218, 282
Mallett, Frank, 140-1, 160
Mallett, Mr, 32
Mallett, Sydney, 251
Manuelle 30, 82, 87, 98, 138, 151, 172
Marley, Harry, 212
Marquand, Mr, 37
Marriette, Jas, 95
Marriette, Jessie, 44
Martel, 41
Martel, Gerald, 66, 90, 118, 121, 144, 162, 172, 175, 179, 183, 187, 224, 243, 254
Martel, Mr (father of Advocate Martel), 280, 283
Matthews, Miss, 32, *passim*
Mauger, Miss, 60, 63, 67, 95, 127, 222, 225, 241
Mauger, Mrs (neé Peek), 180
McCathie, Mr, 252
Messervy, Mr, 25, 31, 98, 118, 153, 154, 157, 197, 207, 212-3, 250-1, 255
Minnie, *see Le Maitre*
Monsell's Pub, 63
Monsell, Evelyn, 105, 276, 287
Mum, 28, *passim*
Murphy, Sister, 278, 281

Naftel, Miss, 240, 282
Ned, Uncle, 32, *passim*
Noyon, Capt. Fred, 228, 257
Noyon, Emile, 46-7

Ogier, Bryan, 194, 225
Ogier, E.H., (Ted), Mr, 193, 271
Ogier, Miss Eunice, 193-4

Ogier, Jackie, 32, 36, 85, 95, 128
Ogier, Jim, 27-29, 128, 200
Ogier, Jocelyn, Mrs, 195, 226
Ogier, Leslie, 181
Ogier, Lionel, 197-8
Ogier, Mr Duvaux, 258
Ogier, Mr P.G., (Dean of the Douzaine), 184, 271
Ogier Shop, 27-9, 44
Ogier, Staff, Stafford, Mr & Mrs, 40, *passim*
Oliver, Capt. (Fire Brigade), 283-5
Oppenheim, Phillips, 66
Ozanne, Ira, 191
Ozanne, Lady, 104
Ozanne, Miss Eliza, 96
Ozanne, Mr Tom (Deputy), 248
Ozanne, Mr, 106
Ozard, Jack, 52, 258
Ozard, Tom, 155

Pattimore, Mr, 41, *passim*
Peek, Mr Gervase, 27, 35, 47, 90, 104, 106, 111, 158-9, 165, 167, 176, 178, 180-1, 194, 198, 200, 214
Peek, Mrs G., 92, 198
Peter, *see Bachmann*
Petruschke, Mrs, 165, 191, 215
Pierce, Miss, 252
Pitcher, 223
Plummer's Shop, 31, 55, 69
Poat, Wilfred, 31, 36, 81, 82, 96, 104, 187, 195, 201, 209, 222, 293
Pommier, Mde, 40
Pontin, Mr, 40, 62, 64
Préciput, 121
Priestley, J.B., 51
"Pullman Car", 29, 31, 45
Purse, Mr, 36, 51

Quinain, 208

Rabbits (wild ones), 227-8, 231
Randall, Miss Marie, 222
Red Cross Bureau, 222, 279

Red Cross Messages, 41, 50, 52, 59
  England, 52, 81, *passim*
  New York, 48
  Switzerland, 77
Registration 34-39, 64, 83 (identity card)
Roberts, *see Tom*
Robin, Wilfred, 25, 58
Romeril, John, 191
Romeril, The Rev. & Mrs P, 76, 148, 156, 191, 193, 214, 216, 256
Roosevelt, 49
Rosemary (granddaughter), 25, *passim*
Rowe, Mrs, 33, *passim*

Salt, 34, 260, 267
Santangelo, Miss Ida, 85
Santangelo, Mr, 43
Santangelo, Mrs S.L., 64
Sauvary, Mary, 61, *passim*
Sauvary, Tom (brother), 223, 224, 249, 275, 281, 283, 285
Sauvary, Willie, 59, *passim*
Shaw (Grange), 67, 82
Sherwill, Major Ambrose, 44
Simon (employee), 25-6, 28, 118, 151, 178
Simon, Guilbert, 207
Smith (N. Side), 167, 202, 232
Smith, Mr (Civil Transport), 198
Stroobant, 168
Stubbs, Mr & Mrs R, 32, *passim*
Sugar Beet, 178, 183, 186, 215-6, 218, 255, 269
Symons, George, 51, 53, 202, 206, 212, 269-71

Tanner, Mr (dentist), 188, 207
Ted, 25, *passim*
Thorn, Mr, 107, 121, 264
Tom Roberts, 25, *passim*
Tooley, Mrs, 222
Tozer, 51
Trésor accounts, 113, 137, 195, 224, 250

Trouteaud, Leonie, 59, 61, 68, 279
Trouteaud, Mr, 36
Trouteaud, Rex, 278, 280
Tuck, 226, 237
Tucker, Mr, 122-3, 209
Typhus, 193

Uncle Ned, *see Honey*
Upham, Joan, 217
Upham, Mr A.A., 148, 217

Valpied, Bob, 92, 105
Vaudin, William, 279

Wanner, Dr, 267-8
Warry, Lloyd, 213, 278, 280, 283
Warry, Mr & Mrs, 167
Warry, Mrs, 179, 189, 282
Waterbury, The Rev., 221, 278
Way, L, 221
Wheadon, Bert, 71, 244, 255
White, Andrew, 108
Williams, Joseph, 96
Wilson, Dr, 71, 119, 196, 198-9
Wirelesses, confiscated, 37, *passim*
  returned, 44, *passim*
  confiscated for good, 150